Canada: A Socio-Political Report

McGraw-Hill Ryerson Series in Canadian Politics

General Editor—Paul W. Fox

Canada: A Socio-Political Report

Ronald Manzer

Department of Political Economy
University of Toronto

McGraw-Hill Ryerson Limited
Toronto Montreal New York London Sydney
Johannesburg Mexico Panama Düsseldorf
Singapore Sao Páulo Kuala Lumpur New Delhi

ISBN 0-07-092666-2 (paperback)

ISBN 0-07-092659-x (hard cover)

2345678910   JD   321098765

Library of Congress Catalog Card
Number 73-16967

Printed and bound in Canada.

ACKNOWLEDGEMENTS

This study had its origins in my efforts to collect Canadian material for classes in political behaviour at the University of Toronto. As the collection has evolved over the past four years, the students in my sophomore political behaviour and public policy courses have variously encouraged, criticized, rejected and ignored it; and each type of response has been helpful in working out the final text.

My colleague Paul Fox encouraged me to develop for publication my suggestion for a collection of social indicators of political goods in Canada and critically reviewed successive versions of the manuscript. Geoffrey Burn tempered his enthusiasm for the manuscript with helpful criticism about the development of its argument, and Professor Michael Whittington provided me with a perceptive criticism of the penultimate draft. Professors Jack McLeod and Donald Smiley also read the manuscript and encouraged me to think it was worthy of publication.

I owe a special debt of gratitude to Professor Donald Forbes. Not only has he permitted me to reproduce some of the results from his survey of Canadian high school students, but he also generously guided me in my computer work on the 1965 and 1968 Federal Election Surveys.

The Canada Council provided me with the financial support of a Leave Fellowship in 1971–2 and kindly permitted me to alter my original research program when the need arose in order to advance the work on this study. I am also grateful to Professor Stefan Dupré, Chairman of the Department of Political Economy, who arranged for the Departmental support of my leave of absence and who has encouraged my work throughout, and to Mrs. Mary Rous and Mrs. Vivian Humphrey who assisted me in the typing and reproduction of the manuscript for use by my students.

My family has shared with me the difficulties of making this book. My best critic and constant helper has been my wife Kathryn. Not only has she willingly accepted additional parental responsibilities to allow me time for research and writing, but she also has listened patiently to the arguments in their several versions and suggested thoughtful resolutions of many problems. My daughters Patricia and Jennifer usually accepted with good grace my prolonged seclusions and otherwise provided happy distractions. Throughout my academic endeavours but especially in the last stages of this project, I have had the loving support of my parents, Margaret and Wendell Manzer, and my parents-in-law, Olive and John Hart. I thank all of them for their help and interest; they know my love.

TABLE OF CONTENTS

LIST OF TABLES

LIST OF FIGURES

FOREWORD

When Professor Manzer first discussed his manuscript with me, I was enthusiastic about everything in it except his proposed title. Now that he has changed the title, I can say that I am more than enthusiastic about the entire book.

For some time many students have felt that the examination of Canadian politics should go beyond an analysis of the "nuts and bolts" in the structure and machinery of government and focus on basic issues in our system. There is a growing belief that we have passed through the initial morphological phase in Canadian political studies and that we should pay less heed now to institutional forms and instead give more attention to the social questions and philosophical considerations implicit in the Canadian political system. Professor Manzer, following his own instincts, decided a few years ago to move in this new direction by concentrating on the problem of human needs and their political fulfilment in this country. *Canada: A Socio-Political Report* is the product of his energetic and industrious labours.

His job was not easy. It involved him in a great deal of hard work digging out the basic facts and finding suitable comparative material to provide a standard of measurement. But I think that any one who reads this book will be impressed by the results of his efforts.

It seems to me that Professor Manzer has accomplished for Canadian politics very much the same sort of thing as Professor John Porter achieved for Canadian society in his outstanding book, *The Vertical Mosaic: An Analysis of Social Class and Power in Canada*. Porter examined the structure of Canadian society on the basis of an accumulation of a very large amount of relevant statistical data. Manzer also makes use of a great deal of empirical evidence, but he begins his analysis at a more fundamental human level than Porter. While the latter commenced by considering various sociological definitions of class, Manzer takes as his departure point the appraisal of human needs presented by Abraham Maslow, a psychologist held in high regard by many contemporaries, including this writer.

Maslow believes that an individual has at least five basic needs that must be satisfied if he or she is to develop. These needs may be described as: Physiological sustenance, safety, belongingness, self-esteem, and self-actualization. To assist the individual to achieve fulfilment in these respects, the state should provide the five instrumental social equivalents to them, namely, welfare, security, fraternity, equality, and liberty. Needless to say, these civic virtues sound familiar since they have long been deemed by political philosophers to be the hallmarks of a benevolent state.

Having identified his criteria for measuring the quality of Canadian democracy, Professor Manzer then leads us step by step through an examination of the extent to which these "political goods" have been achived in our country. How effective is our welfare state, for example, in delivering its benefits fairly to citizens with different needs? Who profits most from our existing panoply of social services—the rich, the middle class, or the poor? Does our publicly funded educational system distribute its advantages impartially to children from different social classes or does it give an edge, particularly in regard to heavily subsidized university education, to the sons and daughters of the middle, professional, and executive class? How much security of persons do we have in Canada? Are we a country that ranks high or low in the observance of law and order? Does civil rights legislation protect and benefit every one equally? How much real fraternity is there in Canadian society? And for that matter, how much genuine individual liberty?

These are the kinds of hard, searching questions that Professor Manzer raises as he pursues his probing analysis of the heart—or maybe one should say, the guts—of Canadian democracy. He would earn his philosopher's stripes if he merely posed the questions, but the great merit of his book is that it is also a major work in social science. The author tries to answer his own questions by looking at the facts, by amassing all the evidence available, and then carefully weighing it to see to what extent each of the five abstract political values has been borne out in reality.

In his research Professor Manzer has not fallen into the trap of the popularizer and seized on a few flamboyant statistics to support his own assertions. On the contrary, he spent several years patiently scouring all the sources he could find, including government blue books, reports from Statistics Canada, and other relevant public documents and monographs. In this respect his work is again reminiscent of Professor Porter's painstaking efforts. What I particularly admire about Professor Manzer's labour is that he also had the initiative and dedication to push his analyses into the comparative realm. He has attempted to answer not only the question "How much equality, liberty, and fraternity do we have in Canada?" but also "How much of each of these political goods do we have in comparison with some other countries?"

As a result, the author has produced a book which in my view is quite unique. I cannot recall any other work which has appraised Canadian democratic values so incisively and thoroughly by testing them on the anvil of cold, hard facts. My guess is that many Canadian social scientists will share my appreciation of Professor Manzer's efforts. I would not be surprised if his book, like Professor Porter's, became the core of a number of courses in Canadian universities. It certainly offers an approach to the study of Canadian politics that is a fresh alternative to the traditional emphasis on institutional forms. It is also in harmony with the contemporary interest in social values and normative theory. Yet at the same time it grounds itself in the social scientists' beloved world of empirical facts.

I would break the rules of editorial etiquette if I gave away here Professor Manzer's conclusions. I will merely say that they are sobering. Although he finds much to commend in Canada's political goods, he shares Professor Porter's belief that we have a long way to go yet in satisfying some of the needs of many of our citizens. Porter was concerned in particular by the lack of equality in Canadian society. Manzer has something to say about this deficiency but even more to add about fraternity. However, this is enough from the editor. I turn you over to something much more interesting, Professor Manzer's own stimulating thoughts.

PAUL W. FOX,
General Editor

January 3, 1974,
University of Toronto

INTRODUCTION

Although government may be justified in many ways, the conclusive justification of government in general must be its ability to
serve human needs and serve them better than would be done without
any government; and any particular system of government must be
justified by its ability to satisfy human needs better than any other
system of government.[1] Acceptance of this view raises three general
problems for students of government and politics. First of all, evidence
must be collected on the broad patterns of unsatisfied human needs
in the community. Then, attention must be directed to the ways in
which the functioning and the product of the governmental process
satisfy the basic needs of citizens. Finally, proposals designed to reform political and other social arrangements must be evaluated for
their probable efficacy in satisfying more of the basic needs of more
people.

Such an approach to the study of politics obviously presents immense challenges of data collection, political analysis, and philosophical argument. My modest contribution to this difficult task consists
of first introducing briefly a simple framework which can be used to
analyze the possibilities for human development in a community and
then presenting within this framework some of the empirical evidence
which is available and relevant for assessing the relative satisfaction
of human needs within the Canadian polity.

In the first chapter, the theory of the modern psychologist Abraham
Maslow, which holds that physiological sustenance, safety, belongingness, self-esteem, and self-actualization constitute the primary
requisites for human development, is considered in relation to the
traditional political ideas of welfare, security, fraternity, equality, and
liberty. The combination of Maslow's concepts of human needs with
long-standing ideas of political good results in a simple framework
which is then used to organize a description of the level of provision
in Canada for each of the basic needs.

Chapters Two through Six present the empirical data for assessing

1

the level of provision in Canada for each political good. The welfare of people living in Canada is considered in terms of the distribution of national income, rates of mortality and morbidity, and the quality of nutrition and housing. Security is presented as dependent on the incidence of war, domestic political violence, and crime. The degree of fraternity is described in terms of the different factors at work promoting the integration and disintegration of the political community. The degree of equality is indicated in terms of differences in Canada between class, status, ethnic, and sex groups in their access to higher-level occupations, educational opportunities, and political power. Liberty is considered in its political aspects in terms of the probability and scope of interference by the various Canadian governments with the actions of citizens.

My approach to Canadian studies is that of a social scientist relying primarily on quantitative and behavioral data. Obviously, among the modes of commentary on human affairs other approaches are possible. A poet expresses the insight that "we are all immigrants to this place even if we were born here"; a film-maker records what it means for two Maritimers to be "goin' down the road"; a painter captures the primal creative achievement of west coast Indian sculpture; a chansonnier remarks that "mon pays ce n'est pas un pays c'est l'hiver"; an historian painstakingly documents the development of the commercial economy of the St. Lawrence River; ordinary citizens write letters to their Prime Minister, collectively providing a painful testimony to the ordeals of an economic depression.[2] Each of these is a valid commentary, revealing something of what it means to live in Canada.

Yet, without proclaiming any exclusive prerogatives for the methods of modern social science, one can still assert their potential usefulness in the study of social behaviour. Descriptions of social reality are inevitably simplifications. Whereas the humanist chooses to simplify by exploring in depth the thoughts, feelings, and actions of a few people living in a particular social situation, the behavioral scientist usually chooses to simplify by summarizing in breadth the thoughts, feelings, attributes, and actions of a great many people. By thus seeking explicitly formulated generalizations within defined theoretical frameworks, the social scientific approach offers the important advantages of inclusiveness and economy in the description of a given social situation. The resulting generalizations are still simplifications, but they have especial value because of the facility with which they can be used to inform political decision-making.

What is proposed here is a social scientific description of the Canadian political community which gives priority to questions concerning the satisfaction of basic human needs. Answers to these questions are not easy to obtain and must of necessity be approximations. Each political good has a number of dimensions, and this makes precise, quantitative measurement of differences in the provision of the good quite impossible. Even so, if the distribution of political goods cannot be measured directly, we can still use series of aggregate statistics, representative surveys, and systematic methods of scaling to produce indicators of the social situation.

In Canada, as in other nations, the selection of indicators is complicated by the incompleteness or unavailability of many social data. Given the limitations, my aim has been to select a few social indicators for each political good which, taken together, will provide enough information to make valid comparative judgements about the enjoyment of political goods and the satisfaction of human needs in the Canadian polity.

Although my subject is contemporary Canada, a comparative perspective is an essential part of my presentation of data. Indeed, comparisons are almost inevitable because welfare, security, fraternity, equality, and liberty are comparative concepts. They raise questions of how much more or less a person enjoys them in comparison with other people in his political community, both past and present, and how much he enjoys them in comparison with people living in other political communities. So the provision of political goods in Canada will be described as fully as possible, not just in terms of recent Canadian performance, but also in terms of the extent to which Canadians enjoy certain political goods in the present compared with the past and in terms of cross-national comparisons of Canada with other nations.

Giving priority to questions concerning the satisfaction of human needs requires comparisons, but viewing the position of Canada in comparative perspective must not divert our attention from the ultimate criterion of human development. Because we view individual development as the ultimate criterion of what is good, in the end we must assess our politics in terms of its contribution to human development. In order to have bench marks for description and evaluation, it is useful to compare the experience of our community with that of others. But such comparisons cannot replace an analysis and evaluation of our national successes and failures against the ultimate criterion of our responsibility for realizing human potential both within our own community and beyond it.

NOTES

1. Christian Bay, "Needs, Wants and Political Legitimacy," *Canadian Journal of Political Science*, I (September 1968), 241.
2. The references are to Margaret Atwood, *The Journals of Susanna Moodie* (Toronto: Oxford University Press, 1970), p. 62; Don Shebib, director, "Goin'

Down the Road" (Evdon Productions, 1970); Emily Carr, "Potlatch Welcome" (1928), "Big Raven" and "Totem Mother, Kitwancool" (circa 1928), "Totem and Forest" (circa 1931), and "Forsaken" (circa 1932—4); Gilles Vigneault, "Mon Pays," *Avec les vieux mots* (Ottawa: Editions de l'arc, 1964), pp. 13–15; Donald Creighton, *The Empire of the St. Lawrence* (Toronto: Macmillan Company of Canada, 1956); and Michael Bliss and Linda Grayson (eds.), *The Wretched of Canada* (Toronto: University of Toronto Press, 1972).

Chapter One

HUMAN NEEDS AND POLITICAL GOODS

A number of political scientists have put forward lists of basic human needs.[1] In one of the most important attempts in modern political science, Graham Wallas early in this century offered an analysis of the basic "political impulses" which he thought included an impulse to feel kindly towards any other human being of whose existence and personality we become vividly aware, an impulse to laugh, a desire for property, a fighting instinct, instincts of suspicion and curiosity and the desire to excel, instincts for sex and food, instincts of anger and fear, intolerance of repeated emotional adjustment, a desire for privacy, and a dread of loneliness.[2]

More recently, Robert E. Lane listed ten human needs which seemed to him to account most adequately for political thinking, at least that of the young middle-class men whom he was studying:

> (1) cognitive needs: learning, curiosity, understanding; (2) consistency needs: emotional and logical and veridical, the kinds of needs satisfied by the reduction of dissonance; (3) social needs: affiliation, approval, being liked; (4) moral needs: satisfied by the appeasing of conscience and/or by giving the impression of rectitude to others; (5) esteem needs: worth, status, importance; (6) needs for personality integration and identity clarification; (7) needs on occasion (but for everyone at some time) for expression of aggression: the desire to injure; (8) needs for autonomy, freedom, the removal of constraint, and the experience of choice; (9) the need for self-actualization: development, growth; (10) the need for adequate instrumental guides to reality, object appraisal and attainment.[3]

James C. Davies, who was concerned with the origins of political behaviour, and Christian Bay, who was concerned to establish "that governments exist in order to safeguard human lives and their free development, with priority for the most basic human rights", have argued that Abraham Maslow's five-fold classification of physiological, safety, belongingness, esteem, and self-actualization needs also provides a useful model of man for political analysis.[4]

Some set of assumptions, either stated or implied, concerning the nature of man underlies, shapes, and stimulates all political and social thought. Each theorist's classification of human needs reflects his interests and research and the general state of thought on the subject at the time.[5] No doubt any of several classifications of human needs would serve as a framework for our assessment of the degree to which human needs are satisfied in Canada, but Maslow's model of man seems the most useful. First, as Bay notes, no one argues that physiological sustenance, safety, belongingness, esteem, and self-actualization are not in some sense prerequisites of human welfare. Second, I have found it possible, without feeling that I was doing injustice to the complexity of human nature, on the one hand, or the purposes and impacts of public policies, on the other, to associate Maslow's scheme of basic human needs with certain concepts of good which have had a durable pre-eminence in the history of political thought.

According to Maslow, five basic needs must be satisfied for full human development: physiological needs such as those for water, food, sex, and shelter; safety needs such as those for order, predictability, dependability of the environment; love, affection, belongingness needs; esteem needs; and self-actualization needs. Maslow's concept of human needs involves not only a series of increasing need gratifications but also a series of increasing degrees of psychological health resulting in his concept of "gratification health". His example illustrates what this means for people with various needs left unsatisfied.

> Let us say that person A has lived for several weeks in a dangerous jungle, in which he has managed to stay alive by finding occasional food and water. Person B not only stays alive but also has a rifle and a hidden cave with a closable entrance. Person C has all of these and two more men with him as well. Person D has the food, the gun, the allies, the cave, and in addition, has with him his best-loved friend. Finally, Person E, in the same jungle, has all of these, and in addition is the well-respected leader of his band. For the sake of brevity we may call these men, respectively, the merely surviving, the safe, the belonging, the loved, and the respected.[6]

Maslow argues that, other things being equal, a person who is safe and belongs and is loved will be healthier than a person who is safe and belongs but who is rejected and unloved. If he also wins respect and admiration and consequently develops his self-respect, he will be even more healthy. Need gratification is thus positively associated with the degree of a person's physiological health and with the degree of his psychological health.

The five political goods which can be associated with Maslow's basic needs are welfare, security, fraternity, equality, and liberty.[7] Each of these is a good in the sense that it represents a condition which we have some reason to regard as agreeable, beneficial, commendable, right, proper, or morally excellent. Each good is political in the sense that it represents a public virtue realizable at least in part through collective action and describes an ideal the fulfilment of which may provide the justification for collectivization.

Physiological Needs and Welfare

Modern psychologists dealing with the problem of motivation and the satisfaction of basic needs have tended to look first to the conditions for existence and the relief of pain.[8] As with general lists of basic needs, it is impossible to make a definitive list of physiological needs because the number of needs can always be increased by making their descriptions more specific; but any list of physiological needs will include in some way the needs to breathe and have food, drink, sleep, sex, and shelter. These physiological needs are prepotent in the sense that a person lacking food, safety, love, and esteem would probably desire food more strongly than anything else.

If all the needs are unsatisfied, and the organism is then dominated by the physiological needs, all other needs may become simply nonexistent or be pushed into the background. It is then fair to characterize the whole organism by saying simply that it is hungry, for consciousness is almost completely preëmpted by hunger. . . . For the man who is extremely and dangerously hungry, no other interests exist but food. He dreams food, he remembers food, he thinks about food, he emotes only about food, he perceives only food, and he wants only food. . . . Another peculiar characteristic of the human organism when it is dominated by a certain need is that the whole philosophy of the future tends also to change. For our chronically and extremely hungry man, Utopia can be defined simply as a place where there is plenty of food. He tends to think that, if only he is guaranteed food

7

for the rest of his life, he will be perfectly happy and will never want anything more. Life itself tends to be defined in terms of eating. Anything else will be defined as unimportant. Freedom, love, community feeling, respect, philosophy, may all be waved aside as fripperies that are useless, since they fail to fill the stomach. Such a man may fairly be said to live by bread alone.[9]

A person's obsession with the satisfaction of his physiological needs can be relevant for explaining his political behaviour. In 1944-45, a group of conscientious objectors underwent a series of starvation experiments conducted by Ancel Keys and his associates at the University of Minnesota. After several weeks of semi-starvation, they grew more restless, irritable, and apathetic; increasingly they came to lack self-confidence and lose interest in other individuals.[10] Reports on the effects of famine conditions from all parts of the world support this relationship between semi-starvation and attitudinal change documented in the Minnesota studies by Keys and his associates. Semi-starved men become apathetic and irritable. In part their apathy results from a lack of biological energy; but this withdrawal into passivity is further accompanied by a diminished sense of social efficiency and an increasing inability to plan, make decisions, and participate in group activities. At the same time semi-starvation appears to create levels of irritability which constitute serious personal and group problems. Keys and his associates found that individuals in their experimental group experienced increased nervousness, outbursts of temper, and periods of sulking and pique. As Robert B. Stauffer has concluded,

even in isolation these attitudes would present a most severe roadblock to social interaction aimed at creating a climate for developing cooperative national political institutions. When accompanying the apathy syndrome, as is typically the case, the impact must be compounded. In more advanced cases of starvation the impact is to destroy all bases for political community. Personality changes may occur to turn men into "mean and hyperegoistic" individuals . . ., aggressive impulses come to the fore as evidenced by an increase in violent crime and thievery, and all social ties are loosened. Extreme starvation, however, precludes forceful or concerted action against the political system, simply because of its direction of all human energies to the problem of individual survival.[11]

For many of the world's inhabitants physical existence is so marginal that any potential capacity for performing the obligations of citizenship is voided by the struggle to stay alive. Comparative data on calorie consumption suggest that the rural populations of the underdeveloped world face a recurring annual period of malnutrition that borders on semi-starvation. Stauffer concludes from this evidence that "rural peoples in the underdeveloped world recurrently suffer biologically created attitude changes of a variety highly destructive of what are frequently assumed to be necessary values for the support of a political community."[12]

In contrast with the situation in poor nations, the physiological needs of people in the advanced industrialized societies are met so regularly for most people that their satisfaction is taken for granted and a basis does exist for a wide participation in political life. Yet even in the advanced industrialized societies severe deprivation with respect to physiological needs is not uncommon for many individuals. Furthermore, we are learning that pollution of the environment, which is one side effect of economic advancement, presents a serious threat to general survival; but this hazard is not yet so serious as to break down normal social relationships and make collective action impossible.

Safety Needs and Security

The fulfilment of the safety needs is the central problem in the political thought of Thomas Hobbes. Writing in Paris in the seventeenth century during a time when his own country, England, was wracked by civil war, Hobbes was, quite understandably, excessively concerned with the maintenance of political order and the ensuring of personal security. His view of human nature as competitive, diffident and vainglorious led him to conclude that "during the time men live without a common Power to keep them all in awe, they are in that condition which is called Warre; and such a warre, as is of every man, against every man". In such a condition, "wherein men live without other security than what their own strength, and their own invention shall furnish them withall", there could be no industrial or agricultural development, no technological innovation or cultural creativity, "and which is worst of all, continual fears, and danger of violent death".[13] The solution was to be found in the Commonwealth which was to be constituted by a group of people accepting a restraint upon themselves in the form of a Common Power, a ruler or an assembly, to settle their disputes authoritatively, remove the continual fear for their personal security, and thus ensure a more contented life for all.

Fear of violent death was for Hobbes the dominant motive for seeking to satisfy safety needs before all others. We have seen how an unsatisfied physiological need can cause a person to ignore all other values in striving to satisfy this need. A person can be dominated in just the same way by the safety needs, so that practically everything looks less important than safety (even physiological needs which, when satisfied, are underestimated) and the person comes to live almost for safety alone.[14] In the political thought of Hobbes we find a convincing account of the kind of political order created by people who are thus dominated by safety needs.

The insecurities of war, crime, and accident remain inevitably with us. As with the physiological needs, however, the safety needs of a person living in an advanced industrialized society are usually satisfied with such regularity that concern for safety does not dominate the personality. As Bay has noted, "most of us take our precautions as best we can as a matter of habit and occupy ourselves with other matters most of the time".[15] Evidence for the continuing potency of the safety needs can still be found, however, in the danger reaction in infants, in the child's preference for some kind of routine rhythm, and in the neurotic adult's compulsive-obsessive ordering and stabilizing of his world so that no threats appear in it. It can also be found in the relative breakdown of social order during periods of war, epidemic, natural catastrophe, excessive crime, or economic depression.[16]

The particular goals pursued by political systems vary greatly, but the maintenance of order and the provision of security for the group as a whole and for its individual members appears as a virtually universal objective of political organization and activity.[17] Davies has argued that this objective is an instrumental one because, unlike the other needs, the safety needs are not basic but instrumental to the satisfaction of other needs. The individual will work and fight to be secure in his ability to satisfy hunger and thirst or to be secure in his self-respect and the pursuit of his dreams, but he does not want to be secure simply for the sake of being secure.[18]

There is a sense in which security is instrumental to the other needs, but then there is also a sense in which the satisfaction of physiological needs is instrumental to the other needs. In fact, human beings do appear to need some degree of order and predictability in their environment, not merely to satisfy other needs but directly to ensure their gratification health. People vary greatly in their ability to cope with prolonged, excessive disorder in their environment, but there are limits beyond which it is impossible for anyone to go without having a nervous breakdown. Widespread anxiety about security also seems to create a kind of collective neurosis which may result in the disruption of accepted social procedures and the imposition of considerable injustices. Hobbes' conception of the state of nature with its war of every man against every man is thus an exaggerated but useful heuristic device which reminds us of the continuing importance of safety needs and the contribution of political order to the realization of human development.

Belongingness Needs and Fraternity

If both the physiological and the safety needs are adequately satisfied, there will emerge the need for love, affection, and belongingness.

> *Now the person will feel keenly, as never before, the absence of friends, or a sweetheart, or a wife, or children. He will hunger for affectionate relations with people in general, namely, for a place in his group, and he will strive with great intensity to achieve this goal. He will want to attain such a place more than anything else in the world and may even forget that once, when he was hungry, he sneered at love as unreal or unnecessary or unimportant.*[19]

The social needs are those which arise from the deep desire people have to get together, be together, and stay together.[20] They must be counted among the most basic and durable needs in view of the overwhelming evidence that humans are social animals and normally choose not to live alone. Aristotle's famous dictum that "man is by nature a political animal" derived from his observation that "men, even when they do not require one another's help desire to live together; not but that they are also brought together by their common interests in proportion as they severally attain to any measure of well-being".[21] Sigmund Freud attempted to explain the psychology of human groups with the supposition that "love relationships (or, to use a more neutral expression, emotional ties) also constitute the essence of the group mind."[22] His concept of the libido makes sexual love the basic force; but it also includes self-love, love for parents and children, friendship, love for humanity in general, and devotion to concrete objects and to abstract ideas. Erich Fromm has concluded that "the necessity to unite with other living beings, to be related to them, is an imperative need on the fulfillment of which man's sanity depends. This need is behind all phenomena which constitute the whole gamut of intimate human relations, of all passions which are called love in the broadest sense of the word".[23]

The human need for love is satisfied in the formation of human communities, from the family to the nation state. Carl Friedrich has described a community as being "composed of persons who are united by one or more of the following aspects of their personality: values— including purposes, interests, ideas and ideologies—myths, utopias and their symbols, and finally, religion and its rituals".[24] A political

11

community is a group of persons united by having some part of all these aspects in common; but it is more comprehensive in its membership than other communities, and this feature weakens the intensity of commitment to it on the part of most of its members. Only a few citizens who are most politically minded normally exhibit the intensity of concern for the political community which most people reserve for their families, churches, or other less comprehensive groupings. Yet political communities can and do satisfy social needs, even if they are not among the most important of human communities in satisfying such needs. At the very least, political communities provide an essential order within which communities better able to satisfy social needs can flourish.

Fraternity is the political good which a political community can provide to satisfy its members' social needs, whether as citizens actively engaged in the political affairs of their community, or as parents, children, friends, or devotees intensively committed to the more private life of a less comprehensive community. Fraternity, as Trevor Lloyd has remarked, sounds a rather sloppy word; but it signifies an essential contribution to the satisfaction of social needs.

> The failure to bring Quebec into a Canadian community, the failure to bring negroes into a United States community, the failure to bring coloured immigrants into a British community are visible signs that people are not living together as brothers. The results of these failures are destructive enough to show that the preservation of the community is a worthwhile objective. . . . Fraternity may be a sloppy word, but the underlying principle of preserving the community is obviously important.[25]

The preservation of a political community and the satisfaction of the social needs of its members must be studied in part by reconstructing the process of political socialization in the community. Political socialization is "the developmental process through which the citizen matures politically" acquiring thereby a "complex of beliefs, feelings, and information which help him comprehend, evaluate, and relate to the political world around him."[26]

One element in the development of a "political self" is the acquisition of basic loyalties to the political community in which the person lives. Indeed, the identification of oneself as a member of the political community appears to be among the first political orientations acquired by a child and also among those orientations which are most enduring in later life.[27]

Political socialization is not just a development limited to the young, however; it is a life-long process. Changes in values, interests, and beliefs can affect a person's identification with a political community. A person's values, beliefs, and political attachments may change with those of the community, of course, and his affiliation remain unchanged. A person's political orientations may also become different from those which prevail in the community, or those in the community may change while those of the individual do not, with the result that the individual becomes alienated from the community. The first case reminds us that even with stable conditions some change in values, interests, and beliefs characterizes any living political community; the second case reminds us that disintegration of the community is always a possibility.

Esteem Needs and Equality

People need self-esteem or self-respect, and they need the esteem of others. From within himself a person needs strength, achievement, adequacy, mastery and competence, confidence in the face of the world, and independence. From other people he needs prestige, status, recognition, attention, importance, and appreciation. "Satisfaction of the self-esteem need leads to feelings of self-confidence, worth, strength, capability, and adequacy, of being useful and necessary in the world. But thwarting of these needs produces feelings of inferiority, of weakness, and of helplessness."[28]

The need for esteem has its political expression in the demand for equality. Much of the attention of social theorists has been directed to the conditions for political equality which may be defined as existing "when in a given community all men are given an undifferentiated *opportunity* to participate in politics and to exert themselves with a view to acquiring power".[29] Equality of opportunity to participate in politics is a special case of general equality of opportunity to participate in various kinds of professional activities. This general equality of opportunity is in turn a special case of "general equality", a term used by Friedrich to designate the status of persons belonging to a political community in which the basis for differentiation is the "prevailing view" of what is just in various kinds of situations. A prevailing view in a democratically organized community is a majority view, but the prevailing view in any community is subject to change as new notions of equality and inequality intrude continually into the political decisions which have to be taken. The essence of politics is an argument about justice, about who may be compared with whom for what treatment.[30]

As with a large number of social beliefs, attitudes toward equality

13

are affected by a person's status, his beliefs about himself, and the degree of his self-esteem. After interviews in depth with fifteen American working men, Robert Lane reached the conclusion that "many members of the working class do not want equality. They are afraid of it. In some ways they already seek to escape from it. Equality for the working classes, like freedom for the middle classes, is a worrisome, partially rejected, by-product of the demand for more specific measures. Inequalities have values for them that have been overlooked."[31]

Lane found that most of the men accepted the view that the United States opens up enough opportunity so that a person must assume responsibility for his own status. Only a few of them took up the theme of differential life chances from birth. To come to terms with the existence of inequality, the men insulated themselves by limiting their outlook and range of comparisons, denied the importance of class position, or reluctantly accepted their fate. They talked about equality of happiness (hardly a man thought the rich were happier than they were) and moral equality, but they also recognized the essence of their need for esteem in a vague demand that being a person was enough in itself to qualify for claims of some undefined equality. As Lane interpreted their argument,

> it seems probable that when men assert their own equality in this vague sense, typically phrased in something like O'Hara's terms: "I think I'm just as good as anybody else. I don't think there's any of them that I would say are better," something other than moral or spiritual equality is at issue. These moral qualities are what the educated commentator reads into the statement, but O'Hara means, if I may put words into his mouth: "Don't put on airs around me; I'm trying to preserve my self-respect in a world that challenges it; I therefore assert my equality with all. I won't be pushed around; I know my rights"; and, to the interviewer, "Just because you're a professor and I'm an oiler, it doesn't mean you can patronize me." And when Sokolsky, a machine operator and part-time janitor, says, in the interview: "The rich guy—because he's got money he's no better than I am—I mean, that's the way I feel," he is not talking about moral or spiritual qualities. He is saying, in effect, to his prosperous older brother and his snobbish wife, "Don't look down on me," and to the world at large, "I may be small, but I will protect my self-esteem." These men are posting notices similar to the motto on the early American colonies' flags, "Don't tread on me."[32]

The men interviewed by Lane accepted differences of status as just where the differences were proportionate to ability or resulted from the wisdom of previous decisions. Moreover, Lane thought that they would fear and resent any strongly equalizing change in the social order which might remove the reassurance of the existing social hierarchy; create difficult problems of social adjustment; and deprive people of their main motivation to work, achieve, and develop their skills—"there is the image of an equalitarian society as a world running down, a chaotic and disorganized place to live."[33] Lane concludes that

> people tend to care less about equality of opportunity than about the availability of some opportunity. Men do not need the same life chances as everybody else; indeed, they usually care very little about that. They need only chances (preferably with unknown odds) for a slightly better life than they now have. Thus: popular satisfaction with one's own status is related less to equality of opportunity than to the breadth of distribution of some opportunity for all, however unequal this distribution may be. A man who can improve his position one rung does not resent the man who starts on a different ladder halfway up.[34]

Although these results may seem to be conservative in their implications, they should not be construed as precluding even marked social change. People do have a strong underlying need to be regarded as equal in worth, value, and dignity; but this need is always expressed within a framework of certain notions about what is just in terms of differences among people. In contemporary industrialized society, the need for esteem may well be satisfied by the availability of some opportunity, given the acceptance of the prevailing social order as more or less just. As notions of justice are widened, however, the meaning of equality will be progressively extended.

Carl Friedrich has made the point that both democratic and totalitarian modern political systems provide for greater political equality than did many systems of the past because "the disbelief in the presence of any manifest innate qualities justifying political inequality is very general, and still spreading."[35] This greater equality in modern systems can be expressed as a quantitatively defined comparative equality of opportunity. In the sphere of politics, the appropriate tests for measuring the advance toward a full realization of equality would include the degree of popular control over political leaders, the degree to which educational advantages are based on ability to profit from them, the opportunity to compete for political office on the basis of completing any necessary educational preparation, and the opportunity to participate through all media of communication in the shaping of political opinion and policy. In the social (status) and economic (class) spheres, the tests for measuring equality of opportunity include the degree of popular control over business and social leaders, the degree to which educational advantages are based on ability to profit from them, the opportunity to compete for occupational positions or socially prestigious positions on the basis of completing the necessary educational preparation, and the opportunity to participate through all media of communication in the shaping of social and economic values and decisions.

Self-actualization Needs and Liberty

The need for self-actualization refers to a person's desire to actualize his full potential as a human being and develop to the utmost what he is capable of becoming. "What a man *can* be, he *must* be."[36]

The fully self-actualizing person is a healthy person. He displays a more efficient perception of reality and a greater ability to come to terms with it. He accepts human nature with all its shortcomings at all levels. His behaviour is marked by spontaneity, simplicity, naturalness, and lack of artificiality. Ordinarily he has some mission in life, some task to fulfill, or some problem outside himself which engages his energies. He has a quality of detachment, preference for privacy, and ability to remain calm in adversity which may be misinterpreted as coldness, snobbishness, or even hostility. He has a capacity for continued freshness of appreciation and for experiencing feelings of great ecstasy, wonder, and awe, the "mystic experience" or the "oceanic feeling." He has for other human beings a deep feeling of identification, sympathy, and affection. He has deeper and more profound interpersonal relations than other adults, including sexual relations. He is a democratic person, able to discriminate between means and ends. He is philosophical, creative, and inventive. He resists becoming enmeshed in the culture of his society, maintaining a certain inner detachment from it.

Not many people would fit this description of a completely self-actualizing person, but any one during a "peak experience" may for a time become self-actualizing. "Not only are these his happiest and most thrilling moments, but they are also moments of greatest maturity, individuation, fulfillment—in a word, his healthiest moments."[37]

The ways in which the need for self-actualization can be realized vary greatly from person to person. "In one individual it may take the form of a desire to be an ideal mother, in another, it may be expressed athletically, and in still another it may be expressed in painting pictures or in inventions."[38] For at least some of the relatively small groups of people who participate intensely in politics, it is reasonable to explain their motivation in terms of their need for self-actualization. In the political involvement of such people the most reasonable, common, fundamental, and basically organic factor appears to be the inherent and profound pleasure which the game of statecraft gives them.[39]

The overwhelming majority of people do not relate their self-actualizing activities to political participation. Moreover, because the ways in which people seek to satisfy their self-actualization needs are so varied, the interest groups using political and governmental action as instruments to promote policies for satisfying needs for self-actualization are likely to be small and politically weak relative to the interest groups seeking the satisfaction of physiological, security, social, or esteem needs through political activity.[40] The absence of important interest groups explicitly concerned with furthering the satisfaction of self-actualization needs does not mean, however, that public policies do not affect the possibilities for individual self-development. On the contrary, public policies may extend or limit the possibilities in important ways.

The political good which is a condition for satisfyng the self-actualization needs is liberty. The political thinker who perhaps more than any other recognized the importance of liberty for self-actualization was John Stuart Mill. Mill's famous essay "On Liberty" is clearly concerned with the self-actualizing aspect of human nature, and Mill's view of man's potential for self-development is not very different from the one expressed by Maslow.

> *Human nature is not a machine to be built after a model, and set to do exactly the work prescribed for it, but a tree, which requires to grow and develop itself on all sides, according to the tendency of the inward forces which make it a living thing. . . . It is not wearing down into uniformity all that is individual in themselves but by cultivating it and calling it forth, within the limits imposed by the rights and interests of others, that human beings become a noble and beautiful object of contemplation; and as the works partake the character of those who do them, by the same process human life also becomes rich, diversified, and animating, furnishing more abundant aliment to high thoughts and elevating feelings, and strengthening the tie which binds every individual to the race, by making the race infinitely better worth belonging to. In proportion to the development of his individuality, each person becomes more valuable to himself, and is therefore capable of being more valuable to others.[41]*

Liberty or freedom, as Carl Friedrich has pointed out, has two dimensions. The first is independence and the second is participation. "In the first type of situation, freedom is . . . a matter of not being personally interfered with by others; in the second, freedom means sharing in the decision-making, which is not being interfered with collectively."[42]

Definitions of the private sphere of freedom have varied according to time and place. Religion and property have been especially important as foundations for the demand that some private sphere be recognized as inviolable. Other common demands have been for protection against arbitrary arrest, search, and seizure; freedom of expression, not only in religion and other basic convictions but also in arts, letters, science, and scholarship; and the freedom of ordering one's family and working life as one chooses. What is common to these demands and accepted as a necessity is "the need for such a personal sphere of freedom of independence from public regulation and interference."[43]

The importance of freedom of independence as a favourable condition for satisfying the self-actualizing needs often results in relative neglect of freedom of participation, but freedom of participation must be as much a part of our concern in reviewing public policies and their consequences for self-actualization as is freedom of independence. Many of a person's most prized experiences arise in the private sphere of family, work, church, club, or concert; but some are attainable only through engagement and commitment in the larger political community. Certainly Mill, who emphasized the importance of the private sphere of freedom, was also aware of the importance of the public sphere. In his consideration of the ideally best form of government in his essay "Representative Government", Mill rejected the "good despot", not only because he would have to have unimaginable talents and energies, but also because the development of citizenship would be effectively prevented. Supposing the talent and energy for a good despot were available, Mill asks,

What should we then have? One man of superhuman mental activity managing the entire affairs of a mentally passive people. Their passivity is implied in the very idea of absolute power. The nation as a whole, and every individual composing it, are without any potential voice in their own destiny. They exercise no will in respect to their collective interests. All is decided for them by a will not their own, which it is legally a crime for them to disobey. What sort of human beings can be formed under such a regimen? What develop-

ment can either their thinking or their active faculties attain under it?[44]

Whether it is freedom of independence or freedom of participation which is at stake, liberty has a crucial psychological aspect for people living in a modern society. Erich Fromm has argued persuasively that people have become more isolated, alone, and afraid as they have become more independent, self-reliant, and critical. Modern man has progressively freed himself from the restraints imposed by traditional economic, religious, and political authorities and has become more an "individual"; but "at the same time he has become isolated, powerless, and an instrument of purposes outside of himself, alienated from himself and others" and "this state undermines his self, weakens and frightens him, and makes him ready for submission to new kinds of bondage."[45]

According to Fromm, concentration on eliminating traditional external restraints on freedom has obscured the growth of internal restrictions on the full realization of the freedom of the personality. Having freedom of worship is less important if a person has lost the spiritual capacity for faith. Having freedom of speech is less valuable if a person does not have the ability to think originally, as this ability gives meaning to the claim for free expression of thought.

> *In other words, we are fascinated by the growth of freedom from powers outside of ourselves and are blinded to the fact of inner restraints, compulsions, and fears, which tend to undermine the meaning of the victories freedom has won against its traditional enemies. We therefore are prone to think that the problem of freedom is exclusively that of gaining still more freedom of the kind we have gained in the course of modern history, and to believe that the defense of freedom against such powers that deny such freedom is all that is necessary. We forget that, although each of the liberties which have been won must be defended with utmost vigour, the problem of freedom is not only a quantitative one, but a qualitative one; that we not only have to preserve and increase the traditional freedom, but that we have to gain a new kind of freedom, one which enables us to realize our own individual self, to have faith in this self and life.*[46]

Extending Fromm's analysis of the psychological aspect of freedom, Christian Bay has argued that there are three types of obstacles to a person's having the capacity, opportunity, and incentive to give expression to what is in him and to develop his potentialities.[47] The first type of obstacle to full freedom of expression consists of various external rewards and punishments which restrain the person's "social freedom" by preventing him from doing something he wants to do, either by physical compulsion or by threat of sanctions.

The second type of obstacle is what Bay calls "defensiveness" which limits an individual's psychological freedom. A variety of unfortunate circumstances in a person's social relationships may contribute to neuroses of various kinds. Inability to cope with excessive anxiety results in a strictly limited consciousness as the individual avoids some of the facts of life with respect to himself and his social surroundings. "The result is an enduring deficiency in communication and, consequently, an enduring disharmony between his fundamental motives and his conscious self and overt behaviour. It is plain that this state of affairs interferes with the free expression of a man's full individuality."[48] Freedom from defensiveness, Bay argues, is more than mere mental health. "Mental health means avoidance of anxieties that one cannot face or capacity to face anxieties that one cannot avoid. Psychological freedom means acceptance of and capacity to cope with all the anxieties to which man in modern society may be exposed."[49]

The third type of restraint on freedom described by Bay puts limitations on a person's "potential freedom" or his freedom from manipulation. Restraints of this type hamper a person's potential behaviour, not his actual behaviour, by the manipulation of his beliefs and wants. Manipulation means "regulating the supply of information in the interest of encouraging or discouraging certain types of behaviour",[50] and Bay concludes that "the most acute problem of potential freedom in our time undoubtedly arises out of the highly developed modern propaganda and advertising techniques."[51]

Evaluating Political Legitimacy

The combination of Maslow's classification of basic needs with traditional ideas of political good provides a useful framework for analyzing the purposes and assessing the results of the political arrangements in a community, but it will not direct us to any obvious resolutions of political differences nor put an end to partisan debate. This is because welfare, security, fraternity, equality, and liberty are comparative ideas; and, for a number of reasons, disagreements can arise about how much of each should be provided in given circumstances.

First, because people can enjoy more or less of them, the question is always open as to how much of each good is necessary in order to satisfy basic physiological, safety, belongingness, esteem, and self-actualization needs. Even if it were generally agreed to provide whatever is required for the gratification health of each member of the community, there is still room for considerable disagreement about what is really "needed" as opposed to what is merely "wanted." Perceptions of need are strongly dependent on the values and beliefs held by the people who make them, and there is rarely any objective test for distinguishing what is basically necessary from what is merely pleasant or luxurious.

Second, people place different weights on the enjoyment of different goods. Some are prepared to have less security and more liberty; others choose the opposite. Some campaign for welfare; others insist on the priority of fraternity or equality. In a community of many individuals, such differences in asserting the priorities for satisfying basic needs are surely inevitable.

Third, people also have quite different time horizons for the enjoyment of political goods. The sacrifice of the welfare of some group in the community now may be accepted as the condition for all to enjoy greater prosperity in the future. Many people have at some time believed that the ultimate sacrifice of their lives was necessary to protect the security of their community or to achieve equality or freedom for those who would live in the future. The misery of the working class was once regarded as the necessary price for national economic growth, and we have enjoyed the fruits of that growth. Now it is apparent that our own forbearance in material consumption is a critical factor in ensuring the welfare of future generations.

Questions as to how much of each good is needed, which goods should have priority, or whether certain sacrifices of present goods for future goods are worthwhile, can rarely be answered with certainty even with the hindsight of history, let alone at the time the questions are being decided. They are simply questions about which people living in a community tend to differ if they take seriously their responsibilities as citizens. The differences cannot be removed by analyzing the questions within a conceptual framework of basic needs; they must be debated and resolved through the political arrangements of the community.

Without providing the means actually to resolve fundamental political differences, Maslow's framework nonetheless helps to organize the debate about them by making us aware of what the differences mean for human development and by providing a useful expression of what matters ought to be politically predominant. A truly self-governing people motivated by a fundamental desire to enlarge the possibilities for human development must be constantly reassessing its beliefs about what it is possible and what it is desirable to accomplish through collective action. Such a people must know what they have done and what they are doing as a community if they are to make mature, responsible, humane resolutions of the recurring, hard choices concerning the distribution of political goods. As Christian Bay has argued, a radically new approach to citizenship is implicit in the acceptance of basic human needs as the criteria for evaluating public policies.

> It is not sufficient to ask, or even moral to ask, if I may take issue with John F. Kennedy, "What you can do for your country," unless you first ask what your country, or your government, is up to. Self-governing individuals do not squander their political commitment on whatever government happens to be in power, in whatever country they happen to inhabit; if they are humane individuals, their first commitment is to humanity, or to the cause of advancing justice, or respect for life and liberties, in their own communities and elsewhere.[52]

The first question for responsible citizens is what our country is up to; and it is this question which has prompted the collection of the data presented in the following chapters of this study. By providing a way of organizing the collection and presentation of these data, the framework of basic needs and political goods outlined here has served both as a fundamental expression of what is politically relevant and as a valuable heuristic device for composing a socio-political report on the state of the nation.

NOTES

1. A human need is an urge or drive or behaviour tendency the gratification of which benefits a person. A need refers to any behaviour tendency whose continued denial or frustration leads to such pathological responses as suicide or serious attempts at suicide, psychosis, severe neurosis, or severe addiction to alcohol or drugs. See Christian Bay, "Needs, Wants and Political Legitimacy," *Canadian Journal of Political Science*, I (September 1968), 242–4.
2. Graham Wallas, *Human Nature in Politics* (London: Constable and Company Ltd., 1948) pp. 50, 58, 59, 61, 63, 68.
3. Robert E. Lane, *Political Thinking and Consciousness* (Chicago: Markham Publishing Company, 1969), p. 31.
4. James C. Davies, *Human Nature in Politics* (New York: Wiley, 1963), p. 9; C. Bay, *op. cit.*, p. 247.
5. R. E. Lane, *op. cit.*, p. 31.
6. Abraham Maslow, *Motivation and Personality* (New York: Harper and Brothers, 1954), p. 115.
7. For a discussion of the concept of political good, see J. Roland Pennock,

"Political Development, Political Systems and Political Goods," *World Politics*, 18 (April 1966), 420. Pennock's list of political goods includes welfare, order, justice, and liberty.

8. R. E. Lane, *op. cit.*, p. 24.
9. A. H. Maslow, *op. cit.*, pp. 82–3.
10. See, for example, the case of "Don" summarized in J. C. Davies, *op. cit.*, pp. 11–14. The original report is found in Ancel Keys et al., *The Biology of Human Starvation* (Minneapolis: University of Minnesota Press, 1950).
11. These excerpts from "The Biopolitics of Underdevelopment," by Robert B. Stauffer are reprinted from *Comparative Political Studies*, Vol. 2, No. 3 (October 1969), p. 365 by permission of the Publisher, Sage Publications, Inc.
12. *Ibid.*, p. 369.
13. Thomas Hobbes, *Leviathan* (London: J. M. Dent and Sons Ltd., 1914, 1953), pp. 64–5.
14. A. H. Maslow, *op. cit.*, pp. 84–5.
15. C. Bay, *op. cit.*, p. 247, note 11.
16. The evidence is listed by A. H. Maslow, *op. cit.*, pp. 85–9.
17. J. R. Pennock, *op. cit.*, p. 421.
18. J. C. Davies, *op. cit.*, pp. 9–10.
19. A. H. Maslow, *op. cit.*, p. 89.
20. J. C. Davies, *op. cit.*, p. 31.
21. Aristotle, *Politics* (New York: The Modern Library, 1943), p. 137.
22. Sigmund Freud, "Group Psychology and the Analysis of the Ego," *The Standard Edition of the Complete Psychological Works of Sigmund Freud,* James Strachey, trans. (London: The Hogarth Press and the Institute of Psychoanalysis, 1955), Vol. xviii, p. 91. U.S.A. (New York: Liveright Publishing Company). Freud's belief that sexual love was the basic force can be seen in his explanation (pp. 90–1) for taking love in a wider sense than sex. "Our justification lies in the fact that psycho-analytic research has taught us that all these tendencies are an expression of the same instinctual impulses; in relations between the sexes, these impulses force their way towards sexual union, but in other circumstances they are diverted from this aim or are prevented from reaching it, though always preserving enough of their original nature to keep their identity recognizable (as in such features as the longing for proximity, and self-sacrifice)."
23. Erich Fromm, *The Sane Society* (New York: Holt, Rinehart and Winston, 1955), p. 36. British Commonwealth: Routledge and Kegan Paul Ltd.
24. Carl J. Friedrich, *Man and His Government* (New York: McGraw-Hill Book Company, 1963), p. 137.
25. Trevor Lloyd, "Introduction: Our Ideological Tradition," in Trevor Lloyd and J. T. McLeod (eds.), *Agenda 1970: Proposals for a Creative Politics* (Toronto: University of Toronto Press, 1968), pp. 13–14.
26. Richard E. Dawson and Kenneth Prewitt, *Political Socialization* (Boston: Little, Brown and Company, 1969), p. 17.
27. *Ibid.*, pp. 20–21. See also David Easton and Jack Dennis, *Children in the Political System* (New York: McGraw-Hill Book Company, 1969). Easton and Dennis argue that socialization provides a crucial support enabling the political system to persist over time.
28. A. H. Maslow, *op. cit.*, p. 91.
29. C. J. Friedrich, *op. cit.*, p. 292.
30. *Ibid.*, p. 256.

31. Robert E. Lane, *Political Ideology* (New York: The Free Press, 1962), p. 60. Copyright © 1962 by the Free Press of Glencoe.
32. *Ibid.*, pp. 67–8.
33. *Ibid.*, p. 78.
34. *Ibid.*, p. 79.
35. C. J. Friedrich, *op. cit.*, p. 294.
36. A. H. Maslow, *op. cit.*, p. 91. The description of the self-actualizing person which follows is summarized from Maslow's discussion on pp. 203–234. See also pp. 235–260 of *Motivation and Personality* on love for self-actualizing people and pp. 135–145 on their creativity in Abraham H. Maslow, *Toward a Psychology of Being*. (Published by Van Nostrand Reinhold Co., copyright 1968 by Litton Educational Publishing, Inc.)
37. A. H. Maslow, *Toward a Psychology of Being*, p. 97. Maslow has defined the peak experience as
   "an episode, or a spurt in which the powers of the person come together in a particularly efficient and intensely enjoyable way, and in which he is more integrated and less split, more open for experience, more idiosyncratic, more perfectly expressive or spontaneous, or fully functioning, more creative, more humorous, more ego-transcending, more independent of his lower needs, etc. He becomes in these episodes more truly himself, more perfectly actualizing his potentialities, closer to the core of his Being, more fully human."
38. A. H. Maslow, *Motivation and Personality*, p. 92.
39. J. C. Davies, *op. cit.*, p. 60.
40. *Ibid.*, p. 54.
41. John Stuart Mill, "On Liberty," *On Liberty, Representative Government, The Subjection of Women: Three Essays* (London: Oxford University Press, 1912, 1960), pp. 73, 77–8.
42. C. J. Friedrich, *op. cit.*, p. 354. Friedrich, unlike some authors, believes the terms "liberty" and "freedom" are synonymous. I accept this view.
43. *Ibid.*, pp. 358–9. Friedrich notes that Plato, however, rejected this notion of personal freedom of independence as a necessary part of a well-ordered community and that he had a good deal of human experience on his side in doing so, there being many political orders which in large degree have lacked such a personal sphere. One can only respond that Plato's model of man is incomplete in this respect and that at least one pattern of need deprivation would be easily identified in any political order lacking a personal sphere.
44. J. S. Mill, "Considerations on Representative Government," in *op. cit.*, p. 180.
45. Erich Fromm, *Escape from Freedom* (New York: Holt, Rinehart and Winston, 1941), p. 270.
46. *Ibid.*, pp 105–6.
47. See Christian Bay, *The Structure of Freedom* (Stanford, California: Stanford University Press, 1958), pp. 16–18.
48. *Ibid.*, p. 16.
49. *Ibid.*, p. 188.
50. *Ibid.*, p. 98.
51. *Ibid.*, p. 331.
52. C. Bay, "Needs, Wants and Political Legitimacy," p. 260.

Chapter Two

WELFARE

Welfare is wealth creating health. A difference in the provision of the political good welfare explains the difference between people who are sick, malnourished, and badly clothed or housed and people who are healthy and well fed, clothed and sheltered. Like its converse, poverty is a relative concept. In an economically advanced society where most people enjoy a high standard of living, the minimum requirements of life are higher than they are in an economically backward society. In part this state of affairs reflects a tendency to define poverty subjectively in terms of the standard of living which prevails in the community, but it is also true that the minimum requirements for life cannot be compared directly between communities at very different levels of economic development.

In a primitive community where there is no electricity, there is no need for electrical appliances, for example, a refrigerator, nor for foods prepared and packaged for use in homes with refrigerators. In an affluent industrialized society, on the other hand, the refrigerator might become a necessity and processed food inevitable. The train and the automobile replace the horse and the mule. Some of the cheapest forms of consumption thus disappear, or if they remain, become expensive. For this reason, the costs of unprocessed foods for the ordinary urban dwelling consumer, for example, live chickens, various fresh vegetables and fruits exceed those of processed foods in the industrialized society, and only the wealthy can afford to ride horses. The net result is that it costs more in real terms to subsist in an industrialized society. Nor is it socially or psychologically acceptable to live without some of the new or improved goods in a society where they are standard consumption. A man wearing rags, which is an acceptable and common form of attire in the

> *countryside of some of the developing areas, would prob-*
> *ably be arrested in London or New York, or at least be un-*
> *able to find employment. In a community where nearly every*
> *family has a radio and television set, it becomes socially and*
> *psychologically more difficult for most people to live without*
> *them.*[1]

Thus, wherever economic differences between communities are marked, valid comparisons can be made only if the minimum requirements for life are defined separately in terms of the appropriate level of economic development.

In addition to its relativity in the present as an idea of political good, welfare must be considered in the dimension of time, in terms of future life and not simply immediate survival. A given provision of welfare may make physical survival possible for many years, but it is inadequate if it does not maintain a person's potential for a long and healthy life. In a society where the average length of life is seventy-five years, a person is still a poor person who has sufficient food, drink, and shelter for day-to-day survival but whose suffering from malnutrition because of ignorance or low income will probably result in illness and death at a relatively early age. Illness and death are inevitable parts of life, but providing people with a sufficient amount of welfare can reduce the likelihood of their illness and expand their possibilities for life within the limits of the medical and health technology of a given time. Providing welfare for the poor in an advanced industrialized society has to be viewed, not as mere provision of the essentials to sustain life, but as provision of adequate access to certain goods and services which are generally available and accepted as the necessary minimum to ensure a long and healthy life.

Length of Life

Other things being equal, the better the physiological needs are satisfied, the longer people will live. Thus, probably the best indicators of the adequacy with which physiological needs are satisfied in a given community are its mortality statistics. Of particular usefulness for our analysis, rates of mortality are available for making cross-national comparisons and for analyzing historical trends.

The average length of life or life expectancy varies widely among nations. In Canada the life expectancy of the average newborn child in the middle of the 1960s was 68.8 years for males and 75.2 for females. As Table 2–1 shows, similar expectations of life, exceeding 65 years for males and 70 years for females, are common in advanced industrialized societies, while expectations of less than 60 years of life for both sexes are common in poor nations throughout most of Asia, Africa, and Latin America.

Table 2–1. *Length of Life, Selected Nations*

Nation	Rate of infant mortality, 1969–1970* (deaths per thousand live births)	Life expectancy at birth, 1960–1970* (years)		Percentage of deaths at age 65 or over, 1967–1970*
		Male	Female	
Canada	18.8	68.8	75.2	61.8
Chile	87.5	54.4	59.9	31.9
Czechoslovakia	22.1	67.3	73.6	65.8
Ecuador	76.6	51.0	53.7	19.5
Egypt	119.0	51.6	53.8	23.0
England and Wales	18.1	68.6	74.9	71.4
France	15.1	67.6	75.3	71.1
Ghana	66.9	37.1	n.a.	15.2
Israel	22.9	69.6	73.0	55.9
Italy	29.2	67.9	73.4	65.9
Japan	13.1	69.1	74.3	61.5
Kenya	55.0	47.5		11.3
Madagascar	62.6	37.5	38.3	18.3
Mexico	68.5	61.0	63.7	23.3
Mozambique	92.5	41.0		10.4
Poland	33.2	66.9	72.8	59.0
Spain	27.9	67.3	71.9	64.1
Sweden	11.7	71.9	76.5	74.5
United States	19.8	66.6	74.0	61.6
Venezuela	48.7	66.4		25.2

* Year of studies varies. See source for details.   n.a. Not available.

Source: United Nations, Department of Economic and Social Affairs, Statistical Office, *Demographic Yearbook 1971* (New York: United Nations, 1972), Table 28, pp. 667–673; Table 34, pp. 746–765; Table 31, pp. 700–726. Reprinted by permission of the United Nations.

Variations in length of life can also be measured by the proportions of deaths occuring at either end of the human life span. Infant mortality, measured as the ratio of annual deaths of infants under one year of age to each one thousand live births, appears to be a particularly sensitive indicator of the degree to which basic physiological needs are being satisfied. At 18.8 deaths per thousand live births in 1970, the rate of infant mortality in Canada was approximately in the middle of the rates prevalent in industrialized societies, which ranged from 12 to 30; but rates of infant mortality in underdeveloped countries such as Chile, Egypt, or Mozambique were very much higher.

A similar international pattern is found in the proportions of all deaths which occur at age 65 or over. The rate in Canada of 61.8 per cent of deaths at age 65 or over in 1970 was relatively modest compared with Sweden (74.5 per cent) or England and Wales (71.4 per

Table 2–2. Average Death Rates for Leading Causes of Death,*
Canada, 1921–1970

(rates per 100,000 population)

Years	Heart Disease	Cancer	Accidents	Tuber-culosis	Diseases of early infancy	Influenza, bronchitis and pneumonia	Gastritis, duodenitis, enteritis and colitis	Communicable diseases
1921–25	221.9	75.9	51.5	85.1	111.0	141.1	72.2	47.1
1926–30	273.1	88.0	58.8	80.3	97.7	133.8	54.9	35.0
1931–35	297.5	100.9	52.4	65.5	74.5	100.6	35.4	17.8
1936–40	337.6	113.8	55.9	56.2	60.2	97.5	24.1	15.6
1941–45	403.3	123.3	60.6	50.1	57.2	69.1	19.2	9.7
1946–50	413.0	129.3	58.9	37.1	58.3	55.3	14.2	4.9
1951–55	414.0	128.7	57.4	14.6	49.5	45.9	7.8	2.5
1956–60	399.9	128.6	55.1	6.2	44.2	44.9	5.7	1.1
1961–65	360.9	132.2	54.5	3.9	35.8	36.3	4.4	0.5
1966–70	347.9	138.5	55.7	2.9	23.3	38.9	2.6	0.2

* For 1921–1960, the detailed international classifications (seventh revision, 1955) are 330-4, 400-68, 592-4; 140-205; E800-962; 001-019; 760-76; 480-3, 490-3, 500-2, 763; 543, 571-2; 055-6, 085, 050, 040-1. For 1961-8, the intermediate classifications (seventh revision, 1955) are B22, B24-9; B18; BE47-8; B1-2; B42-4; B30-2; B36; B4, B7-9, B14. For 1969, the intermediate classifications (eighth revision, 1965) are B25-30; B19; BE47-8; B5-6; B43-4; B31-3; B4; B2, B8-10; B14. For 1970, the international classifications (eighth revision, 1965) are A80-8; A45-60; AE138-46; A6-10; A131-5; A90-3; A5, A99; A2, A15-7, A25.

Sources: M. C. Urquhart and F. A. H. Buckley (eds.), Historical Statistics of Canada (Toronto: Macmillan Company of Canada Ltd., 1965), p. 40; Canada, Dominion Bureau of Statistics, Canada Year Book 1965 (Ottawa: Queen's Printer, 1965), pp. 247-8; Canada Year Book 1967 (Ottawa: Queen's Printer, 1967), pp. 255-6; Canada Year Book 1969 (Ottawa: Queen's Printer, 1969), pp. 243-4; Canada Year Book 1970-71 (Ottawa: Information Canada, 1971), pp. 304-5; Statistics Canada, Canada Year Book 1972 (Ottawa: Information Canada, 1972), pp. 262-3; Statistics Canada, Vital Statistics 1970 (Ottawa: Information Canada, 1972), Table D8, pp. 84-103. Statistics from Canada Yearbooks and Vital Statistics reproduced by permission of Information Canada.

cent), but far superior to such poor countries as Ecuador (19.5 per cent), Kenya (11.3 per cent), and Mozambique (10.4 per cent).

In its 1964 Report, the Royal Commission on Health Services raised the question "whether our longer life today, beset as it is with chronic illness and exposed to such insidious risks as radiation and carcinogenic matter, is really healthier than the shorter life span of former generations which may have ended more abruptly as a result of some acute infectious disease."[2] This question is probably not answerable; but it deserves consideration, if only because it forces us to examine the results of the spectacular advances in health care in the twentieth century. Certainly the prospects for a longer life have improved remarkably in Canada in the twentieth century.

The death rate, adjusted for age composition, declined from 12.9 to 6.9 per thousand population between 1921 and 1970, from 13.3 to 8.5 for males and from 12.4 to 5.4 for females; infant mortality declined from 102 deaths per thousand live births in 1921 to 18.8 in 1970; and life expectancy at birth increased from 60.00 for males and 62.10 for females in 1931 to 68.75 and 75.18 respectively in 1966.[3]

Table 2–2 shows the trends in Canada for the effective control of some diseases which were once fatal, and the elimination of fatality or its postponement in the case of other diseases. Since 1921, there have been important advances in reducing mortality from diphtheria, whooping cough, measles, scarlet fever, and typhoid fever; gastritis, duodenitis, enteritis, and colitis; tuberculosis; influenza, bronchitis, and pneumonia; and diseases of early infancy. Accidents continue to be an important cause of death; but, with Canadians on the average living longer, cancer and heart disease have become by far the most important causes of their deaths.

That this change in the pattern of mortality is related to increases in national prosperity is suggested by Figure 2–1. Mortality patterns broadly similar to the Canadian one are found in other economically advanced nations. Economically underdeveloped nations have mortality patterns more like the Canada of fifty years ago, when heart disease and cancer were relatively less important and influenza, bronchitis, pneumonia, and gastrointestinal and communicable diseases were more important as causes of death.

The improvement in this century in the prospects of life for the average Canadian should not be allowed to obscure the persistence of different life chances for some groups of citizens. First, there are continuing regional differences in the average length of life. As Figure 2–2 shows, life expectancy varied much more among the regions of Canada in 1931 than it did in 1966; but slight regional differences still remain. Rates of infant mortality also reveal regional differences in the prospects for life in Canada. Substantial differences among the provinces in rates of infant mortality during the inter-war years were gradually reduced in the 1950s and 1960s; but some areas still had relatively high rates, notably Newfoundland, Prince Edward Island, Saskatchewan, and the Yukon and Northwest Territories.

Second, two ethnic groups whose prospects for life are markedly shorter than those of other Canadians are Canadian Indians and Eskimos. The life expectancy for Indians in 1968 was 60.5 years for males and 65.6 years for females, while that of Eskimos was 50.5 years. Table 2–4 shows that, except for the three Maritime Provinces, mortality among infants of Eskimo and Indian origin in 1961–3 was much

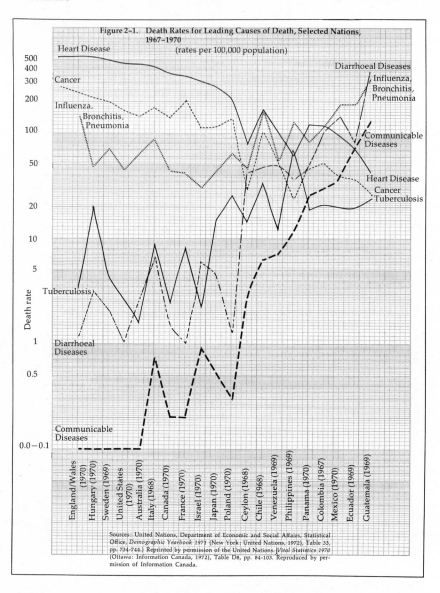

Figure 2–1. Death Rates for Leading Causes of Death, Selected Nations, 1967–1970 (rates per 100,000 population)

Sources: United Nations, Department of Economic and Social Affairs, Statistical Office, *Demographic Yearbook 1971* (New York: United Nations, 1972), Table 33, pp. 734–744.) Reprinted by permission of the United Nations. *Vital Statistics 1970* (Ottawa: Information Canada, 1972), Table D8, pp. 84–103. Reproduced by permission of Information Canada.

higher than that for infants of other ethnic origins. Taken together, the available evidence on regional and ethnic group differences with respect to life expectancy and infant mortality indicates that much remains to be done to improve the welfare of many Canadians.

Incidence of Illness

One important effect of advances in health care has been a change in the pattern of illness in economically advanced societies. The im-

Table 2–3. Infant Mortality, Canada and Provinces, 1921–1970
(average number of deaths of persons under one year of age per thousand live births)

Years	Canada	Newfoundland	Prince Edward Island	Nova Scotia	New Brunswick	Quebec	Ontario	Manitoba	Saskatchewan	Alberta	British Columbia	Yukon	Northwest Territories
1921–1925	98.8	115.9	77.1	94.0	105.1	124.5	82.8	84.0	82.9	85.8	60.5	n.a.	n.a.
1926–1930	93.9	115.4	70.3	84.8	100.7	127.1	74.1	71.6	73.2	75.0	55.1	131.4	136.0
1931–1935	76.1	116.9	66.6	73.1	82.0	98.3	60.9	61.0	62.0	60.2	46.3	86.1	109.6
1936–1940	65.4	98.7	68.9	64.8	82.2	82.4	49.6	57.2	54.9	53.3	43.9	101.7	125.4
1941–1945	55.9	91.7	52.4	57.5	73.7	68.3	42.1	51.4	46.5	43.9	38.6	100.8	188.5
1946–1950	44.6	61.1	39.7	42.2	60.1	53.7	36.1	41.9	40.3	36.6	33.6	63.0	138.7
1951–1955	35.0	45.6	32.4	32.1	43.5	44.1	28.2	31.7	31.5	28.7	27.3	52.8	117.1
1956–1960	29.7	39.2	32.7	29.3	34.2	35.8	24.5	30.0	26.3	25.5	26.0	43.6	143.2
1961–1965	25.9	35.6	28.2	27.1	26.6	29.4	22.2	24.9	25.9	24.7	22.9	42.1	93.7
1966–1970	20.8	24.8	24.1	21.3	21.6	22.2	18.7	20.9	24.1	19.8	20.0	36.4	65.7

n.a. Not available.

Sources: Canada, Dominion Bureau of Statistics, *Selected Statistics on Children* (Ottawa: Queen's Printer, 1965), Table 32, p. 44; Statistics Canada, *Vital Statistics 1970* (Ottawa: Information Canada, 1972), Table D11, p. 147. Reproduced by permission of Information Canada.

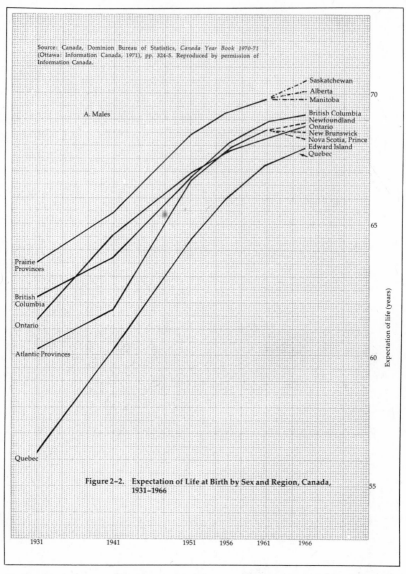

Figure 2-2. Expectation of Life at Birth by Sex and Region, Canada, 1931–1966

pact of many long-term diseases which now constitute the main health problems in Canada and other industrialized countries does not arise so much from their fatality (some, like mental illness or arthritis, have low mortality rates) as from their duration, the extent and degree of disability they cause, and the amount of health services they require for their treatment.[4] Such a situation is not very well described by mortality statistics. Morbidity statistics are needed; but, unfortunately, reliable data in this area are difficult to obtain.

One way to obtain information on the incidence of illness is to

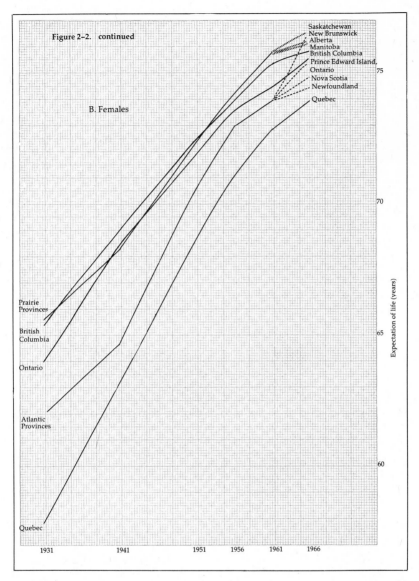

Figure 2-2. continued

B. Females

question a random sample of the total population. To date, the only available national survey of illness among Canadians has been the Canadian Sickness Survey, carried out in 1950–51 with a sample of ten thousand households.[5] Although these data are now two decades old, similar surveys in other industrialized nations suggest that the general pattern of illness found by the Canadian Sickness Survey is probably still valid. Thus, although the specific incidence of illness may have changed, it is unlikely that the pattern of illness found in 1950–51 has changed very much; and the results of the survey can

Table 2–4. Infant Mortality for Indians, Eskimos, and Others,
Canada and Provinces*, 1961–1963
(average rates per thousand live births)

Region	Total	Indians	Eskimos	Others
Canada*	28.6	65.5	178.9	26.9
Prince Edward Island	28.3	34.5	**	28.3
Nova Scotia	28.8	36.4	**	28.8
New Brunswick	28.0	21.8	**	28.0
Quebec	31.1	76.8	176.6	30.7
Manitoba	25.4	64.7	115.4	21.5
Saskatchewan	26.3	70.1	**	22.3
Alberta	25.3	61.1	**	23.2
British Columbia	23.7	64.6	**	21.0
Yukon	41.1	71.0	**	29.5
Northwest Territories	111.7	79.4	181.7	28.5

*Excludes Newfoundland and Ontario.
**Rate too small to be expressed.

Source: Canada, Dominion Bureau of Statistics, *Selected Statistics on Children* (Ottawa: Queen's Printer, 1965) Table 37, p. 52. Reproduced by permission of Information Canada.

still be usefully studied to improve our understanding of the health status of Canadians.[6]

Table 2–5 shows the average number of disability days per thousand Canadians in 1950–51 for the nation and its regions by classes of illness. Diseases of the respiratory system, infective and parasitic diseases, and diseases of the circulatory system were the most important in accounting for the total disability days in the nation as a whole and in all the regions, except for Quebec where diseases of the digestive system and symptoms of senility and ill-defined conditions were more important. Some variations can be observed among the provinces in the total disability days caused by the different diseases, but whether these can be taken to reflect regional variations in the health status of the Canadian people is open to question.[7]

Table 2–6 shows four indicators of the volume of health care available to Canadians in 1968–70, and regional differences are readily apparent. Especially, the provincial population–physician ratios and population–dentist ratios indicate differences among the provinces in their capacities to respond to the demands of people for health services. If we assume that the regional variations shown in Table 2–5 do have some basis in reality and study the data of Table 2–6 in relation to them, the tentative conclusion is that provincial variations in the capacity to provide health services seem to be largely unrelated to variations in the need for such services. To take the extreme cases, the

Table 2-5. Disability Days per Thousand Population for Selected Classes of Illness, Canada and Regions, 1950–1951

Region	Total disability days	Infective and parasitic diseases	Allergies, endocrine metabolic and nutritional diseases	Diseases of nervous system and sense organs	Disease of circulatory system	Diseases of digestive system	Deliveries and complications of pregnancy, childbirth and puerperium	Symptoms, senility and ill-defined conditions	Accidents, poisonings and violence	Diseases of respiratory system
Canada	12,162	1,316	183	882	1,271	955	346	1,136	795	3,899
Newfoundland	16,915	4,307	..	1,312	1,647	1,331	387	1,606	524	4,814
Maritimes	11,063	1,497	185	305	940	888	360	842	833	3,960
Quebec	12,566	802	122	518	993	1,408	465	1,391	928	4,924
Ontario	13,280	1,598	216	1,446	1,717	718	300	1,222	823	3,205
Prairies	10,447	1,261	190	797	1,244	778	232	838	552	3,411
British Columbia	9,766	1,003	193	625	796	631	330	714	787	3,719

Source: Canada Dominion Bureau of Statistics and Department of National Health and Welfare, *Illness and Health Care in Canada: Canadian Sickness Survey, 1950–51*. (Ottawa: Queen's Printer, 1960), pp. 148–9. Reproduced by permission of Information Canada.

Table 2–6. *Regional Differences in Provision of Health Manpower and Hospital Facilities, Canada and Provinces, 1968–1970.*

	Population per physician, 1970	Population per dentist, 1968	Hospital beds per thousand population, 1970
Newfoundland	1,118	9,236	7.8
Prince Edward Island	1,134	4,231	10.4
Nova Scotia	744	4,720	9.6
New Brunswick	1,102	5,531	10.2
Quebec	682	4,031	10.0
Ontario	654	2,697	9.6
Manitoba	701	3,627	10.0
Saskatchewan	804	5,005	11.2
Alberta	720	3,353	12.3
British Columbia	627	2,519	9.5
Yukon and Northwest Territories	1,150	9,200	12.6
Canada	692	3,319	10.0

Sources: Canada, Statistics Canada, *Canada Year Book 1972* (Ottawa: Information Canada, 1972), pp. 316, 336; Department of National Health and Welfare, *Earnings of Dentists in Canada 1959–1968* (Ottawa: Queen's Printer, 1970), Table A 2, p. 18. Reproduced by permission of Information Canada.

average number of disability days was highest in Newfoundland while the population–physician ratio and the population–dentist ratio were among the highest in the nation and the number of hospital beds per thousand population was the lowest. In British Columbia the average number of disability days was the lowest in the nation while the indicators of health manpower show the province to be the most favoured.

Table 2–7 attempts to show the volume of health care received during the Sickness Survey while controlling for variations in the need for health care by relating various types of health care received to the number of disability days. Each of the indicators in Table 2–7 shows some regional variation; and, assuming that we can project this pattern forward in time, we are led again to the conclusion that there is little association between variations in need as indicated by disability days and the amount of health care received in the six regions.

Provincial differences in the provision of health care can be given additional perspective by Tables 2–8 and 2–9, which serve to remind us of the existence of important international and intraprovincial variations in the availability of health personnel. First, Canadians are not the most favoured people in the world in terms of access to physi-

Table 2–7. *Types of Health Care Received by Region, Canada,*
1950-1951

Region	Physicians' office and home calls and clinic visits per 100 disability days	Hospital days per 100 disability days	Operations per 100 disability days	Dental visits per 1,000 population
Canada	14.7	14.2	0.3	323
Newfoundland	4.2	10.4	0.1	50
Maritimes	14.2	18.7	0.3	326
Quebec	13.2	9.6	0.3	123
Ontario	16.1	12.2	0.3	407
Prairies	13.3	23.1	0.4	390
British Columbia	23.8	21.6	0.6	633

Source: Canada, Dominion Bureau of Statistics and Department of National Health and Welfare, *Illness and Health Care in Canada: Canadian Sickness, Survey, 1950–51.* (Ottawa: Queen's Printer, 1960), pp. 157, 179, 186, 188. Reproduced by permission of Information Canada.

Table 2–8. *Ratios of Population to Health Personnel, Selected*
Nations, 1967–1968

Nation	Population per physician	Population per dentist	Population per pharmacist	Population per nurse
Brazil	2,220	54,720	75,390	3,150
Canada	740	3,050	1,960	170
Chile	1,810	2,950	5,040	4,020
Czechoslovakia	500	2,660	2,650	210
England and Wales	860	3,870	3,060	330
Ethiopia	65,380	1,314,830	483,000	23,180
France	780	2,550	2,200	380
Ghana	15,540	226,380	23,460	1,530
Hungary	580	4,630	2,460	250
Indonesia	27,560	146,380	131,830	8,310
Israel	420	1,380	1,760	320
Japan	910	2,820	1,650	400
Madagascar	9,890	81,250	85,530	3,250
Mexico	1,850	13,650	55,610	5,250
Nigeria	28,740	870,140	77,540	5,100
Peru	1,950	6,320	6,160	3,270
Spain	770	10,110	2,240	1,760
Sweden	800	1,260	2,910	230
United States	650	2,020	1,630	200
Venezuela	1,120	4,770	4,060	530

Source: World Health Organization, *World Health Statistics Annual 1968* (Geneva: World Health Organization, 1971), Volume III, Table 2, pp. 40–55.

Table 2–9. Ratios of Population to Health Personnel by Population
             of Area, Ontario, 1961

Population of area	Population per physician	Population per dentist	Population per pharmacist	Population per graduate nurse
Over 100,000	603	2,195	1,655	232
30,000–100,000	680	2,344	1,891	191
10,000–30,000	602	1,918	1,719	198
Under 10,000	2,626	7,951	5,560	431
TOTAL	776	2,713	2,092	254

Source: Ontario, Committee on the Healing Arts, *Report* (Toronto: Queen's
Printer, 1970), Volume I, p. 154.

cians, dentists, pharmacists, and nurses; but the Canadian population
ratios for health personnel do compare favourably with those in other
industrialized nations, and are very much better than those in underdeveloped countries. Second, given both the relatively high level of
health care by international standards and the existence of provincial
differences within the nation, it is important to remember that there
are also differences in the provision of health care within each of the
provinces. To illustrate this point, evidence on the variations of population–health personnel ratios between rural and urban areas is presented in Table 2–9 for the province of Ontario; but the pattern in
Ontario would certainly be repeated in the other provinces.

Adequate provision for the welfare of citizens would ensure that
there was no relationship between illness and social class in the community. Either people would be provided with health care when they
needed it, regardless of the level of their income; or their incomes
would be supplemented, if necessary, to permit them to buy adequate
care. The Canadian Sickness Survey did not report directly on the
incidence of illness in the nation by income group, but it did attempt
to establish the nature of the relationship between the need of a person for health care, the amount of health care received by him, and the
level of his income by giving the volume of various types of health
care received per hundred disability days for different income groups.

The indicators in Table 2–10 show that in relation to their need as
measured in terms of disability days people in the low-income group
on average had fewer physicians' calls and clinic visits, fewer operations, fewer nursing visits, and fewer hospital days than people in the
middle-income group. The only exception was the group of low-income
males aged fifteen to forty-four who averaged more hospital days
than middle-income males of the same age. People in the high-income
group had on average more physicians' calls and clinic visits and more

Table 2–10. Types of Health Care Received by Income Group, Canada, 1950–1951

Income group	Types of health care provided: Physicians' calls and clinic visits per 100 disability days	Operations per 100 disability days	Dental visits per 1,000 population	Nursing visits per 100 disability days	Average number of hospital days per 100 disability days: Male	Female	Total
Low income	8.5	0.2	163	1.1	15.4	14.1	14.9
Middle income	16.4	0.3	302	1.3	13.7	17.3	15.5
High income	19.2*	0.5	416*	n.a.	11.0	15.0	13.2

* In presenting the data I have collapsed the Survey's two "high" classes into one. This slightly affects physicians' calls and clinic visits where the figure given is for high (lower) and the figure for high (upper) is 19.1. It also affects dental visits per 1,000 population where the figure given is for high (lower) and the figure for high (upper) is 542.

n.a. Not available.

Source: Canada, Dominion Bureau of Statistics and Department of National Health and Welfare, *Illness and Health Care in Canada: Canadian Sickness Survey, 1950–51.* (Ottawa: Queen's Printer, 1960), pp. 50, 53, 54, 55, 179. Reproduced by permission of Information Canada.

operations but fewer hospital days than those in the middle- and low-income groups. The number of dental visits per thousand population increased significantly with income. Taken together, the indicators shown in Table 2–10 leave a strong impression that the level of a person's income was an important factor in determining how much health care he was likely to receive.[8]

Food Consumption

Food is necessary for life, and a balanced diet is needed for a long and healthy life. Patterns of food consumption vary widely from country to country and often among different parts of the same country. The kind and quality of foods consumed depend on available food supplies, levels of income, and local food habits and customs. National food balance sheets can be studied to identify at least some of the variations among different countries in the contents of their diets, particularly diet variations between developed and underdeveloped countries, which result from gross differences in agricultural productivity and average income.

Comparative studies, like those shown in Table 2–11, of food supplies available for human consumption carried out by the Food and Agriculture Organization indicate that food supplies in the less economically developed nations consist of a relatively high proportion of energy foods (cereals and other carbohydrate foods) and much smaller amounts of protective foods (milk, meat, fish and eggs, pulses, fruits, and vegetables). In the economically developed nations, including Canada, there are relatively large supplies of protective foods and lower amounts of cereals, starchy roots, and tubers.

Some further differences in national diets between rich and poor nations can be observed in the calories and protein content of average food supplies which are shown in Table 2–12. The caloric content is generally lower in the less developed nations where the average daily intake ranges from 1,900 to 2,500 calories per capita, and in the majority of these nations the calories supplied are below requirements. For most nations, net protein intake does exceed requirements; but the shortage of calorie supplies in many poor countries requires that a part of the daily protein supplies be utilized as an energy source rather than as a tissue builder, and the overall result is protein-calorie malnutrition.[9]

International differences in the nutritional quality of average food supplies are indicated in Table 2–12 by the percentages of total calories derived from cereals, starchy roots, and sugar and by the percentages of total protein intake from animal protein. In the economically advanced nations where there are adequate food supplies, the percentage of calories derived from cereals, starchy roots, and sugar is generally below 50 per cent; it is well below that level in Canada (41.8 per cent). In poorer nations this percentage rises above 65 per cent; and sometimes, as in the cases of Ethiopia, India, or Madagascar, it is well above that level. The rich nations also generally derive 50 per cent or more of their protein intake from animal protein (in Canada, 67.6 per cent), while the percentage in poorer nations is much lower, falling as low as 11.0 per cent in Ethiopia and 5.6 per cent in India.

Data on national average food supplies can conceal wide disparities in the distribution within the nation. Stauffer has noted that

> calories are not . . . distributed equally spatially, socially, nor temporally. Poor communication systems, administrative and and political watertight bulk-heads within nations, and other conditions of isolation prevent some areas from sharing even limited national average caloric supplies. People in those areas starve. National aggregate figures are affected, further, by the economics of the distribution system. Some groups can afford to eat well and regularly in nations that habitu-

Table 2–11. Food Supplies Available for Human Consumption, Selected Nations, 1970
(grams per capita per day)

Nation	Cereals	Potatoes and other starchy foods	Sugars and sweets	Pulses, nuts, and seeds	Vegetables	Fruits	Meat	Eggs	Fish	Milk	Fats and oils
Brazil	272	537	128	81	40	150	84	11	7	195	18
Canada	180	215	136	12	213	230	257	41	n.a.	619	51
Chile	321	128	86	20	265	196	108	17	18	231	35
Ecuador	188	402	78	33	161	230	57	4	5	179	17
Ethiopia	403	82	10	67	24	14	55	7	0	66	11
France	219	268	94	13	358	237	256	36	22	630	73
India	384	48	49	53	10	48	4	1	3	116	10
Israel	304	107	107	30	331	410	155	62	18	403	52
Japan	352	161	73	44	362	142	48	45	88	137	26
Madagascar	382	414	26	21	77	68	67	1	10	26	4
Sweden	168	236	114	8	110	262	n.a.	35	56	723	56
United Kingdom	200	279	136	16	170	155	209	44	24	592	63
United States	176	151	140	22	318	276	310	50	18	689	66
Venezuela	252	409	99	27	36	114	99	16	13	221	27

n.a. Not available.

Source: Food and Agriculture Organization, *Production Yearbook 1971* (Rome: Food and Agriculture Organization of the United Nations, 1972), Volume 25, Table 135, pp. 435–441. Reproduced by permission of FAO.

Table 2–12. Estimated Calories and Protein Content of Daily Average Food Supplies, Selected Nations, 1970

Nation	Calories per capita		Protein per capita (grams)			Percentage of calories from cereals, starchy roots, and sugar	Percentage of gross protein intake from animal protein
	Intake	Require-ment	Gross intake	Net intake*	Net re-quire-ment		
Brazil	2,820	2,350	66.8	38.1	36.1	68.9	21.4
Canada**	3,130	2,640	95.7	60.3	39.8	41.8	67.6
Chile	2,560	2,490	65.9	39.5	37.4	62.3	28.0
Ecuador	1,970	2,320	45.5	26.8	32.4	66.3	15.1
Ethiopia	1,980	2,210	66.3	35.8	32.1	74.0	11.0
France	3,270	2,530	102.6	62.6	42.7	40.9	64.0
India	1,990	2,220	49.4	29.6	30.0	79.7	5.6
Israel	2,990	2,530	91.5	59.5	39.5	52.7	44.3
Italy	3,020	2,460	87.9	55.3	38.6	53.6	38.3
Japan	2,470	2,360	76.9	46.1	36.5	66.2	31.8
Madagascar	2,240	2,220	51.2	33.8	33.2	84.4	12.6
Sweden	2,850	2,800	80.0	52.0	45.3	41.9	54.9
United Kingdom	3,170	2,630	86.8	57.3	42.1	45.2	53.4
United States	3,300	2,590	98.6	62.1	40.4	39.1	71.5
Venezuela	2,430	2,350	59.7	35.8	37.2	66.7	26.2

* Net protein intake is obtained by multiplying gross protein intake by NPU, the proportion of nitrogen intake which is retained.

** The estimate for per capita intake of fish is based on 1966–68 data. All other estimates of food supplies are based on 1970 data.

Sources: Food and Agriculture Organization, Production Yearbook 1971 (Rome: Food and Agriculture Organization of the United Nations, 1972), Volume 25, Table 136, pp. 442–448; Table 137, pp. 449–455. Reproduced by permission of FAO. United Nations, Department of Economic and Social Affairs, Report on the World Social Situation 1967 (New York: United Nations, 1969), pp. 36–7. Reprinted by permission of the United Nations.

ally appear in the caloric deficit column. Finally, the temporal pattern in food availability is of considerable relevance. For the 70–85% of the population of developing nations living in rural areas, the availability of food is affected by the cycle of nature as it influences supply and consumption.[10]

These factors probably affect the distribution of calories in all systems, at least to some extent; but they are much less important in richer nations. Nonetheless, the high quantity and quality of average food supplies in Canada do conceal many specific nutritional problems. During 1970-72, a comprehensive national nutrition survey involving over nineteen thousand individuals of all ages was carried out in Canada. The preliminary analysis of the responses to this survey has not turned up any serious distributional shortcomings of the sort described by Stauffer, but it has finally documented the existence of many nutritional problems which had been suspected for many years.[11]

The initial analysis of the results from the Nutrition Canada survey indicates that there is no consistent effect of season, income, or community type on nutrition in the general population in Canada. Canadian nutritional problems are essentially the same in summer and winter; in metropolitan, urban, and rural areas; and in low-income and other-income areas. The Nutrition Canada report therefore concludes that the food distribution system in Canada seems to be effective and that the critical factor in Canadian nutritional problems is apparently not the number of food dollars spent. However, it does not exclude the possibility that the nutritional status of families living on very low incomes is adversely affected and anticipates that further analysis in terms of individual family incomes may give some indication of income levels below which nutritional problems are related primarily to the income available to spend on food rather than to nutritional knowledge and dietary practices.

Although no serious distributional shortcomings have been discovered, Nutrition Canada has revealed a number of specific, serious nutritional problems in Canada: overweight, which affects a very large proportion of adults and which results primarily from inadequate physical activity; iron deficiency among a large proportion of Canadians, both women and men; a protein deficit for women during pregnancy and for a small but noteworthy proportion of children under five years of age; shortage of calcium and vitamin D in the diets of many infants, children, and adolescents; thiamin deficiency among adults and pregnant women in the general and Indian populations; vitamin C deficiency in the Eskimo population and to a lesser extent in the Indian population; and a moderate vitamin A deficit among pregnant Indians and Eskimos. These problems of malnutrition are different from those which prevail in poor countries; but their implications for the welfare of Canadians are sufficiently serious to warrant strong corrective measures, especially since the results of Nutrition Canada probably present an optimistic view of our nutritional status.

Housing Conditions

Compared with other nations, the quantity and quality of shelter with which Canadians have provided themselves are indeed impressive. Table 2–13 shows that Canadian housing conditions combine a

Table 2–13.   Density of Occupation and Facilities of Occupied Dwellings, Selected Nations, 1960–1970

Nation and year	Average number of rooms per dwelling	Average number of persons per room	Percentage of dwellings with less than 1.5 persons per room	Percentage of dwellings with piped water inside	Percentage of dwellings with flush toilet	Percentage of dwellings with fixed bath or shower
Brazil (1970)	4.6	1.1	73.9	32.8*	17.5	n.a.
Canada (1967)	5.4	0.7	96.6	95.2	92.5	89.8
Chile (1960)	3.2	1.7	40.6	62.0*	44.8	46.0
Colombia (1964)	2.9	1.9	39.4	60.0	62.0	62.3
Czechoslovakia (1961)	2.7	1.3	62.1	49.1	39.5	33.3
Ecuador (1962)	2.1	2.5	21.4	37.5*	21.7	n.a.
Egypt (1960)	3.6	1.6	42.3	39.5*	n.a.	n.a.
England and Wales (1961, 1966)	5.5	0.6	98.2	98.7	98.2	85.1
France (1968)	3.4	0.9	80.2	91.5	53.2	48.9
Hungary (1970)	2.6	1.2	64.3	36.4	32.7	32.2
Israel (1966)	2.3	1.6	48.4	89.5	80.9	92.5
Italy (1961)	3.3	1.1	66.0	62.3	n.a.	28.9
Japan (1968)	3.7	1.1	72.8	94.9*	17.1	65.6
Mexico (1960, 1970)	2.3	2.5	18.1	38.8	n.a.	31.8
Nigeria (urban, 1961)	1.4	3.0	16.1	n.a.	7.0	n.a.
Peru (1961)	2.3	2.3	26.3	14.6	22.6	16.4
Sweden (1965)	3.6	0.8	93.2	95.2	85.3	72.9
United States (1960, 1970)	5.0	0.6	97.8	92.9	89.7	88.1
Venezuela (1961)	3.3	1.6	45.3	67.1*	49.5	52.9
Zambia (1969)	1.9	2.4	25.7	12.4	15.1	n.a.

*Piped water inside or outside.

n.a. Not available.

Source: United Nations, Department of Economic and Social Affairs, Statistical Office, Statistical Yearbook 1971 (New York: United Nations, 1972), Table 202, pp. 716-739. Reprinted by permission of the United Nations.

relatively low density of occupation with a wide provision of basic dwelling facilities. These housing conditions are rivalled only by those in the United States, Sweden, and England and Wales, and are vastly superior to those available in all other nations.

Canada also enjoys the highest ratio of new additions to its housing stock in the Western world. In the years 1945–68, a total of 2,839,251 new dwelling units were built in Canada, representing 49 per cent of

Table 2–14. *Average Number of Persons per Room in Occupied Dwellings by Region, Canada, 1941–1971*

Region	1941	1951	1961	1971
Atlantic Provinces*	0.8	0.7	0.7	0.7
Quebec	0.9	0.8	0.8	0.7
Ontario	0.7	0.7	0.7	0.6
Prairie Provinces	1.0	0.8	0.8	0.6
British Columbia	0.8	0.7	0.7	0.6
Yukon and Northwest Territories	n.a.	n.a.	1.2	0.9
Canada	0.8	0.7	0.7	0.6

* Includes Newfoundland 1951–1971.

n.a. Not available.

Source: Canada, Dominion Bureau of Statistics, *Eighth Census of Canada 1941*, Volume V (Ottawa: King's Printer, 1947), Table 4; *Ninth Census of Canada 1951*, Volume III (Ottawa: Queen's Printer, 1953), Table 52; *Census of Canada 1961*, Bulletin 2.2–2 (Ottawa: Queen's Printer, 1963), Table 30; Statistics Canada, *1971 Census of Canada*, Volume II–Part 3 (Bulletin 2.3–5) (Ottawa: Information Canada, 1973), Table 19. Reproduced by permission of Information Canada.

Table 2–15. *Incidence of Selected Dwelling Characteristics by Region, Canada, 1951–1971*
(percentages)

Region	Crowded dwellings			Hot and cold running water			Installed bath or shower facilities			Flush toilet		
	1951	1961	1971	1951	1961	1971	1951	1961	1971	1951	1961	1971
Atlantic Provinces	21.9	21.4	15.7	40.0	60.9	78.3	38.0	58.0	78.3	45.9	65.7	83.7
Quebec	25.3	21.8	12.4	52.7	79.1	94.0	63.0	81.8	93.6	83.7	95.3	98.5
Ontario	12.8	11.8	6.8	68.7	89.1	96.4	72.8	89.1	96.2	76.4	91.0	97.0
Prairie Provinces	21.8	17.7	8.9	38.8	67.5	87.5	39.5	66.5	87.5	39.9	65.5	86.7
British Columbia	14.2	12.1	6.8	81.4	92.0	96.3	79.6	91.6	96.9	81.2	92.4	97.2
Yukon and Northwest Territories	n.a.	45.4	30.7	n.a.	44.0	64.5	n.a.	44.0	65.9	n.a.	43.9	63.6
Canada	18.8	16.5	9.4	56.8	80.1	92.7	60.8	80.3	92.5	68.3	85.2	94.5

n.a. Not available.

Sources: Canada, Dominion Bureau of Statistics, *Ninth Census of Canada 1951*, Volume III (Ottawa: Queen's Printer, 1953), Tables 12, 32, 52; *Census of Canada 1961* (Ottawa: Queen's Printer, 1963), Bulletin 2.2–2, Table 30 and Bulletin 2.2–3, Tables 36, 40; Statistics Canada, *Advance Bulletin (AH–2): 1971 Census of Canada* (Ottawa: Statistics Canada, 1972), Table 2. Reproduced by permission of Information Canada.

the entire Canadian housing stock.[12] Given this recent expansion of our national housing stock, it is perhaps not surprising to find a steady decline during the post-war period in the average number of persons per room (Table 2–14) and in the percentage of crowded dwellings (Table 2–15), and a wider provision of basic housing equipment such as plumbing facilities.

The increases in the quantity and quality of housing in Canada have been outstanding. Yet the data which show a high level of provision in terms of the average quantity and quality of housing in Canada conceal significant differences in its distribution. Four of the five indicators presented in Tables 2–14 and 2–15 display noticeable regional differences.

Except for the Yukon and Northwest Territories, the average number of persons per room in each region varied only sightly from the national average at each census from 1941 to 1971; but there were substantial regional differences in the incidence of overcrowded dwellings. The percentage of crowded dwellings (defined as having more than one person per room) was 18.8 per cent for the nation as a whole in 1951, ranging among the regions from 25.3 in Quebec to 12.8 per cent in Ontario. By 1971, the percentage of crowded dwellings had declined to 6.8 per cent in Ontario and British Columbia; but it was 15.7 per cent in the Atlantic Provinces and 30.7 per cent in the Yukon and Northwest Territories.

Improvements in the provision of basic plumbing facilities between 1951 and 1971 are evident for each region. The differences which existed between Quebec, Ontario, and British Columbia in 1951 had disappeared by 1971. Although the improvements in the Prairie Provinces and the Atlantic Provinces were also considerable, they still left those regions clearly below the national average in 1971, as they were in 1951; and the Yukon and Northwest Territories had average dwelling facilities in 1971 comparable to those which were prevalent in the rest of Canada twenty years earlier.

Table 2–16 shows that income differences between families are associated with the quantity and, especially, the quality of their accommodation. A national survey of household facilities in 1968 found that the average number of rooms per household increased consistently from 4.53 rooms per household with incomes under $1,000 and 4.40 rooms per household with incomes between $1,000 and $2,000 to 6.68 rooms per household with incomes $15,000 and over. Because the average number of persons per household was smaller in the lowest income groups, however, the average number of persons per room was lower for household income groups below $4,000. The percentage of crowded dwellings tended to first rise and then decline as incomes rose, from 16.8 and 13.1 per cent for the two income groups

Table 2–16. Average Size of Households and Dwellings and Percentage of Households with Selected Dwelling Characteristics by Household Income Group, Canada, 1968

1967 household income group (dollars)	Persons per household (average number)	Rooms per household (average number)	Persons per room (average number)	Crowded dwellings: one or more persons per room (percentage)	Period of construction before 1940 (percentage)	Central heating by furnace (percentage)	Piped running water supply (percentage)	Flush toilet (percentage)	Bath facilities (percentage)
Under 1000	2.17	4.53	0.48	16.8	58.0	63.7	87.1	84.4	77.8
1000–1999	1.91	4.40	0.43	13.1	57.9	56.5	86.5	82.2	74.3
2000–2999	2.73	4.87	0.56	19.4	57.7	62.6	90.1	87.1	78.8
3000–3999	3.20	4.90	0.65	25.3	52.3	66.1	93.4	90.3	84.5
4000–4999	3.52	5.03	0.70	29.4	49.0	71.1	95.7	93.8	88.5
5000–5999	3.66	5.08	0.72	31.0	45.3	75.4	97.0	94.8	92.1
6000–6999	3.84	5.22	0.74	29.3	37.0	79.3	97.7	96.6	94.1
7000–7999	3.98	5.39	0.74	27.3	37.3	82.5	98.6	98.0	96.5
8000–8999	4.00	5.44	0.74	26.6	30.6	84.4	99.2	98.5	96.7
9000–9999	3.95	5.51	0.72	25.2	27.9	87.0	99.2	99.0	98.2
10000–11999	4.17	5.77	0.72	23.8	28.4	88.3	99.0	98.3	97.8
12000–14999	4.34	6.10	0.71	22.0	27.7	89.1	99.5	99.1	98.7
15000 and over	4.58	6.68	0.69	19.4	30.3	91.9	99.2	99.0	98.6
National average	3.59	5.29	0.68	24.6	41.3	76.9	95.9	94.3	90.9

Source: Canada, Statistics Canada, *Household Facilities by Income and Other Characteristics 1968* (Ottawa: Information Canada, 1972), Table 2A, p. 26; Table 2B, p. 42. Reproduced by permission of Information Canada.

under $2,000, up to 31 per cent for the income group $5,000-$5,999, and then down to 19.4 per cent for the income group $15,000 and over. Taken together, the first four columns in Table 2–16 indicate that, on the average, groups at both the upper and the lower ends of the income scale enjoy more favourable circumstances with respect to the quantity of housing than do the middle-income groups.

In contrast with this curvilinear association between the level of household income and the quantity of housing, the last five columns of Table 2–16 indicate a straightforward linear association between the quality of housing accommodation and the level of household income. Dwellings occupied by low-income households consistently tended to be older, less likely to have central heating, and less adequately provided with plumbing facilities than dwellings occupied by higher-income households.

Within the low-income group, housing conditions for Indians and Eskimos are especially below standard. A housing survey conducted by the Indian Affairs Branch in 1962–63 reported that 56 per cent of Indian housing was three rooms or less compared with 11 per cent for the general population, 9 per cent of Indian housing was six rooms or larger compared with a national average of 44 per cent, 13 per cent of Indian dwellings were equipped with running water, 9 per cent had indoor toilets, and 7 per cent had indoor baths.[13] The changes between 1962–63 and 1968–69 in the percentages of Indian housing with running water, indoor toilets, and indoor baths (Table 2–17) indicate that improvements were made in Indian housing during the 1960s in all provinces except Saskatchewan and Manitoba; but Indian housing conditions in 1968–69 were still far below those enjoyed on the average by other Canadians, and appeared to be especially bad in Ontario and the Prairie Provinces.

The impressions recorded by the Federal Task Force on Housing and Urban Development after an examination which carried it across the nation in 1968 provide supporting evidence for the nature of the differences recorded in surveys and census data. The Task Force found the housing situation in rural Canada "both confusing and contradictory". On the one hand, they saw giant farm complexes, which were big businesses in organization and method of operation, providing their owners with economic gains equal to or greater than those open to urban businessmen, while continuing to make possible the enjoyment of life on the land. On the other hand, beside these agricultural giants they saw

> the small farms and the large families which industrialization too often has swept aside, leaving them to scratch the most meagre of existences from land often capable of different and more productive use. In most cases the physical

*Table 2–17. Percentages of Indian Housing with Running Water,
Indoor Toilets, and Indoor Baths, 1962–63 and 1968–69*

Region and year	Total number of houses	Running water (percentage)	Indoor toilet (percentage)	Indoor bath (percentage)
Maritimes				
1962–3	993	33.6	9.3	5.1
1968–9	1,145	73.5	43.2	33.9
Quebec				
1962–3	2,523	34.2	32.3	25.7
1968–9	3,184	64.6	48.8	40.0
Ontario				
1962–3	3,478	10.5	7.2	6.6
1968–9	4,627	23.1	16.4	15.8
Manitoba				
1962–3	3,489	0.1	0.5	0.6
1968–9	4,142	1.4	8.4	1.3
Saskatchewan				
1962–3	3,221	0.2	0.3	0.3
1968–9	4,026	0.7	1.1	0.5
Alberta				
1962–3	3,136	1.1	0.9	1.0
1968–9	3,436	10.2	9.7	9.6
British Columbia and Yukon				
1962–3	5,319	34.4	20.3	13.9
1968–9	5,426	57.9	32.5	29.2
Canada				
1962–3	25,786	13.3	9.1	6.7
1968–9	28,398	26.6	18.7	21.3

Source: Canada, Department of Indian Affairs and Northern Development, "Brief
to the Special Senate Committee on Poverty," *Proceedings of the Special Senate
Committee on Poverty*, January 20, 1970, Appendix, p. 81. Reproduced by permission of Information Canada.

> *setting reflects the economic barrenness. Houses are old and
> dilapidated. Gardens and lawns have become muddy bare
> patches intermixed with weedy scruff. In a few exceptions
> the landscape belies the overall economic problem. Here one
> finds well-kept houses and neatly tended fields to disguise
> the facts of low income and economic under-development.
> But these are the exceptions and not the rule.*[14]

In the cities of Canada the Task Force noted the benefits of large
population centres in providing wide opportunities for economic,
social, and cultural development; but it also found some very serious
problems. The growth of urban Canada has been self-generated and
little controlled, whereas urban planning has been reactive and not
pre-emptive in its effect. The result is that suburban sprawl, crowded

schools and recreation areas, inadequate transportation systems, and air and water pollution have become commonplace in Canadian cities. There is more.

> *Here, too, is poverty in its rawest and ugliest form. No pretty gardens or painted cottages here to camouflage economic depression. Poverty in the worst areas of the city core is abundantly visible in the decrepit structures which form its housing, the cracked pavement of the streets which are its recreational area, and the rodents which are its wild life. This poverty you can see—and hear—and taste—and smell. Its residents are not simply families struggling to catch up to the average national income; too often they are people fighting to retain a vestige of human dignity and self-respect. No Task Force impression is more vivid of mind or depressing of spirit than those formed amid the blight and slum of Canada's larger cities.[15]*

Table 2–18. Selected Indicators of the Physical Volume of Canadian Economic Output, 1920–1972.

	1920	1946	1972
Net generation of hydro-electric power (million kilowatt hours)	5,730	40,692	179,114
Crude petroleum (thousand barrels)	196	7,856	622,500
Natural gas (million million cubic feet)	17	48	3,214
Pig iron (thousand tons)	158	684	9,363
Steel ingots and steel castings (thousand tons)	869	1,256	13,073
Newsprint (thousand tons)	876	4,162	8,661
Copper (million pounds)	82	368	1,563
Zinc (million pounds)	40	471	2,510
Milk (million pounds)	10,976	16,131	17,731
Cattle slaughtered (thousand head)	1,091	2,216	2,879
Wheat flour (thousand hundred-weight)	26,771	53,218	37,319
Refined sugar (million pounds)	782	960	2,262
Passenger cars (thousand units)	79	84	1,155
Domestic washing machines (thousand units)	25*	115	421
Dwelling units completed (thousand units)	34*	67	232

* 1921

Sources: M. C. Urquhart and K. A. H. Buckley (eds.), *Historical Statistics of Canada* (Toronto: Macmillan Company of Canada, 1965), pp. 373-4, 412-4, 437, 448, 482-5, 510, 535; Canada, Statistics Canada, *Canadian Statistical Review April 1973*, Volume 48, Number 4 (Ottawa: Information Canada, 1973), pp. 69-74 76, 79, 84-7. Statistics from *Canadian Statistical Review* reproduced by permission of Information Canada.

Income

Some of the effects of different levels of income on the satisfaction of physiological needs have been indicated already in our presentation of statistics on the length of life, incidence of illness, patterns of food consumption, and standards of housing in Canada and elsewhere. Because of its pervasive effects in determining how many resources are available to satisfy various physiological needs, the material wealth of a country is one of the most widely used and useful measures of the welfare of its citizens.

One common measure of national wealth is the gross national product, which represents the aggregate of all goods and services produced in a country in a given year. Using per capita figures to control for population increases and constant dollars to control for price increases, the increasing material wealth of Canadians can be indicated by the change in gross national expenditure per capita in constant 1949 dollars from $858 in 1927 down to $598 in 1933 and up to $846 in 1939, $1,333 in 1944, $1,480 in 1956 and $1,815 in 1967.[16] These increases in wealth per capita have only been possible because of a remarkable expansion in the productive capacity of the Canadian economy, some indicators of which are given in Table 2–18.

The wealth of Canada measured in terms of national income per capita has ranked third in the world in recent years behind the United States and Sweden, making possible a level of welfare for most Canadians which is available only to small elite groups in nations such as Tanzania, Indonesia, Ecuador, or Brazil, and is still quite limited even in more economically advanced countries like Japan or Italy.

Whether compared with other countries or with its own past, the capacity of the Canadian economy to provide for the welfare of its members is obviously very great; but all members of the community do not share equally in the wealth produced. In the first place, the distribution of wealth in Canada is characterized by persistent regional disparities.

Personal income, the flow of income to individuals, is an indicator of the level of economic output, degree of productivity, and general economic welfare, so that one way to measure regional income disparities is to compare the levels of personal income in each of the regions. Figure 2–4 shows the changing levels of personal income per capita for six regions of Canada from 1926 to 1971. Because Figure 2–4 has been drawn on a semi-logarithmic scale, the rates of change in personal income per capita can be compared directly between regions with different levels of personal income per capita. The slope of each regional line reflects the rate of change in the personal income per capita of that region, and the vertical distance between regional lines

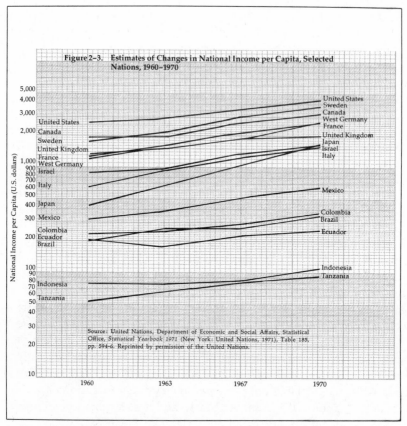

Figure 2-3. Estimates of Changes in National Income per Capita, Selected Nations, 1960–1970

Source: United Nations, Department of Economic and Social Affairs, Statistical Office, *Statistical Yearbook 1971* (New York: United Nations, 1971), Table 185, pp. 594-6. Reprinted by permission of the United Nations.

is a measure of the relative disparity in personal income per capita between regions.

Even with the fluctuations of personal income per capita in the Prairie Provinces and the Yukon and Northwest Territories, Figure 2–4 reveals a consistent pattern of regional disparities from 1926 to 1971. Since the nadir of 1933, personal income per capita in each region has increased with only minor interruptions, and the rate of increase in each region has been more or less the same. Consequently, the pattern and relative size of regional income disparities in 1971 and 1926 were very similar.

From 1926 to 1935, the relative disparity between British Columbia ($524 per capita in 1926 and $407 per capita in 1935) and the Atlantic Provinces ($282 per capita in 1926 and $220 per capita in 1935) remained constant. There followed a gradual reduction in the distance between the richest and poorest regions until 1946 (Ontario, $930 per capita; British Columbia, $924 per capita; and Atlantic Provinces, $638 per capita) when the smallest disparity in the forty-five year period was registered. Thereafter, the distance increased until 1951

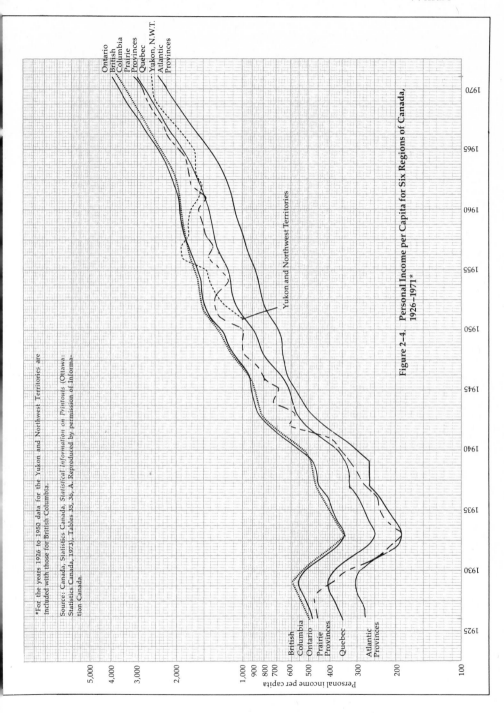

Figure 2-4. Personal Income per Capita for Six Regions of Canada, 1926–1971*

*For the years 1926 to 1950 data for the Yukon and Northwest Territories are included with those for British Columbia.

Source: Canada, Statistics Canada, *Statistical Information on Printouts* (Ottawa: Statistics Canada, 1973), Tables 35, 36, A. Reproduced by permission of Information Canada.

Personal income per capita

53

(British Columbia, $1,429 per capita; Ontario, $1,418 per capita; and Atlantic Provinces, $755 per capita) when the relative disparity between richest and poorest again approximated that prevalent from 1926 to 1935. Beginning in 1959, the relative distance between Ontario and the Atlantic Provinces again decreased gradually until 1971 (Ontario, $3,967 per capita; Atlantic Provinces, $2,443 per capita). It remains to be seen whether this modest reduction in regional income disparities is temporary, as it was from 1935 to 1946, or permanent.

Analysis of regional disparities is a useful first step in describing inequalities of income in Canada, but our concern is with the needs of individuals and the regional data hide very different positions for individual Canadians. Another approach is to compare the sharing of national income among different groups of families by ranking all families in terms of their incomes, dividing them into five equal income groups, and calculating the percentage of total income which goes to each income group. If total income were equally distributed, each income group containing one-fifth of the families would gain one-fifth of the total income. In fact, available estimates of the distribution of incomes within the nation since 1931 show marked disparities among income groups. In 1931, for example, the lowest quintile of families shared only 5.3 per cent of wages and salaries; but the highest quintile of families gained 42.6 per cent of wages and salaries. By 1967, some equalization had occurred in the distribution of income, as the lowest quintile of families shared 6.4 per cent of total income and the highest quintile had 38.9 per cent; but this tendency toward greater equality was neither strong nor persistent.

Table 2–19 shows that there was a slight shift towards greater

Table 2–19. Upper Limits of Wage and Salary Quintiles and Percentage Distribution of Wages and Salaries by Quintiles for Wage and Salary Earning Families, Canada, 1931 and 1951.

	Lowest quintile	Second quintile	Middle quintile	Fourth quintile	Highest quintile
Upper limits (current dollars)					
1931	616	1,060	1,529	2,157	
1951	2,010	2,712	3,387	4,452	
Shares of wages and salaries (percentages)					
1931	5.3	11.3	17.3	23.5	42.6
1951	8.0	13.9	17.9	22.6	37.5

Source: Simon A. Goldberg and Jenny R. Podoluk, "Income Size Distribution Statistics in Canada—A Survey and Some Analysis," in Milton Gilbert and Richard Stone (eds.), *Income and Wealth, Series VI* (London: Bowes and Bowes, 1957), p. 163.

Table 2–20. *Upper Limits of Income Quintiles and Percentage Distribution of Total Income by Quintiles for Families, 1951 to 1967*

	Lowest quintile	Second quintile	Middle quintile	Fourth quintile	Highest quintile
Upper limits (current dollars)					
1951*	1,820	2,700	3,480	4,640	
1954*	2,220	3,240	4,150	5,680	
1957*	2,380	3,600	4,680	6,350	
1959*	2,650	3,920	5,000	6,690	
1961*	2,800	4,270	5,460	7,180	
1965*	3,495	5,248	6,808	9,033	
1965**	3,320	5,139	6,699	8,944	
1967**	3,900	5,949	7,794	10,379	
Shares of total income (percentages)					
1951*	6.1	12.9	17.4	22.4	41.1
1954*	6.5	13.5	18.1	24.4	37.5
1957*	6.3	13.1	18.1	23.4	39.1
1959*	6.8	13.4	17.8	23.0	39.0
1961*	6.6	13.5	18.3	23.4	38.4
1965*	6.6	13.3	18.0	23.5	38.6
1965**	6.2	13.1	18.0	23.6	39.0
1967**	6.4	13.1	18.0	23.6	38.9

 * Non-farm families only.

 ** All families.

Sources: Canada, Dominion Bureau of Statistics, *Incomes of Non-Farm Families and Individuals in Canada, Selected Years 1951–65* (Ottawa: Queen's Printer, 1969), Table 12, p. 78; Canada, Dominion Bureau of Statistics, *Comparative Income Distributions 1965 and 1967*, (Ottawa: Information Canada, 1971), Table 32, p. 53. Reproduced by permission of Information Canada.

equality in the distribution of wages and salaries between 1931 and 1951, as there was a definite decrease in the share of total wages and salaries going to the highest quintile of families, a slight decrease for the fourth quintile, and modest gains for the first two quintiles. After 1954, however, there were no significant changes in the distribution of income. Table 2–20, based on returns from the consumer finance surveys carried out by Dominion Bureau of Statistics on the distribution of non-farm (beginning in 1965, all) family incomes in Canada, shows almost no variation in the shares of total income going to each income quintile between 1954 and 1967.

The upper limits of each income quintile also given in Table 2–20 (except for the highest) show how the persistence of relative inequalities in the distribution of income ensures that the richer become even better off than the poor with the passage of time. The upper limit of incomes in the lowest quintile was $1,820 in 1951 and $3,900 in 1967, a difference of $2,080. The differences between 1951 and 1967 were $3,249 for the second quintile, $4,314 for the middle quintile, and $5,739 for the fourth quintile. Part of the increases in upper limits may be attributed to inflation; but, assuming that inflation affected each group more or less equally, it is evident that while the lowest income group was perhaps gaining some real improvement in its standard of living the higher income groups were gaining even more. Given the existing inequalities in the distribution of income, increasing the economic welfare of the lowest income group by even a small amount entails the additional provision of much larger amounts of welfare to the highest income groups.

The effect of governmental tax policies and transfer payments in reducing inequalities in the distribution of income is illustrated by the Lorenz curves drawn in Figure 2–5. "Income" includes both money income (wages and salaries, net income from farm operations and non-farm unincorporated businesses, paid rents, interest, dividends, and private pension payments) and non-money income (imputed rents and interest; investment income of insurance companies, fraternal societies and trusteed pension funds; supplementary labour income; food and fuel grown and consumed on farms; transfers from corporations; corporate retained earnings; and unshifted corporate profits tax payments). Family units may be either families or unattached individuals. With the cumulative percentages of family units measured on the horizontal axis and the cumulative percentages of their income on the vertical axis, the diagonal line represents the situation of perfect equality in which each 10 per cent of family units shares 10 per cent of total income, and the distance between the diagonal line and the Lorenz curves measures the degree of income inequality.

The Lorenz curve for income distribution in 1969 before governmental taxes and transfer payments shows that the lowest income group of family units (those with money incomes under $2,000) was 12.3 per cent of all family units, but had only 0.8 per cent of all income. The two lowest income groups (those with money incomes under $3,000) were 20.3 per cent of all family units and had 2.4 per cent of all income; the seven lowest income groups (those with money incomes under $8,000) were 60.0 per cent of all family units and had 36.7 per cent of all income; and the highest income group (those with money incomes $15,000 and over) was 8.3 per cent of all family units and had 27.5 per cent of all income.

The Lorenz curve for income distribution in 1969, after taxes paid to all levels of government and transfer payments received from governments are taken into account, is shown in Figure 2–5 to be inside

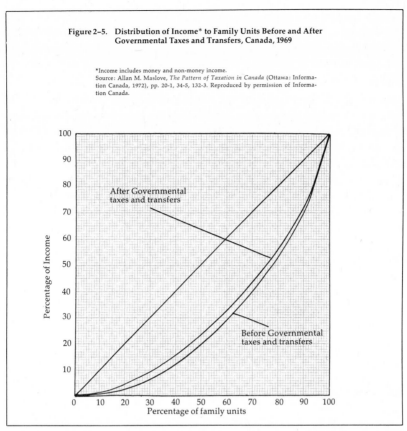

Figure 2–5. Distribution of Income* to Family Units Before and After
Governmental Taxes and Transfers, Canada, 1969

*Income includes money and non-money income.
Source: Allan M. Maslove, *The Pattern of Taxation in Canada* (Ottawa: Information Canada, 1972), pp. 20-1, 34-5, 132-3. Reproduced by permission of Information Canada.

the Lorenz curve for the pre-government income distribution and closer to the line of perfect equality. After governmental taxes and transfer payments, the lowest income group of family units (money incomes under $2,000, 12.3 per cent of all family units) had 1.6 per cent of all income; the two lowest income groups (money incomes under $3,000, 20.3 per cent of all family units) had 4.4 per cent of all income; the seven lowest income groups (money incomes under $8,000, 60.0 per cent of all family units) had 40.4 per cent of all income; and the highest income group (money incomes $15,000 and over, 8.3 per cent of all family units) had 25.4 per cent of post-government income. The leftward shift of the Lorenz curve when governmental taxes and transfers are taken into account illustrates the modest reduction in inequalities of income distribution which occurred as a result of governmental tax and transfer policies in 1969.

The Incidence of Poverty

Unequal distribution of income is a factor in the satisfaction of physiological needs only if those individuals or families receiving the lowest incomes cannot achieve the minimum acceptable level of welfare. There is persuasive evidence that low-income families in Canada have less than the minimum level of welfare required to make a long and healthy life possible, and that many of them in fact suffer severe poverty.[17]

In an attempt to estimate the extent of poverty in Canada, Jenny R. Podoluk began with the data on the expenditures of all families living in urban areas, which show that on the average they allocated about one-half of their income to the basic essentials of food, clothing, and shelter.[18] Low-income families, then, would be those whose incomes are insufficient to purchase much more than these essentials because they spend much more than half their incomes on them. To make her estimate of the extent of poverty in Canada, Podoluk defined as low-income families and individuals those who were spending 70 per cent or more of their incomes for essentials. By this definition, low-income families and individuals in 1961 would include single persons with incomes below $1,500 and families of two, three, four, and five or more with incomes of less than $2,500, $3,000, $3,500, and $4,000 respectively. In 1961, 916,000 non-farm families and 416,000 individuals, making a total of 4.2 million people or 27 per cent of the non-farm population, had incomes below these levels. In addition, about 150,000 farm families comprising 550,000 people were also spending more than 70 per cent of their incomes on essentials, and thus the percentage of people living in poverty was almost 29 per cent of the national population.

Similar studies based on the results of consumer finance surveys indicate that the incidence of low income declined during the economic expansion of the 1960s. The percentage of non-farm families with incomes below the defined poverty lines was 25.9 per cent in 1961, 22.3 per cent in 1965, and 15.5 per cent in 1967, while the percentage of all families with incomes below the poverty lines was 21.2 per cent in 1965, 18.4 per cent in 1967, 17.3 per cent in 1969, and 16.4 per cent in 1971.[19] In 1967, there were 832,000 families and 585,000 unattached individuals, making a total of 3.9 million people in a nation of 20.4 million (18.9 per cent), who had incomes below the current poverty lines.

These estimates of the incidence of low incomes have been criticized as understating the real extent of poverty in Canada in the 1960s. For example, the Special Senate Committee on Poverty argued in its 1971 Report that the adopted poverty lines were too stringent, providing no allowance for families larger than five and making adjustments for changes in the cost of living without any adjustments for a rising standard of living.[20] Using a more generous standard of poverty lines ranging from $2,140 for an individual to $9,290 for a

Table 2–21.   *Poverty Rates by Family Unit Size, 1969, as Estimated by the Special Senate Committee on Poverty*

Family unit size	Poverty line income (dollars)	Number of family units below poverty line (thousands)	Number of individuals below poverty line (thousands)	Poverty rate (percentage)
1	2,140	629	629	38.7
2	3,570	408	816	28.4
3	4,290	161	483	16.8
4	5,000	157	628	15.6
6.2*	6,570	416	2,579	28.5

* Used as, the average size of all families of five or more persons.

Source: Canada, Special Senate Committee on Poverty, *Poverty in Canada*, (Ottawa: Queen's Printer, 1971), p. 12. Reproduced by permission of Information Canada.

family of ten, the Senate Committee estimated that 5.1 million people, approximately 25 per cent of the nation, were living below a minimum acceptable level of welfare in 1969.

The characteristics of low-income families differ from those of the average Canadian family in a number of respects besides income. Although the incidence of low income was greater in 1961 than it was in 1971, Table 2–22 shows that in both years, families were more likely to have a low income if they lived in rural areas, their heads were women, or they included four or more children. Families living in the Atlantic Provinces were more likely to have low incomes than those in other regions, and families living in Quebec and the Prairie Provinces were more likely to have low incomes than those living in Ontario and British Columbia.

In the data for both 1961 and 1967, a strong association appears between the incidence of low-income families and the schooling and occupations of family heads. The incidence of low-income families was about 4 per cent among families whose heads had university degrees, rising to 37 per cent among families whose heads had no formal education beyond elementary school. The percentage of low-income families was lowest among the families of professional and technical workers and highest among the families of farmers and farm workers, loggers, fishermen, trappers, and hunters. In general, the incidence of low-income families in 1961 and 1967 was lower among families whose heads were white-collar workers than it was among families whose heads were blue-collar workers.

Consideration of these characteristics helps define the sources of low income in Canada, but they can be misleading. While rates of

Table 2–22. Incidence of Low Income Among Families by Selected Characteristics, Canada, 1961* and 1971

	Incidence of low-income families as a percentage of all families			Incidence of low-income families as a percentage of all families	
	1961*	1971		1961*	1971
Place of residence:			Number of children under sixteen		
Metropolitan centres	16.5	11.1			
Other cities	21.7	16.0	None	23.9	17.4
Small urban areas	31.8	18.0	One	20.5	13.6
Rural areas	45.9	32.0	Two	23.0	13.8
Region:			Three	33.1	17.4
Atlantic	45.3	27.2	Four or more	33.1	22.7
Quebec	27.9	18.1	Schooling of head:**		
Ontario	18.6	11.6	None or elementary	37.2	37.0
Prairies	27.0	21.5	Some high school	19.5	17.3
British Columbia	21.3	12.8	Some university	10.9	8.3
Sex of head:			University degree	4.4	3.5
Male	23.8	14.2	Occupation of head:**		
Female	42.6	44.7	Managerial	10.3	6.7
Age of head:			Professional and		
Under 25	29.0	17.1	technical	4.8	3.3
25–34	24.1	12.2	Clerical	12.0	5.6
35–44	22.5	14.0	Sales	14.2	7.2
45–54	19.3	12.5	Service and		
55–64	22.2	16.5	recreation	23.5	16.7
65–69	37.9	28.2	Transportation and		
70 and over	47.5	40.8	communication	23.7	14.9
Size of family:			Farmers and farm		
Two	29.2	21.6	workers	56.1***	52.8
Three	20.2	14.1	Loggers, fishermen,		
Four	20.8	12.2	trappers, hunters	60.5	42.3
Five or more	28.1	15.7	Miners, quarrymen and		
			related workers	17.7	8.9
			Craftsmen, production process, and related		
			workers	18.6	9.6
			Labourers	40.9	21.4
			Did not work	54.4	49.2

* Non-farm population only.

** Data shown are for 1961 and 1967. The schooling categories are not exactly the same for 1961 and 1967. For 1961, the four categories are no schooling or elementary only; secondary, one to three years; secondary, four to five years or some university, and university degree. For 1967, the four categories are none or some elementary, completed elementary or some high school, completed high school or some university, and university degree.

*** Farm workers only.

Sources: Jenny R. Podoluk, *Incomes of Canadians*, Dominion Bureau of Statistics, 1961 Census Monograph (Ottawa: Queen's Printer, 1968), pp. 187, 197, 200-1;

incidence of low income are high among certain groups, the absolute numbers of low-income families may be much higher in other groups. Thus, in spite of the high rate of rural poverty, 35 per cent of low-income families lived in metropolitan centres in 1967. In addition, 84 per cent of low-income families lived elsewhere than in the Atlantic Provinces; 73 per cent of them had family heads under sixty-five years of age; and 85 per cent were headed by men.

Because of their very different implications for remedial policies, perhaps the most important differences in the characteristics of poverty are those between urban and rural areas. A cross-tabulation of 1967 data on income distribution has been made by N. H. Lithwick according to type of locality; type of family unit; and the age, sex, and labour-force status of the head. The incidences of poverty which he calculated for the resulting sub-groups are shown in Table 2–23 for cities over 500,000 population and for rural areas. Lithwick concludes that there is a sharp difference in kind between poverty in the large urban areas and that in rural areas of Canada.

> In both, the incidence of poverty among the aged is high, although it is somewhat higher in rural areas. In urban areas, the incidence of family poverty is quite low, with the exception of those families headed by females. In rural areas, the incidence of family poverty is four times as high and twice the national average—with the bulk of this among families with male heads. Indeed, in these units, there is little difference in the incidence of poverty among the various age groups: the probability of a young rural family being poor is no less than that of an old rural family! The difference then is critical. In rural areas, poverty is general; in urban areas, it is specific to certain groups. Solutions in rural areas require overall transformation of their economies, from backward to dynamic. In urban areas, only income redistribution can solve the poverty problem. . . . But despite its magnitude, engendering support for this problem, now that its profile is clearer, will be more difficult precisely because no material benefits can be derived from solving this problem. Rural development can yield a high return to all Canadians by expanding the economy's potential. In the cities, only the poor will benefit—they will not be more productive only better off, while the rest of society will be mar-

Dominion Bureau of Statistics, *Statistics on Low Income in Canada 1967* (Ottawa: Information Canada, 1971), Table 1, p. 25; Statistics Canada, *Income Distributions by Size in Canada: Preliminary Estimates 1971* (Ottawa: Information Canada, 1972), Table 7, p. 15. Reproduced by permission of Information Canada.

Table 2–23. Incidence of Poverty Cross-tabulated by Selected Characteristics for Cities over 500,000 Population and Rural Areas, 1967

(percentages)

Region, sex, and age of head	Individuals					Families				
	Paid workers	Unem-ployed	Self-employed	Not in labour force	Total	Paid workers	Unem-ployed	Self-employed	Not in labour force	Total
A. Cities over 500,000 (total incidence: 16)										
Males										
Under 25	22	17	0	44		4	0	49	31	
25–44	4	22	0	58		5	22	15	41	
45–65	2	60	0	76		3	20	10	27	
Over 65	13	100	0	56		7	53	0	39	
Total male					21					9
Females										
Under 25	31	28	0	80		23	0	0	100	
25–44	9	15	0	70		16	38	100	67	
45–65	13	46	32	67		12	100	31	33	
Over 65	16		76	70		0	0	65	22	
Total female					40					29
TOTAL CITIES					31					10

B. Rural areas (total incidence: 44)

Males								
Under 25	27	0	0	79	18	58	52	32
25–44	19	24	41	100	22	48	54	70
45–65	28	62	50	74	16	43	50	62
Over 65	100	50	60	85	30	33	50	66
Total male				51				40
Females								
Under 25	58	100	0	0	56	0	0	0
25–44	20	0	0	100	74	0	43	82
45–65	39	0	88	82	21	100	54	52
Over 65	80	0	100	85	0	0	0	49
Total female				71				52
TOTAL RURAL AREAS				58				41

Source: From "Urban Canada: Problems and Prospects," a report by N. H. Lithwick for the Minister of State for Urban Affairs, Government of Canada, and published by Central Mortgage and Housing Corporation, Ottawa, December 1970.

> ginally worse off. This, then, is the ultimate challenge of
> urban poverty—a challenge to the conscience of an abund-
> ant society, and one that in the history of man has never
> been met.[21]

Even a cursory inquiry into poverty in Canada reveals that many
people are suffering a persistent pattern of physiological need deprivation. People attempting to live on very low incomes have fewer
health services, poorer housing conditions, and shorter prospects for
life. In cases such as those of Canadian Indians and Eskimos, the poor
are easily identified. In cases such as those of ill-educated, low-paid
farm or factory workers, they are more difficult to locate. Their numbers vary from perhaps three to five million people and their personal
circumstances are altered marginally depending on general economic
conditions. They usually have a supply of welfare sufficient for their
immediate physical survival, but undeniably their potential for a long
and healthy life is severely damaged by poverty.

The existence of this poverty provides a strong justification for
governmental intervention to alter the pattern of production and distribution of goods and services in order to provide an acceptable level
of welfare for these disadvantaged members of the community. The
concept of gratification health proposes a hierarchy of human needs
with the physiological needs prepotent. Such a hierarchy implies that in
the provision of political goods the first claim on community resources
should be to ensure the welfare of every citizen. That some such governmental intervention has occurred in Canada is evident, for example, in
Figure 2–5 where a modest redistribution of income is shown to occur
between upper and lower income groups as a result of governmental
tax and transfer policies. It is equally evident from our selection of
social indicators that more strenuous governmental intervention will
be necessary in order to achieve a distribution of welfare which is consistent with the criterion of promoting human development.

Finally, the existence of a minority living in poverty must not be
allowed to obscure the very high standard of welfare now available
to most Canadians. Canadians enjoy a blend of welfare which includes
longer expectations of life, less likelihood of illness, more nutritious
supplies of food, higher quantity and quality of housing, and lower
incidence of general poverty than are to be found in any other nations
except the equally prosperous United States and Sweden; and, compared with most nations, Canadian welfare is not just marginally
better but vastly superior. Through individual and collective enterprise (and with much good luck) Canadians have achieved an enormous growth of real economic product in the twentieth century; and
by individual and collective choice they have converted it, in part, into

patterns of food consumption, standards of housing, and facilities for health care which serve to satisfy the physiological needs of most citizens on a regular basis at a level sufficient to ensure their potential for a long and healthy life.

NOTES

1. United Nations, Department of Economic and Social Affairs, *Social Policy and the Distribution of Income in the Nation* (New York: United Nations, 1969), pp. 52–3. Reprinted by permission of the United Nations.
2. Canada, Royal Commission on Health Services, *Report*, Vol. I (Ottawa: Queen's Printer, 1964), p. 225.
3. M. C. Urquhart and K. A. H. Buckley (eds.), *Historical Statistics of Canada* (Toronto: Macmillan Company of Canada Ltd., 1965), p. 40; Dominion Bureau of Statistics, *Canada Year Book 1970–71* (Ottawa: Information Canada, 1971), p. 323; Statistics Canada, *Vital Statistics 1970* (Ottawa: Information Canada, 1972), Table D6, pp. 76–77.
4. Royal Commission on Health Services, *op. cit.*, p. 141.
5. The final report of the Canadian Sickness Survey is found in Canada, Dominion Bureau of Statistics and Department of National Health and Welfare, *Illness and Health Care in Canada: Canadian Sickness Survey 1950–51* (Ottawa: Queen's Printer, 1960).
6. This is the opinion of R. A. Jenness. See Canada, Privy Council, Special Planning Secretariat, *Profile of Poverty in Canada* (Ottawa: Privy Council, mimeographed, 1965), p. 17.
7. The survey is hesitant about concluding that these regional differences are real. "It is not possible to ascertain to what extent the regional differences were due to real differences in the geographical and social characteristics of the various regions, or to sampling and non-sampling errors. However, it cannot be over-emphasized that the regional differences in the Tables of this report are not necessarily real differences." (Dominion Bureau of Statistics, *Illness and Health Care in Canada: Canadian Sickness Survey 1950–51*, p. 18.) Reproduced by permission of Information Canada.
8. More recent studies indicate that poverty and illness continue to be closely related. The Health Department of Winnipeg reported in 1968 that numerous cases of infant dysentery were caused by poverty and "poor environment". A 1968 survey of three hundred multi-problem families living on low or marginal incomes in Vancouver showed they had a significantly greater number of health defects than families having higher incomes. A study conducted in Montreal in 1969 found that stress syndromes were inversely related to income as well as being higher for welfare recipients than for those who were self-supporting. A Saskatchewan study in 1967 showed that symptomatology associated with physical and mental illness existed to a greater degree in the low-income group and that men on low incomes made greater use of medical services than those with higher incomes, but that women in the low-income group, despite a higher illness rate, did not take advantage of medical services as much as women in higher income groups. See Canadian Medical Association, "Brief to the Special Senate Committee on Poverty," *Proceedings of the Special Senate Committee on Poverty*, May 28, 1970, Appendix B, p. 41.

9. United Nations, Department of Economic and Social Affairs, *Report on the World Social Situation 1967* (New York: United Nations, 1969), p. 37.

10. This excerpt from "The Biology of Underdevelopment," by Robert B. Stauffer is reprinted from *Comparative Political Studies*, Vol. 2, No. 3 (Oct. 1969), pp. 367, 369, by permission of the publisher, Sage Publications, Inc.

11. See Canada, Nutrition Canada, *Nutrition: A National Priority* (Ottawa: Information Canada, 1973).

12. Canada, Federal Task Force on Housing and Urban Development, *Report* (Ottawa: Queen's Printer, 1969), p. 6. Excerpts from this report reproduced by permission of Information Canada.

13. Martin P. O'Connell, *Canadian Standards of Housing in Indian Reserve Communities* (mimeographed, May 1965), p. 6.

14. Federal Task Force on Housing, *op. cit.*, p. 9.

15. *Ibid.*, p. 11.

16. Richard M. Bird, *The Growth of Government Spending in Canada* (Toronto: Canadian Tax Foundation, 1970), p. 307.

17. During 1965, the Canadian Welfare Council carried out two surveys covering 290 poor rural families and 201 poor urban families. The reports of these interviews provide one of the best illustrations of what poverty in Canada means for particular families. The results of the two surveys are reported in Canadian Welfare Council, *A Preliminary Report of Rural Poverty in Four Selected Areas* (Ottawa: Agricultural Rehabilitation and Development Agency, Department of Forestry, 1965); D. E. Woodsworth, project director, *Rural Need in Canada, 1965: The Background of Rural Poverty in Four Selected Areas* (Ottawa: Canadian Welfare Council, 1966); and D. E. Woodsworth, project director, *Urban Need in Canada, 1965: A Case Report on the Problems of Families in Four Canadian Cities* (Ottawa: Canadian Welfare Council, 1965).

18. Jenny R. Podoluk, *Incomes of Canadians* (Ottawa: Queen's Printer, 1968), p. 185.

19. Canada, Dominion Bureau of Statistics, *Statistics on Low Income in Canada 1967* (Ottawa: Information Canada, 1971), p. 20; Statistics Canada, *Income Distributions by Size in Canada: Preliminary Estimates 1971* (Ottawa: Information Canada, 1972), p. 7. By 1971, the income limits had been increased to $2,013 for one-person units; $3,355 for two-person units; $4,026 for three-person units; $4,697 for four-person units; and $5,368 for units with five or more.

20. Canada, Special Senate Committee on Poverty, *Report: Poverty in Canada* (Ottawa: Queen's Printer, 1971), pp. 6–7. The same criticisms have been made by Ian Adams et al., *The Real Poverty Report* (Edmonton: M. G. Hurtig Ltd., 1971), pp. 9–10. Adams et al. suggest poverty lines ranging from $1,100 for an unattached individual to $8,900 for a family of ten.

21. From "Urban Canada: Problems and Prospects," a report by N. H. Lithwick for the Minister of State for Urban Affairs, Government of Canada, and published by Central Mortgage and Housing Corporation, Ottawa, December, 1970.

Chapter Three

SECURITY

Satisfying the safety needs of a person may require anything from a comforting embrace to a world war, but for the political scientist who is concerned with identifying broad patterns of unsatisfied needs and with studying the political implications of the fear of violent death there appear to be two aspects of security which are of particular importance. The first is political violence between members of different political communities and between members of different social groups living in the same political community. The second is criminal violence which is non-political and usually involves only members of the same political community.

External Aggressiveness

If the number of fatalities is used as the criterion, violence between political communities seems to represent the greatest threat to security. Between 1820 and 1949, 2.9 million people in the world died in minor forms of group violence and 9.7 million more in murders involving one to three persons; but 46.8 million people died as a result of major wars during the same period.[1]

The incidence of war appears to be fairly constant over time. Table 3–1 shows no upward or downward secular trend in the number of interstate wars begun during five successive periods between 1816 and 1965. The number of nation months of war per period did rise from 48.4 in 1816–45 to 1,542.6 in 1936–65; but when the increase in the size of the international system from an average of 27.1 to 80.4 nations is taken into account, the upward secular trend tends to disappear. The number of battle deaths per period also increased from 134.2 thousand in 1816–45 to 18,216.4 thousand in 1936–65; but, when the figures for battle deaths are also normalized to take account of changes in system size over time, the upward secular trend again disappears. Finally, the correlation between the chronological occurrence of interstate wars and battle deaths per nation month of inter-

Table 3–1. Amount of Interstate War Begun in Five Successive
Periods, 1816–1965

Period	Average number of nations	Number of wars	Average number of wars per nation	Nation months of war	Average number of war months per nation	Battle deaths (thousands)
1816–1845	27.1	3	0.11	48.4	1.8	134.2
1846–1875	37.4	17	0.45	423.9	11.3	586.3
1876–1905	37.7	8	0.21	280.9	7.4	469.1
1906–1935	55.0	12	0.22	899.3	16.3	9,001.3
1936–1965	80.4	10	0.12	1,542.6	19.2	18,216.4
TOTALS		50	1.12	3,195.1	56.1	28,407.3
Means		10.0	0.22	639.0	11.2	5,681.5

Source: J. David Singer and Melvin Small, The Wages of War, 1816–1965: A Statistical Handbook (New York: John Wiley and Sons, Inc., 1972), p. 191. Copyright © 1972 by John Wiley & Sons, Inc.

state war is only 0.13 and that between chronological occurrence and battle deaths per capita (based on the pre-war size of the belligerents' total populations) is 0.11. As Singer and Small conclude, "Whether we look at the number of wars, their severity or their magnitude, there is no significant trend upward or down over the past 150 years."[2]

Different nations have quite different histories of involvement in war-making. The twelve states in Table 3–2 which participated in five or more wars in the period 1816 to 1965 make up 8.3 per cent of the 144 states included by Singer and Small in their study; but, as a group, these twelve states accounted for 61.7 per cent of the total nation war months from 1816 to 1965, and 90.4 per cent of all battle deaths. Probably the best indicator of the variable impact of war is the number of battle deaths. Among the twelve states, this number ranged from 9.6 million for Russia and 5.4 million for Germany to 189,000 for Spain and 53,000 for Greece. In terms of total months at war during the period, France was at war for 494.3 and England for 409.8 months, while Greece was at war for 104.1 months and Austria-Hungary for 78.4 months.

The Canadian experience of 147.4 war months was much less than the total months France and England were at war; but it was quite similar to the experiences of the major powers of Germany, Italy, and the United States. The hundred thousand Canadian battle deaths are comparable to the battle deaths suffered by Greece and Spain, especially when the figures for total deaths are normalized to take account of years in the international system and total months at war; but the number of Canadian battle deaths is small in comparison with the

Table 3–2. *National War Experience of Canada Compared with Twelve Nations Participating in More than Five Wars, 1816–1965*

Nation	Total years in system	Number of wars	Total battle deaths	Total war months	Battle deaths per year in system	Battle deaths per war month
Canada*	52	3	100,270	147.4	1,928	680
Austria-Hungary	103	8	1,287,200	78.4	12,497	16,418
China	106	8	3,110,500	204.6	29,344	15,203
England	150	19	1,295,280	409.8	8,635	3,161
France	148	19	1,943,840	494.3	13,134	3,933
Germany/Prussia	130	6	5,353,500	140.0	41,181	38,239
Greece	134	7	53,270	104.1	398	512
Italy/Sardinia	150	12	759,500	155.7	5,063	4,878
Japan	99	7	1,365,300	196.2	13,791	6,959
Turkey	150	17	757,120	339.0	5,047	2,233
Russia	150	15	9,662,560	249.0	64,417	38,805
Spain	150	9	188,900	262.0	1,259	721
United States	150	6	608,800	165.9	4,059	3,670

* Singer and Small date the entry of Canada into the international system from 1920. In order to include Canadian participation in World War I in this table, the entry date for Canada has been advanced to 1914.

Source: J. David Singer and Melvin Small, *The Wages of War, 1816–1965: A Statistical Handbook* (New York: John Wiley and Sons, Inc., 1972), pp. 275–280, copyright © 1972 by John Wiley & Sons, Inc.; G. W. L. Nicholson, *Canadian Expeditionary Force 1914–1919* (Ottawa: Queen's Printer, 1962), pp. 49, 535.

hundreds of thousands or even millions of battle deaths suffered by each of the major powers from 1816–1965.

The relatively moderate impact of war on the security of Canadians in the twentieth century is shown in another way in Table 3–3 which sets forth indicators of the magnitude, severity, and intensity of World Wars I and II and the Korean War for each of their participants. Canadian forces participated for most of the duration of these wars, but the severity and intensity of the wars varied considerably for Canada. The cost of the first war to Canada was especially heavy. Over 60,000 Canadian military personnel died during World War I, compared with 39,000 in World War II. Whether measured by battle deaths per nation month of war or battle deaths per million pre-war population, World War I (1,351.0 battle deaths per war month, 7,641 battle deaths per million population) also greatly exceeded World War II (552.0 battle deaths per war month, 3,447 battle deaths per million population) in its intensity for Canadians. In comparison, the impact of the Korean War on Canada was slight—310 battle deaths, a rate of 9.9 deaths per month of war, or 23 deaths per million population. Obviously, the loss of 100,000 Canadian lives in these three wars is not a negligible occurrence; but, as before, when the Canadian experience is viewed from a comparative perspective, these wars were much less severe and intense for Canadians than they were for the people whose nations were among the major combatants.

Another study of the dimensions of conflict between nations, carried out by Rudolph J. Rummel, collected data on thirteen measures of

Table 3–3. *Magnitude, Severity, and Intensity of World Wars I and II and the Korean War for Participants in Each War*

Nation and war	Magnitude: Nation months of war	Severity: Number of battle deaths	Intensity: Battle deaths per nation month of war	Battle deaths per million population
A. World War I				
Austria-Hungary	51.2	1,200,000	23,437.5	22,642
Belgium	51.3	87,500	1,705.7	11,513
Bulgaria	35.6	14,000	393.3	2,917
Canada	44.9	60,661	1,351.0	7,641
England	51.2	908,000	17,734.4	19,654
France	51.3	1,350,000	26,315.8	32,927
Germany	51.4	1,800,000	35,019.5	26,866
Greece	16.5	5,000	303.0	1,852
Italy	41.7	650,000	15,587.5	18,466
Japan	50.7	300	5.9	6
Portugal	32.4	7,000	216.0	1,129
Rumania	15.4	335,000	21,753.2	47,183
Russia	40.2	1,700,000	42,288.6	10,494
Serbia	51.5	48,000	932.0	10,667
Turkey	48.5	325,000	6,701.0	17,568
United States	18.9	126,000	6,666.7	1,313
TOTAL	607.8	9,000,000	14,076.7	14,137
B. World War II				
Australia	71.4	29,400	411.8	4,324
Belgium	0.6	9,600	16,000.0	1,143
Brazil	10.1	1,000	99.0	25
Bulgaria	40.9	10,000	399.3	1,588
Canada	71.2	39,300	552.0	3,447
China	44.3	1,350,000	30,474.0	2,495

TABLE 3–3 continued

Intensity:

Nation and war	Magnitude: Nation months of war	Severity: Number of battle deaths	Battle deaths per nation month of war	Battle deaths per million population
England	71.4	270,000	3,781.5	5,684
Ethiopia	5.3	5,000	943.4	500
Finland	38.9	42,000	1,079.7	10,769
France	19.4	210,000	10,824.7	5,109
Germany	68.2	3,500,000	51,319.6	44,416
Greece	5.9	10,000	1,694.9	1,408
Holland	0.2	6,200	31,000.0	713
Hungary	42.8	40,000	934.6	4,348
Italy	57.5	77,500	2,482.2	1,777
Japan	44.3	1,000,000	22,573.4	14,164
Mongolia	0.2	3,000	15,000.0	5,000
New Zealand	71.4	17,300	242.3	10,813
Norway	2.0	2,000	1,000.0	690
Poland	0.9	320,000	355,555.6	9,169
Rumania	46.0	300,000	8,877.3	15,000
South Africa	71.3	8,700	122.0	870
Soviet Union	46.7	7,500,000	160,599.6	43,988
United States	44.3	408,300	9,216.7	3,141
Yugoslavia	0.4	5,000	1,250.0	325
TOTAL	875.6	15,000,000	17,318.8	10,912
C. Korean War				
Australia	31.6	270	8.5	33
Belgium	30.2	100	3.3	11
Canada	31.3	310	9.9	23
China	33.0	900,000	27,272.7	1,607
Colombia	25.7	140	5.4	10
England	35.0	670	19.1	13
Ethiopia	26.9	120	4.5	8
France	30.8	290	9.4	7
Greece	30.2	170	5.6	22
Holland	30.2	110	3.6	11
North Korea	37.1	520,000	14,016.2	53,608
Philippines	34.4	90	2.6	4
South Korea	37.1	415,000	11,186.0	19,952
Thailand	30.2	110	3.6	5
Turkey	33.3	720	21.6	34
United States	37.0	54,000	1,459.5	348
TOTAL	514.0	2,000,000	3,681.1	1,936

Source: J. David Singer and Melvin Small, *The Wages of War, 1816–1965: A Statistical Handbook* (New York: John Wiley and Sons, Inc., 1972), pp. 66–9, copyright © 1972 by John Wiley & Sons, Inc.; G. W. L. Nicholson, *Canadian Expeditionary Force 1914–1919* (Ottawa: Queen's Printer, 1962), pp. 49, 535.

foreign conflict behaviour for seventy-seven nations during 1955–57.[3] Table 3–4 shows the foreign conflict behaviour in 1955–57 of the twelve nations which, as Singer and Small found, had been involved in five or more wars in the period 1816–1965. Only Austria is excluded from this study since the data needed were not available. Although Italy, Spain, and East and West Germany were not very active during 1955–57, the other nations appearing in Table 3–2 were prominent in the foreign conflict events of the middle 1950s. In addition, data are shown for Egypt, India, Iraq, Israel, Jordan, Pakistan, and Syria, nations which were also prominent in foreign conflict during 1955–57 but which did not appear in Table 3–2. Finally, the incidence of foreign conflict behaviour for Canada is also shown in Table 3–4; and Canada's relatively limited foreign conflict behaviour during 1955–57 offers further evidence of the comparatively temperate nature of the nation's external relations.

Of the seventy-seven nations studied by Rummel, the twenty-two listed in Table 3–4 account for well over half the incidence of every type of foreign conflict behaviour during 1955–57 except for expulsion or recall of ambassadors. If the relatively restricted behaviour of Canada, East Germany, Italy, Spain, and West Germany is excluded from consideration, then just over one-fifth of the nations studied account for 63 per cent of anti-foreign demonstrations, 79 per cent of negative sanctions, 72 per cent of protests, 79 per cent of severances of diplomatic relations, 29 per cent of expulsions or recalls of ambassadors, 56 per cent of expulsions or recalls of lesser officials, 92 per cent of threats, 77 per cent of military actions, 86 per cent of engagements in war, 87 per cent of troop movements, 60 per cent of mobilizations, and 83 per cent of accusations.

The combined evidence of Tables 3–2 to 3–4 leads to the conclusion that certain nations have histories of relatively high involvement in foreign conflict, and that others are relatively uninvolved. The addition of seven nations to the list in Table 3–4 and the restricted behaviour of East Germany, Italy, Spain, and West Germany in 1955–57 serve to remind us that any cross-sectional analysis has its limitations. Patterns of international conflict can change quite quickly, and the foreign conflict behaviour of any nation may vary from one time to another. Nor should we underestimate the great sacrifices of human life and development which the Canadian people have made as a result of the wars and other foreign conflict incidents which have punctuated the history of our community. Yet, given these caveats, the continuing unobtrusive position of Canada among belligerent nations surely permits the modest conclusion that members of the Canadian community, who have faced death in relatively few of the fatal quarrels of the world and who sponsor a government relatively unaggressive

Table 3–4. Foreign Conflict Behaviour, Selected Nations, 1955–1957

Nation	Anti-foreign demonstrations	Negative sanctions	Protests	Severance of diplomatic relations	Expel or recall ambassador	Expel or recall lesser official	Threats	Military action	War	Troop movements	Mobilizations	Accusations	Number killed in foreign violence
Canada	1	1	1	–	–	1	1	–	–	–	–	1	–
China	2	–	2	1	–	–	–	3	–	1	–	8	2,385
East Germany	–	–	–	–	–	–	–	–	–	–	–	2	–
Egypt	16	2	4	2	–	3	19	3	1	1	1	79	4,875
France	15	4	12	–	–	–	3	1	1	1	1	21	4,486
Greece	4	1	3	–	1	–	–	–	–	1	–	2	–
Hungary	3	–	5	1	–	4	–	–	1	–	–	10	13,350
India	27	1	4	1	1	2	3	2	–	1	–	28	16
Iraq	7	–	2	–	1	1	2	–	–	–	–	8	–
Israel	2	–	11	–	–	–	13	3	1	1	1	141	5,228
Italy	2	–	1	–	–	–	–	–	–	–	–	2	–
Japan	13	–	4	–	–	–	–	–	–	–	–	44	263
Jordan	22	2	–	2	–	3	5	3	–	–	–	21	20
Pakistan	3	1	10	2	–	–	3	2	–	–	–	–	–
Soviet Union	6	–	26	–	2	6	25	–	1	3	–	142	13,350
Spain	1	–	–	1	–	–	1	–	–	–	–	2	–
Syria	2	2	5	–	–	2	8	3	–	2	2	60	56
Taiwan	–	–	2	–	–	–	3	3	–	3	–	45	2,385
Turkey	3	–	3	–	–	2	2	1	–	1	–	7	–
United Kingdom	1	1	30	–	–	2	9	3	1	2	1	25	4,509
United States	23	8	33	1	1	7	19	–	–	3	–	63	–
West Germany	–	–	–	–	–	–	–	–	–	–	–	2	–
TOTALS, 22 nations	153	23	158	11	6	33	116	27	6	20	6	713	Not available
TOTALS, 77 nations	242	29	220	14	21	55	126	35	7	23	10	858	Not available

Source: Rudolph J. Rummel, "Dimensions of Conflict Within and Between Nations," *General Systems*, Volume VIII (New York and Ann Arbor: Society for General Systems Research, 1963), pp. 36–9.

in its external relations, have enjoyed a greater degree of security, both physical and psychological, than people living in the more belligerent nations.

Internal Instability

Continual disruption and disorder in social relationships tend to cause anxieties and create insecurity. Consequently, any failure to maintain public order in the community will certainly jeopardize the satisfaction of safety needs. While internal political instability is usually not as serious in terms of deaths as engagements in major wars, it is often just as inhibiting to human development.

Empirical analysis of domestic political violence reveals an ordered and scalable universe of events rather than arbitrary and random occurrences. Betty A. Nesvold studied twelve types of violent political events which occurred in eighty-two nations between 1948 and 1961 and concluded that events in the non-Communist nations could be rank-ordered according to four classes of increasing political turmoil. The four positions shown in Table 3–5 with their related violent political events form a Guttman scale in that the occurrence of an event at a position denoting more violence is almost always accompanied in the same time period by one or more events at each of the positions denoting less violence. Thus, countries which experienced events at position four would probably also experience events at positions three, two, and one; other countries would experience events

Table 3–5. A Scale of Political Violence

Position 1	Position 2	Position 3	Position 4
Riots and demonstrations	Martial law	Guerilla warfare	Politically motivated executions
Boycotts against the government	Coup d'état	Politically motivated assassinations	Civil war
Politically motivated arrests	Revolt		
Government action against specific groups			
Sabotage			

Source: This table excerpted from "Scalogram Analysis of Political Violence," by Betty Nesvold is reprinted from *Comparative Political Studies*, Vol. 2, No. 2 (July 1969) p. 175, by permission of the publisher, Sage Publications, Inc.

at positions three, two, and one without experiencing the extreme events listed at position four; there would be countries where the pattern of violence was limited to events at positions two and one; and so on.

The existence of a perfect scale would mean that the pattern of violence would be completely known from the occurrence of the most extreme event, but perfect scales are rarely found in empirical data. Guttman's suggested test for a reasonable approximation to a perfect scale is to count the number of events which do not fit the scale and then accept the scale only if the percentage of errors is 10 per cent or less. Nesvold found an acceptable coefficient of reproducibility of 0.94 for the scale of violent events in eighty-two nations over the fourteen-year period, but noticed that the Communist countries had a high proportion of errors. The coefficient of reproducibility for seventy-one non-Communist nations for the fourteen-year period was 0.97, but it was only 0.77 for eleven Communist nations.

Examination of the data revealed that the misplaced events in the Communist countries were a result of coding politically motivated executions under position four. In all other nations politically motivated executions were almost always associated with civil war or incipient civil war, and events of lesser violence under positions one to three were also present. In Communist countries, however, a politically motivated execution was a much more routine event, not associated with civil war and not necessarily accompanied by events of lesser violence. In this respect, the pattern of violence in Communist countries represents a systematic departure from the pattern found in all other nations.[4]

The number and rate of occurrence of four types of violent political events are shown in Table 3–6 for twenty nations from 1948 to 1967. There was a remarkable range among the twenty nations in the number and rate of deaths from domestic political violence, from 615,000 deaths in Indonesia, a rate of 5,841 per million population, to no deaths in Australia and Sweden. Although no pattern is evident in the numbers of deaths from domestic political violence, nations with a high level of economic development tended to have lower rates of deaths from domestic violence than those at lower levels of development. One study has reported a linear correlation coefficient of −0.43 between the rates of death from domestic group violence between 1950 and 1962 and per capita gross national product; but it was noted that rates of violent death tended to be lower in nations with very low levels of gross national product, such as Liberia and Saudi Arabia, than in those with somewhat higher levels of development.[5] These findings and those of other studies support the theory that political violence tends to be low in very traditional societies where knowledge,

Table 3–6. Incidence of Riots, Armed Attacks, Assassination Events,
and Deaths from Domestic Political Violence,
Selected Nations, 1948–1967

Nation	Deaths from domestic political violence		Riots		Armed attacks		Assassination plots and attempts	
	No.	Rate*	No.	Rate*	No.	Rate*	No.	Rate*
Indonesia	615,000	5,840.46	82	0.78	7,900	75.02	5	0.05
Hungary	40,000	3,941.66	31	3.05	106	10.45	1	0.10
Kenya	14,000	1,494.93	93	9.93	439	46.88	n.a.	n.a.
Venezuela	1,700	194.91	170	19.49	509	58.36	12	1.38
Ethiopia	475	21.02	16	0.71	74	3.27	2	0.09
Mexico	446	10.45	131	3.07	82	1.92	3	0.07
Soviet Union	399	1.73	44	0.19	43	0.19	0	0
United States	320	1.64	683	3.51	779	4.00	16	0.08
Brazil	143	1.74	95	1.16	117	1.42	12	0.15
Ecuador	128	25.18	73	14.36	78	15.34	3	0.59
France	112	2.29	127	2.60	550	11.24	14	0.29
Italy	109	2.11	310	6.01	249	4.83	3	0.06
Czechoslovakia	74	5.23	48	3.39	6	0.42	5	0.35
Chile	62	7.24	64	7.47	41	4.79	0	0
Israel	49	19.12	59	23.02	91	35.51	3	1.17
Japan	28	0.29	159	1.62	35	0.36	9	0.09
United Kingdom	9	0.16	82	1.50	45	0.82	0	0
Canada	8	0.41	29	1.48	113	5.76	1	0.05
Australia	0	0	3	0.26	8	0.70	2	0.17
Sweden	0	0	10	1.29	1	0.13	0	0

* All rates are per million 1965 population.

n.a. Not available.

Sources: Charles L. Taylor and Michael C. Hudson, *World Handbook of Political and Social Indicators* (New Haven and London: Yale University Press, second edition, 1972), pp. 94–115, 295–8; James F. Kirkham, Sheldon G. Levy and William J. Crotty, *Assassination and Political Violence* (New York: Praeger Publications, 1970), pp. 156–9.

aspirations, and expectations are limited; development at first brings an increase in the level of civil unrest and a resulting increase in deaths from domestic political violence; but as relatively high levels of national wealth are achieved, this unrest is much reduced and the rate of deaths from political violence declines.[6]

Armed attacks are acts of political violence carried out by an organized political group with the object of weakening or destroying the power exercised by another organized group, usually that of a regime, government, or political leader, but also possibly that of a religious, ethnic, racial, linguistic, or special interest minority.[7] Examples of armed attacks include attacks on government buildings and personnel, public utilities, roads and transportation facilities, homes, factories, and marketplaces. As is to be expected, the rank order of the twenty nations according to both the number and rate of armed attacks is approximately the same as their rank order according to the number and rate of deaths from domestic political violence; but in the case of Canada this relationship was rather weak for the period between 1948 and 1967. With 113 armed attacks, a rate of 5.76 per million 1965 population, Canada ranked eighth among the twenty nations in both the number and the rate of attacks, whereas it ranked eighteenth in the number and sixteenth in the rate of deaths from domestic political violence.

Riots are violent demonstrations or disturbances involving large numbers of people. They are characterized by spontaneity and by tumultuous group behaviour. They imply the use of physical force which is usually manifested in the destruction of property; the wounding or killing of people by the authorities; the use of riot control equipment such as clubs, gas, guns, or water cannons; and the use of various weapons by the rioters.[8] In general, riots appear to be less related to deaths from domestic violence than are armed attacks; but among the twenty nations listed in Table 3-6 Canada ranked seventeenth in the number of riots (twenty-nine) and fourteenth in the rate of riots (1.48 per million population) between 1948 and 1967.

A time profile showing the occurrence of riots, armed attacks, and deaths from domestic political violence in Canada from 1948 to 1967 is presented in Figure 3-1. Most, if not all, of this violence is attributable to the actions of two political groups: that from 1948 to 1962 to terrorist groups belonging to the Sons of Freedom sect of the Doukhobors in British Columbia, and that from 1963 to 1967 to members of the Front de Libération du Québec in the province of Quebec.[9] The Sons of Freedom terrorists were evidently responsible for more armed attacks than the F.L.Q., with the year 1962 being a high point for this type of political violence; but the armed attacks by members of the F.L.Q. were more serious in terms of deaths, as six of the eight deaths recorded as resulting from domestic political violence occurred between 1963 and 1967.

Deaths as a result of political assassinations merit consideration in assessing the provision of security, first, because the occurrence of assassinations implies the occurrence of a whole set of events of lesser violence such as demonstrations, riots, and boycotts; and, second, because the death of a prominent political leader may have important implications for the psychological state of ordinary citizens. As Hobbes saw, fear of violent death obstructs human development; and that fear can be strongly aroused in a person by the demonstration

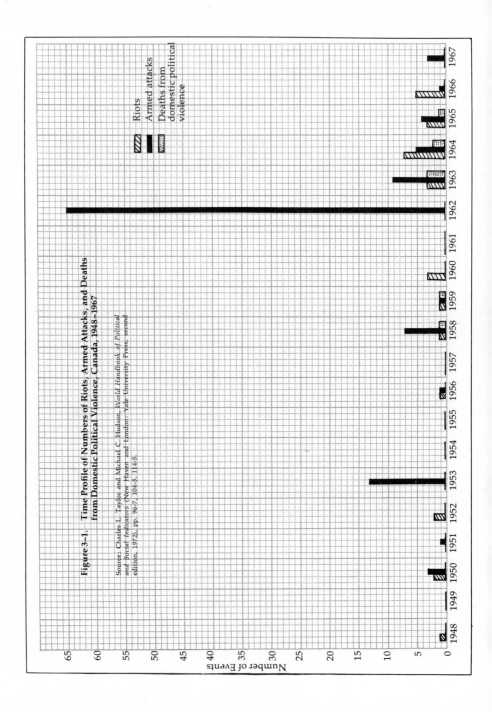

Figure 3-1. Time Profile of Numbers of Riots, Armed Attacks, and Deaths from Domestic Political Violence, Canada, 1948–1967

Source: Charles L. Taylor and Michael C. Hudson, *World Handbook of Political and Social Indicators* (New Haven and London: Yale University Press, second edition, 1972), pp. 96–7, 104–5, 114–5.

effect of an assassination, however remote the possibility of his own death from political violence may be.

At least three separate elements of the political act of assassination make it a particular kind of murder: a target who is a prominent political figure, a political motive for killing, and the potential political impact of the event.[10] Most murders which can be called "assassinations" contain in greater or lesser degree these three elements. Thus, Pierre LaPorte, the Minister of Labour in the Government of Quebec, was kidnapped and later murdered by the Chénier cell of the Front de Libération du Québec which seems to have been motivated by a desire to actualize its ideology by a propaganda of the deed and to terrorize and destroy the legitimacy of the ruling elite in order to effect substantial political changes in Quebec. As a result, martial law was invoked by the Federal Government.

Pierre LaPorte's death was not the first death to result from the activities of militant revolutionaries in the province of Quebec in recent years. In 1963, a guard at the Army Recruitment Centre in Montreal was killed when a bomb exploded, and a second explosion claimed the life of a police sergeant of the bomb detonation squad. In 1964, two employees were killed in a raid on a Montreal armament factory. An explosion at the LaGrenade factory in 1966 killed a female worker, and an F.L.Q. activist was killed by the bomb he was transporting to the Dominion textile factory. A female employee was killed in an explosion at the Department of Defence headquarters in Ottawa in June 1970. However, these deaths between 1963 and 1970 were incidental to acts of violence directed against symbols of English-speaking domination. The victims were not the intended targets of the terrorism,[11] and their deaths cannot properly be described as political assassinations. Thus, in Table 3–6 only one assassination event is recorded for Canada during the period from 1948 to 1967, and that attempt was unsuccessful. On May 18, 1966, a bomb which apparently was meant to be tossed into the Chamber of the House of Commons exploded prematurely in a washroom of the Parliament Buildings and killed the assassin, Paul Joseph Chartier, before he could carry out his plot.

Another approach to producing quantitative measures of national differences in levels of domestic political instability is found in the work of a study group led by Ivo Feierabend at San Diego State College.[12] The Feierabend study group attempted to sort political instability events in terms of the intensity of aggressive behaviour by creating a seven-point scale of political events ranging from zero (denoting extreme stability) to six (denoting extreme instability), and using the scale to weight political events in eighty-four nations for the period from 1948 to 1965. In this scale, typical events were rated as follows: a peaceful general election was given a weight of zero; the resignation of a cabinet official had a weight of one; peaceful demonstrations were scaled at position two; the assassination of a significant political figure, but not the head of a state, was weighted three; mass arrests or the assassination of a chief of state were at position four; a *coup d'état* was weighted five; and a civil war was given the highest rating for political instability.

Using this scale, nations were first assigned to groups on the basis of the most unstable event that occurred during the period, and then ranked within the groups according to the sum totals of their stability ratings for all political events studied. Thus, nations which had experienced civil wars were placed in group six, those which had had *coups d'état* were assigned to group five, those with mass arrests were placed in group four, and so on. Then each nation's ranking in the group was determined by summing its political instability events, each weighted appropriately from zero to six. To prevent distortion of the results, the stability ratings were calculated separately for three six-year periods (1948–53, 1954–59, 1960–65); and the rank within the group was determined by the average of the highest strife events occurring in each six-year period.

The resulting political instability ratings for each nation are set forth in Table 3–7. Each nation is listed with the group of nations having the same average of highest strife events, and ranked within its group according to the sum of the stability ratings for the three periods analyzed. The first two of the five digits in the scale are the sum of the highest strife events occurring in each six-year period. The last three digits show the summed scores for all (weighted) political events for the eighteen-year period.

Only Indonesia among the eighty-four nations studied experienced a civil war during each of the three six-year periods and thus found itself alone at the most unstable scale position. No country was placed at scale position zero, but Luxembourg and the Netherlands were at position one. Canada was at scale position three and at rank–order position eighteen. Approximately 20 per cent of the eighty-four nations studied experienced less civil strife than Canada during the period from 1948 to 1965, while 79 per cent experienced more. The Canadian rating was only slightly higher than the median for advanced industrialized democracies, which was somewhere in the upper third of group two, well removed from Netherlands and Luxembourg on the one hand and the United States and France on the other.

The method for deriving national profiles of political instability shown in Table 3–7 gives special weight to the highest strife event experienced by a nation. Although giving special weight to the highest strife event offers a useful perspective on political violence, it does

Table 3–7. Political Instability Profiles for Eighty-four Nations, 1948–1965

1		2		3		4		5		6	
Netherlands	04021	United Kingdom	07112	Belgium	10162	France	13435	Argentina	16445	Indonesia	18416
Luxembourg	03012	Ghana	07106	Chile	10156	South Africa	13422	Bolivia	16318		
		Austria	07057	Mexico	10111	Brazil	13209	Cuba	16283		
		Denmark	07030	Uruguay	10100	Morocco	13194	Iraq	16274		
		Iceland	07026	Israel	10064	Portugal	13190	Colombia	16244		
		West Germany	06087	Liberia	10036	Turkey	13189	Burma	16213		
		Finland	06056	Ethiopia	10034	Poland	13179	Venezuela	15429		
		Taiwan	06039	Italy	09192	Thailand	13152	Syria	15329		
		Australia	06026	Libya	09069	Jordan	13145	Korea	15291		
		Sweden	06020	Rumania	09060	Cyprus	13123	Haiti	15205		
		Ireland	05031	Costa Rica	09058	Hungary	13113	Peru	15196		
		Saudi Arabia	05018	Afghanistan	09029	Philippines	13105	Greece	14236		
		New Zealand	05015	Canada	08084	Czechoslovakia	13100	Guatemala	14234		
				Switzerland	08042	China	13086	Lebanon	14212		
				Norway	08034	Cambodia	13071	Egypt	14152		
						India	12360	Paraguay	14141		
						Iran	12237	East Germany	14138		
						Pakistan	12231	Laos	14129		
						Sudan	12189	Tunisia	14126		
						U.S.S.R.	12165	Honduras	14105		
						Ecuador	12117	Panama	14101		
						Nicaragua	12096	El Salvador	14079		
						United States	11318				
						Spain	11284				
						Dominican Rep.	11195				
						Ceylon	11152				
						Japan	11123				
						Malaya	11108				
						Yugoslavia	11077				
						Bulgaria	11071				
						Albania	11067				

Source: James F. Kirkham, Sheldon G. Levy and William J. Crotty, *Assassination and Political Violence* (New York: Praeger Publishers, 1970), p. 168.

Table 3–8. Political Instability Profiles for Eighty-four Nations,
Summed Scores of Weighted Events,* 1948–1965

Nation	Score	Nation	Score
Luxembourg	12	Japan	123
New Zealand	15	Tunisia	126
Saudi Arabia	18	Laos	129
Sweden	20	East Germany	138
Netherlands	21	Paraguay	141
Iceland	26	Jordan	145
Australia	26	Ceylon	152
Afghanistan	29	Thailand	152
Denmark	30	Egypt	153
Ireland	31	Chile	156
Ethiopia	34	Belgium	162
Norway	34	U.S.S.R.	165
Liberia	36	Poland	179
Taiwan	39	Sudan	189
Switzerland	42	Turkey	189
Finland	56	Portugal	190
Austria	57	Italy	191
Costa Rica	58	Morocco	194
Rumania	60	Dominican Republic	195
Israel	64	Peru	196
Albania	67	Haiti	205
Libya	69	Brazil	208
Bulgaria	71	Lebanon	212
Cambodia	71	Burma	213
Yugoslavia	77	Pakistan	231
El Salvador	79	Guatemala	234
Canada	83	Greece	236
China	86	Iran	237
West Germany	87	Colombia	244
Nicaragua	96	Iraq	274
Czechoslovakia	100	Cuba	281
Uruguay	100	Spain	284
Panama	101	Korea	291
Honduras	105	United States	319
Philippines	105	Bolivia	323
Ghana	106	Syria	329
Malaya	108	India	360
Mexico	111	Indonesia	416
Hungary	113	South Africa	427
United Kingdom	116	Venezuela	429
Ecuador	117	France	435
Cyprus	123	Argentina	445

* Events include elections, vacation of office, significant change of laws, acquisition of office, crisis within a non-governmental organization, organization of opposition party, repressive action against specific groups, microstrikes, general strikes, macrostrikes, microdemonstrations, macrodemonstrations, microriots, macroriots, severe macroriots, arrests of few insignificant persons, execution of

tend to favour nations which have experienced many political instability events but none at the most extreme levels. To avoid special weighting of the highest strife events, the nations can be rank-ordered according to the last three digits of scores shown in Table 3–7, which give the sum of the scores for all instability events for the eighteen-year period.

The ranking of nations according to these summed scores for all political instability events studied is shown in Table 3–8. Most of the nations remain more or less in the same rank-order position. Luxembourg, Netherlands, New Zealand, and Saudi Arabia are still at the most stable end of the ranking; and Indonesia, Argentina, and Venezuela are at the most unstable end. Yet there are important differences in the rankings. In particular, the advanced industrialized democracies are much less concentrated in the first quarter of the summed scores, indicating that many of these nations experienced considerable political turmoil but most of it was moderate rather than extreme. Thus, the United Kingdom, United States, and France ranked fifteenth, thirty-ninth, and sixty-first on the grouped scores, but were fortieth, seventy-sixth, and eighty-third on the summed scores. Giving special weight in ranking to the highest strife event rather than to the summed total of all scores also favoured Canada, although the change in ranking was a moderate one from eighteenth on the grouped scores to twenty-seventh on the summed scores. On the rankings by summed scores, 31 per cent of the eighty-four nations experienced less civil strife than Canada between 1948 and 1965, while 68 per cent experienced more; and, as before, the Canadian rank is slightly above the median for advanced industrialized democracies.

Viewed in comparative perspective, domestic political violence is very low in Canada. Incidents of political violence tend to be brief episodes in the Canadian political experience, little remembered by the nation in general, although often deeply impressed in the memories of particular groups (for example, the Riel Rebellion and the French Canadians, or the Winnipeg General Strike and the labour movement). Only with a new outbreak of violence are we reminded that order cannot always be taken for granted.

The episodic character of political violence in Canada should serve to remind us of a major limitation in using social indicators of the

insignificant persons, assassination, martial law, execution of significant persons, terrorism and sabotage, guerilla warfare, civil war, *coups d'état*, revolts and exile. The events for each nation are weighted on a zero to six scale and the scores are summed.

Source: James F. Kirkham, Sheldon G. Levy and William J. Crotty, *Assassination and Political Violence* (New York: Praeger Publishers, 1970), p. 170.

type shown here to measure the provision of security. Cross-national studies may provide useful information about the comparative provision of security, but they do not permit evolutionary or developmental analysis.[13] From the perspective of need satisfaction, however, the dimension of time in the life of the community may be ignored only with considerable loss of understanding of the evolving political community and the possibilities for human development within it. The Canadian index of political violence was only 3.08084 according to the Feierabend group's study of the period 1948–65. Obviously, if the period selected were 1960–70, this index would be somewhat higher, primarily as a result of the political violence perpetrated by the Front de Libération du Québec. Yet the violence in Quebec during the 1960s had its roots in the preceding period of stability, and cannot be understood without reference to earlier years. The social indicators of political violence tell us something about the immediate provision of security for Canadians, but their descriptions are incomplete. In this case, ignoring the dimension of time and the unique configuration of politics in the Canadian community might result in a false sense of security if the period examined were 1950–60, or an unwarranted pessimism if the period were 1960–70.

Crime

The incidence of criminal violence is obviously an important factor in determining how well the safety needs of the people in a community are met, and controlling crime is an essential aspect of maintaining public order. Alarming descriptions of increases in crime and threats to public safety have become commonplace in Canada; but, while it is fair to conclude that some increases in crime have occurred, they have not represented a serious threat to law and order nor disrupted the expectations of citizens concerning public safety.

Total convictions for offences of all types rose from 42,148 in 1901 to 1,773,586 in 1969. If we control for population increases by considering the rate of convictions per 100,000 population at risk (those aged sixteen years and over), the rate of convictions rose from 1,236 to 19,456 per 100,000 population. An increase in the rate of convictions for more serious (indictable) offences, from 165 to 686 convictions per 100,000 population, contributed to this rising rate of crime. As Figure 3-2 shows, however, the increase in the rate of convictions for less serious (summary conviction) offences accounted for most of the increase in the total rate; and an increasing rate of convictions for traffic offences was, in turn, largely responsible for the rising rate of non-indictable convictions. What seems to be indicated by overall conviction statistics is not a dramatic upsurge in violent or predatory crime, but a phenomenal growth in the use and misuse of motor vehicles.[14]

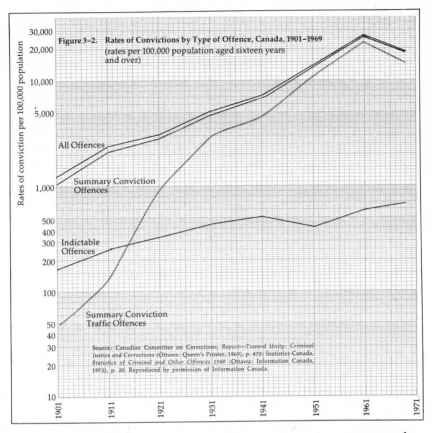

Figure 3-2. Rates of Convictions by Type of Offence, Canada, 1901–1969 (rates per 100,000 population aged sixteen years and over)

Source: Canadian Committee on Corrections, *Report—Toward Unity: Criminal Justice and Corrections* (Ottawa: Queen's Printer, 1969), p. 470; Statistics Canada, *Statistics of Criminal and Other Offences 1969* (Ottawa: Information Canada, 1973), p. 20. Reproduced by permission of Information Canada.

When trends in the separate classifications of convictions for indictable offences are examined, as in Table 3-9, it appears that the rates of conviction for offences against the person for both juveniles and adults continued at a fairly low level during the 1960s, so that such offences became a smaller percentage of the total than in earlier years. Rates of conviction for offences against property with violence did increase during the 1960s for juveniles, though not for adults; but "90 per cent of the offences are simple cases of breaking and entering, with no weapons used and without actual violence—an affluent society in which the average householder possesses valuable and easily portable goods presents a high degree of opportunity for this type of offence."[15]

Tables 3–10 and 3–11 are based on offences reported to the police rather than on convictions. The five types of violent crimes included in these two tables represent an annual average of 5.5 per cent of all offences reported to the police, ranging from 4.4 per cent in 1962 to 5.9 per cent in 1970. The pattern which emerges for Canada and for each province shows that the least frequent violent crime was attempted murder, followed closely by criminal homicide. Rape and

*Table 3–9. Adults Convicted of Indictable Offences and Juvenile
Delinquents, Canada, 1960–1969*

Year	Adults (rates per 100,000 population aged sixteen years and over)				Juveniles (rates per 100,000 population aged seven to fifteen years for 1958–66 and seven to seventeen years for 1967–9)			
	Offences against the person	Offences against property with violence	Offences against property without violence	Total	Delinquencies against the person	Delinquencies against property with violence	Delinquencies against property without violence	Total
1960	43	66	159	307	11	92	177	434
1961	47	67	169	330	11	103	189	477
1962	49	65	164	324	13	102	204	475
1963	50	72	179	354	14	108	206	489
1964	51	68	173	340	14	119	229	528
1965	51	63	168	330	14	111	207	492
1966	54	61	184	352	14	115	223	529
1967	49	61	179	341	17	139	242	579
1968	50	66	185	363	19	153	238	616
1969	58	70	216	417	21	160	261	640

Sources: Canada, Dominion Bureau of Statistics, *Canada Year Book 1963–64*
(Ottawa: Queen's Printer, 1964), pp. 388–9; *Canada Year Book 1966* (Ottawa:
Queen's Printer, 1966), pp. 420–1; *Canada Year Book 1968* (Ottawa: Queen's
Printer, 1968), pp. 439–40; *Canada Year Book 1970–71* (Ottawa: Information
Canada, 1971), pp. 512–3; Statistics Canada, *Canada Year Book 1972* (Ottawa:
Information Canada, 1972), pp. 489–90, 501; *Statistics of Criminal and Other
Offences 1969* (Ottawa: Information Canada, 1973), p. 10. Reproduced by per-
mission of Information Canada.

robbery ranked third and second respectively in order of frequency,
and wounding and assaults were by far the most frequent crimes of
violence. On the average in Canada between 1962 and 1970, there
were three hundred and ten wounding and assaults for every forty-
two robberies, five rapes, two criminal homicides, and one attempted
murder.

The total incidence of the five types of violent crimes increased
118.2 per cent from 1962 to 1970, but the different types of violent
crimes increased at different rates. The largest increase of 180.0 per
cent occurred for attempted murder, from 0.5 to 1.4 reported offences
per 100,000 population. An increase of 125.1 per cent was recorded
for reported wounding and assault offences, and 94.7 per cent for
robberies. The rate of criminal homicide rose by 35.3 per cent, from
1.7 to 2.3 offences reported per 100,000 population; and the incidence
of rape showed a slightly greater increase of 52.6 per cent. Except for
attempted murder, which tends to be unreliably reported, the percentage increases of the more violent crimes, criminal homicide and rape,

Table 3–10. Changes in the Rates of Crimes of Violence,
Canada, 1962–1970

(rates per 100,000 population aged seven years and over)

Year	Criminal homicide	Attempted murder	Wounding and assaults	Rape	Robbery	Total*
1962	1.7	0.5	188.5	3.8	32.1	226.6
1963	1.6	0.7	216.4	3.5	37.4	259.6
1964	1.6	0.8	257.3	4.6	35.3	299.6
1965	1.7	0.7	276.6	3.9	34.0	316.9
1966	1.5	0.8	324.4	3.9	34.0	364.6
1967	1.9	0.8	346.7	4.5	41.6	395.5
1968	2.1	1.0	382.2	5.0	47.1	437.4
1969	2.1	1.2	405.0	5.6	55.1	469.0
1970	2.3	1.4	424.4	5.8	62.5	494.4
Per cent change	+35.3	+180.0	+125.1	+52.6	+94.7	+118.2

* The totals here are those for the five categories of violent crime.

Source: Ezzat Abdel Fattah, A Study of the Deterrent Effect of Capital Punishment with Special Reference to the Canadian Situation, Department of the Solicitor General, Research Centre Report 2 (Ottawa: Information Canada, 1972), pp. 94, 108–114. Reproduced by permission of Information Canada.

Table 3–11. Average Rates for Different Violent Crimes, Canada
and Provinces, 1962–1970

(rates per 100,000 population aged seven years and over)

Region	Criminal homicide	Attempted murder	Wounding and assaults	Rape	Robbery
Newfoundland	0.9	0.2	248.2	2.6	6.8
Prince Edward Island	1.0	0.2	186.7	2.5	12.3
Nova Scotia	1.6	1.6	343.7	3.2	19.1
New Brunswick	1.0	0.2	260.7	1.5	10.0
Quebec	1.6	1.3	141.1	4.2	70.8
Ontario	1.6	0.5	352.3	3.3	27.8
Manitoba	2.5	0.9	227.5	6.0	36.2
Saskatchewan	2.5	1.2	413.8	5.7	18.2
Alberta	2.1	0.9	482.4	7.3	39.5
British Columbia	3.2	1.1	539.3	7.8	55.7
Canada	1.8	0.9	313.5	4.5	42.1

Source: Ezzat Abdel Fattah, A Study of the Deterrent Effect of Capital Punishment With Special Reference to the Canadian Situation, Department of the Solicitor General, Research Centre Report 2 (Ottawa: Information Canada, 1972), p. 165. Reproduced by permission of Information Canada.

were substantially below those recorded for the somewhat less serious crimes of robbery and wounding and assaults.

Although the general pattern of violent crimes was the same in each province between 1962 and 1970, the rankings of the provinces for each type of violent crime were not the same. British Columbia had the highest average rates of criminal homicide, rape, and wounding and assaults; and Quebec had the highest rates of attempted murder and robbery. Newfoundland had the lowest average rates of criminal homicide and robbery; Quebec, the lowest rate of wounding and assaults; New Brunswick, the lowest average rate of rape; and Newfoundland, New Brunswick, and Prince Edward Island shared the lowest rate for attempted murder.

In order to provide overall ratings for the provinces for four types of violent crime (excluding attempted murder), Ezzat Abdel Fattah used a simple scoring system which distributed points among the provinces on the basis of the ranks the provinces occupied for each type of crime. The province with the lowest average rate of reported offences would get one point; and the province with the highest average rate would get ten points. The maximum possible score for the four offences would be forty points, and the minimum would be four points.

The overall ratings for the provinces for criminal homicide, rape, robbery, and wounding and assaults were: British Columbia, 39.0; Alberta, 33.0; Saskatchewan, 27.5; Manitoba, 26.5; Ontario, 23.0; Quebec, 22.0; Nova Scotia, 20.0; New Brunswick, 10.5; Prince Edward Island, 9.5; and Newfoundland, 9.0.[16] Thus, except for ranking Nova Scotia before New Brunswick, the overall ratings of the provinces show a consistent increase from east to west in the incidence of violent crime.

In an attempt to make a more careful statistical test of the "conventional wisdom" of rapidly rising crime rates, Lynn McDonald analyzed the general trends in crime rates by regressing a number of indicators of crime, both serious and non-serious, as dependent variables on the independent variable of time.[17] If the crime rate has been rising, then the results of the regression calculations (R^2) should show that a large amount of the variation in the indicators of crime can be explained simply by the passage of time. The two general indicators of more serious crimes—convictions for indictable offences and charges for indictable offences—showed no significant increases (or decreases) between 1950 and 1966. Only 2 per cent of the variation in convictions for indictable offences and none of the variation in charges for indictable offences was explained by the variable of time. Within the category of serious crimes, the amount of variation in the rates which is explained by time ranged from 17 per cent for manslaughter rates to 36 per cent for attempted murder rates. McDonald's calculations showed slight percentage increases in annual rates of murder (0.5 per cent) and attempted murder (5.4 per cent), but percentage decreases for manslaughter (–0.5 per cent), aggravated assault (–3.0 per cent), and shooting and wounding (–1.6 per cent). The rise in the murder rate may well result from the separation of murder into categories of capital and non-capital offences in 1961, with more charges being laid under the new, non-capital category.

Table 3–12. *Summary of Trends in Crime Rate Statistics, Canada, 1950–1966**

	Percentage of variation in rate explained by time trend (R^2)	t	Estimated percentage rate of change per year (r)	Rate significantly increasing or decreasing**
A. Indicators of more serious crime:				
Convictions for indictable offences	0.02	0.40	0.5	neither
Charges for indictable offences	0.00	0.40	0.2	neither
Murder	0.20	2.21	0.5	increasing
Attempted murder	0.36	3.15	5.4	increasing
Manslaughter***	0.17	–1.82	–0.5	neither
Shooting and wounding	0.21	–2.29	–3.0	neither
Aggravated assault	0.28	–2.68	–1.6	neither
B. Indicators of less serious crime:				
Convictions for Criminal Code summary conviction offences***	0.55	3.83	5.5	increasing
Children adjudged delinquent	0.86	9.78	0.5	increasing
All summary conviction convictions	0.92	13.78	0.5	increasing
Traffic convictions	0.91	12.17	0.6	increasing
Parking offences known to police	0.68	4.92	5.2	increasing

* A semi-logarithmic fit was employed to obtain an estimate of the compound growth rate in the crime indicator. Thus, the estimating equation was of the form $\log Y = a + bt$. It can be shown that the regression coefficient b is an estimate of $(1 + r)$ where r is the compound annual growth rate. The growth rate r is shown in percentage terms in the third column. The t statistic is the ratio of the regression coefficient (b) to its standard error.

** Statistically significant at the 5 per cent level (one-tailed test).

*** Rates for 1955 to 1966.

Source: Lynn McDonald, "Crime and Punishment in Canada: A Statistical Test of the Conventional Wisdom", *Canadian Review of Sociology and Anthropology,* 6 (November 1969), pp. 218, 221.

Among McDonald's indicators of less serious crime, the percentage rates of annual change all show significant increases: 5.5 per cent for convictions for Criminal Code summary conviction offences (1955–66), 0.5 per cent for children judged delinquent (1950–65), 0.5 per cent for all summary conviction convictions (mostly traffic offences), 0.6 per cent for traffic convictions, and 5.2 per cent for parking offences known to the police. Moreover, the amount of variation which is explained by time in each of these rates of less serious crime is very much greater than was the case with the rates of serious crime. Time explains 55 per cent of the variation in the rates of convictions for Criminal Code summary conviction offences, 86 per cent of the variation in rates of juvenile delinquency, 92 per cent of the variation in summary conviction convictions, 91 per cent of the variation in rates of traffic convictions, and 68 per cent of the variation in rates of parking offences known to police. Thus, McDonald's findings confirm that general increases in crime rates from the 1950s to the 1960s resulted primarily from increases in non-serious offences and offer no support for the hypothesis that crimes of violence have been increasing and endangering personal security more and more. McDonald concludes that "the alarmed discussion of swiftly rising crime rates is simply not warranted by the few increases which are the exception rather than the rule. It would be more appropriate to refer to sharply rising rates of parking tickets, although this would not coincide with popular notions of a crime wave."[18]

Part of the explanation for the long-run increase in crime in Canada can be found in the change from a predominantly rural nation dependent on primary production to an urban industrialized society. Urban communities have higher rates of crime than rural ones. Given the higher rates of persons convicted on indictable offences among urban Canadians, as shown in Table 3–13, the growth of the proportion of the population classified in the census as urban, from 37.5 per cent in 1901 to 73.6 per cent in 1971, should in itself account for some increase in the rate of serious crime.

Changes in the age structure of the Canadian population may also be related to increases in the rate of crime. In Canada, as in other industrialized nations, the crime rate is highest among juveniles and young adults and decreases markedly with age.[19] In 1969, for example, the rate of persons convicted of indictable offences was 1,849.1 per 100,000 population among males aged sixteen to nineteen but only 65.9 among those aged sixty or over. The tendency for conviction rates to decline with age was true for virtually all categories of indictable offences, with the exception of convictions for offences against the person and for forgery in the two youngest age groups; and it was true for both males and females. This probably means that recent

Table 3–13. Urban–Rural Differences in Rates of Conviction of Adults for Indictable Offences, Canada and Provinces*, 1969

(rates per 100,000 population aged sixteen years and over**)

Region	Persons convicted of indictable offences by residence		Persons convicted of indictable offences by place of crime	
	Urban	Rural	Urban	Rural
Newfoundland	380.0	232.9	398.9	207.9
Prince Edward Island	380.8	108.9	365.4	122.2
Nova Scotia	426.6	233.0	465.2	195.3
New Brunswick	532.0	339.9	569.0	329.8
Ontario***	440.3	243.0	445.2	234.8
Manitoba	427.6	34.2	443.6	76.3
Saskatchewan	564.3	185.5	678.5	187.5
British Columbia	509.7	387.0	555.3	341.9
Yukon and Northwest Territories	1,536.4	437.5	1,545.5	450.0
Canada	298.1	194.4	336.6	209.3

* Excluding Quebec and Alberta.

** Populations based on 1969 estimates distributed between urban and rural locations according to the 1971 census.

*** Ontario rates have been weighted to take account of a much larger number of cases than occurred in the other provinces where residence of persons convicted and place of crime were not stated.

Sources: Canada, Statistics Canada, *Statistics of Criminal and Other Offences 1969* (Ottawa: Information Canada, 1973), Table 1, pp. 27, 29; *1971 Census of Canada*, Volume 1–Part 1 (Bulletin 1.1–9) (Ottawa: Information Canada, 1973), Table 10. Reproduced by permission of Information Canada.

increases in crime rates are due in part to increases in the proportion of young people in the population.

The incidence of crime is related to the socio-psychological conditions prevalent in the community. In Table 3–15 three indicators of disruptive socio-psychological conditions in the provinces are compared with the average rates for crimes of violence during the 1960s. Like the separate types of violent crimes, average suicide rates, average divorce rates, and the percentages of the drinking population consuming hazardous amounts of alcohol provide the provinces with different rankings, none of which are exactly the same as the rankings for crimes of violence; but some association among the indicators is also evident. If the scoring system used above to obtain an overall rating for each province for crimes of violence is employed here to combine the three indicators of suicide, divorce, and hazardous consumption of alcohol, the overall ratings of the ten provinces are:

Table 3–14. Persons Convicted of Indictable Offences by Sex and
Age Groups, Canada, 1969

(rates per 100,000 population aged sixteen years and over*)

| Offence class | | Age groups | | | | 60 and |
and sex	16–19	20–29	30–39	40–49	50–59	over
Males:						
Against the person	153.2	187.5	99.9	50.2	22.3	9.9
Against property with violence	498.1	195.0	58.2	25.8	8.3	1.9
Against property without violence	867.1	441.2	243.0	189.8	104.6	44.3
Malicious offences against property	60.7	36.3	12.9	7.0	2.4	1.0
Forgery	27.7	31.0	21.5	9.9	4.1	0.8
Other criminal code	85.4	76.9	41.1	26.8	14.8	7.4
Federal statutes	157.0	82.0	12.1	4.0	2.0	0.6
TOTAL, males	1,849.1	1,049.9	488.8	313.5	158.6	65.9
Females						
Against the person	7.3	8.3	7.7	2.9	1.0	0.2
Against property with violence	11.2	3.5	0.8	0.4	0	0
Against property without violence	141.0	97.2	79.0	56.4	37.7	14.4
Malicious offences against property	1.2	2.0	1.4	0.6	0.3	0
Forgery	5.7	7.1	2.4	1.6	0.2	0
Other criminal code	7.7	7.7	4.2	2.7	0.6	0.4
Federal statutes	20.6	10.8	3.2	0.5	0	0
TOTAL, females	194.7	136.5	98.7	65.1	39.8	15.0

* Populations based on 1969 estimates distributed between sex and age groups according to the 1971 census.

Source: Canada, Statistics Canada, *Statistics of Criminal and Other Offences 1969* (Ottawa: Information Canada, 1973), Table 5, pp. 38–41. Reproduced by permission of Information Canada.

British Columbia, thirty; Alberta, twenty-five; Ontario, twenty-four; Manitoba, twenty-one; Saskatchewan, sixteen; Nova Scotia, fifteen; Quebec, twelve; Prince Edward Island, ten; New Brunswick, nine; and Newfoundland, three. As was the case with violent crimes, a strong tendency is evident for disruptive socio-psychological conditions to increase as one moves from east to west. The Spearman's rank–order correlation coefficient between the overall provincial ratings for crimes of violence and the overall ratings of socio-psychological conditions is 0.92, which is statistically significant at the 1 per cent level on a one-tailed test.

Increases in the strength of police forces may also form part of

Table 3–15. *Average Annual Rates for Crimes of Violence, Suicide, Divorce, and Percentage of Drinking Population Consuming Hazardous Amounts of Alcohol, Canada and Provinces, 1961–1970*

Region	Average rates* for crimes of violence, 1962–1970	Average rates* of suicide, 1961-1968	Average rates* of divorce, 1961–1968	Percentage of drinking population consuming hazardous amounts of alcohol, 1968**
British Columbia	607.1	13.1	103.9	6.38
Alberta	532.2	9.5	98.5	5.58
Saskatchewan	441.4	9.2	34.3	4.78
Ontario	385.5	9.4	55.7	5.94
Nova Scotia	369.2	6.8	44.4	4.20
New Brunswick	273.4	5.1	32.3	3.59
Manitoba	273.1	9.6	43.9	5.10
Newfoundland	258.7	2.9	1.6	3.27
Quebec	219.0	5.8	9.3	5.17
Prince Edward Island	202.7	7.1	11.3	3.54
Canada	362.8	8.3	45.6	5.45

* All rates are per 100,000 population.

** A hazardous amount of alcohol consumption is defined as average consumption per day exceeding ten centilitres of absolute alcohol which is the equivalent of nine ounces of whiskey, twenty-one ounces of wine or 5½ twelve-ounce bottles of beer.

Sources: Ezzat Abdel Fattah, *A Study of the Deterrent Effect of Capital Punishment With Special Reference to the Canadian Situation*, Department of the Solicitor General, Research Centre Report 2 (Ottawa: Information Canada, 1972), pp. 105, 165; Dominion Bureau of Statistics, *Canada Year Book 1970–71* (Ottawa: Information Canada, 1971), p. 320. Reproduced by permission of Information Canada. Alcoholism and Drug Addiction Research Foundation, *Appendices to the Nineteenth Annual Report* (Toronto: Addiction Research Foundation, 1970), Appendix IV, Table IV, p. 35. Reprinted with permission of the Addiction Research Foundation of Ontario.

the explanation for increases in crime rates which are based on charges or convictions. Police forces presumably give highest priority to the most dangerous crimes such as murder, robbery, and rape, which are thoroughly investigated even if the forces are understaffed. Larger forces permit more attention to less serious offences, so that an increase in the number of traffic policemen would probably result in the detection of more violations and hence an increase in the crime rate.

To test this hypothesis, McDonald estimated the relationship between changes in the number of police personnel per capita and various crime rate indicators and found that the rates of charges for the most serious offences (murder, manslaughter, attempted murder, shooting and wounding, and aggravated assault) did not increase with the size of the police force. Among serious non-violent crimes, only breaking and entering showed a significant association with police force strength, with 16 per cent of the variation in the rate of convictions explained by increases in the number of police personnel per capita; but, among the less serious offences, police force strength explained 68 per cent of the variation in the rate of all summary conviction convictions, 68 per cent of the variation in the rate of traffic convictions, 53 per cent of the variation in convictions for Criminal Code summary conviction offences, 23 per cent of the variation in known parking offences, and 16 per cent of the variation in children adjudged delinquent.[20]

There is no way to judge whether the increases in crime in Canada in this century are more or less than should be expected in view of the great social changes which have occurred.[21] Figure 3–3 and Table 3–16 show that rates of violent crime in Canada during the 1960s were higher than they were in England and Wales but much lower than they were in the United States. Valid comparisons are difficult because of differences among the three countries in law, social development, and methods of collecting and categorizing offences. On the whole, however, we can probably accept the conclusion of the Canadian Committee on Corrections that there is no evidence that Canada has been experiencing a marked increase in serious crime in recent years. We should also note their warning that these findings underline the danger of attaching too much significance to reports of

Table 3–16. *Average Rates of Reported Offences for Rape, Robbery, and Wounding in Canada, England and Wales, and United States, 1963–1967*

(rates per 100,000 population)

Nation	Rape	Robbery	Wounding*
Canada	4	37	6
England and Wales	2	9	56
United States	12	77	110

* Termed aggravated assault in the United States.

Source: Donald J. Mulvihill and Melvin M. Tumin (co-directors), *Crimes of Violence*, Volume 11, Staff Report Submitted to the National Commission on the Causes and Prevention of Violence (Washington, D.C.: United States Government Printing Office, 1969), p. 124.

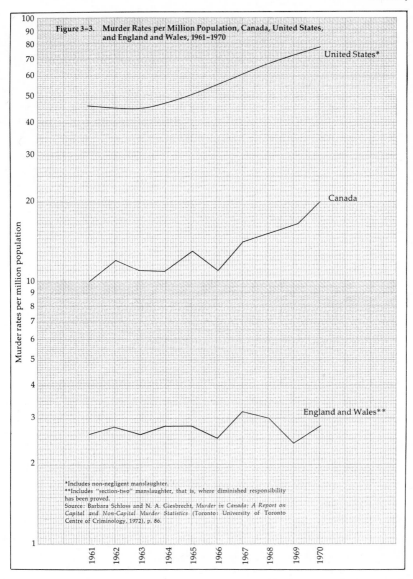

Figure 3–3. Murder Rates per Million Population, Canada, United States, and England and Wales, 1961–1970

United States*

Canada

England and Wales**

Murder rates per million population

*Includes non-negligent manslaughter.
**Includes "section-two" manslaughter, that is, where diminished responsibility has been proved.
Source: Barbara Schloss and N. A. Giesbrecht, *Murder in Canada: A Report on Capital and Non-Capital Murder Statistics* (Toronto: University of Toronto Centre of Criminology, 1972), p. 86.

annual fluctuations in unfamiliar statistics or of extrapolating to the Canadian situation the much-publicized trends of crime in large cities in the United States. Many of the circumstances cited as causes of the apparently rising crime rates in the United States are either absent or much less severe in Canada.[22]

Patterns of Violence

Political violence is not a random occurrence. The patterned character of domestic political instability can be extended to include international aggressiveness and non-political violence. The Feierabend group reported finding interrelationships among foreign conflict behaviour, political stability, and homicide rates in their cross-national studies of political violence.[23] They developed a dichotomous political instability variable from their summed political instability scores (see Table 3–8) by dividing nations into "stable" (012-125) and "unstable" (126-445) groupings. An external aggression variable was derived from the studies of foreign conflict behaviour carried out by Rummel[24] and Raymond Tanter.[25] Their studies cover the period from 1955 to 1960 and include counts of protests, accusations, threats, antiforeign demonstrations, expulsion of diplomatic officials, mobilizations, negative sanctions, troop movements, severing of diplomatic relations, and military actions. The data on homicide rates were taken from the statistical compilations of the United Nations.

When two-by-two contingency tables were constructed, in each case positive associations were found to exist between the dichotomous variables. First, nations involved in external conflict were more likely to be politically unstable internally than nations with less hostile external relations. Second, nations which were politically unstable tended to have high rates of homicide, and those with low rates of homicide tended to be politically stable; but there was only a weak tendency for nations which were politically stable to have low homicide rates, and none at all for high-homicide nations to be politically unstable. Third, although the Feierabend group did not test the association directly, their data make it evident that high-aggression nations tended to have high rates of homicide and low-homicide nations tended to be low in external aggression; but there was little evidence that low-aggression nations tended to be low-homicide, and none that nations with high rates of homicide were high in external aggression. Viewed together in terms of the safety needs of citizens, these findings suggest that citizens threatened by one aspect of violence are likely to be threatened by other aspects as well.

Violence appears to be related to a number of conditions in the environment of political systems.[26] Inevitably, there are many difficulties in explaining the occurrence of political events by environmental conditions, and only the most tentative generalizations are possible. Yet, even with reservations, at least one definite pattern emerges from a consideration of the relationship between the elements of violence and certain social conditions. In Table 3–17 we analyze the relationship between political instability, homicide rate, and external aggression on the one hand, and level. of development, degree of systemic satisfaction, and rate of socio-economic change on the other.

The derivation of the variables denoting violence has already been described. The index of development was devised by the Feierabend study group using various indicators, based primarily on United Nations statistics for gross national product, literacy, radios, newspapers, telephones, urbanization, caloric intake, and physicians. In the construction of Table 3–17, the development variable has been dichotomized by calling the nations which are in the upper third of the scores on the Feierabend index "modern" and calling the other nations "transitional". Systemic satisfaction refers to the gap or ratio between social wants and social satisfactions in a nation.[27] Here the Feierabend study group constructed a ratio from the eight indicators used in the development index. Literacy and urbanization comprised the numerator of the ratio, indicating the level of want formation in the society; the remaining six indicators were regarded as measures of want satisfaction, and formed the denominator of the ratio. In order to measure the rate of socio-economic change, data on literacy, primary and post-primary education levels, infant mortality, caloric intake, radios, urbanization, and national income were collected for the period from 1935 to 1962; and the rate of change in these indicators was calculated in percentage terms.[28]

With the exception of the first and last rows and columns, the ordering of the rows and columns in Table 3–17 is somewhat arbitrary. The rows combine three forms of violence into eight patterns of violence, and an attempt has been made to order them from the most aggressive pattern (high external aggression, political instability, and high rate of homicide) to the most peaceful (low external aggression, political stability, and low rate of homicide) following the argument of this chapter. The columns combine three variables of social conditions and are ordered from the combination which seems to have the lowest potential for violence (modern, high satisfaction, and low rate of change) to that with the highest potential for violence (transitional, low satisfaction, and high change).

Two observations are suggested immediately from an examination of Table 3–17. First, three-quarters of the cells are empty. If information were available on more nations, some of these empty cells would become occupied;[29] but most would not. As many as two-thirds of the possible combinations of variables do not appear to exist, and this again shows the interrelationships of these variables. If chance alone were operating and if there were no relationship among these variables, such a large proportion of cells would not remain empty.[30] Second, while a variety of patterns of violence are found for both modern and transitional nations, the concentration of nations in the lower left-hand corner of Table 3–17 identifies a definite syndrome of political non-aggression in the contemporary world. Ten nations are classed as modern, politically stable, and low in external aggression, and have high levels of satisfaction and low rates of change and

Table 3–17. *Relationship of Development, Systemic Satisfaction, and Rate of Socio-economic Change to Political Instability, Homicide Rate, and External Aggression, Thirty-eight Nations*

	1 Modern High satisfaction Low change	2 Modern High satisfaction High change	3 Transitional High satisfaction Low change	4 Modern Low satisfaction Low change	5 Transitional High satisfaction High change	6 Modern Low satisfaction High change	7 Transitional Low satisfaction Low change	8 Transitional Low satisfaction High change	TOTALS
1 High aggressive Unstable High homicide	United States	—	—	—	—	—	Chile Guatemala	Egypt India	5
2 High aggressive Unstable Low homicide	France	—	—	—	—	—	—	—	1
3 High aggressive Stable High homicide	Australia	—	—	—	—	—	Mexico	—	2
4 Low aggressive Unstable High homicide	—	—	—	—	—	—	—	Brazil Ceylon Colombia Dominican Rep. Peru	5

High aggressive 5 Stable Low Homicide	United Kingdom West Germany	—	—	—	—	—	—	2
Low aggressive 6 Unstable Low homicide	Belgium	—	—	Portugal	—	—	Greece Italy Spain	5
Low aggressive 7 Stable High Homicide	Finland Uruguay	—	—	Costa Rica	—	Ecuador Philippines Bulgaria	Japan Panama	8
Low aggressive 8 Stable Low homicide	Austria Canada Denmark Iceland Ireland Netherlands New Zealand Norway Sweden Switzerland	—	—	—	—	—	—	10
TOTALS	18	0	0	2	0	9	9	38

Source: James F. Kirkham, Sheldon G. Levy and William J. Crotty, *Assassination and Political Violence* (New York: Praeger Publishers, 1970), pp. 174, 178, 181, 188, 193.

homicide. These nations are all small-power liberal democracies, and Canada is in fact the largest (in terms of population and territory) of the ten nations which enjoy this most peaceful combination.

The peaceful pattern into which Canada is allocated by the combination of socio-economic and conflict variables included in Table 3–17 provides a convenient summary of the general evidence on foreign conflict behaviour, domestic political instability, and criminal violence. Canadians have gone to war three times in this century at a cost of a hundred thousand lives, but their national war experiences have been much less severe than those suffered by the peoples of the major powers in these and other conflicts. Similarly, violence has left its mark on our political history, most recently as a result of the terrorist campaigns of the Sons of Freedom and the F.L.Q.; but the number and rates of assassinations, armed attacks, riots, and deaths from political violence have been low and have not occasioned more than temporary interruptions in a record of basic political stability. Finally, rates of criminal violence have risen modestly in recent years; but this rise seems to derive from relatively benign social changes, such as those in the age composition or urban–rural balance of the population, rather than from a manifest shift in the use of non-political violence within the society. Taking the three aspects of political and criminal violence separately, Canadians have not enjoyed the most favourable circumstances among modern nations. When the three aspects are taken together and viewed in a comparative perspective, however, the Canadian community must be judged to be among the most favoured, peaceful few.

NOTES

1. C. E. Black, *The Dynamics of Modernization* (New York: Harper and Row, 1966), p. 33.
2. J. David Singer and Melvin Small, *The Wages of War, 1816–1965: A Statistical Handbook* (New York: John Wiley and Sons, Inc., 1972), p. 201. Copyright © 1972 by John Wiley & Sons, Inc.
3. Rudolph J. Rummel, "Dimensions of Conflict Within and Between Nations," *General Systems*, Vol. VIII (New York and Ann Arbor: Society for General Systems Research, 1963), pp. 1–50. The measures of foreign conflict were defined (p. 5) as follows:
   "(1) number of anti-foreign demonstrations: any demonstration or riot by more than a hundred people directed at a foreign country or its policies; (2) number of negative sanctions: any non-violent act against another country, such as boycott or withdrawal of aid, the purpose of which is to punish or threaten that country; (3) number of protests: any official diplomatic communication or governmental statement complaining about or objecting to the policies of another country; (4) number of countries with which diplomatic relations were severed: complete withdrawal from official contact with

a country; (5) number of ambassadors expelled or recalled: any expulsion of an ambassador from a country or recalling an ambassador for other than administrative reasons, but not including expulsion and recall resulting from severance of diplomatic relations; (6) number of diplomatic officials of less than ambassador's rank expelled or recalled; (7) number of threats: any official diplomatic communication or governmental statement asserting that if a particular country does or does not do a particular thing it will incur negative sanctions; (8) presence or absence of military action: any military clash between one country and another involving gunfire but not war; (9) number of wars: any military clash between one country and another in which more than 0.02 per cent of its population are militarily involved in the clash; (10) number of troop movements: any rapid movement of large bodies of troops, naval units, or air squadrons to a particular area for the purpose of deterring the military action of another country, gaining concessions, or as a show of strength; (11) number of mobilizations: any rapid increase in military strength through the calling up of reserves or activation of additional military units or equipment; (12) number of accusations: any official diplomatic or governmental statement involving charges and allegations of a derogatory nature against another country; and (13) number of people killed in all forms of foreign conflict behaviour: the total number of deaths resulting directly from any violent interchange between countries."

4. Betty A. Nesvold, "Scalogram Analysis of Political Violence," *Comparative Political Studies*, 2 (July 1969), 177.

5. Bruce R. Russett et al., *World Handbook of Political and Social Indicators* (New Haven and London: Yale University Press, 1964), pp. 306–7.

6. See, for example, Betty A. Nesvold, *op cit.*, and the report on the work of the Feierabend study group in James F. Kirkham, Sheldon G. Levy and William J. Crotty, *Assassination and Political Violence* (New York: Praeger Publishers, 1970), pp. 164–207.

7. Charles L. Taylor and Michael C. Hudson, *World Handbook of Political and Social Indicators* (New Haven and London: Yale University Press, second edition, 1972), p. 67.

8. *Ibid.*, p. 67.

9. The numbers of events reported by Taylor and Hudson are based on those recorded in *The New York Times Index* and the Associated Press card file and judged by the coders to satisfy *a priori* definitions of domestic political violence. (*Ibid.*, Appendix 1.) They provide a useful comparative indicator of domestic political violence in Canada, but they also understate the violence for which the Doukhobors or the F.L.Q. properly may be held responsible. Thus, Hawthorn attributes 114 depredations to the Sons of Freedom terrorists for the year 1953 while Woodcock and Avakumovic mention 106 bombings and burnings committed by them in 1961 and 274 depredations in 1962, "the classic year of terrorist activity." [See Harry B. Hawthorn (ed.), *The Doukhobors of British Columbia* (Vancouver: University of British Columbia and J. M. Dent and Sons Ltd., 1955), p. 255; and George Woodcock and Ivan Avakumovic, *The Doukhobors* (Toronto/New York: Oxford University Press, 1968), p. 350.)]

10. J. F. Kirkham, S. G. Levy and W. J. Crotty, *op. cit.*, p. 1.

11. Denis Szabo, "Assassination and Political Violence in Canada," Supplement G in *ibid.*, pp. 710, 713.

12. The members of the Feierabend study group were Ivo Feierabend, Rosalind Feierabend, Betty A. Nesvold, and Franz N. Jaggar, with assistance from

Rosemary J. Roth, K. Linden Smithson, Robert Kaufman, and Antonia E. Williams.

13. See also Richard Hofstadter's comment on the attempts of the experts of the United States National Commission on the Causes and Prevention of Violence to measure violence quantitatively:

"in some ways their comparisons are crudely mechanical. The 'measurement' of civil strife by the numbers of participants, the duration of incidents, or the casualties per 100,000 of population has no way of taking account of the decisive *qualitative* aspects of violence. The political importance of an act of violence need not be at all proportionate to its cost in casualties—witness the Boston Tea Party, in which not a soul was hurt. Like so many other positivistic inquiries in social science, such 'measurement' jars our sense of proportion by setting down with mathematical exactitude data that have in actuality little of the precision apparently conveyed by the figures in which they are reported. . . . Nonetheless, the figures compiled by the National Commission's experts constitute the only check we have thus far against arbitrary impressions . . ." See Richard Hofstadter and Michael Wallace (eds.), *American Violence: A Documentary History* (New York: Alfred A. Knopf, 1970), p. 8. This work represents an important contribution toward understanding the qualitative aspects of violence in the United States.

14. Canada, Canadian Committee on Corrections, *Report—Towards Unity: Criminal Justice and Corrections* (Ottawa: Queen's Printer, 1969), p. 23.

15. P. J. Giffen, "Rates of Crime and Delinquency," in W. T. McGrath (ed.), *Crime and Its Treatment in Canada* (Toronto: Macmillan Company of Canada, 1965), pp. 68, 70.

16. Ezzat Abdel Fattah, *A Study of the Deterrent Effect of Capital Punishment With Special Reference to the Canadian Situation*, Department of the Solicitor General, Research Centre Report 2 (Ottawa: Information Canada, 1972), pp. 169-70.

17. Lynn McDonald, "Crime and Punishment in Canada: A Statistical Test of the Conventional Wisdom." Reprinted from *The Canadian Review of Sociology and Anthropology*, 6:4 (1969) pp. 212–36, by permission of the author and publisher. In using time as the independent variable, McDonald notes (p. 223) that "although time accounts for a substantial amount of variation in crime, it can only be the beginning of an explanation. The changing of the calendar each January 1 is not of course what really affects the crime rate, although it is treated in the analysis as the independent variable. What is really meant is that unknown factors which vary with time and for which time is simply a proxy, are acting to change the crime rate."

18. *Ibid.*, p. 223.

19. Canadian Committee on Corrections, *op. cit.*, p. 28.

20. L. McDonald, *op. cit.*, pp. 223–6.

21. Canadian Committee on Corrections, *op. cit.*, p. 26.

22. *Ibid.*, p. 30.

23. J. F. Kirkham, S. G. Levy and W. J. Crotty, *op. cit.*, pp. 188, 193.

24. R. J. Rummell, *op. cit.*

25. Raymond Tanter, "Dimensions of Conflict Behaviour Within and Between Nations, 1958–60," *Journal of Conflict Resolution*, X (March 1966), 41–64.

26. J. F. Kirkham, S. G. Levy and W. J. Crotty, *op. cit.*, p. 172.

27. *Ibid.*, p. 176.

28. *Ibid.*, p. 179.

29. For example, Pakistan had a low level of development, high satisfaction, and

a low rate of change, was politically unstable and high in external aggression; it would occupy column three, row one or two, depending on its rate of homicide. The Soviet Union had a high level of development and a high rate of change, was unstable and high in aggression; thus it would fall into column two or six, row one or two, depending on its ranking on satisfaction and homicide.

30. J. F. Kirkham, S. G. Levy and W. J. Crotty, *op. cit.*, p. 204.

Chapter Four

FRATERNITY

A political community is a group of people united by sharing some of their fundamental purposes, interests, and beliefs. The degree of fraternity in a community depends on the degree to which members share and are aware of sharing basic aspects of their personalities. A political community is preserved and enhanced by the promotion of a widespread sense of belonging, trust, and responsiveness in a human group. By thus developing fraternity, the satisfaction of the human needs for love, affection, and belongingness is facilitated.

Two approaches will be adopted here in an attempt to measure the degree to which fraternity exists in contemporary Canada. First, since the development and maintenance of a political community requires extensive, stabilized patterns of communication, one approach to measuring the degree of fraternity is by comparing the quantity and character of communications within the community with communications to points outside it. In making such comparisons, it is assumed that the rates of communication in a wide range of activities are much greater among the members of a strong political community than they are with outsiders. In the first section of this chapter, patterns of communication will be explored in four areas of activity which involve exchanges both within and without Canada: language and culture, migration, travel, and trade.

Second, because the development and maintenance of a political community presupposes some broad agreement among members on their purposes, interests, and beliefs, another general approach to measuring the degree of fraternity is by studying patterns of agreement and disagreement in the orientations of members toward their community. Since a survey of the attitudes of every member of the community is not feasible, the usual technique is to choose a representative group of people, question them for their opinions, and examine their responses for patterns of agreement and disagreement. The underlying assumption of this second approach is that value consensus and conflict will be revealed directly or indirectly in the attitudes expressed by respondents and that these agreements and disagreements in the perceptions of the community relate directly to the actuality of fraternity.

Patterns of Communication

The first obvious characteristic of communication through language in Canada is its separation into English and French. Approximately two-thirds of Canadians speak English as their official language, one-fifth speak French, and just over one-tenth speak both languages. People of other language groups who were here before the French and British or who also have immigrated to Canada have progressively adopted one of the two official languages, usually English, and consequently the number of Canadians who speak neither English nor French is only 1 per cent of the population.

The sense of community between two language groups is likely to grow stronger as bilingualism increases and the possibilities for communication are correspondingly widened. A useful measure of the degree of potential communication among different language groups is the index of mutual intelligibility shown in Table 4–1. It describes the probability that two members chosen at random from the population will be able to communicate because they have at least one language in common. The index may range from 1.0 (where every possible pair of speakers has at least one language in common) to 0 (the unlikely extreme where every speaker has a different lan-

Table 4–1. Percentages of Canadians Speaking Official Languages and Index of Mutual Intelligibility, 1911–1971

Official language	Ten years of age and older			All ages				
	1911	1921	1931	1931	1941	1951	1961	1971
English only	68.0	68.1	69.6	67.5	67.2	67.0	67.4	67.1
French only	19.3	13.2	13.6	17.1	19.0	19.6	19.1	18.0
English and French	7.4	16.7	15.1	12.7	12.8	12.3	12.2	13.4
Neither	5.2	2.0	1.8	2.7	1.0	1.1	1.3	1.5
Index of mutual intelligibility*	0.634	0.78	0.777	0.716	0.725	0.715	0.717	0.729

* The index of mutual intelligibility describes the probability that if two members of the population are chosen at random, they will have at least one official language in common.

Sources: Stanley Lieberson, *Language and Ethnic Relations in Canada* (New York: John Wiley and Sons, Inc., 1970), pp. 31–2; Statistics Canada, *Advance Bulletin (AP–8): Census of Canada* (Ottawa: Statistics Canada, 1973).

guage and has not learned the language of anyone else).[1] In a nation which is divided by language differences, an increasing index of mutual intelligibility might not necessarily mean a growing sense of community; but at least it would indicate a reduction in the barriers to the development of fraternity.

In Canada from 1911 to 1921 the index of mutual intelligibility did increase from 0.634 to 0.781 for the population ten years of age and older. This change reflected an increase in official-languages bilingualism coupled with decreases in the groups speaking French only and neither English nor French. Since 1921, however, the index of mutual intelligibility has remained very stable at approximately 0.72. Because the index was calculated on the basis of the national population and the official-language groups are not randomly distributed, the index tends to understate the degree of mutual intelligibility in actual conversations which occur in specific localities. Nonetheless, the index does serve to summarize both "the striking stability of potential communication in Canada through an official language"[2] and the persistent barrier which language differences present for the development of Canadian community.

Compared with the unilingual English- and French-language groups, the official-languages bilingual group is relatively small; and it is made up mainly of people whose first language is French. Table 4–2 shows the percentage distributions of the respondents to a 1965 survey according to their ethnic origins and their facility in a second language, either French or English. Among the respondents who had British or Canadian-English ethnic origins, those who were not able to speak or read French at all ranged from 56 to 69 per cent; and only 3 to 5 per cent reported that they could speak or read French without difficulty. In contrast, among those of French origin 32 per cent said that they could read English and 29 per cent said that they could speak it without difficulty. Among the respondents who described themselves as Canadians and whose first language was French, over two-thirds reported that they spoke or read English without difficulty. As for the respondents of other ethnic origins, the high proportion of them who reported reading or speaking English without difficulty or with some difficulty bespeaks the extent to which this group has been integrated into the English-language group on coming to Canada; and they do not appear to contribute disproportionately to the official-languages bilingual group.

An important aspect of the relationship between English-speaking and French-speaking people in Canada is their increasing territorial segregation. Richard Joy has described Canada as a state which is steadily developing into two unilingual territories separated by a "bilingual belt".[3] During the nineteenth century, it was common for

Table 4–2. *Percentages of Canadians Able to Speak or Read a Second Language (English or French) by Ethnic Origin, 1965*

Language facility	British origins in French	French origins in English	Other origins in French	Other origins in English	Canadian origins*			
					English in French	French in English	Other language in French	Other language in English
Read second language:								
Without difficulty	4	32	5	36	5	72	26	66
With some difficulty	17	23	16	39	1	21	12	15
With great difficulty	16	14	10	10	20	1	6	6
Not at all	63	30	69	12	56	6	57	2
Speak second language:								
Without difficulty	3	29	4	44	5	67	34	69
With some difficulty	13	27	15	47	15	22	7	16
With great difficulty	15	16	12	3	16	7	13	1
Not at all	69	28	69	3	63	4	46	2

* Respondents who said they were simply Canadian or that they belonged to no particular ethnic group were classified by their principal language into English, French, and Other language groups.

Source: From an unpublished study, *A Study of Interethnic Relations in Canada*, by the Social Research Group, prepared for the Royal Commission on Bilingualism and Biculturalism, with permission of the authors.

English-speaking and French-speaking people (as well as people speaking other languages, such as Gaelic or German) to intermingle within the same geographical region; but this pattern now exists only along the borders of Quebec Province in northern Ontario, the Ottawa Valley, Montreal, the Eastern Townships of Quebec, and the northern counties of New Brunswick.

Within the "Soo-Moncton" area live 93 per cent of all Canadians of French mother tongue, and an even higher percentage of those who still use French as the language spoken at home. Elsewhere in Canada the French language is hardly ever heard, and the assimilation of the French-speaking minorities is accelerating. Conversely, in the heartland of French Canada north and east of Montreal, 95 per cent of the population speak French as their mother tongue; and this region is only slightly less a unilingual French region than the Western Provinces, southern Ontario, and the Atlantic Provinces are unilingual English regions.

> *The forecast, therefore, emerges of a Canada in which the relative strengths of the two major language groups may remain similar to those found today but within which there will be a much more pronounced linguistic segregation: French within Quebec and English elsewhere. Although Montreal may well retain its bilingual character, the English-speaking population of other parts of Quebec will probably decline in actual numbers, not merely in relative strength. Outside Quebec, French will continue to be spoken in the border counties of Ontario and New Brunswick but will virtually disappear from southern Ontario, the Atlantic Region and the Western Provinces.*[4]

Joy argues that political leaders in Canada must begin to prepare the public for this eventuality by showing that the disappearance of linguistic minorities is a natural phenomenon rather than the consequence of ethnic subversion. Otherwise the psychological shock when the minorities do disappear could be far more harmful to Canadian unity than the actual disappearance.

Whether the public needs to be prepared for the assimilation of minorities or not, facilitating communication between the two language groups in Canada obviously presents a serious, long-term problem. Canada is a bilingual nation; and, assuming its existing territorial integrity is maintained, it will remain bilingual. Yet most of the people of Canada are not bilingual, and there is no reason to think this situation will improve. The capacity for direct communication between the two language communities tends to be restricted to a relatively small group of Canadians most of whom live in the "Soo-Moncton" bilingual belt and have French as their first language. At the same time, over a quarter of the French-language group and three-fifths of the English-language group are unable to communicate at all in the other official language of the nation. In such circumstances the development of the Canadian political community is continually impeded by the difficulties which the two language groups have in communicating enough of each other's world to be able to act jointly for the attainment of common values.

Since there are 2,500 languages spoken in the world and about 150 states, problems of communication among different language

Table 4-3. Percentage Distributions of Population by Mother Tongue and Region, Canada, 1941–1971

(percentages)

Mother tongue	Atlantic region	Northern New Brunswick	Interior Quebec	Southern and western Quebec	Eastern and northern Ontario	Southern Ontario	Western region	Canada
1941:								
English	90	40	4	23	56	87	60	57
French	7	59	95	69	33	2	4	29
Other**	3	1	1	7	11	11	36	14
Total**	100	100	100	99	100	100	100	100
1951:								
English	94	39	4	23	59	86	70	59
French	4	60	96	71	32	2	4	29
Other	1	1	1	6	9	11	26	12
Total**	99	100	100	100	100	99	100	100
1961:								
English	94	40	4	21	60	81	73	59
French	4	59	95	70	29	2	3	28
Other	2	1	1	9	11	17	24	13
Total	100	100	100	100	100	100	100	100
1971:								
English	95	41	3	20	64	80	77	60
French	4	58	96	71	27	2	3	27
Other	1	1	1	9	9	18	20	13
Total	100	100	100	100	100	100	100	100

* The boundaries of the regions generally follow those suggested by Richard J. Joy, *Languages in Conflict* (Toronto/Montreal: McClelland and Stewart Limited, 1972), pp. 17–23.

** Totals may not add to 100 per cent because of rounding errors.

Sources: Canada, Dominion Bureau of Statistics, *Census of Canada 1941*, Volume II (Ottawa: King's Printer, 1944), Table 54; *Census of Canada 1951*, Volume I (Ottawa: Queen's Printer, 1953), Table 56; *1961 Census of Canada*, Bulletin 1.2–9 (Ottawa: Queen's Printer, 1963), Table 66; Statistics Canada, *1971 Census of Canada: Advance Bulletin*, Catalogue 92-758 (Ap-7) (Ottawa: Information Canada, 1972), Table 2. Reproduced by permission of Information Canada.

groups living in the same state are obviously not unique to Canada; but the Canadian situation is unique in that English and French both vie for the highest international rank.[5] The situation is further complicated by the fact that one of the two official national languages is also the national language of the United States. The Royal Commission on Bilingualism and Biculturalism has remarked that

> as the national language of the United States, one of the most powerful countries of the world, English has a massive preponderance in North America. Thus the English-language group in this country draws much of its strength from the English-speaking population of our neighbour. The French-language group is, on the other hand, a minority on the North American continent and suffers from its isolation not only from France but from other French-speaking peoples of the world.[6]

The preponderance of English in North America undoubtedly gives the English-language group in Canada a considerable advantage over the French, as the Royal Commission argues; and it also weakens the sense of Canadian community by facilitating the flow of cultural transactions between English-speaking Canadians and Americans at the expense of an internal production and exchange. The substantial penetration of American culture is reflected in the origins of the films, television programs, books, and magazines consumed in Canada.

Table 4–4 shows that over six hundred feature films were released each year for theatrical bookings in Canada from 1966 to 1969. The majority of films each year came from the United States, which was the country of origin for one-third of the films released in 1967 and for almost one-half of those released in 1968. France, Italy, and Britain were the other important sources of feature films in each of these years, while Canadian films constituted a slight 1.2 to 1.7 per cent of the totals.

In 1968 the percentage distribution of the channels selected by Canadians for their television viewing was as follows: American stations, 17 per cent; C.B.C. English network and its affiliates, 35 per cent; C.T.V. stations, 19 per cent; independent stations, 15 per cent; and C.B.C. French network and its affiliates, 14 per cent. Given the preponderance of American programs on the C.T.V. and C.B.C. English networks, especially in prime time, it is clear that the viewing hours of most English-speaking Canadians were spent watching American programs.[7] Table 4–5 makes it plain, however, that this is what Canadians overwhelmingly preferred. Whether referring to

Table 4–4. National Origins of Feature Films Released in Canada,
1966–1969

(percentages)

Nation	1966	1967	1968	1969
United States	35.8	33.7	48.4	37.8
France	24.6	23.8	18.6	5.1
Italy	17.0	17.0	12.3	14.6
Britain	9.7	11.2	8.0	24.7
Canada	1.7	1.3	1.2	1.5
Other Countries	11.1	13.0	11.4	16.3
TOTALS*				
Percentage	99.9	100.0	99.9	100.0
Number	637	623	649	669

* Totals may not add to 100 per cent because of rounding errors.

Sources: Canada, Dominion Bureau of Statistics, *Canada Year Book 1968* (Ottawa: Queen's Printer, 1968), p. 901; *Canada Year Book 1969* (Ottawa: Queen's Printer, 1969), p. 932; *Canada Year Book 1970–71* (Ottawa: Information Canada, 1971), p. 1018; Statistics Canada, *Canada Year Book 1972* (Ottawa: Information Canada, 1972), p. 1002. Reproduced by permission of Information Canada.

television shows or the television medium in general, substantial majorities in all areas of the nation, except French-speaking Quebec, said that they preferred American television to its Canadian counterpart.

Even at the best of times the Canadian magazine industry has been weak; and the evidence suggests that it is growing weaker, in part because of the competition and attractiveness of American magazines.[8] The national survey of opinions on the media in 1969 found that only about one-fifth of the respondents in French-speaking Quebec expressed a preference for American magazines over Canadian ones, but elsewhere two-fifths to two-thirds of the respondents said that they preferred American magazines. The two strongest magazines in the country are actually Canadian editions of the American magazines, *Time* and *Reader's Digest*, which together earned 42 per cent of the total revenue spent on advertising in major Canadian consumer magazines in 1958 and 56 per cent in 1969.[9] However, the most important reason for the continuing difficulties of the Canadian magazine industry is not the competition from *Time* and *Reader's Digest* for advertising revenue but the overflow circulation of American magazines into Canada.

Unhampered by tariff barriers, by language barriers, or by any form of protective legislation, foreign magazines—

111

Table 4-5. Percentages of Respondents Expressing Preferences for Canadian Versus American Media by Province,*
Canada, 1969

Media	Total	British Columbia	Alberta	Saskat-chewan	Manitoba	Ontario	Quebec English	Quebec French	New Brunswick	Nova Scotia	Newfound-land
Television shows:											
Canadian	35	28	26	23	23	24	33	69	32	16	18
American	60	66	70	70	74	70	60	29	68	82	80
Did not state	5	6	4	7	3	6	7	2	–	2	2
Total	100	100	100	100	100	100	100	100	100	100	100
Television:											
Canadian	43	34	33	31	32	29	45	80	35	32	29
American	54	59	63	68	67	66	50	20	65	68	71
Did not state	3	7	4	1	1	5	5	–	–	–	–
Total	100	100	100	100	100	100	100	100	100	100	100
Radio:											
Canadian	92	89	92	91	97	92	95	94	84	93	88
American	4	3	5	5	3	4	1	4	5	6	8
Did not state	4	8	3	4	–	4	4	2	11	1	4
Total	100	100	100	100	100	100	100	100	100	100	100
Magazines:											
Canadian	56	41	55	59	54	51	44	76	49	49	29
American	37	46	40	39	44	41	46	18	38	49	67
Did not state	7	13	5	2	2	8	10	6	13	2	4
Total	100	100	100	100	100	100	100	100	100	100	100

* Prince Edward Island and French-speaking Maritimes not included.

Source: Special Senate Committee on Mass Media, Report, Volume III (Ottawa: Queen's Printer 1970), p. 131. Reproduced by permission of In-formation Canada.

mostly American, naturally—pour into the country by the tens of millions, swamping our newsstands and occasionally overloading our postal system. The fact of overflow circulation is of course obvious, but its sheer magnitude is seldom appreciated. Playboy, to cite one example, collects about as much money selling its magazine in Canada as do the seventeen largest English-language consumer magazines combined. Chatelaine, with a circulation of 980,000, has one of the world's highest per capita penetrations of its available audience; yet Life sells more magazines in Canada than Chatelaine does. Canadians buy almost twice as many copies of True Story as they do of Saturday Night. We buy more than sixteen times as many copies of the National Geographic Magazine as we do of Canadian Geographic. We spend more money buying American comic books than we do on the seven leading Canadian-owned magazines.[10]

The popular literature read by Canadians shows a significant American penetration; but the Canadian content is somewhat higher than it is in the case of films, television, and magazines. Table 4–6 shows the percentage distribution by the authors' nationalities of the best-selling books in Canada during 1972 as published in the weekly lists of Montreal's *La Presse* and the *Toronto Daily Star*. Because the *Star* compiles separate lists for fiction and non-fiction

Table 4–6. *Best-selling Books in Canada Listed by* La Presse *and* Toronto Daily Star *by Nationalities of Authors, 1972*

(percentages)

Nationalities of authors	La Presse fiction and non-fiction Titles	Entries*	Toronto Daily Star fiction Titles	Entries*	Toronto Daily Star non-fiction Titles	Entries*
Canadian	52	38	28	28	58	64
American	8	16	30	43	21	18
British	1	**	33	25	10	11
French	23	27	2	**	2	**
Other	16	19	7	4	8	7
TOTAL						
Percentage***	100	100	100	100	99	100
Number	75	422	43	519	48	521

* Entries refers to the number of titles weighted by the number of weeks each title appeared on the best-seller list.

** Less than 0.5 per cent.

*** Totals may not add to 100 per cent because of rounding errors.

and *La Presse* combines fiction and non-fiction in a single list, the English-language and French-language lists are not directly comparable; but, taken together, the three lists indicate a significant Canadian content in the consumption of popular literature in Canada during 1972. Two-thirds of the best-selling fiction books in English were written by American and British authors but over one-quarter of them were Canadian in origin, and a majority of both the best-selling non-fiction books in English and the best-selling books in French were authored by Canadians.

Overall, the proportion of best-selling books which have Canadian origins probably does not differ very much between English Canada and French Canada; but clearly the two Canadian communities show very different cultural attachments in their consumption of popular literature. English Canadians appear to make up a regional bloc in an international common market for English-language popular literature. Although the international market is dominated by American and British writers, a number of English Canadians make a proportionate contribution; and in the book consumption of the English-Canadian regional bloc the representation of the English-Canadian writers is obviously very much higher.

This impression of an English-Canadian regional bloc within a larger English-language market for popular literature is strengthened by a comparison of the non-Canadian titles on the *Star's* lists with those appearing on the best-seller lists of *The New York Times* during 1972. All of the best-selling books authored by the American writers and most of those authored by the British which appeared on the *Star's* lists in 1972 also appeared on the lists published by *The New York Times*. The pattern of the evidence, then, shows an English-Canadian regional bloc consuming in large part the books which hold sway in the international English-language market for popular literature, making a modest contribution to the offerings of that international market, and supporting a specific regional market which reflects its own particular concerns and interests.

The cultural attachments of French Canada in its consumption of popular literature are very different from those of English Canada. The fact that nearly one-tenth of the books on the French-Canadian best-seller list in 1972 were authored by Americans indicates that, given a time lag for translation, French Canada is also subject to a significant penetration of American popular literature. However, the American presence was much less pronounced than it was in English Canada; and the larger representation of French writers combined with an insignificant representation of British writers provided virtually a mirror-image of the English-Canadian lists.

An inspection of the titles which appeared on the French-language list also supports the impression, which is gained from the percentage distributions of authors' nationalities, of a mutual separation between French and English Canada. In contrast with the shared core of the best-seller lists of the *Toronto Daily Star* and *The New York Times*, there were only four titles which appeared on both the French-language and English-language lists in 1972; and they represented only 5 per cent of the titles and 6 per cent of the entries on the *La Presse* list and 4 per cent of the titles and 7 per cent of the entries on the two *Toronto Daily Star* lists.

The cultural separation of French Canada from the rest of North America is also evident in its preferences in television viewing. Table 4–5 shows that French-speaking viewers in Quebec preferred Canadian television shows to American ones by a great majority; and, no doubt because of language differences, they stated an even stronger preference for Canadian television as a medium. A Gallup poll taken in 1966 found that 41 per cent of the national sample thought American television programs were better than Canadian ones and 36 per cent thought Canadian programs were better. On a regional basis, 52 per cent of respondents in Ontario and 51 per cent in the West said American programs were better, and 24 per cent in Ontario and 23 per cent in the West favoured Canadian programs. Conversely, in Quebec 66 per cent thought Canadian programs were better, while only 15 per cent favoured American programs.[11]

On the whole the newspapers of Canada are barely distinguishable from those of the United States,[12] but there are some noticeable differences between the newspapers of French Canada and those of English Canada. An analysis of the attention given to various subjects in twenty-nine daily newspapers between January 11 and June 30, 1965 showed that newspaper readers in different regions of the nation were offered information which varied widely in terms of amount, subjects stressed, and editorial comment; but the differences between French-language and English-language newspapers were even greater than those between regions.

Table 4–7 shows the different emphasis given to fifteen subject areas by the newspapers in five regional and two language groups in the first half of 1965; and Table 4–8 attempts to summarize the regional differences by presenting indices of similarity between the respective percentage distributions over the fifteen subject areas for each pair of regions. The index of similarity between English-language and French-language newspapers was 0.676 during this period. There were some notable regional differences, such as those between the newspapers of the Atlantic Provinces and British Columbia, and similarities, such as those between the newspapers of On-

Table 4–7. *Average Weighted* Column Inches for Fifteen Subject Areas in Twenty-nine Canadian Newspapers by Region and Language, 1965*

Subject area	Region					Language	
	British Columbia	Prairie Provinces	Ontario	Quebec	Atlantic Provinces	French	English
Federal administration	693.7	1,023.7	998.2	753.7	692.2	653.2	927.5
Federal politics	6,935.2	5,670.7	6,752.0	6,137.2	4,278.7	5,770.1	5,740.2
Provincial politics	1,258.1	1,024.4	1,843.9	3,553.1	597.2	3,580.5	1,421.2
Biculturalism	948.6	1,669.8	2,243.7	2,953.3	1,009.4	3,406.2	1,753.6
Crime and legal	4,965.2	4,579.5	6,222.9	5,619.6	2,796.6	4,888.0	5,198.9
Natural disasters	1,159.5	827.4	963.1	639.6	595.5	497.3	908.2
Business and economic	1,558.0	2,230.7	2,691.4	1,821.8	1,194.9	1,583.7	2,187.4
Religion and education	461.3	565.8	814.2	612.7	354.7	560.7	629.6
Social	550.6	554.0	759.5	281.7	281.1	237.9	589.7
Agriculture	175.0	455.1	181.6	121.1	139.6	126.7	240.7
Maritime	77.1	131.6	169.8	116.7	134.4	77.1	149.6
Obituaries	72.0	143.9	136.7	89.1	124.6	59.3	133.8
Foreign affairs	732.1	893.6	1,067.7	929.9	501.6	884.0	886.0
Medicine and science	705.6	747.6	910.0	385.1	458.0	267.8	770.1
Armed services	212.3	247.6	274.1	171.1	185.2	167.9	240.1

* Reports were weighted to take account of where they were printed in the paper and how much prominence was given to them.

Source: From an unpublished study, *National News in Canadian Newspapers* by Donald Gordon, prepared for the Royal Commission on Bilingualism and Biculturalism, with permission of the author.

Table 4–8. *Indices of Similarity Among Twenty-nine Canadian Newspapers by Region, 1965**

	Atlantic Provinces	Quebec	Ontario	Prairie Provinces	British Columbia
Atlantic Provinces	—	0.656	0.808	0.878	0.711
Quebec		—	0.774	0.694	0.653
Ontario			—	0.892	0.819
Prairie Provinces				—	0.755
British Columbia					—

* The indices of similarity were calculated by changing the average weighted column inches for each subject area to a ratio of the total average weighted column inches for each region. The algebraic sums of the differences between the distributions of ratios for each pair of regions were calculated and then subtracted from 1.000.

Source: Table 4–7.

tario and Quebec. In general, however, the indices of regional similarity were higher than the index of language similarity, except for the indices of similarity between Quebec and the Atlantic Provinces, the Prairies, and British Columbia; and the best explanation of these regional differences appears to be the existence of language differences. Donald Gordon, the author of the study, concluded that to a large extent the differences in selection and emphasis of national news "can be summed up as mutual separation. French language newspapers tend to be preoccupied with the affairs of their nation—Quebec. English language newspapers tend to be preoccupied with their nation too."[13]

Communication is likely to be easier and more effective in a community where the membership is not changing too much. In this connection, John Porter has argued that "a strongly held set of beliefs or a basic personality structure would seem to require a relatively stable population or one with relatively stable rates of growth over some considerable time. Shared culture and shared habits are broken up, or never get established, where demographic trends are erratic."[14]

Historically the foreign-born population of Canada has increased rather erratically in three periods of rapid growth separated by two periods of stagnation. The proportion of foreign-born people in the Canadian population was one-fifth in 1871 because of the high rate of immigration during the growth period in the first half of the nineteenth century; but the proportion of people who were foreign-born dropped and emigration exceeded immigration during the last four decades of the century.

During the second period of growth in the first decades of the twentieth century, the rate of emigration continued to be very high; but the rate of immigration was even higher, reaching nearly 25 per cent of the population between 1901 and 1911 and then decreasing over the next two decades. The enormous turnover in the decade from 1901 to 1911 resulted in a net gain of 810,000 people and raised the proportion of the foreign-born in Canada to 22 per cent of the population where it remained until the 1930s. The depression of the 1930s was accompanied by a drop in rates of migration, and the rates increased only slightly during World War II so that the proportion of the foreign-born in Canada had fallen to 14.7 per cent by 1951.

After World War II the rate of emigration remained relatively low, but a sizable increase in the rate of immigration resulted in a slight increase in the proportion of foreign-born Canadians in 1961. Overall, between 1851 and 1961 Canada gained 8.32 million by immigration and lost 6.15 million by emigration.

Table 4–9. *Immigration as a Factor in the Composition and Growth of the Canadian Population, 1861–1971*

Period	Population at end of decade (thousands)	Foreign-born in Canadian population at end of decade	
		Number (thousands)	Percentage of total population
1861–1871	3,689	625	20.8
1871–1881	4,325	603	13.9
1881–1891	4,833	644	13.3
1891–1901	5,371	699	13.0
1901–1911	7,207	1,587	22.0
1911–1921	8,788	1,956	22.3
1921–1931	10,377	2,308	22.2
1931–1941	11,507	2,019	17.5
1941–1951	14,009	2,060	14.7
1951–1961	18,238	2,844	15.6
1961–1971	21,568	3,269	15.3

Sources: Canada, Department of Manpower and Immigration, *Immigration Statistics 1968* (Ottawa: Queen's Printer, 1969); Statistics Canada, *Advance Bulletin (AP–10): 1971 Census of Canada* (Ottawa, Statistics Canada, 1973). Reproduced by permission of Information Canada.

Table 4–10. *Size and Rates of External Migration, Canada, 1851–1961*

Period	Average population* (millions)	Emigration (millions)	Rate of emigration (percentage)	Immigration (millions)	Rate of immigration (percentage)	Net migration (millions)	Rate of net migration (percentage)
1851–1861	2.84	−.17	−5.99	0.35	12.32	0.18	6.34
1861–1871	3.46	−.41	−11.85	0.26	7.51	−0.15	−4.34
1871–1881	4.01	−.39	−9.73	0.35	8.73	−0.04	−1.00
1881–1891	4.58	−.83	−18.12	0.68	14.85	−0.15	−3.27
1891–1901	5.10	−.38	−7.45	0.25	4.90	−0.13	−2.55
1901–1911	6.29	−.74	−11.76	1.55	24.64	0.81	12.88
1911–1921	8.00	−1.09	−13.63	1.44	18.00	0.31	4.37
1921–1931	9.59	−.97	−10.11	1.20	12.51	0.23	2.40
1931–1941	10.95	−.24	−2.19	0.15	1.37	−0.09	−0.82
1941–1951	12.76	−.37	−2.90	0.55	4.31	0.18	1.41
1951–1961	16.13	−.46	−2.85	1.54	9.55	1.08	6.70

* Average of the populations at the start and at the end of each period.

Source: Pierre Camu, E. P. Weeks, and W. Z. Sametz, *Economic Geography of Canada* (Toronto: Macmillan Company of Canada, 1964).

The detrimental effects of excessive migration for the emergence of a sense of Canadian community have been mitigated since the

1930s by the relatively lower rate of overall turnover and by the downward trend in the rate of emigration of native Canadians. Camu, Weeks, and Sametz have pointed out that a large part of the population lost by emigration since 1851 has been made up of short-term immigrants and that this tendency has become stronger in recent decades. During the decade from 1951 to 1961, for example, 77 per cent of the 462,000 emigrants were born outside Canada and admitted to Canada during that period.[15] When the United States was rapidly industrializing, there was a significant outflow of native Canadians to the United States; but there has been a steady decline in the relative size of the Canadian-born population in the United States since 1930. In 1900, the number of Canadian-born people living in the United States equalled 25.3 per cent of the number of Canadian-born people then living in Canada. By 1961, the Canadian-born population of the United States was only 6.2 per cent of the Canadian-born population living in Canada and 5.3 per cent of the total population of Canada.[16]

In terms of facilitating or impeding the development of fraternity, a very important aspect of Canadian migration has been its different impact on French Canada and English Canada. There has been a sizable emigration of French Canadians to the United States involving a net loss of 800,000 people, but most of this emigration occurred between 1850 and 1930 and effectively ended with the depression. At the same time, immigration has had only a negligible effect on the French-Canadian population, as its growth from 65,000 in 1763 to 5.8 million in 1971 was almost entirely the result of natural increase. Thus, most of the turnover in the Canadian population has occurred in English Canada, which Porter has likened to a "huge demographic railway station".[17] It seems reasonable to conclude that these different demographic developments have contributed to the differences between the French-speaking and English-speaking societies in Canada. The demographic history of French Canada does show the persistence within the nation of a relatively stable population sub-group, which potentially provides the locus for the development of strong collective sentiments. Conversely, the presence of very many people in English-speaking Canada who have been either newcomers or potential migrants or both has almost certainly inhibited the emergence of a coherent, deeply held set of traditions, values, and commitments.

The rate of immigration into Canada decreased to 7.19 per cent during the decade 1961–1971 (total immigration was 1.43 million compared with an average population of 19.9 million). Yet this rate of immigration continued to be relatively high among advanced industrialized nations. Table 4–11 shows the average annual inflow of

119

Table 4–11. *Average Annual Immigration, Selected Nations, 1962–1969*

Nation	Average annual number of long-term immigrants	Average annual number of immigrants per million population
Australia	185,267	16,110
Israel	34,993	13,616
New Zealand	32,160	12,136
West Germany	665,857	11,706
Canada	148,778	7,488
Belgium*	66,517	7,002
Netherlands	56,151	4,547
Sweden**	34,468	4,459
Japan	378,490	3,843
United Kingdom	177,120	3,705
Norway	13,516	3,614
France**	123,824	2,546
United States	341,329	1,747
Italy	10,640	206

* 1963–1969.

** 1962–1968.

Source: United Nations, Department of Economic and Social Affairs, Statistical Office, *Demographic Yearbook 1970* (New York: United Nations, 1971), Tables 4, 25. Reprinted by permission of the United Nations.

long-term immigrants per million population for fourteen nations during the 1960s. At 7,488 per million population, the average annual rate of immigration into Canada between 1962 and 1969 was relatively high compared with other industrialized nations, most of which have not had in addition the modern history of demographic flux experienced by Canada.

Few people would dispute the value of the contributions made to Canada by successive groups of immigrants, but the identity problem created by this inflow of new citizens also needs to be recognized. Thus, while there has been a lower rate of turnover since the 1930s, the decrease is too recent and the stock of new immigrants is too constantly renewed for English Canada to have yet attained a degree of population stability which is conducive to a strong sense of community.

High rates of immigration and emigration impede the development of fraternity by preventing a relatively stable population, but high rates of internal migration further fraternity by strengthening primary relationships among people of different regions. In the case of Canada, "interesting and important as the external migration streams may be, they are dwarfed in volume by the migration streams flowing *within* Canada. The Canadian population is in a perpetual state of flux from migration as people change residence from one locality to another."[18] Much of the population mobility within Canada is accounted for by movement within municipalities or provinces and has little significance for national integration, but a pattern which is partially integrative and affects mainly English Canada is observable for the 4 per cent of the population which moves between provinces.

The mobility ratios in Table 4–12 show all those who were intra-municipal, intraprovincial, or interprovincial movers at least once between 1956 and 1961 as a percentage of the total population. During the five-year period, 43.5 per cent of Canadians moved at least once, with 39.9 per cent of the population moving within munici-palities and provinces and only 3.6 per cent between provinces. There were significant differences among ethnic groups in their ratios of interprovincial movers, and these differences are probably accounted for by language differences. Table 4–12 shows that the interprovincial mobility ratio was greatest among those who spoke English, closely followed by those who spoke English and French; and the ratio was a very low 0.5 per cent of those who spoke French only and 1.5 per cent of those who spoke neither English nor French.

The relatively low rate of interprovincial mobility and the marked differences in interprovincial mobility between language groups reduce the importance of domestic migration as a factor in national

Table 4–12. *Five-year Internal Mobility Ratios by Ethnic Origins and Language Group, Canada, 1956–1961*

Ethnic origin or language group	(percentages) Mobility ratios			
	Intramunicipal	Intraprovincial	Interprovincial	Total
Ethnic origin:				
British	23.7	14.4	4.6	42.7
French	26.9	13.4	1.8	42.1
Other	29.6	13.8	3.8	47.2
Language group:				
English only	25.2	14.2	4.4	43.8
French only	24.2	12.2	0.5	37.9
English and French	30.0	14.9	3.9	48.8
Neither English nor French	43.3	9.2	1.5	54.0
All groups	26.0	13.9	3.6	43.5

Source: Leroy O. Stone, *Migration in Canada*, Dominion Bureau of Statistics, 1961 Census Monograph (Ottawa: Queen's Printer, 1969), pp. 81–2. Reproduced by permission of Information Canada.

integration. The interprovincial migration which does occur shows a familiar ambiguity between centralizing and decentralizing tendencies.

Tables 4–13 and 4–14 show the provincial destinations for the out-migrants from each province between 1956 and 1961 and for families with children in 1970-1971. What is immediately striking is the importance of Ontario as the destination for migrants from other parts of the nation. During both periods Ontario was by far the most important province of destination for people moving out of the Atlantic Provinces, Quebec, and Manitoba; and it was the second most important province of destination for those moving out of Alberta and British Columbia.

A study of geographic mobility within Canada during 1964 and 1965 concluded that the majority of all moves were made for economic and job-related reasons and over 70 per cent of the interprovincial moves were primarily concerned with the labour market.[19] Migration in Canada thus appears to be strongly associated with finding employment; and, given the concentration of wealth and productive capacity in Ontario and its record of superior economic growth, the flow of migrants into that province is not surprising. Thus, although regional disparities continue to cause resentment, the superior growth of the Ontario economy must be seen as a strong tie binding Canadians together in a common interest and enterprise. Where Maritimers and French Canadians once made their way to New England (and the family ties thus created across the border persist), now the Maritimers at least and their compatriots from the Western Provinces migrate to Ontario for improved employment opportunities; and the relationships of family and friendship established across regional boundaries increasingly contribute to national integration.

Tables 4–13 and 4–14 also reveal significant patterns of regional migration in the Atlantic Provinces and in the West, with the most important regional exchange being that among the Western Provinces. Alberta and British Columbia were each other's most important destination in addition to being first and second in importance for Saskatchewan (and the Yukon and Northwest Territories) and only slightly less important than Ontario for families moving from Manitoba. For the same reasons of economic growth and employment opportunities which draw people to Ontario, people in the Western Provinces move to the centres of economic growth in Alberta and British Columbia, thus strengthening Western regionalism and mitigating the centralizing tendencies of the Ontario economy.

Travel is supposed to be broadening, and to the extent that it is concentrated within a community it should work to enhance poten-

Table 4–13. *Relative Shares of Provincial Destinations of the Five-year Out-migrants from Each Province of Origin, Canada, 1956–1961*

(percentages)

Province of destination

Province of origin	New- found- land	Nova Scotia	Prince Edward Island	New Brunswick	Quebec	Ontario	Manitoba	Saskat- chewan	Alberta	British Columbia
Newfoundland	–	18.2	0.5	6.6	13.7	46.9	2.9	2.0	4.3	4.8
Nova Scotia	3.3	–	4.0	18.5	11.1	46.9	3.3	0.9	3.9	8.1
Prince Edward Island	3.7	17.4	–	17.9	8.2	40.7	2.0	1.4	5.4	3.4
New Brunswick	2.3	13.8	2.8	–	30.0	42.2	1.7	0.7	3.2	3.2
Quebec	1.2	4.4	0.6	5.8	–	73.0	3.1	1.2	4.6	6.1
Ontario	1.8	8.8	1.1	6.6	35.4	–	13.2	5.2	12.6	15.3
Manitoba	0.5	2.2	0.3	2.2	6.0	34.1	–	15.3	17.8	21.7
Saskatchewan	0.1	0.7	0.2	0.3	1.4	13.7	16.2	–	39.8	27.5
Alberta	0.4	1.3	0.3	1.1	4.8	20.8	9.0	15.9	–	46.4
British Columbia	0.3	3.8	0.3	1.9	5.7	28.7	9.6	11.1	38.6	–

Source: Leroy O. Stone, *Migration in Canada*, Dominion Bureau of Statistics, 1961 Census Monograph (Ottawa: Queen's Printer, 1969), pp. 35–8. Reproduced by permission of Information Canada.

Table 4–14. Relative Shares of Provincial Destinations of Families With Children Moving from Each Province of Origin, Canada, 1970–71

(percentages)

Province of destination

Province of origin	Newfoundland	Prince Edward Island	Nova Scotia	New Brunswick	Quebec	Ontario	Manitoba	Saskatchewan	Alberta	British Columbia	Yukon and Northwest Territories	Total*
Newfoundland	—	1.0	12.9	6.7	7.2	63.2	1.8	0.7	2.4	33.6	0.4	99.9
Prince Edward Island	3.8	—	18.5	18.4	3.8	41.2	3.0	1.4	4.8	4.8	0.4	100.1
Nova Scotia	5.6	4.0	—	12.5	7.8	52.2	2.9	1.0	5.1	8.4	0.4	99.9
New Brunswick	3.3	2.6	15.3	—	15.1	46.1	3.9	1.2	5.7	6.6	0.2	100.0
Quebec	1.6	0.6	3.5	6.3	—	70.2	2.9	0.8	4.7	8.9	0.6	100.1
Ontario	6.0	1.8	12.1	10.4	26.5	—	8.7	3.0	11.0	19.7	0.7	99.0
Manitoba	0.5	0.4	1.8	2.8	5.5	33.0	—	12.6	20.6	21.6	1.1	99.0
Saskatchewan	0.3	0.1	1.4	0.5	1.2	14.0	19.3	—	36.7	24.4	2.0	99.9
Alberta	0.6	0.3	1.9	1.4	3.3	21.3	8.2	14.3	—	44.7	4.0	100.0
British Columbia	0.7	0.2	2.9	1.4	4.9	30.2	8.4	8.8	37.8	—	4.7	100.0
Yukon and Northwest Territories	1.3	0.2	—	1.2	3.9	10.7	4.2	4.1	37.9	36.5	—	100.0
TOTAL	2.3	1.0	5.4	5.1	8.6	31.4	7.0	5.1	14.6	17.7	1.7	99.9

* Totals may not add to 100 per cent because of rounding errors.

Source: Canada, Statistics Canada, *Interprovincial Movement of Children in Canada 1970–71* (Ottawa: Department of Industry, Trade and Commerce, 1971), p. 3. Reproduced by permission of Information Canada.

tial communication. The evidence on the patterns of travel by Canadians indicates, however, that the centrifugal attraction of the United
States and the persistence of regionalism are much stronger than
any integrating pattern of national travel.

Table 4–15 shows that over two-thirds of the vacation travel by
Canadians in 1970 took place in Canada, but the areas which they
visited in Canada were mainly in their own regions of residence.
The percentage of total trips involving visits overnight or longer to
areas in Canada ranged from 64 per cent of all trips by Quebec
residents to 78 per cent of all trips by the residents of Manitoba
and Saskatchewan, and the percentage of trips which included at
least some visiting in Canada ranged from 67 per cent in Quebec to

Table 4–15. Vacation Travel by Canadians, 1970

(percentages of total trips)
Place of residence at time of trip

Areas visited overnight or longer	Atlantic Provinces	Quebec	Ontario	Manitoba	Saskat-chewan	Alberta	British Columbia
Canada only	77	64	71	78	78	77	67
Canada at all	85	67	74	82	89	88	73
Atlantic Provinces	63	5	5	3	1	0	1
Newfoundland	19	*	1	0	*	0	*
Prince Edward Island	6	2	2	*	0	0	*
Nova Scotia	25	2	4	3	1	0	1
New Brunswick	19	4	3	*	*	0	*
Quebec	11	52	9	3	3	2	2
Ontario	15	10	58	14	7	7	6
Prairie Provinces	4	2	7	56	78	47	21
Manitoba	2	1	5	28	13	9	5
Saskatchewan	1	1	2	19	51	7	5
Alberta	2	1	3	16	26	33	16
British Columbia	1	2	4	19	16	41	56
Yukon and Northwest Territories	0	*	0	0	0	*	1
Continental United States	21	29	20	16	14	14	26
All other countries	2	7	9	6	8	9	7
Any other province	53	17	20	58	49	63	27

* Less than 1 per cent

Source: Traveldata Limited, *Vacation Travel by Canadians in 1970* (Toronto:
mimeographed March 1971), p. 14. Study carried out for the Canadian Government Travel Bureau.

89 per cent in Saskatchewan. However, 63 per cent of the trips by the residents of the Atlantic Provinces were spent in the Atlantic Provinces; 52 per cent of the trips by Quebec residents were spent in Quebec; 58 per cent of Ontario residents visited areas in Ontario; the Prairie Provinces were the destination of 56 per cent of the trips of Manitoba residents, 78 per cent of the trips of Saskatchewan residents, and 47 per cent of the trips of Alberta residents; and British Columbia residents spent 56 per cent of their total trips in British Columbia.

The regional concentration of vacation travel in 1970 is summarized by the percentages of total trips which involved visits to "any other province". The vacation trips of the residents of the Atlantic and Prairie Provinces were likely to involve an overnight stay in a neighbouring province, but clearly most of this interprovincial travel took place within the same region. As for Ontario, British Columbia, and Quebec—the three provinces which are also regions—the trips taken by residents of Ontario and British Columbia included visits to other provinces about as often as they included visits to the United States, while the residents of Quebec visited the United States on 29 per cent of their trips and other Canadian provinces on only 17 per cent of their trips.

In the context of this regional concentration of vacation travel by Canadians, the percentage of trips which involve visits to the United States assumes greater significance. Canadians on vacation tend to visit the United States more often than any region of Canada outside their own region of residence, with the important exception of the residents of the Prairie Provinces, particularly those of Alberta, who travel to British Columbia more often than to the United States. Of course, much vacation travel is interregional, but the effect of such travel is relatively small compared with the flow of travel within each region and across the border.

Economic transactions constitute communications through the medium of dollars offered in exchange for goods or services. To the extent that they are contained within the community, they give rise to integrating relationships which are potentially very important for the development of fraternity. The great majority of Canadian economic transactions are contained within the community, and these domestic economic transactions do tend to form an integrating pattern of national economic exchange. However, the centripetal tendencies of the national economy are strongly counteracted by its extensive integration into the economy of the United States.

The best available indicator of the general pattern of domestic economic transactions is the distribution of shipments of Canadian manufacturing industries.[20] Table 4–16 shows that 83.7 per cent of

Table 4-16. *Percentage Distribution of Shipments of Canadian Manufacturing Industries by First Destination of Shipments, 1967*

(percentages)
First destination of shipments

Region of origin	Atlantic Provinces	Quebec	Ontario	Prairie Provinces	British Columbia and Territories*	All Canadian destinations	Other countries	Total
Atlantic Provinces	54.4	8.4	8.7	1.8	0.7	74.0	26.0	100.0
Quebec	3.8	54.2	19.4	4.6	2.7	84.7	15.3	100.0
Ontario	3.3	13.2	57.8	7.3	3.9	85.5	14.5	100.0
Prairie Provinces	1.0	6.2	8.2	70.9	7.0	93.3	6.7	100.0
British Columbia and Territories*	0.6	2.0	3.9	8.5	48.6	63.6	36.5	100.0
Canada	4.9	23.1	36.9	11.5	7.3	83.7	16.3	100.0

*Yukon and Northwest Territories

Source: Canada, Dominion Bureau of Statistics, *Destination of Shipments of Manufacturers, 1967.* (Ottawa: Information Canada, 1971), p. 9. Reproduced by permission of Information Canada.

the first shipments of Canadian manufacturing industries in 1967 went to Canadian destinations. This percentage ranged among the regions from 63.6 per cent of the shipments from British Columbia, Yukon, and the Northwest Territories, to 93.3 per cent of those from the Prairie Provinces. Not surprisingly, destinations located in the region of origin were in every case the most important for the manufacturers of the region. The percentage of shipments which originated in each region and went to destinations within the region ranged from a low of 48.6 per cent for British Columbia and the Territories to a high of 70.9 per cent for the Prairie Provinces.

The regional concentration of shipments can also be seen in Table 4–17 which shows the relative participation of the manufacturers of each region in the five regional markets and in other countries. For each region, the manufacturers of that region had the highest rate of participation in its market, but the rate ranged from the 81.7 per cent of shipments destined for Ontario which originated within Ontario to the 40.1 per cent of shipments to destinations in the Atlantic Provinces which originated within the Atlantic Provinces.

Besides showing the importance of local markets, Table 4–16 indicates that each region of Canada, except for British Columbia and the Territories, has trading links with other regions which rival or exceed its transactions with other countries. In 1967, 19.6 per cent of the shipments of manufacturing industries located in the Atlantic Provinces had first destinations in other regions of Canada compared with 26.0 per cent of shipments which went to other countries; 30.5 per cent of Quebec shipments went to other regions compared with 15.3 per cent to other countries; 27.7 per cent of Ontario shipments went to other regions compared with 14.5 per cent to other countries; and 22.4 per cent of shipments originating in the Prairie Provinces had first destinations in other regions compared with only 6.7 per cent destined for other countries. As for British Columbia and the Territories, only 15.0 per cent of their shipments went to other regions of Canada while 36.5 per cent went to other countries.

Because of the concentration of manufacturing activity in Ontario and Quebec, the integrating effect of interregional trade in Canada is also a centralizing one. This concentration of Canadian manufacturing industries in the two central regions is evident in Table 4–17. In 1967 Ontario was the region of origin for 52.1 per cent of all Canadian shipments and Quebec accounted for another 28.2 per cent. The presence of the manufacturing industries located in Ontario is felt in every region of Canada as Ontario was the region of origin for 35.5 per cent of shipments sent to the Atlantic Provinces, 29.8 per cent of shipments to Quebec, 33.2 per cent of ship-

Table 4–17. Sources of Supply of Shipments by Canadian Manufacturers to Regions of Canada and to other Countries, 1967

(percentages)

First destination of shipments

Region of origin	Atlantic Provinces	Quebec	Ontario	Prairie Provinces	British Columbia and Territories*	All Canadian destinations	Other countries	Total
Atlantic Provinces	40.1	1.3	0.8	0.6	0.3	3.2	5.7	3.6
Quebec	21.7	66.1	14.8	11.2	10.3	28.5	26.5	28.2
Ontario	35.5	29.8	81.7	33.2	27.4	53.3	46.3	52.1
Prairie Provinces	1.7	2.1	1.8	49.0	7.6	8.8	3.3	7.9
British Columbia and Territories*	1.0	0.7	0.9	6.0	54.4	6.2	18.2	8.2
Canada	100.0	100.0	100.0	100.0	100.0	100.0	100.0	100.0

* Yukon and Northwest Territories.

Source: Canada, Dominion Bureau of Statistics, *Destination of Shipments of Manufacturers, 1967.* (Ottawa: Information Canada, 1971), p. 10. Reproduced by permission of Information Canada.

ments to the Prairie Provinces, and 27.4 per cent of shipments to British Columbia and the Territories. Shipments originating in Quebec also had a substantial share of each regional market across the country; but they were well behind Ontario, as they varied from 21.7 per cent in the Atlantic Provinces to 10.3 per cent in British Columbia and the Territories. None of the other regions has an industrial establishment with national interests comparable to those of Ontario and Quebec; and, while this situation undoubtedly gives rise to some interregional resentment, it does ensure a strong centre of economic attraction for a dispersive community.

The integrating, centralizing tendencies of Canadian domestic economic transactions are balanced by a substantial foreign trade with the United States. Viewed in comparative perspective, the striking aspect of Canadian foreign trade is not its general openness to the import and export of goods and services but its heavy dependence on one external market, that of the United States. Table 4–18 shows that the Canadian economy is indeed a relatively open one with imports comprising 24.5 per cent and exports 27.0 per cent of the national income in 1968; but Austria, Denmark, the Nether-

Table 4–18. *Relative Size of Foreign Trade and Most Important Trading Partners of Twelve Industrialized Democracies, 1968*

Nation which imports and exports	Imports and exports as percentage of national income		Trading partner providing largest percentage of imports		Trading partner taking largest percentage of exports	
	Imports	Exports	Nation	Percentage	Nation	Percentage
Australia	16.1	14.2	United States	25.8	Japan	21.1
Austria	29.6	23.6	West Germany	41.4	West Germany	23.4
Canada	24.5	27.0	United States	73.2	United States	67.9
Denmark	34.4	28.0	West Germany	18.8	United Kingdom	20.6
France	14.4	13.1	West Germany	21.4	West Germany	18.6
Italy	16.8	16.6	West Germany	17.9	West Germany	18.7
Japan	11.5	11.4	United States	27.2	United States	31.9
Netherlands	45.1	40.5	West Germany	26.4	West Germany	27.8
Norway	39.2	28.1	Sweden	19.2	United Kingdom	19.3
United Kingdom	22.9	18.4	United States	13.5	United States	14.2
United States	4.6	4.7	Canada	27.0	Canada	23.4
West Germany	19.4	23.9	France	12.1	France	12.3

Source: United Nations, *Statistical Yearbook 1970* (New York: United Nations, 1971), Tables 145, 184; *Yearbook of International Trade Statistics 1969* (New York: United Nations, 1971), pp. 69, 79, 151, 246, 293, 318, 434, 457, 596, 644, 877, 888. Reprinted by permission of the United Nations.

lands, and Norway are as open or even more open than Canada. However, no nation listed in Table 4–18 comes close to Canada in its dependence on one market for imports and exports. Austria obtained 41.4 per cent of its imports from Germany, and Japan sent 31.9 per cent of its exports to the United States in 1968; but, however significant, these percentages are modest beside the 73.2 per cent of Canadian imports from the United States and the 67.9 per cent of Canadian exports to the United States.

Figure 4–1 shows that changes in the pattern of Canadian foreign trade during the post-war period have not affected Canadian reliance on the American market for both imports and exports, while the Canadian share of the historically important United Kingdom market has declined in favour of more trade with other industrialized countries, principally Japan and West Germany. By 1970, Canadian trade with Japan was approaching in importance its trade with the United Kingdom, as 4.9 per cent of Canadian exports went to Japan and 4.2 per cent of Canadian imports came from there, and 8.9 per cent of Canadian exports went to the United Kingdom and 5.3 per cent of Canadian imports came from there.

The dependence of Canada on the United States as an international trading partner is accompanied by a considerable American presence in the ownership and control of Canadian industries. The overall level of foreign ownership in Canada is significantly higher than that in any other economically developed nation as well as in most underdeveloped nations, and this foreign investment in Canada has come overwhelmingly from the United States.[21]

Canadian economic development has always depended on foreign capital, but the implications of this reliance for national economic and political integration were not serious in the first half-century following Confederation because the inflow of foreign capital mainly took the form of debt securities rather than equity. The London bond market was the main external source of Canadian capital in the nineteenth century, and direct investment seems to have constituted no more than one-third of total foreign investment.

The shift from the United Kingdom to the United States as a source of capital evidently began before World War I, and it was virtually completed by 1930 when 61.2 per cent of the estimated book value of foreign capital invested in Canada came from the United States. Thereafter the percentage of foreign capital in Canada which was American increased during the 1940s and again during the 1960s to reach 80.7 per cent of all foreign investment in 1967.

A shift from reliance on borrowing to direct investment coincided with the increase in American investment in Canada, but it proceeded more slowly. Although American investors were more inter-

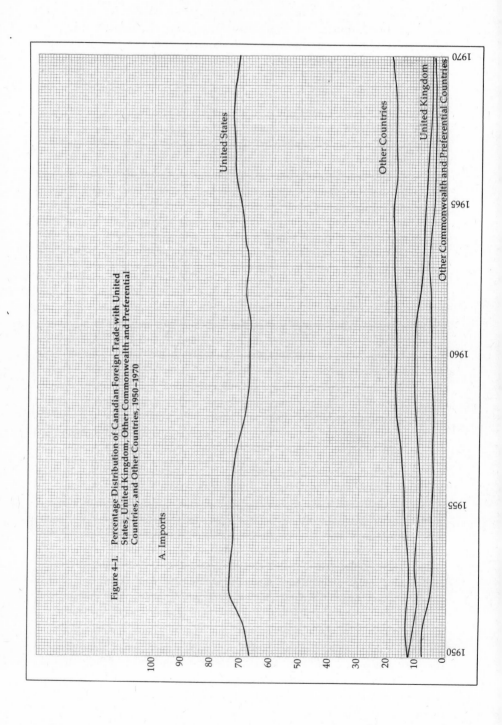

Figure 4-1. Percentage Distribution of Canadian Foreign Trade with United States, United Kingdom, Other Commonwealth and Preferential Countries, and Other Countries, 1950–1970

A. Imports

United States

Other Countries

United Kingdom

Other Commonwealth and Preferential Countries

1950   1955   1960   1965   1970

0   10   20   30   40   50   60   70   80   90   100

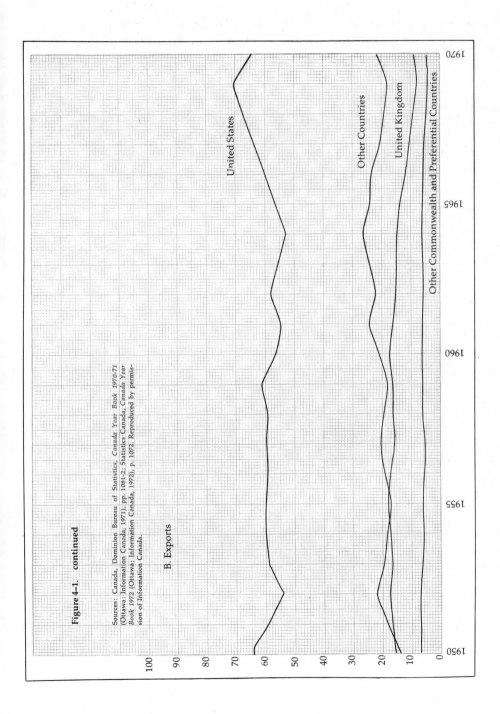

Figure 4-1. continued

Sources: Canada, Dominion Bureau of Statistics, *Canada Year Book 1970-71* (Ottawa: Information Canada, 1971), pp. 1081-2; Statistics Canada, *Canada Year Book 1972* (Ottawa: Information Canada, 1972), p. 1072. Reproduced by permission of Information Canada.

B. Exports

United States

Other Countries

United Kingdom

Other Commonwealth and Preferential Countries

ested in direct investment than investors in the United Kingdom, the majority of American investment and 68.1 per cent of total foreign investment in 1930 were still portfolio investments (principally debt). Table 4–19 shows, however, that by the end of World War II American direct investment exceeded American portfolio investment and that during the 1950s direct investment became the predominant form of external investment in Canada. By 1967, 59.6 per cent of the book value of all foreign capital invested in Canada was in the form of direct investment; and 48.9 per cent of the foreign capital was direct investment from the United States.[22]

"International" trade unions represent another long-standing form of Canadian-American economic association. American trade unions first began to enter Canada about 1860; and within a decade they had become the dominant force in the Canadian labour movement, reaching a high point in 1911 when 90 per cent of Canadian union members were in international unions.[23] The position of the international unions weakened after World War I, dropping to 50 per cent of union membership by 1935; but the resurgence of the American trade union movement after 1935 provided the impetus for a rapid recovery in the Canadian membership in international unions to 60 per cent of all union workers by 1939 and 70 per cent by 1955. International union membership held at roughly this level until the middle of the 1960s when union organization in the public service had the effect of increasing the share of total Canadian union membership belonging to national unions.

Two features of the American penetration into Canadian labour organization may be thought to pose special difficulties for Canadian integration by according a subordinate place to Canadian national labour interests inside the international unions. First, international unions enrol the majority of Canadian trade union members; but Canadian members generally are not a strong force inside the international unions. Of the 190 unions listed in the *Directory of National and International Unions in the United States 1967*, 109 had members in Canada; but the Canadian membership was only 6.5 per cent of total membership. Of the unions listed in the 1967 Directory, 70 had less than 10 per cent and 101 had less than 20 per cent of their membership in Canada. Only 2 unions, the relatively small National Association of Broadcast Employees and Technicians and the much larger International Woodworkers of America, had a majority of their members working in Canada. Second, the international unions tend to be among the more powerful unions in Canada and represent the workers in the leading sectors of the economy.[24] This is illustrated, for example, in Table 4–20 where it can be seen that 7 of the 10 largest unions operating in Canada in 1970 were international

Table 4-19. Estimated Book Value of Foreign Capital Invested in Canada, Selected Year-ends, 1900–1967

(millions of dollars)

Residence of foreign investors	1900	1914	1930	1939	1946	1950	1960	1967
United States								
Direct	n.a.	n.a.	1,993	1,881	2,428	3,426	10,549	17,000
Portfolio and other	n.a.	n.a.	2,667	2,270	2,730	3,123	6,169	11,030
Totals	168	881	4,660	4,151	5,158	6,549	16,718	28,030
Britain								
Direct	n.a.	n.a.	392	366	335	468	1,535	2,152
Portfolio and other	n.a.	n.a.	2,374	2,110	1,335	1,282	1,824	1,424
Totals	1,050	2,778	2,766	2,476	1,670	1,750	3,359	3,576
Other foreign nations								
Direct	n.a.	n.a.	42	49	63	81	788	1,547
Portfolio and other	n.a.	n.a.	146	237	290	284	1,349	1,549
Totals	14	177	188	286	353	365	2,137	3,096
All foreign nations								
Direct	n.a.	n.a.	2,427	2,296	2,826	3,975	12,873	20,699
Portfolio and other	n.a.	n.a.	5,187	4,617	4,355	4,689	9,342	14,003
Totals	1,232	3,837	7,614	6,913	7,181	8,664	22,214	34,702

n.a. Not available.

Source: Canada, *Foreign Direct Investment in Canada* (Ottawa: Information Canada, 1972), p. 15. Reproduced by permission of Information Canada.

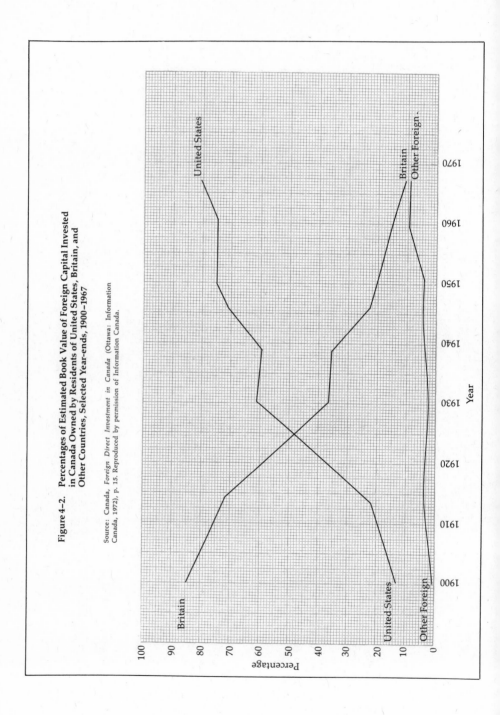

Figure 4-2.   Percentages of Estimated Book Value of Foreign Capital Invested in Canada Owned by Residents of United States, Britain, and Other Countries, Selected Year-ends, 1900–1967

Source: Canada, *Foreign Direct Investment in Canada* (Ottawa: Information Canada, 1972), p. 15. Reproduced by permission of Information Canada.

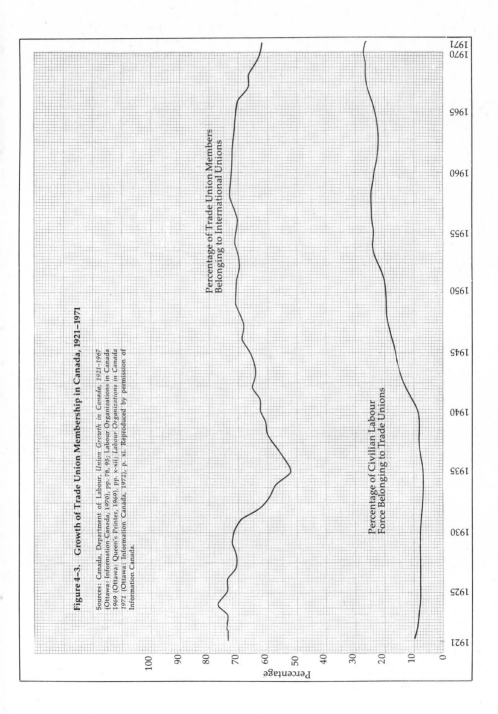

Figure 4-3. Growth of Trade Union Membership in Canada, 1921–1971

Sources: Canada, Department of Labour, *Union Growth in Canada, 1921–1967* (Ottawa: Information Canada, 1970), pp. 78, 95; *Labour Organizations in Canada 1969* (Ottawa: Queen's Printer, 1969), pp. x-xii; *Labour Organizations in Canada 1971* (Ottawa: Information Canada, 1972), p. xi. Reproduced by permission of Information Canada.

Percentage of Trade Union Members Belonging to International Unions

Percentage of Civilian Labour Force Belonging to Trade Unions

Percentage

100 90 80 70 60 50 40 30 20 10 0

1921 1925 1930 1935 1940 1945 1950 1955 1960 1965 1970 1971

Table 4–20.   Ten Largest Trade Unions in Canada, 1970

Union	Type	Affiliation	Membership
United Steelworkers of America	International	A.F.L.–C.I.O./C.L.C.	150,000
Canadian Union of Public Employees	National	C.L.C.	136,127
Public Service Alliance of Canada	National	C.L.C.	119,743
International Union United Automobile, Aerospace and Agricultural Implement Workers of America	International	C.L.C.	109,274
United Brotherhood of Carpenters and Joiners of America	International	A.F.L.–C.I.O./C.L.C.	72,209
International Brotherhood of Teamsters, Chauffeurs, Warehousemen and Helpers of America	International	Independent	58,178
International Brotherhood of Electrical Workers	International	A.F.L.–C.I.O./C.L.C.	56,918
International Association of Machinists and Aerospace Workers	International	A.F.L.–C.I.O./C.L.C.	53,003
Fédération Nationale des Services-Service Employees' Federation	National	C.S.N./C.N.T.U.	49,362
International Woodworkers of America	International	A.F.L.–C.I.O./C.L.C.	48,904

Source: Canada, Department of Labour, *Labour Organizations in Canada 1970* (Ottawa: Queen's Printer, 1970), pp. viii–ix. Reproduced by permission of Information Canada.

unions organized among workers in the leading sectors of the Canadian economy.

As with the degree of American ownership and control of the Canadian economy, a degree of external penetration equal to that of the American trade unions into labour organization in Canada is not to be found in any other nation of comparable size and industrial importance.[25] The fact that it does exist is another telling indicator of the remarkable scope of the North American continental community, not merely with respect to economic transactions but also in social organization and cultural exchange.

Perceptions of Community

Basic differences in the orientations of Canadians towards their nation are evident in their perceptions of what the community has been, is now, and ought to become. As it travelled across the nation in 1963–1964, researching and reporting on the degree of our fraternity, the Royal Commission on Bilingualism and Biculturalism found, *as might have been expected, that conflicts in opinion were rooted in widely differing conceptions of the Canadian state and society. The image of his country that each Canadian had forged for himself inevitably determined his assessment of the present predicament [of ethnic division] and formed the background and basis of his participation in the discussions. At once striking contrasts emerged between French and English-speaking Canadians, and even more between French-speaking Quebec and the rest of Canada, as each tried to relate the implications of the co-existence of two cultures to the Canada he recognized.*[26]

French-speaking Canadians for the most part accepted without question the Commission's terms of reference which referred to an "equal partnership", pointed to the failures to implement it in the past, and argued strenuously for a different course in the future. The Commission also found that French Canadians more and more were thinking and speaking of themselves as "a nation".

This idea of a French-Canadian nation, having a common language, territory, history and a common culture or way of life, was expressed in Quebec by many people who have no association with separatism. In their mind, it provides the foundation for the ideal of a partnership on equal terms. And when these Quebec French Canadians think of themselves as one nation, it is easy—if not logical—for them to lump all the others together as a nation. Thus concentrating on themselves, and on what we may call their own self-conquest, they view the rest of Canada as a single entity— "les Anglais"—the non-self. The expression "two nations" still rings in our ears, it was so often heard in our Quebec meetings.[27]

The English-speaking group's view of Canada generally rejects ethnic nationalism. Historically, there have been times when strong feelings of ethnic identification on the part of Canadians of British origin were in evidence, as for example in the United Empire Loyalist tradition, the Imperial Federation movement, the Ontario and Manitoba schools questions, and the conscription crises. On the whole, however, the ethnic component has become steadily less important in the English-speaking view, according with its anticipation of a Canadian nationality in which the aspect of ethnic origins will diminish over time rather than increase.[28] Thus, the Royal Commission on Bilingualism and Biculturalism found that dualistic concepts of Canada whether expressed in the terms of "equal partnership" or "two founding races" or "two nations" encountered strong opposition from English-speaking Canadians who have defined their nation as a single entity. In their appearances before the Commission, English-speaking Canadians persistently questioned the meaning of equal partnership in the Commission's terms of reference and gave "nation" a meaning quite different from that assumed by most French-speaking Canadians. "When English-speaking Canadians talked of 'the nation' they usually meant all the people who live in Canada. They did not think of themselves as forming a national group or 'nation' in the same sense that so many French-speaking Canadians do."[29]

Not surprisingly, Canadians who do not identify themselves with one or the other of the two founding ethnic groups find themselves in a difficult position. The Royal Commission found that the idea of Canada having a dual character aroused particular fears among members of European and Asian ethnic groups. They saw themselves and their part in the development of Canada being forgotten in a dialogue defined as being between Canadians of French and British origin, and wanted more emphasis on the multi-cultural character or "mosaic" of Canadian society. For them, "in the complex ethnic situation existing in Canada, the only kind of unity which can reasonably be striven for and achieved is unity in diversity: the harmonious cooperation of all ethnic groups in the Canadian country as a whole."[30]

The native ethnic groups of Canada also find themselves isolated from and alienated by disagreement between the French and British ethnic groups. Their position is typified perhaps by the Indian who asked the Royal Commission, "Why is the Indian always forgotten? This was the first culture and this was the first language in Canada. We are told that the BNA Act was between the French and the English—where was the Indian during this time?" and by the other Indians who wondered, "If the French people think that they lost a lot of their rights since Confederation, what should the Indian say? They lost the whole land".[31]

Evidence gathered in the 1968 federal election survey provides support for the impression reported by the Royal Commission on Bilingualism and Biculturalism that Canadians belonging to different ethnic groups have different perceptions of Canada. Respondents were asked how they viewed Canada and how they thought of themselves in relation to their political community. The pattern of responses reveals a basic dualism between French and non-French Canadians in their perceptions of the community and their identification with it. When asked how they viewed Canada, the majority of the French-speaking respondents (40 per cent) described their nation as an English-French partnership; and the majority of non-French respondents (63 per cent) described their nation as a "homeland of various people".

In addition to this prevailing dualism between the French and non-French views of Canada, a number of other similarities and differences among language and regional sub-groups may be noted in Table 4–21. First, only 8 per cent of the respondents said that they viewed Canada as an"English country". French-speaking respondents in Quebec and English-speaking respondents in the Atlantic Provinces and British Columbia were slightly more likely to express this view than respondents in other regions.

Second, two-thirds of the respondents who viewed Canada as an English-French partnership were French-speaking. Among the non-French sub-groups, the English-speaking respondents in Quebec presumably would be the ones most aware of the "French fact"; but, even though they were more likely to agree with the French-speaking groups, only 22 per cent of them mentioned this view of an English-French partnership.

Third, the perception of Canada as a homeland of various people was especially strong among English-speaking Canadians in Ontario and the West and among those who spoke neither English nor French at home. It was also the view of a clear majority of the English-speaking respondents in Quebec and the Atlantic Provinces. Altogether, 88 per cent of the respondents describing Canada as a homeland of various people were non-French; but it should be added that French-speaking respondents outside Quebec were about as likely to express this view as they were to describe Canada as an English-French partnership.

Finally, 21 per cent of the respondents described their nation as "just Canada". This proportion was more or less the same in each language group, although within the English-speaking group there was a slight decrease across the nation from 28 per cent in the Atlantic region to 14 per cent in British Columbia.

In identifying themselves in relation to Canada, two-thirds of the French-speaking respondents said that they thought of themselves as "French-Canadian"; and 78 per cent of the non-French respondents described themselves as "simply Canadian". Again, however, there were interesting variations among language and regional sub-groups.

First, a clear majority of the French-speaking respondents chose to think of themselves as French-Canadian. This ethnic national identification was more prevalent among the Quebec respondents,

Table 4-21. Canadians' Perceptions of Their Political Community by Language Spoken at Home and Region, 1968

(percentages)

View of Canada	French		English					Other	Total
	Quebec	Non-Quebec	Atlantic Provinces	Quebec	Ontario	Prairie Provinces	British Columbia		
English country	11	4	12	4	8	5	11	4	8
English–French partnership	40	38	11	22	6	3	4	10	15
Homeland of various people	22	36	44	49	63	72	69	60	52
Just Canada	24	19	28	23	21	17	14	24	21
Other	1	0	*	0	*	*	0	0	*
No opinion	3	4	4	1	1	2	1	2	2
TOTAL Percentage**	101	101	99	99	99	99	99	100	98
Number	632	84	249	90	868	462	238	144	2,767

*Less than 0.5 per cent

**Totals may not add to 100 per cent because of rounding errors.

Source: John Meisel, Queen's University, 1968 Federal Election Survey. Some of the data supplied by John Meisel here and elsewhere in this book are analyzed and discussed in John Meisel, *Working Papers on Canadian Politics*, enlarged edition, (Montreal and London: McGill-Queen's University Press, 1973).

Table 4-22. Canadians' Perceptions of Their Identification with Their Political Community by Language Spoken at Home and Region, 1968

(percentages)

Perception of self	French		English					Other	Total
	Quebec	Non-Quebec	Atlantic Provinces	Quebec	Ontario	Prairie Provinces	British Columbia		
English Canadian	2	4	26	9	14	8	16	3	10
French Canadian	69	52	3	4	1	1	1	3	19
Simply Canadian	27	39	61	83	79	85	79	68	65
Ethnic Canadian	*	0	3	2	3	3	2	19	3
Other	1	1	1	1	2	1	1	7	2
No opinion	1	4	6	0	1	1	*	1	1
TOTAL Percentage**	100	100	100	99	100	99	99	101	100
Number	632	84	249	90	868	462	238	144	2,767

*Less than 0.5 per cent.

**Totals may not add to 100 per cent because of rounding errors.

Source: John Meisel, Queen's University, 1968 Federal Election Survey.

as French-speaking people outside Quebec were more inclined to see themselves as simply Canadian.

Second, among the non-French respondents, those speaking English who lived in the Atlantic Provinces and those speaking neither English nor French at home were somewhat less likely than the rest to identify themselves as simply Canadian. In the Atlantic Provinces 26 per cent said that they thought of themselves as English-Canadian; and 19 per cent of the non-French, non-English respondents also expressed an ethnic identification.

Third, among the English-speaking respondents of Ontario, British Columbia, and the Prairie Provinces the identification overwhelmingly expressed was simply Canadian with only one-tenth, more or less, viewing themselves as English Canadians.

A 1968 survey of 1,825 high school students in Quebec City, Montreal, Oakville, and Winnipeg carried out by H. D. Forbes produced results very similar to those found during the 1968 federal election survey.[32] Forbes asked the students an open-ended question, "How do you prefer to think of yourself—as English-Canadian, or French-Canadian , or German- or Italian-Canadian, as simply Canadian, or how?" The pattern of responses (Table 4-23) shows a strong similarity among the English-speaking students in the four cities, and a marked difference between the English-speaking students and

Table 4-23. Canadian High School Students' Perceptions of Their Identification with Their Political Community by Language and Province, 1968

(percentages)

Perception of self	English			French
	Manitoba	Ontario	Quebec	Quebec
Emphatically Canadian	32	34	30	10
Simply Canadian	38	42	41	9
Qualified Canadian	12	7	8	10
Hyphenated Canadian	14	11	16	61
Another Nationality	2	4	4	3
Provincialist	0	*	1	5
Internationalist	1	1	1	1
TOTAL				
Percentage**	99	99	101	99
Number	367	498	203	719

*Less than 0.5 per cent.

**Totals do not add to 100 per cent because of rounding errors.

Source: H. D. Forbes, "Conflicting National Identities Among Canadian Youth" (Toronto: mimeographed, 1973), p. 5.

the French-speaking students. Seven out of ten English-speaking students said they were simply Canadian, and three out of ten even put a special emphasis on the idea that they were simply Canadian and nothing else.[33] Only two out of ten French-speaking students responded by describing themselves as simply or emphatically Canadian, while about seven out of ten identified themselves with the French ethnic group in Canada, most of them by describing themselves as "Canadien français".

The contrast between English-speaking and French-speaking students was even more pronounced in the responses to another question Forbes asked them, "Of the three terms below, which one comes closest to describing you? Canadian, English-Canadian, French-Canadian." Among the French-speaking students, 70 per cent chose "French-Canadian" as the best term to describe their national identity, and 29 per cent chose "Canadian". Among the English-speaking students "Canadian" was chosen as the term closest to describing their national identity by 87 per cent of the Winnipeg students, 81 per cent of the Oakville students, and 78 per cent of the Montreal and Quebec students. It is interesting that the English-speaking students closer to French Quebec were slightly more likely to identify themselves as "English-Canadian". Only 11 per cent of the students in Winnipeg chose "English-Canadian" as the best term for their national identity, but 17 per cent of the Oakville students and 20 per cent of the students in Montreal and Quebec City did so.

In a national survey of Canadians thirteen to twenty years of age, carried out in 1965 for the Royal Commission on Bilingualism and Biculturalism, respondents were given a blank map of Canada and asked to write in five words or phrases which described Canada for them.[34] Not surprisingly, given the cue of a map, a large percentage of the respondents in every language–regional group cited some geographical feature of the country; but other references indicated that the images of Canada held by French-speaking young people, especially those living in Quebec, differed from those of the non-French.

More references to Canadian economic development, climatic conditions, and personal characteristics of the Canadian people were made by the English-speaking and other-language students than were made by the French-speaking students either inside or outside Quebec. The English-speaking and other-language students as well as the French-speaking students outside Quebec were also more likely to mention the form of government or way of life in Canada than were the French-speaking students in Quebec. Conversely, the French-speaking students in Quebec were much more likely than other students to mention a provincial political subdivision as a feature of Canada which was salient for them. Johnstone concludes,

Table 4–24. Salient Features of Canada for Young Canadians by Language Spoken at Home and Region, 1965

(percentages)

Salient features	French			English						Other
	Quebec	Non-Quebec	Total	Atlantic Provinces	Quebec	Ontario	Prairie Provinces	British Columbia	Total	
Natural terrain or geography	65	66	66	65	70	81	76	72	75	77
Economic resources or industries	42	51	44	69	69	64	66	69	67	61
Climatic conditions	4	5	4	16	7	11	20	18	15	7
Form of government or way of life	11	21	13	34	32	29	23	19	27	36
Political subdivisions:										
Regional	18	17	18	7	19	15	18	13	14	12
Provincial	55	38	52	18	21	9	11	12	12	16
Municipal	26	24	26	9	15	7	12	19	11	18
Social environment:										
Demographic	8	4	8	14	14	15	16	16	15	6
Social and cultural subdivision	15	7	13	17	23	16	14	10	15	14
Personal characteristics of Canadian people	3	5	4	25	20	16	18	13	18	11
Symbolic–patriotic content	6	17	8	16	12	9	10	11	11	2
TOTAL*	253	255	256	290	302	272	284	272	280	260

*Totals may add to more than 100 per cent because most respondents entered more than one type of salient features.

Source: John C. Johnstone, *Young People's Images of Canadian Society, Studies of the Royal Commission on Bilingualism and Biculturalism, Number 2* (Ottawa: Queen's Printer, 1969), pp. 2, 5. Reproduced by permission of Information Canada.

The results would suggest that Francophones learn very early in life to think of their country in political terms, while Anglophones and "Others" become much more conscious of Canada as an economic entity.[35]

The dualism found in the perceptions by Canadians of their state and society can be found again in their political myths and historical memories. The Royal Commission on Bilingualism and Biculturalism has remarked that historical conflicts between French-speaking and English-speaking Canadians are remembered in quite different ways.[36] To the French-speaking, Lord Durham is the great assimilator; Riel, the defender of minority rights, was judicially murdered by the English; and conscription in 1917 and 1944 dragged a peaceful French people into conflicts of concern only to those of British origin. To the English-speaking, Lord Durham is the great decolonizer; Riel, the traitor and murderer, was justly hanged; and conscription was a necessity for a nation committed to victory in world wars.

This dualism in political myths and historical memories is illustrated by the results of the National History Project which surveyed ten thousand grade 12 students in 1967. The students were asked to list five important Canadians since Confederation and to identify events in Canadian history which were a source of pride to them.[37] French-Canadian students identified exclusively with historical figures of their own nationality. English-speaking students named leaders of "English" Canada like Macdonald, Borden, King, and Pearson or made references to mutually acceptable leaders like Laurier and Vanier with occasional recognition of Louis Riel. The major source of pride in Canadian history for English-speaking students was Canada's part in wars—the War of 1812, World War I, and World War II—and the achievement of Confederation. French-Canadian students found no reason for pride in either wars or Confederation. The main response from French-speaking students was pride in "our forefathers who fought to preserve our language, customs and religion" and pride in the early colonists who struggled "to build a French-Canadian land".

As might be expected, these ethnic differences in historical memories are reflected in the content of school history textbooks and courses. Marcel Trudel and Geneviève Jain compared fourteen representative Canadian history textbooks and concluded that French-language and English-language textbooks differed widely in organization, themes, and objectives.[38]

In terms of organization, the "heroic" period of French colonization to 1663 received very full treatment in French-language books and only brief accounts in English-language books. Both English and French textbooks were fairly balanced in their accounts of the regime of New France from 1663 to 1760, but the two groups of textbooks diverged again in recording the periods of the British regime and Confederation.

> Here the two groups do not even seem to be talking about the same country! The English-speaking authors do their best to give an overall history of Canada, while the French authors take less and less interest in regions other than Quebec. If the latter still talk about the Maritimes it is because of the Acadians; if they talk about the West it is mostly about the role played by the French Canadians there; in short, they hardly talk about anything but the history of Quebec and its expansion beyond its borders.[39]

Group differences were found to pervade the interpretation of crises and the assessment of institutions and historical figures. The English histories described Cabot as the discoverer of Canada and Iberville as an aggressor; the French regarded Cartier as the discoverer and Iberville as a defender. According to the French textbooks, the policy of New France to pursue the peaceful civilization of the New World aroused English "covetousness"; the English-language books viewed the defeat of the French regime as the outcome of inevitable conflict between two vast commercial empires. The English textbooks recorded the two World Wars of the twentieth century as very serious threats to national survival; the French did not agree. When historical pairs such as Baldwin–La Fontaine and Macdonald–Cartier were considered, each author gave the main attention to the representative of his own group. Depending on language, the textbooks presented conscription in 1917 as necessary or unnecessary, Riel as a valiant defender of minority rights or a rebel and murderer, the achievement of Confederation as blessed or dangerous, and the land of free institutions in the eighteenth century as New England or New France.

In their educational objectives, the French-language histories aimed to inculcate a moral education, while the English-language books used history to give future citizens a political and social education. The French-language textbooks displayed continual anxiety about the survival of the French ethnic group; the English-language textbooks showed no anxiety about the survival of either their own or the French group. In the English-language books, the frontier was said to be a very important experience, imparting desirable developments of culture and attitude, making men more realistic, innovative, progressive, and independent; the French-language authors viewed the colonists as unchanged by the frontier experience and denigrated the spirit of adventure and individualism. Economic development was a constant and basic theme of English-language books; the French books touched on economic history as a minor interest apart from their constant and basic preoccupation with religion. The French-language textbooks advocated the ideals of courage, the hard and simple life of the forefathers, unselfishness, and the spirit of sacrifice; the English-language textbooks recommended courage, individualism, and the spirit of adventure.

The report of the National History Project supports the findings of Trudel and Jain on the different contents of textbooks and extends them to cover classroom practices. According to the Project's report, the main difficulties arise at the level of secondary schooling.

> It is fair to say that Canadian history in the French Roman Catholic schools of Quebec is preoccupied with the survival of their own society, giving little attention to what happened in the rest of Canada. It is equally fair to say, however, that the developments and interests of French Canada are sadly neglected in the other provinces. Although there is no evidence of intolerance or lack of sympathy, the textbooks and courses of study outside of Quebec are also guilty of assuming a somewhat patronizing and self-assured attitude toward French Canada. Judging from the textbooks and from classroom observations, it is our opinion that the particular bias from which French-Canadian history is interpreted is not destructive at the elementary school level. The younger children develop a strong love for and identification with their own ancestors, but this is not done at the expense of English-speaking Canadians. It is possible, however, to detect a change of tone in secondary school books and classes. The interpretations tend to become bitter, resentful and vindictive, with frequent references, in somewhat belligerent terms to resistance and, in the economic field at least, to revenge.[40]

The report of the National History Project is quite clear in its conclusion that dualism in the content of civic education in Canada is a major factor in contributing to the development of our "two solitudes". Trudel and Jain agree that the teaching of history has not fostered mutual understanding or a more objective view of our shared adventure. Rather, "more often than not it has only tended to set one group against the other. If Canada is more than ever before threatened with schism, we believe we must look for the cause very largely in the manner in which today's citizens have learned the history of their country".[41]

Unfortunately, neither the Trudel and Jain study nor the National History Project attempted to analyze the relationship between the content of history textbooks and the political attitudes, if any, acquired by young people from their studies. Other studies have indicated that the effect of formally taught civic education in shaping the political beliefs, feelings, and understandings of young people is not clearly established. One study of American high school students found that a civics course had no significant effect on levels of political knowledge and sophistication, political interest, discussion of politics, feelings of political efficacy or cynicism, degree of civic tolerance, or participative orientation.[42] Another study concluded that the content of a civics course was only effective where it attempted to inculcate or reinforce the prevailing values of the community. Where the course content ran counter to prevailing values it had no significant effect in changing students' attitudes.[43]

The difficulty of achieving either English-Canadian or French-Canadian educational objectives in the face of American penetration into Canadian culture and society perhaps serves to illustrate the tenuous connection between formal education and political attitudes. In his 1968 survey of high school students in Quebec, Montreal, Oakville, and Winnipeg, Forbes asked the students to name the two or three great people, living or dead, whom they most admired. Most of the students made two choices, and the percentage distributions of their responses by the nationalities of the great men named are shown in Table 4–25.

The pattern of ethnic dualism in the students' responses is weak, but it is consistent with the findings of Trudel and Jain and the National History Project. Both in their first and in their second choices the French-speaking students were more likely to name French-Canadian or French heroes than English-Canadian or British ones. The English Canadians chose equally between English-Canadian and French-Canadian heroes, 6 per cent each on their first choice and 8 per cent each on their second choice.

What is striking about Table 4–25, however, is not the pattern of ethnic dualism but the pattern of ethnic agreement in naming Americans as the great men. For their first choice, 52 per cent of the English-speaking students and 74 per cent of the French-speaking students chose American heroes; and Americans were also the second choice of 38 per cent of the English-speaking and 31 per cent of the French-speaking students. In his analysis, Forbes notes the possible objection that Canada has produced few world-historical figures and thus the results of Table 4–25 are to be expected;

Table 4–25. *Nationality of Great Men Named by Canadian High School Students by Language of Respondents, 1968*

(percentages)

Nationality of great men	English		French	
	First choice	Second choice	First choice	Second choice
English Canadian	6	8	*	2
French Canadian	6	8	5	13
American	52	38	74	31
British	15	15	3	9
French	3	3	7	11
Other	11	8	8	17
No response	7	19	4	17
TOTAL				
Percentage**	99	99	101	100
Number	1,049	1,042	740	731

*Less than 0.5 per cent.

**Totals may not add to 100 per cent because of rounding errors.

Source: H. D. Forbes, "Conflicting National Identities Among Canadian Youth" (Toronto: mimeographed, 1973), p. 7.

but he also observes that world-historical figures were not prominent among the "great men" named by the students. Plato, Caesar, Shakespeare, and Beethoven were chosen by only a few students. Most of them named less remote figures such as Pope John, Billy Graham, Timothy Leary, Dag Hammarskjöld, or Frank Zappa; and the most frequently chosen person was John Kennedy.[44] What Forbes found, then, was not the ethnic dualism promulgated in the formal teaching of Canadian national history but the overwhelming impact of American political and popular culture.

Without knowing more than we do about the link between course content and attitude formation, it is difficult to evaluate the socializing effects of formal teaching or to prescribe corrective public policy. Nonetheless, the contents of textbooks and classroom presentations described in the studies of Trudel and Jain and in the National History Project remain valuable indicators of the weakness of Canadian fraternity. For whether school history studies positively shape the political and social orientations of young people or only purvey (and perhaps reinforce) orientations already learned through other socializing agencies, in either case the results of these two studies of Canadian history teaching as indicators of the provision of fraternity remain unchanged. Collectively we have chosen to teach two quite different versions of our historical experience, and this must be taken to reflect the wide and persistent division of the Canadian political community between French and English Canada.

The differences which emerged between French Canada and English Canada over the design of a national flag provide another illustration of a persistent ethnic division in perceptions of the national political community. The red maple leaf on a white and red background became the national flag in 1965 only after a bitter and prolonged debate.[45] Without recounting the details of the flag debate, something of the persistent attachment to different symbols and therefore to different perceptions of the political community can be indicated by the pattern of responses in surveys of public opinion on the flag question in the years immediately preceding its adoption.

After World War II, public opinion generally came to favour a Canadian national flag, but significant minorities continued to choose the Union Jack or the Red Ensign. According to a Canadian Institute of Public Opinion poll in 1952, 46 per cent of respondents thought that Canada should design a flag of its own, 30 per cent supported continued use of the Union Jack, and 16 per cent wanted to use the Red Ensign. On the same question in 1963, 45 per cent of a national sample thought that Canada should design a new flag, 25 per cent wanted to use the Union Jack, and 16 per cent favoured the Red Ensign.[46] The surveys indicated, however, that there were significant regional differences in public support for the design of a new flag. In 1963, for example, 74 per cent of the respondents in Quebec thought that Canada should design a new flag; but only 23 per cent in the Maritimes and 35 per cent in Ontario and the West agreed. The simplest explanation for these differences of opinion about a new flag would appear to be that behind the failure to agree on this important symbol of the national political community there lay a failure to agree on certain basic views of the community and of the values comprehended within it.

The question of the place of the monarchy as a primary political symbol in the Canadian constitution also results in a familiar pattern of disagreement among those of different ethnic origins. Table 4–26 shows that the opinions held by Canadians concerning the role of the monarchy in Canada differed significantly between respondents in Quebec and those in the rest of Canada on a number of questions asked by the Canadian Institute of Public Opinion between 1966 and 1971. Quebec respondents were more likely than other Canadians to see the importance of the monarchy as decreasing and to believe it should play a less important role; and they were less likely to

Table 4–26. *Opinions on the Role of the Monarchy in Canada by Region, 1966–1971*

Release date	Item	Percentage of respondents expressing agreement				
		National	Maritimes	Quebec	Ontario	West
27/1/66	Importance of monarchy represented by Queen Elizabeth is decreasing in Canada	61	n.a.	73	57	56
8/2/67	Queen should be invited to visit the World Exposition in Montreal	60	*	42	66	72
2/10/68	Canada should continue to pay allegiance to the Queen	50	**	23	54	68
17/7/71	Monarchy should play a less important role in Canada	40	31	55	36	32
14/7/71	Government is downgrading the role of monarchy	36	48	26	33	49

n.a. Not available.

*Approximately the same as Ontario but number of respondents too small to be reported with required statistical accuracy.

**Approximately the same as the West but number of respondents too small to be reported with required statistical accuracy.

Source: Canadian Institute of Public Opinion, *The Gallup Report* (Toronto: mimeographed).

favour an invitation to the Queen to visit Expo, to want to continue paying allegiance to the Queen, and to agree that the Government is downgrading the role of the monarchy.

These differences between Quebec and other Canadian respondents on the role of the monarchy result from ethnic, not regional, differences. This is shown clearly by the results of a question put by the C.I.P.O. in 1970, on whether respondents wanted Canada to abolish the monarchy at the end of Queen Elizabeth's reign or to recognize Charles the Third as King.[47] On the whole, 52 per cent expressed themselves in favour of recognizing King Charles, 29 per cent wanted to become a Republic, and 19 per cent were undecided. Among English-speaking respondents 67 per cent wanted to recognize King Charles, 21 per cent favoured becoming a Republic, and 12 per cent were undecided—a result almost exactly the same as that obtained when the same question was put to an Australian sample (of whom 65 per cent favoured recognizing King Charles,

25 per cent wanted to become a Republic, and 19 per cent were undecided). Among French-speaking respondents in Canada, however, only 27 per cent wanted to recognize Charles; 45 per cent favoured a Republic; and 28 per cent were undecided.

As Table 4–27 shows, the respondents to the 1968 federal election survey were equally divided between those who agreed and those who disagreed with the statement that Canada should abolish the monarchy; but again the pattern of responses of people grouped according to their language and region were rather different. The sharpest differences existed between the French Quebec respondents, 48 per cent of whom strongly agreed with abolishing the monarchy, and the English Atlantic respondents, 45 per cent of whom strongly disagreed with abolishing it. The non-Quebec French, the English in Quebec, and other-language groups tended to favour abolishing the monarchy; but the proportion agreeing strongly, about one-third of each group, was lower than in the French Quebec group. Conversely, English-speaking respondents in Ontario, the Prairies, and British Columbia tended to disagree with abolishing the monarchy; but their opinions were generally not as strongly expressed as they were in the Atlantic Provinces. There was a full spectrum of opinion in each group from strong agreement to strong disagreement on the question of abolishing the monarchy, and this kind of opinion distribution could be important for maintaining unity while continuing to debate the meaning of the Canadian political community. The fact remains that one of the most important political symbols of the nation tends to be divisive rather than unifying in its effect; and this, along with other disagreements over national political myths and symbols, reflects the existence of significant disruptions and discontinuities in the sense of Canadian community.

Mutual Responsiveness

The togetherness of a political community expresses not only what already exists but also what is explicitly willed.[48] Social indicators of patterns of communication and perceptions of the community help describe the extent to which a community of values, interests, and beliefs actually exists; but conclusions from these data may also be quite misleading if the factor of the will to create a strong political community is not considered.

Social indicators which reveal something of the will to create a Canadian community as well as the existential quality of the Canadian community are those which describe mutual responsiveness. Deriving from the togetherness of belonging to a community, mutual

Table 4–27. Responses to the Statement that Canada Should Abolish the Monarchy by Language Spoken at Home and Region, 1968

	French		English					Other	Total
	Quebec	Non-Quebec	Atlantic Provinces	Quebec	Ontario	Prairie Provinces	British Columbia		
Agree strongly	48	32	10	32	16	12	20	34	24
Agree mildly	15	20	10	19	24	22	22	22	20
Disagree mildly	8	16	22	26	27	26	24	15	21
Disagree strongly	6	19	45	18	26	31	29	12	23
No opinion/ no answer	23	13	12	6	7	9	5	17	12
TOTAL Percentage*	100	100	99	101	100	100	100	100	100
Number	632	84	249	90	868	462	238	144	2,767

*Totals may not add to 100 per cent because of rounding errors.

Source: John Meisel, Queen's University, 1968 Federal Election Survey.

responsiveness is the "we-feeling" which inspires a basic trust and consideration among members of a community and nourishes their ability to perceive one another's needs and predict one another's behaviour.[49] Some evidence of mutual responsiveness between English-speaking and French-speaking Canadians is revealed in the patterns of attitudes presented in Tables 4–28 to 4–37.

In the first place, Table 4–28 suggests that there are many personal contacts across ethnic groups in Canada; and many of them are close relationships, at least insofar as the frequency of contacts is any indication. In the 1965 sample taken by the Social Research Group, over half the English and two-thirds of the French respondents said they had contacts with members of the other "founding" ethnic group; and frequent contacts were indicated by 43 per cent of English Canadians and 53 per cent of French Canadians. English Canadians reported both more contacts and more frequent contacts with members of other ethnic groups than with French Canadians, while French Canadians tended to have more contacts with English Canadians than with other groups. Members of other ethnic groups had many more contacts and many more frequent contacts with English Canadians and with other groups than they had with French Canadians. Even so, 46 per cent said they had contacts with French Canadians and 40 per cent reported frequent contacts.

The incidence of interethnic contacts between French and English Canadians is subject to substantial regional variation as Table 4–29 shows. The Social Research Group found that English-Canadian respondents in Quebec were much more likely to have frequent contacts with French Canadians than were English Canadians in other regions, and French Canadians in other regions were much more likely to have frequent contacts with English Canadians than

Table 4–28. *Percentages of Respondents Reporting Interethnic Contacts by Ethnic Group, Canada, 1965*

	English Canadians	French Canadians	Others
Contacts with:			
English Canadians	—	68	93
French Canadians	56	—	46
Another group	78	46	85
Frequent contacts with:			
English Canadians	—	53	79
French Canadians	43	—	40
Another group	56	40	68

Source: From an unpublished study, *A Study of Interethnic Relations in Canada*, by the Social Research Group, prepared for the Royal Commission on Bilingualism and Biculturalism, with permission of the authors.

Table 4–29. *Frequency and Desirability of Contacts Between English and French Canadians by Region, 1965*

Type of contact	Percentage of respondents by region				
	National	Maritimes	Quebec	Ontario	West
English Canadians who have contacts with French Canadians	56	47	94	55	53
French Canadians who have contacts with English Canadians	68	92	61	98	93
English Canadians who have frequent contacts with French Canadians	43	29	69	32	28
French Canadians who have frequent contacts with English Canadians	53	61	30	81	77
English Canadians who have French Canadians among best friends	17	11	27	19	16
French Canadians who have English Canadians among best friends	15	36	8	44	26
English Canadians who would like to have French Canadians among best friends	48	41	67	46	50
French Canadians who would like to have English Canadians among best friends	57	44	59	46	58
English Canadians who have French Canadians among close relatives	12	12	19	13	10
French Canadians who have English Canadians among close relatives	15	33	9	39	40
English Canadians who would like to have French Canadians among close relatives	38	30	61	36	38
French Canadians who would like to have English Canadians among close relatives	50	38	52	41	45

Source: From an unpublished study. *A Study of Interethnic Relations in Canada,* by the Social Research Group, prepared for the Royal Commission on Bilingualism and Biculturalism, with permission of the authors.

were French Canadians in Quebec. Only about 30 per cent of French Canadians in Quebec and English Canadians outside Quebec reported frequent contacts with members of the other official group; but, given the national distribution of the two ethnic groups, this seems a fairly high rate of interaction. Perhaps the most interesting evidence of mutual responsiveness is that when English and French Canadians were questioned on the desirability of having members of the other ethnic group among best friends or close relatives, they appeared much closer to each other in their desire for contact than they were in terms of actual frequency of contact.

Table 4–30 provides evidence of regional–ethnic divisions on certain questions concerning the satisfaction of Quebec's interests, but it also suggests an underlying agreement on some important questions of political procedure. On the three issues of political procedure involving French–English relations, there was a notable degree of uniformity among the regions in the distribution of public opinion. First, about half the sample in each region in 1968 agreed that the principle of alternating the Prime Minister's Office between French and English leaders was a good one. Second, of those who expressed their opposition to separatism in 1968, an overwhelming 98 per cent in Ontario and the West also opposed a special status for Quebec; but a substantial 72 per cent of the Quebec respondents also were opposed to special status for their province. Third, two-fifths of the national sample in 1971 agreed that Quebec had the right to separate if the majority of its people wanted it. Surprisingly, the percentage of agreement with this principle was somewhat higher in the Maritimes, Ontario, and the West than it was in Quebec.

Table 4–30. Selected Opinions Indicating Variations in Mutual Responsiveness by Region in Canada, 1965–1972

Release date	Item	Percentage expressing agreement by region				
		National	Maritimes	Quebec	Ontario	West
27/3/68	Principle of alternation of Prime Minister's Office between English-speaking and French-speaking leader is a good one	50	n.a.	51	55	44
19/10/68	Quebec should have the same powers as all other Provinces, not a special status with more powers*	91	n.a.	72	98	98
17/4/71	Accept the principle that Quebec should have the right to separate from Canada if the majority of its people want it	40	41	30	41	49
1/9/65	French should be a compulsory subject like spelling, writing, and arithmetic in all grades of public schools in English-speaking Canada	64	n.a.	91	63	35

4/9/65	English should be a compulsory subject like spelling, writing and arithmetic in all grades of public schools in French-speaking Canada	84	n.a.	92	84	76
23/3/68	Prime Minister should encourage Quebec's wish for full equality	38	n.a.	61	32	24
20/4/68	Would approve a law by which all traffic signs and all labels on goods were in both English and French	70	n.a.	93	65	51
4/5/68	Would be a bad thing if Quebec continues to develop closer ties with France	67	n.a.	28	76	88
24/5/69	Approve proposed bill of Federal Government to establish minority right to deal with federal officials in own official language	56	n.a.	85	52	30
9/12/70	Prime Minister is paying too much attention to Quebec	20	26	3	21	35
19/7/72	Steps being taken to strengthen bilingualism through civil service areas, signposts, package information, and other ways are a good thing for the future of the country.	59	53	83	53	46

n.a. Not available because number of respondents was too small to be reported with required statistical accuracy.

* Question asked of respondents who disapproved of separatism for Quebec.

Source: Canadian Institute of Public Opinion, *The Gallup Report* (Toronto: mimeographed).

When opinions were sought on several specific proposals for further accommodating the interests of French Canada, the disagreement among the regions followed a predictable pattern. Respondents in Quebec were more likely than respondents in other regions to believe that French (and English) should be a compulsory school subject, to agree that the Prime Minister should encourage Quebec's wish for full equality, and to approve legislation concerning bilingual signs and minority language rights throughout the nation. They were less likely to think that it would be a bad thing for Quebec to continue to develop close ties with France, or that the Prime Minister was paying too much attention to the province of Quebec. Outside Quebec, respondents in the Western Provinces showed a certain lack of enthusiasm for compulsory French in English schools (though they supported compulsory English in French

schools), minority language rights, and Prime Ministerial encouragement of Quebec's wish for equality. They were more likely than
those in other regions to think that it would be a bad thing for
Quebec to develop closer ties with France and that the Prime Minister
was paying too much attention to Quebec. Somewhere between
these sets of contrasting opinions held in Quebec and the West
were the opinions of the respondents in Ontario (and probably
those in the Maritimes as well).

Additional evidence of mutual responsiveness in perceptions of
the place of Quebec in the Canadian community is found in Tables
4–31 and 4–32 which show regional opinions on the likelihood and
the consequences of Quebec's leaving Confederation. During the
1960s there was a growing opinion that relations between the French
and the English were growing worse. Feelings between English-
speaking and French-speaking Canadians were thought to be worse
than they were five years before by 27 per cent of a national sample in
1963, 33 per cent in 1966, 38 per cent in 1967 and 42 per cent in
1970.[50] Interestingly enough, respondents in Quebec were less and

Table 4–31. *Canadians' Opinions on the Likelihood of Quebec's
Leaving Confederation by Region, 1964–1973*

Release date	Item	National	Mari- times	Quebec	Ontario	West
			Percentage agreed			
7/11/64	Quebec's leaving Confederation and becoming a separate state might happen	20	n.a.	24	17	18
16/4/66	Differences between various parts of Canada are so great they will never be solved and Confederation will break up	15	21	26	9	16
17/2/68	The wish for separation among Quebec people is very strong	19	n.a.	12	19	23
12/7/69	Quebec will likely be separated from the rest of Canada in five years	18	n.a.	19	15	15
8/3/72	The wish for separatism among the people of Quebec is very strong	16	12	13	17	21
16/6/73	Quebec will likely be separated from the rest of Canada in five years	16	17	25	8	15

n.a. Not available.

Source: Canadian Institute of Public Opinion, *The Gallup Report* (Toronto:
mimeographed).

Table 4–32. Percentage Distribution of Opinions on the Seriousness of the Consequences for Canada if Quebec Should Leave Confederation by Region, 1964–1972

Region	Very or fairly serious				Not serious				No opinion			
	1964	1966	1970	1972	1964	1966	1970	1972	1964	1966	1970	1972
Canada	64	48	61	58	28	28	29	32	8	24	10	10
Maritimes	n.a.	n.a.	64	55	n.a.	n.a.	21	39	n.a.	n.a.	15	6
Quebec	80	51	74	64	10	20	17	26	10	29	9	10
Ontario	58	43	53	60	35	32	35	30	7	25	12	10
West	53	49	56	49	39	32	36	39	8	19	8	12

n.a. Not available.

Source: Canadian Institute of Public Opinion, The Gallup Report (Toronto: mimeographed), March 4, 1972; July 18, 1970; July 20, 1966; November 11, 1964.

those in the West and Ontario were more inclined to perceive relations as worsening. The percentage of those who said feelings were worsening between the English and the French increased in Quebec from 14 per cent in 1963 to 28 per cent in 1970, while fully half the respondents in the West and Ontario thought feelings were worse by 1970.[51]

Yet, during this period when a growing number of Canadians believed that feelings were worsening, there was no obvious upward trend in the percentages of respondents, always fairly low in each region, who agreed that separation was likely. Nor was there any marked change in the distribution of opinion on how serious the consequences of Quebec's leaving Confederation would be. The 1966 sample of opinions revealed considerable indecision, and the only trend occurred in Quebec where the percentage expecting very or fairly serious consequences declined somewhat and the percentage expecting no serious consequences increased. By 1972, the pattern of expectations in Quebec on the seriousness of the consequences of separation was similar to that in other regions; and the opinion that consequences would be very or fairly serious was still in the majority, as it had been in 1964.

A blending of responsiveness and unresponsiveness is also evident on the part of the participants in the 1968 federal election survey in their answers to questions on whether the Canadian constitution should be changed, how Quebec should be treated, whether Quebec is likely to separate, how they would feel about such a separation, and what the federal government should do if separation occurred.

On the general question of the status of the Canadian constitution, 52 per cent of the respondents agreed that it should be changed and 27 per cent disagreed. The French and the English in Quebec were the only groups in which a majority expressed strong agreement on the need for constitutional change. Elsewhere both agreement and disagreement tended to be mild rather than strong, a situation which at least seems to offer some room for political leaders to manoeuvre in persuading the majority to accommodate the two different, strongly interested minorities living in Quebec.

The rather wide potential for agreement which appears to exist on the general question of changing the constitution tends to narrow significantly when more specific proposals for constitutional change are considered. We have already seen in Table 4–27 that language and regional group opinions on the abolition of the monarchy were rather more divided than they were on the general question of constitutional change shown in Table 4–33. Similarly, on the more specific constitutional question of how Quebec should be treated, the sub-groups living outside Quebec overwhelmingly responded that Quebec should be treated like the other provinces. Majorities of the French and English groups in Quebec also took this view, but in each of the Quebec groups there was also a strong minority concerned with achieving a special position for Quebec in Canada's national political arrangements.

On the question of the possible separation of Quebec, the majority of respondents in each sub-group believed Quebec will not separate, although French-speaking respondents, English-speaking respondents in the Atlantic Provinces, and the group of non-English, non-French respondents seemed less certain of this. In every group, most respondents were strongly opposed to the separation of Quebec from the rest of Canada (Table 4–36). Not surprisingly, the English-speaking Quebec group had the largest proportion of strong opponents to separation (89 per cent), while the French Quebec group (53 per cent) and, curiously, the English Atlantic Provinces group (52 per cent) had the smallest proportions of strong opponents.

From the perspective of mutual responsiveness, the most important question regarding separation is what the Government of Canada should do if Quebec voted to separate (Table 4–37). Here, on the basic question of making Quebec stay or letting it go, the French-speaking respondents in Quebec and those living outside Quebec were in clear disagreement: 29 per cent of the Quebec French favoured letting Quebec go and 15 per cent recommended making it stay, whereas 20 per cent of the non-Quebec French favoured letting Quebec go and 44 per cent thought the Federal Government should make Quebec stay.

Elsewhere in the nation, language and regional groups were also divided on whether Quebec should be forced to stay or allowed to

Table 4–33. Responses to the Statement that Canada's Constitution Should Be Changed by Language Spoken at Home and Region, 1968

(percentages)

	French		English					Other	Total
	Quebec	Non-Quebec	Atlantic Provinces	Quebec	Ontario	Prairie Provinces	British Columbia		
Agree strongly	42	19	13	40	16	16	18	21	23
Agree mildly	24	26	18	29	32	34	38	29	29
Disagree mildly	9	11	18	14	24	21	25	8	18
Disagree strongly	6	14	12	7	11	8	9	4	9
No opinion/no answer	19	30	37	10	17	20	10	38	20
TOTAL Percentage*	100	100	98	100	100	99	100	100	99
Number	632	84	249	90	868	462	238	144	2,767

* Totals may not add to 100 per cent because of rounding errors.

Source: John Meisel, Queen's University, 1968 Federal Election Survey.

Table 4–34. *Canadians' Opinions on How Quebec Should Be Treated by Language Spoken at Home and Region, 1968*

(percentages)

Treatment of Quebec	French		English					Other	Total
	Quebec	Non-Quebec	Atlantic Provinces	Quebec	Ontario	Prairie Provinces	British Columbia		
Same as other provinces	55	87	87	67	90	85	90	82	80
Special position	36	4	4	28	5	8	6	8	13
Other	2	2	1	2	4	4	4	1	3
No opinion/no answer	7	7	8	3	1	3	1	9	4
TOTAL Percentage*	100	100	100	100	100	100	101	100	100
Number	632	84	249	90	868	462	238	144	2,767

* Totals may not add to 100 per cent because of rounding errors.

Source: John Meisel, Queen's University, 1968 Federal Election Survey.

Table 4-35. *Canadians' Opinions on Whether Quebec Will Separate in the Future by Language Spoken at Home and Region, 1968*

(percentages)

Quebec will separate	French		English					Other	Total
	Quebec	Non-Quebec	Atlantic Provinces	Quebec	Ontario	Prairie Provinces	British Columbia		
Yes	26	24	22	7	16	18	12	16	19
No	47	50	48	69	67	64	74	47	60
Don't know	27	26	28	23	16	17	12	36	21
No answer	1	0	2	1	*	*	2	1	1
TOTAL Percentage**	101	100	100	100	99	99	100	100	101
Number	632	84	249	90	868	462	238	144	2,767

* Less than 0.5 per cent.

** Totals may not add to 100 per cent because of rounding errors.

Source: John Meisel, Queen's University, 1968 Federal Election Survey.

Table 4-36. Canadians' Feelings About the Possibility of Quebec's Separating in the Future by Language Spoken at Home and Region, 1968

(percentages)

	French		English					Other	Total
	Quebec	Non-Quebec	Atlantic Provinces	Quebec	Ontario	Prairie Provinces	British Columbia		
Strongly in favour	4	1	3	0	3	2	3	1	3
Slightly in favour	7	1	4	2	5	5	3	2	5
Undecided	21	12	23	6	10	11	6	12	14
Slightly opposed	14	17	12	3	12	14	11	12	13
Strongly opposed	53	68	52	89	70	68	76	70	65
No answer	1	1	6	0	1	*	0	2	1
TOTAL Percentage**	100	100	100	100	101	100	99	99	101
Number	632	84	249	90	868	462	238	144	2,767

* Less than 0.5 per cent.

** Totals may not add to 100 per cent because of rounding errors.

Source: John Meisel, Queen's University, 1968 Federal Election Survey.

Table 4–37. *Canadians' Opinions on the Job of the Federal Government If Quebec Voted to Separate by Language Spoken at Home and Region, 1968*

(percentages)

Job of the Federal Government	French		English					Other	Total
	Quebec	Non-Quebec	Atlantic Provinces	Quebec	Ontario	Prairie Provinces	British Columbia		
Make Quebec stay	15	44	30	20	29	25	32	32	26
Let Quebec go	29	20	25	16	36	30	33	23	30
Nothing can be done	6	1	2	11	3	4	3	4	4
Compromise	6	1	*	11	3	4	6	1	4
Other	14	5	10	16	12	11	14	9	12
Don't know	27	29	31	26	17	24	13	31	23
No answer	3	0	1	1	1	1	0	1	1
TOTAL Percentage**	100	100	99	101	101	99	101	101	100
Number	632	84	249	90	868	462	238	144	2,767

* Less than 0.5 per cent.

** Totals may not add to 100 per cent because of rounding errors.

Source: John Meisel, Queen's University, 1968 Federal Election Survey.

go. In the English Atlantic, the English Quebec, and the other-language groups majorities favoured making Quebec stay, while respondents in the English Ontario, the Prairie, and the British Columbia groups were more inclined to let Quebec go.

In general, two points of mutual responsiveness seem worth noting in this expression of public opinion. First, the proportion which favoured letting Quebec go was actually higher among English-speaking respondents in Ontario, the Prairie Provinces, and British Columbia than it was in French-speaking Quebec. Second, there were at least some French-speaking respondents in Quebec (15 per cent) who favoured making Quebec stay in Confederation. As with other issues of constitutional change, on the question of what the Federal Government should do if Quebec voted to separate we find the full spectrum of opinion represented in each language and regional group; and this situation offers at least some promise of intergroup communication and responsiveness on the fundamental issues concerning the integrity of the political community.

After its hearings, the Royal Commission on Bilingualism and Biculturalism concluded that the great bulk of English-speaking opinion was moderate, without animus against French-speaking Canadians, and eager to see French Canada happy and participating vigorously in the development of Canada. Admittedly, the rapidity of political and social change in Quebec had left English-speaking Canadians quite bewildered with the result that "throughout English-speaking Canada there was tragically little awareness of the feelings and aspirations of French-speaking Canadians. Few had come to grips with the questions that Quebec's resurgence poses for all Canadians."[52] Yet the Royal Commission continued to be optimistic about the prospects of a good relationship developing between English and French Canada, since it found, for example, that the number of English-speaking Canadians with an understanding of French Canada was growing and that many more were eager to learn.

On the whole, the social indicators of mutual responsiveness shown in Tables 4–28 to 4–37 tend to support this optimism. There appears to be at least some desire for more personal contacts between English and French Canadians and, more important, significant agreement exists on certain political procedures which reflect an underlying mutual responsiveness. Differences between the two language groups are found on specific issues of recognition for Quebec; but opinion is certainly not uniformly against Quebec in Ontario and the West, and it varies markedly from issue to issue. This situation indicates at least some potential for accommodation. The mutual responsiveness of English and French Canada cannot be properly assessed, however, without some reference to the opinions of Canadians on their economic and social ties with the United States, for mutual responsiveness between the two language groups in Canada is rendered much more difficult by the towering presence of the American community.

Canadian perceptions of the general relationship between Canada and the United States during the period since World War II show a constant, fairly high awareness of growing dependence on the United States; but there was a marked shift from the 1950s to the 1960s in how this situation was evaluated. In response to the question as to whether Canada was becoming more or less dependent on the United States than it was ten years ago, 42 per cent of a national sample agreed in 1948 that Canada was becoming more dependent; and 43 per cent said Canada was becoming more dependent in 1961. Between 1961 and 1963, the percentage of respondents who perceived a growing dependence on the United States increased to 49 per cent; in 1969, 48 per cent agreed that Canada and the United States had been drawing close together recently; and in 1970, 50 per cent said Canada was becoming more dependent than it was ten years before.[53] As Table 4–38 shows, respondents in Ontario and the West were more likely to perceive a growing dependence on the United States in 1970 than they were in 1961, while there was no change in Quebec opinion.

During the 1950s, the majority of Canadians apparently were not concerned by this perceived situation of growing dependence on the United States. Asked whether the Canadian way of life was

Table 4–38. Canadians' Opinions on the Growing Dependency of Canada on the United States by Region, 1961–1970

| Release date | Percentage agreed Canada becoming more dependent* | | | | |
	National	Maritimes	Quebec	Ontario	West
25/1/61	43	38	40	45	46
3/7/63	49	41	47	52	50
30/7/69	48	n.a.	40	54	49
28/3/70	50	n.a.	42	57	54

* Canada becoming more dependent on the United States than ten years ago except for 30/7/69 where opinion expressed was Canada and U.S. drawing closer together recently.

n.a. Not available.

Source: Canadian Institute of Public Opinion, The Gallup Report (Toronto: mimeographed), March 28, 1970; Mildred A. Schwartz, Public Opinion and Canadian Identity (Berkeley: University of California Press, 1967), pp. 70, 72. Originally published by the University of California Press, reprinted by permission of The Regents of the University of California.

being influenced too much by the United States, 47 per cent of respondents in 1951 said it was not being influenced too much. This percentage rose to 63 per cent in 1956 and then dropped to 57 per cent in 1957 and to 49 per cent in 1961. The opinion that Canada was too much influenced by the United States became more widely accepted in the early 1960s. By 1966 the favourable attitudes of the 1950s had been completely reversed as 53 per cent thought the Canadian way of life was being influenced too much by the United States and only 36 per cent thought it was not. Moreover, the reversal of opinion occurred in all regions. Too much influence was perceived by 56 per cent of respondents in Quebec, 52 per cent in Ontario, and 60 per cent in the West.[54]

Opinions on the excessive influence of the United States in Canada clearly changed in all regions in the 1960s, but the American presence continued just the same to complicate the problem of mutual responsiveness between Quebec and the rest of Canada. Canadians, both English-speaking and French-speaking, became progressively concerned about the growth of American economic power in their country, presumably because of the threat it posed to their political independence; but the two language groups responded quite differently on the whole to the continued presence of American culture.

Opinions recorded at various times since World War II show a

Table 4–39. *Canadians' Opinions on Economic Relations with the United States by Region, 1943–1972*

Release date	Item	National	Mari-times	Quebec	Ontario	West
			Percentage agreed by region			
2/6/43	Canada would be better	67	n.a.	——63——		78
6/6/53	off if there were free	49	n.a.	37	44	n.a.
18/5/68	trade with the United States	56	n.a.	69	51	52
18/7/56	Good thing for Canada	68	n.a.	70	68	69
10/8/63	that development has been	55	n.a.	55	59	54
15/7/67	financed by the United States	57	——54——		63	54
19/7/67	Enough United States	60	——61——		59	62
28/11/70	capital now invested in Canada	62	53	48	70	67
12/2/72		67	61	58	73	69

n.a. Not available.

Source: Mildred A. Schwartz, *Public Opinion and Canadian Identity* (Berkeley: University of California Press, 1967), pp. 67, 68; Canadian Institute of Public Opinion, *The Gallup Report* (Toronto: mimeographed).

fairly strong belief in all regions of Canada in the advantages of free trade with the United States, a decline in all regions between 1956 and 1963 in the percentage who thought American investment had been good for Canadian development (although a majority in both 1963 and 1967 still held that American investment had been beneficial), and a growing opinion in all regions from 1967 to 1972 that there was now enough American capital in Canada. Surveys taken in 1965 and 1971 indicate that favourable attitudes towards free trade with the United States have also declined in recent years. In 1965, 59 per cent of English Canadians and 47 per cent of French Canadians and Canadians of other ethnic origins favoured an economic union with the United States. In 1971, following a change in economic policy in the United States which threatened to impede Canadian exports, only 18 per cent of the respondents in the British ethnic groups, 17 per cent in the French ethnic group, and 23 per cent in the other ethnic groups thought Canada should now seek to enter some form of economic union with the United States.[55]

In contrast with this growing opinion throughout both French and English Canada against further strengthening economic connections with the United States, there was no comparable joint concern about American cultural penetration into the Canadian community. The high rate of consumption of American television, magazines, films, and books and the expressed preferences of English Canadians for American cultural products have already been recorded. Perhaps the differences between the two language groups in their relative concerns about American economic and cultural penetration are also revealed in their different responses to two recent questions concerning possible national remedial policies.[56] In 1970, on the question about the plan advanced by the Canadian Radio and Television Commission to require that all television and radio stations have 60 per cent Canadian content during prime time, approval was expressed by 65 per cent of French Canadians; 48 per cent of Canadians having non-French, non-British ethnic origins; and only 39 per cent of English Canadians. In contrast with this mixed response to controlling the penetration of American culture, 69 per cent of a national sample in early 1972 favoured a plan to set up an organization to screen the introduction of more American capital into Canada; and the level of support was high in all regions of the country— 66 per cent in the Maritimes, 68 per cent in Quebec, 67 per cent in Ontario, and 75 per cent in the West.

Additional evidence underlining the difficulties which the presence of the American community creates for mutual responsiveness between the two language groups in Canada comes from the national survey of young people carried out in 1965 by John C. Johnstone.

Questions in the survey asked respondents to compare Canadians with Americans on a number of specific traits and characteristics, to make an overall judgement on the degree of their similarities and differences, to make similar judgements for English and French Canadians, and to rate the strength of interethnic ties within Canada in comparison with ties across the border.

Most Canadian young people, particularly the English-language and the other-language respondents but also a majority of the French, viewed themselves collectively as more similar to than different from Americans (Table 4–40). A majority of young people in each ethnic group rated the English and the French as being alike in most ways, as shown in Table 4–41; but, whereas 79 per cent of the English-language group rated Canadians and Americans as being alike, only 50 per cent gave a similar rating to the French and the English

Table 4–40. Young Canadians' Perceptions of Similarity between Canadians and Americans by Language Spoken at Home, 1965

(percentages)

Perception of Americans and Canadians	English	French	Other
Alike in most ways	79	56	75
Different in most ways	18	37	25
I'm not sure	3	7	—
TOTAL	100	100	100

Source: John C. Johnstone, Young People's Images of Canadian Society (Ottawa: Queen's Printer, 1969), p. 23. Reproduced by permission of Information Canada.

Tale 4–41. Young Canadians' Perceptions of Similarity between English and French Canadians by Language Spoken at Home, 1965

(percentages)

Perception of English and French Canadians	English	French	Other
Alike in most ways	50	54	42
Different in most ways	41	38	40
I'm not sure	10	8	18
TOTAL	101	100	100

Source: John C. Johnstone, Young People's Images of Canadian Society (Ottawa: Queen's Printer, 1969), p. 28. Reproduced by permission of Information Canada.

in Canada. For the non-English, non-French group the discrepancy was even greater—75 per cent compared with 42 per cent. Of the three groups, it was the French who most often saw English and French Canadians as alike, and Americans and Canadians as different.[57]

When the strength of interethnic ties within Canada is compared with that of ties across the border (Tables 4–42 and 4–43), it is apparent that many English-speaking respondents felt closer ties to Americans than to French Canadians; and that non-English, non-French respondents strongly agreed with this appraisal. The views of the French respondents were quite different. They tended to see stronger ties between the English and the French in Canada, and

Table 4–42. *Young Canadians' Perceptions of Closeness of Ties of English Canadians with Americans and French Canadians by Language Spoken at Home, 1965*

(percentages)

Groups perceived as having more in common	English	French	Other
English Canadians and Americans	68	41	69
English Canadians and French Canadians	20	39	9
I'm not sure	12	20	22
TOTAL	100	100	100

Source: John C. Johnstone, *Young People's Images of Canadian Society* (Ottawa: Queen's Printer, 1969), p. 33. Reproduced by permission of Information Canada.

Table 4–43. *Young Canadians' Perceptions of Closeness of Ties of French Canadians with Americans and English Canadians by Language Spoken at Home, 1965*

(percentages)

Groups perceived as having more in common	English	French	Other
French Canadians and Americans	8	21	10
French Canadians and English Canadians	70	60	63
I'm not sure	21	19	27
TOTAL	99	100	100

Source: John C. Johnstone, *Young People's Images of Canadian Society* (Ottawa: Queen's Printer, 1969), p. 33. Reproduced by permission of Information Canada.

weaker ties between English-speaking Canadians and Americans. Finally, respondents from all three language groups thought French Canadians had more in common with English Canadians than with Americans.

Questions similar to those put to the young people in 1965, regarding who has more in common, were asked in the 1968 federal election survey; and the results shown in Tables 4–44 to 4–46 were generally the same. In the 1968 national sample, clear majorities of the English-speaking respondents in British Columbia, Ontario, and the Prairie and Atlantic Provinces said that they thought English Canadians and Americans had more in common than English Canadians and French Canadians. Conversely, majorities of the French-speaking respondents inside and outside Quebec and of the English-speaking respondents in Quebec said that they thought English Canadians and French Canadians had more in common than English Canadians and Americans. Somewhat surprisingly, majorities of the English-speaking respondents in British Columbia, Ontario, and the Prairie Provinces also thought English Canadians had more in common with the British than with French Canadians; and once more the converse was true for both groups of French-speaking respondents and for the English-speaking respondents in Quebec. Finally, French-speaking respondents in Quebec were about equally divided as to whether they had more in common with English Canadians or the French; but the preponderant opinion in each of the other sub-groups was towards the interethnic rather than the cross-national tie.

In view of the similarity of the results, Johnstone's conclusion with respect to the 1965 sample of young people may also be applied to the findings of the 1968 national survey.

> Together, then, these reactions describe a grossly unbalanced set of relationships. The social orientation of the Anglophones crosses national lines much more frequently than ethnic lines, while that of the Francophones is exactly the reverse. The most interesting feature here, perhaps, is that this situation seemed to be clear to everyone: it was obvious to the Anglophones and the "Others", and even the Francophones recognized it more often than not. The French did tend to overestimate the ties English Canadians felt toward them, and this can perhaps be interpreted as a reaction to the uncomfortable situation of recognizing attachments which are not reciprocated. The results suggest a rather weak foundation for intergroup solidarity among Canadian young people. And while it would be foolish

Table 4-44. *Canadians' Opinions on Who Has More in Common, English Canadians and French Canadians, or English Canadians and Americans, by Language Spoken at Home and Region, 1968*

(percentages)

Groups perceived as having more in common	French		English					Other	Total
	Quebec	Non-Quebec	Atlantic Provinces	Quebec	Ontario	Prairie Provinces	British Columbia		
English Canadians and French Canadians	44	56	28	58	28	24	26	28	33
English Canadians and Americans	34	21	43	27	59	61	63	33	49
No difference	*	0	0	1	1	0	*	0	*
Don't know	22	23	28	14	12	15	11	38	18
No answer	*	0	*	0	0	*	0	0	*
TOTAL Percentage**	100	100	99	100	100	100	100	99	100
Number	632	84	249	90	868	462	238	144	2,767

* Less than 0.5 per cent.

** Totals may not add to 100 per cent because of rounding errors.

Source: John Meisel, Queen's University, 1968 Federal Election Survey.

Table 4–45. Canadians' Opinions on Who Has More in Common, English Canadians and French Canadians, or English Canadians and the British, by Language Spoken at Home and Region, 1968

(percentages)

Groups perceived as having more in common	French		English					Other	Total
	Quebec	Non-Quebec	Atlantic Provinces	Quebec	Ontario	Prairie Provinces	British Columbia		
English Canadians and French Canadians	52	62	34	62	38	36	29	33	41
English Canadians and British	27	10	33	27	49	49	60	29	41
Don't know	20	29	32	11	12	15	10	38	18
No answer	*	0	*	0	0	0	*	0	*
TOTAL Percentage**	99	101	99	100	99	100	99	100	100
Number	632	84	249	90	868	462	238	144	2,767

* Less than 0.5 per cent.

** Totals may not add to 100 per cent because of rounding errors and because two respondents who said "the same" have been omitted.

Source: John Meisel, Queen's University, 1968 Federal Election Survey.

Table 4-46. *Canadians' Opinions on Who Has More in Common, French Canadians and English Canadians, or French Canadians and the French, by Language Spoken at Home and Region, 1968*

(percentages)

Groups perceived as having more in common	French		English					Other	Total
	Quebec	Non-Quebec	Atlantic Provinces	Quebec	Ontario	Prairie Provinces	British Columbia		
French Canadians and English Canadians	45	67	52	72	69	59	62	43	58
French Canadians and French	42	16	18	14	16	23	24	18	24
Don't know	13	18	29	13	14	18	14	38	17
No answer	*	0	*	0	0	0	0	0	*
TOTAL Percentage**	100	101	99	99	99	100	100	99	99
Number	632	84	249	90	868	462	238	144	2,767

* Less than 0.5 per cent.

** Totals may not add to 100 per cent because of rounding errors and because two respondents who said "neither" have been omitted.

Source: John Meisel, Queen's University, 1968 Federal Election Survey.

> to suggest specific implications of this imbalance, it should
> be clear enough that a tendency to identify stronger social
> ties outside the national borders than within could become
> extremely significant in situations of either individual or
> collective cross-pressure.[58]

The Political Problem of Fraternity

A political community may disintegrate in two ways.[59] It may
sever through disnomie if values, interests, and beliefs come to
polarize rather than unify it, by dividing the community into a
part which continues to espouse the former integrating values,
interests, and beliefs and an anti-community which insists on their
disvalue and cherishes their opposites. It may also disappear through
anomie if integrating values, interests, and beliefs no longer serve to
separate it from other communities by sustaining its particular
myths, symbols, and utopias, its organizational structure and decision-
making capacity, and its communications networks.

Neither of these processes of disintegration is easy to identify.[60]
Anomie may be mistaken for the continuous change in values, interests, and beliefs which characterizes any live community. Disnomie
may be mistaken for the healthy antagonism of values, interests,
and beliefs which is a vital part of any pluralistic community. Yet
even the most cautious interpretation of the social indicators used
above to describe patterns of communication, perceptions of the
community, and mutual responsiveness reveals serious strains on
the Canadian community; and the strains are made more serious
by the fact that they derive partly from disnomie and partly from
anomie.

The danger of disnomie results from the coexistence of two
distinct communities in a single state. The state is bilingual; but
increasingly one of its two communities is unilingual in English
and the other is unilingual in French. As the territorial locations of
these two language communities become increasingly well-defined
by the bilingual frontier running from Moncton to Sault Ste. Marie,
the potential for intercommunity contacts seems to narrow; and
the difficulties in exchanging communications respecting common
goals become correspondingly greater.

In addition to the basic differences of language, the English and
French communities are divided by their perceptions of the national
political community and their identifications with it. The English
Canadians strongly reject ethnic community identifications. Most
of them think of themselves as simply Canadian and of their nation
as just Canada. Conversely, most of the French Canadians are

strongly oriented towards an ethnic community identification and think of Canada as an English–French partnership.

The dualism of the prevailing French and English views of Canada is reflected clearly in the formal schooling that the young people of each language community have received in their national history. Disagreements between the English and the French communities are evident in their contradictory memories of intercommunity conflicts, their rival lists of heroes and villains, and their different attributions of pride in their historical achievements. They are also evident in the opposing sets of values, interests, and beliefs which their respective educational programs purpose to inculcate.

Regional and cultural differences within English Canada are sometimes thought to present another danger of disnomie, but this fear seems exaggerated. Definite disparities in economic prosperity separate the regions of Canada; and domestic trade, migration, and travel show well-defined patterns of regional concentration. The "golden horseshoe" of southern Ontario continues to be the core area of English Canada, while Calgary and Vancouver represent an increasingly attractive alternative. Subtle differences in their perceptions of Canada do appear to exist among the regional and ethnic sub-groups of English Canada, and these groups differ also in their responsiveness to the problem of Canadian dualism. More direct and more sensitive social indicators would undoubtedly reveal a lot more about these very interesting regional and ethnic variations in the English-language community, but they would be unlikely to alter this basic conclusion. None of the regional and ethnic differences within the English community appears to present the kind of barrier to national political integration which is posed by the existence of the French community.

Although regional and ethnic differences in the English-language community do not present a serious danger of disnomie, they do underline another important dimension of the fundamental differences between the English community and the French community in Canada. The French community has had a relatively stable demographic history; except for the Atlantic Provinces, the English community has had a very unstable demographic history. The members of the French community generally have French ethnic origins; the members of the English community do not necessarily have English or even British ethnic origins. The people of English Canada have many ethnic origins; and their local sub-communities throughout English Canada have become increasingly multi-ethnic and multi-cultural in their populations and life-styles and in their collective values and social goals—a development which is not found in the local sub-communities of French Canada.

The problem of anomie results from the overwhelming presence of the United States. The people of the United States and Canada broadly agree on the basic values of constitutionalism and democracy in political arrangements and modified free enterprise in economic activity. Without many of the formalities of economic union, countless private and public decisions concerning their mutual economic activities have created an immense area of common interest between the two nations. Through common media of communications, especially television but also magazines, books, popular music, and films, they share exposure to the same propaganda concerning preferred values, appropriate interests, and views of the world.

Not surprisingly, it is English Canada which is most exposed to American penetration. The English community, living on the border and speaking the language of this powerful American community, presents few barriers to the penetration of American news, books, films, and television. The continual infusion of new members who have diverse ethnic origins has produced in English Canada a nascent, variegated set of social and cultural orientations which is still too recent to be well-defined and which consequently appears to be in constant danger of disappearing into the American melting pot.

In contrast, the French community, separated from English Canada and the United States by language, seems more detached from American culture. Like other nations in which the spread of American popular culture has required translation, French Canada has sustained its own actors, authors, musicians, poets, and other intellectuals who collectively provide a distinctive French-Canadian statement of the international popular culture and hence help to define the membership and meaning of their community in a more cosmopolitan world. The actors, authors, musicians, poets, and intellectuals of English Canada also work to provide such distinctive statements, and their value to their community is gaining recognition; but their work in terms of cultural definition is constantly undermined by the fact that it is unprotected by the natural tariff barrier of language.

The problems of disnomie and anomie are not separate ones. The presence of the United States constantly intrudes upon efforts within Canada to accommodate its dualism. American penetration, especially cultural penetration tends to reinforce internal divisions, weakening English responsiveness to French Canada and strengthening French consciousness of its minority status. Accommodation with the French-language group surely seems much less imperative to English-speaking Canadians living in the predominantly English-speaking environment of North America than it would in an environment more balanced in its bilingualism and biculturalism.

This is not to say that French-speaking Canadians are not deeply involved in the North American culture. They are also North American and share its popular culture, but the barrier of their language and the stability of their community have both impeded American penetration and nourished mutual separation. Nor is it to say that English-speaking Canadians favour political integration into the United States. It is clear that a great majority want very much to retain their political independence.[61] However, this desire for political independence is not accompanied by any reinforcing desire to be separated from the American cultural community, at least not for the great majority of English-speaking Canadians.

The political problem of Canadian fraternity is thus two-fold: first, to preserve the political independence of the State, which means preserving the real capacity to make and enforce binding collective decisions in the face of the powerful economic, cultural, and political attractiveness of the United States; and, second, to continue to develop national political arrangements which will encourage the maintenance and growth of each of the distinctive sub-communities contained in the binational state. Thus stated, the political problem of Canadian fraternity has existed for at least two centuries; and during that time the preservation and enhancement of a separate national identity have become permanent fixtures among the main goals of public policy in Canada.

A succession of governmental policies has been directed at creating and maintaining continent-wide patterns of communication. Among the matters of highest concern to policy-makers in the nineteenth century was the support of the northern commercial empire converging on Montreal by the construction of canals and railways. This concern evolved into the larger goal of a continent-wide northern community reflected in the "national policy" of railway development, tariff protection, and free lands to western settlers; and, as technology advanced, the aim to achieve continent-wide patterns of communication was reasserted in policies for national airlines, energy, broadcasting, and arts and letters.

There is a formidable list of legislative decisions and governmental undertakings since the British conquest which have been directed at creating a set of mutually acceptable political arrangements and ensuring an harmonious national association between English Canada and French Canada. The list includes such historic legislative decisions as the Quebec Act, 1774, the Constitutional Act, 1791, the Act of Union, 1840, and the British North America Act, 1867; and it includes such contemporary governmental arrangements as opting-out clauses for Quebec in national fiscal policies and designated bilingual areas for federal public services.

There have also been policies which have proved harmful to the development of Canadian fraternity. Sometimes they have been inspired by ethnic nationalism, as seems to have been the case with the conscription policies of 1917 and 1944; and sometimes, as seems to have been the case with the unwillingness in English Canada to give French a preferred place in school curriculum regulations, they have reflected the evolution of English Canada into a multi-ethnic, multi-cultural community very different in make-up from mono-ethnic French Canada.

The omissions and commissions of the policy-makers and the beneficial and the harmful effects of their actions for the development of fraternity attest to the fact that the mixture of mutual responsiveness and unresponsiveness revealed in the political orientations of Canadians by current social indicators has been part of the Canadian political culture for a very long time. In the course of that time, much love has been lost from our life as a people because of our collective failure to create an enduring harmony of values, interests, and beliefs among the various sub-groups which inhabit this country. Nor is there any evidence in the prevailing patterns of communication or in the perceptions of the community to indicate that our situation will soon improve; but there is evidence of at least a modicum of mutual responsiveness, which may provide the leeway necessary to accommodate the distinctive aspirations of the people of English and French Canada.

Communities do not simply spring into existence; they are created. Patterns of communications, perceptions of the community, and mutual responsiveness may be fixed in the short-term; but in the long-term they are open to improvement through political persuasion and leadership. In this respect, after three centuries English Canadians and French Canadians have only begun to know themselves and to understand each other; and they have only begun to explore the array of political arrangements which have the potential to accommodate the values and goals of their distinctive sub-communities within a larger national political community.

NOTES

1. Stanley Lieberson, *Language and Ethnic Relations in Canada* (New York: John Wiley and Son, Inc., 1970), pp. 31, 33.
2. *Ibid.*, p. 33.
3. Richard J. Joy, *Languages in Conflict* (Toronto/Montreal: McClelland and Stewart Limited, 1972). Reprinted by permission of The Canadian Publishers, McClelland and Stewart Limited, Toronto and the Carleton Library Editorial Board.
4. *Ibid.*, pp. 135–6.

5. Canada, Royal Commission on Bilingualism and Biculturalism, *Report,* vol. I (Ottawa: Queen's Printer, 1967), p. 15.

6. *Ibid.* Reproduced by permission of Information Canada.

7. Frank Peers, "Oh Say, Can You See?" in Ian Lumsden (ed.), *Close the 49th Parallel Etc.* (Toronto: University of Toronto Press, 1970), pp. 150-151.

8. Canada, Special Senate Committee on Mass Media, *Report,* vol. I (Ottawa: Queen's Printer, 1970), p. 152.

9. *Ibid.,* vol. III, p. 213.

10. *Ibid.,* vol. I, p. 152. Reproduced by permission of Information Canada.

11. Canadian Institute of Public Opinion, *The Gallup Report* (Toronto: mimeographed, May 18, 1966).

12. John W. Warnock, "All the News It Pays to Print," in Ian Lumsden (ed.), *op. cit.,* pp. 126-7.

13. From an unpublished study, *National News in Canadian Newspapers,* by Donald Gordon, prepared for the Royal Commission on Bilingualism and Biculturalism, with permission of the author.

14. John Porter, "Canadian Character in the Twentieth Century," *The Annals of the American Academy of Political and Social Science,* 370 (March 1967), p. 50.

15. Pierre Camu, E. P. Weeks, and Z. W. Sametz, *Economic Geography of Canada* (Toronto: Macmillan Company of Canada, 1964), p. 58.

16. T. J. Samuel, *The Migration of Canadian-Born Between Canada and United States of America 1955 to 1968,* Research Branch, Program Development Service, Department of Manpower and Immigration (Ottawa: Queen's Printer, 1970), p. 4.

17. John Porter, *The Vertical Mosaic* (Toronto: University of Toronto Press, 1965), pp. 32-3.

18. Leroy O. Stone, *Migration in Canada,* Dominion Bureau of Statistics, 1961 Census Monograph (Ottawa: Queen's Printer, 1969), p. 22. Reproduced by permission of Information Canada.

19. May Nickerson, *Geographic Mobility in Canada, October 1964 to October 1965,* Dominion Bureau of Statistics, Special Labour Force Studies, Number 4 (Ottawa: Queen's Printer, 1967), p. 16.

20. Statistics based on first destination tend to understate the percentage of exports, since many goods first shipped to points in Canada are eventually exported; but this does not affect the validity of first destination as a useful measure of internal economic transactions, since the shipments constitute internal transactions, whatever the eventual destination.

21. Canada, Task Force on the Structure of Canadian Industry, *Foreign Ownership and the Structure of Canadian Industry* (Ottawa: Queen's Printer, 1968), pp. 300-301.

22. About half of the increase from 2.4 to 17 billion dollars in direct investment from the United States between 1945 and 1967 was for the development of natural resources. The rest was largely directed into manufacturing industries for beginning new enterprises, expanding existing plants, or taking over Canadian-owned firms. The Gray Report has noted that:
"a large proportion of the investment in resource exploitation reflected the needs of the United States investors for raw materials for their processing and manufacturing plants in the United States. These captive export markets were a particularly important factor in a number of developments, as the very heavy capital costs involved were apparently very difficult to justify without assured markets for the output, such as was the case for the Quebec-

Labrador iron ore fields and newsprint, and sufficiently large markets were not then available in Canada. This so-called "backward vertical integration" —the integration of the earlier stages of the productive process—by United States processors and manufacturers had the practical impact, in some cases, of reducing the likelihood of further processing activity of Canadian natural resources in Canada."

See Canada, *Foreign Direct Investment in Canada* (Ottawa: Information Canada, 1972), p. 14. Reproduced by permission of Information Canada.

23. John Crispo, *International Unionism* (Toronto: McGraw-Hill Company of Canada Ltd., 1967), pp. 1–6.
24. I. Brecher and S. S. Reisman, *Canada–United States Economic Relations* (Ottawa: Queen's Printer, 1957), p. 202, quoted by J. Crispo, *op. cit.*, p. 5.
25. Canada, Department of Labour, *Union Growth in Canada 1921-1967* (Ottawa: Information Canada, 1970), p. 36.
26. Canada, Royal Commission on Bilingualism and Biculturalism, *Preliminary Report* (Ottawa: Queen's Printer, 1965), p. 45. Reproduced by permission of Information Canada.
27. *Ibid.*, pp. 47–8. Reproduced by permission of Information Canada.
28. Kenneth McNaught, "The National Outlook of English-Speaking Canadians," in Peter Russell (ed.), *Nationalism in Canada* (Toronto: McGraw-Hill Company of Canada Ltd., 1966), pp. 63–4.
29. Royal Commission on Bilingualism and Biculturalism, *op. cit.*, p. 122. Reproduced by permission of Information Canada.
30. *Ibid.*, p. 52. Reproduced by permission of Information Canada.
31. *Ibid.*, p. 49. Reproduced by permission of Information Canada.
32. H. D. Forbes, "Conflicting National Identities among Canadian Youth" (Toronto: mimeographed, 1973).
33. Forbes has defined the four categories which describe the different styles of Canadian identification as follows: emphatically Canadian—those who put a special emphasis on the idea that they were simply Canadians and nothing else; simply Canadian—those who wrote down, in ordinary script, the word "Canadian" or "Canadien"; qualified Canadian—those who indicated they were Canadians but with some qualification or elaboration, for example, "Canadien de langue française," "Canadian of German descent," "Canadian citizen and British subject"; hypenated Canadian—those who said "English-Canadian," "Canadien français," "German-Canadian," and so on. The Internationalist category includes those who said that they did not think of themselves as being of any particular nationality, that they were human beings, that they did not believe in national distinctions, and so on. See *ibid.*, p. 5.
34. John C. Johnstone, *Young People's Images of Canadian Society*, Studies of the Royal Commission on Bilingualism and Biculturalism, Number 2 (Ottawa: Queen's Printer, 1969).
35. *Ibid.*, p. xiii. Reproduced by permission of Information Canada.
36. Royal Commission on Bilingualism and Biculturalism, *Preliminary Report*, pp. 134–5.
37. A. B. Hodgetts, *What Culture, What Heritage*, Report of the National History Project (Toronto: Ontario Institute for Studies in Education, 1968), p. 81.
38. Marcel Trudel and Geneviève Jain, *Canadian History Textbooks: A Comparative Study*, Studies of the Royal Commission on Bilingualism and Biculturalism, Number 5 (Ottawa: Queen's Printer, 1970).
39. *Ibid.*, p. 124. Reproduced by permission of Information Canada.

40. A. B. Hodgetts, *op. cit.*, p. 33.

41. Marcel Trudel and Geneviève Jain, *op. cit.*, p. 133. Reproduced by permission of Information Canada.

42. Kenneth P. Langton and M. Kent Jennings, "Political Socialization and the High School Civics Curriculum in the United States," *American Political Science Review*, LXII (September 1968), 852–867.

43. Edgar Litt, "Civic Education, Community Norms and Political Indoctrination," *American Sociological Review*, 28 (February 1963), 69–75.

44. H. D. Forbes, *op. cit.*, pp. 7–8.

45. See George F. G. Stanley, *The Story of Canada's Flag* (Toronto: Ryerson Press, 1965).

46. Mildred Schwartz, *Public Opinion and Canadian Identity* (Berkeley: University of California Press, 1967), pp. 107–8.

47. Canadian Institute of Public Opinion, *The Gallup Report*, August 15, 1970.

48. Carl J. Friedrich, *Man and His Government*, (New York: McGraw-Hill Book Company, 1963), p. 143.

49. Karl W. Deutsch et al., *Political Community and the North Atlantic Area* (Princeton, N.J.: Princeton University Press, 1957, 1968), p. 129.

50. Canadian Institute of Public Opinion, *The Gallup Report*, February 19, 1966; April 1, 1967; December 20, 1970.

51. The events of autumn 1970 did not noticeably affect the relationship between French-speaking and English-speaking Canadians. On December 23, 1970, the Canadian Institute of Public Opinion reported the following distribution of responses to its question "Would you say you feel more friendly, or less friendly, towards the English (French)-speaking Canadians than you did, say a year ago?"

	More friendly	Less friendly	About the same	Undecided
English-Canadian attitudes	7	9	81	3
French-Canadian attitudes	13	6	72	9

52. Royal Commission on Bilingualism and Biculturalism, *Preliminary Report*, p. 125. Reproduced by permission of Information Canada.

53. Mildred Schwartz, *op. cit.*, p. 70; Canadian Institute of Public Opinion, *The Gallup Report*, March 28, 1970; July 30, 1969.

54. Canadian Institute of Public Opinion, *The Gallup Report*, July 16, 1966.

55. Social Research Group, *A Study of Interethnic Relations in Canada*, Research report for the Royal Commission on Bilingualism and Biculturalism, Division IX, Contract 2 (Montreal: mimeographed, 1965), p. 189; Canadian Institute of Public Opinion, *The Gallup Report*, December 11, 1971.

56. Canadian Institute of Public Opinion, *The Gallup Report*, July 4, 1970; February 16, 1972.

57. J. C. Johnstone, *op. cit.*, p. 28.

58. *Ibid.*, pp. 33–4. Reproduced by permission of Information Canada.

59. Carl J. Friedrich, *op. cit.*, pp. 144–6.

60. *Ibid.*, pp. 144, 146.

61. In 1964, the Canadian Institute of Public Opinion reported that only 13 per cent of Canadians wanted to join the United States while 81 per cent wanted to remain independent. The percentage favouring union had not varied much over the previous two decades. Nor did it vary much among regions, as it was 20 per cent in the East, 11 per cent in Ontario, and 8 per cent in the West. The poll taken following the change in U.S. economic policy in 1971

showed an even lower percentage than usual favouring union, as only 3 per cent of English Canadians, 10 per cent of French Canadians, and 5 per cent of other Canadians wanted a political union with the United States. See Canadian Institute of Public Opinion, *The Gallup Report*, October 3, 1964; December 11, 1971.

Chapter Five

EQUALITY

Equality among citizens is necessary to ensure satisfaction of the need for esteem; but equality is a comparative, not an absolute condition. Who shall be treated alike for what purposes is a recurring question in politics, and the criteria for its answer vary with prevailing social conditions. Equality has a meaning in traditional society different from its meaning in modern industrial society, and it has a meaning in Britain or Japan different from its meaning in Canada or Australia.

These societal differences make it difficult to find cross-national social indicators suitable for measuring inequalities, and the development of social indicators for even a single political community is beset by two further difficulties. The question of who shall be treated alike raises the problem of identifying appropriate social groups for analysis, and the question for what purposes particular social groups are to be treated equally raises the problem of identifying appropriate social activities for analysis. People may be divided by such characteristics as age, sex, or race; and they will usually have different criteria for equality respecting a variety of personal, social, economic, and political activities. Certain group characteristics or areas of social activity may have particular importance for a political community at its current stage of development; and, if so, these must be identified and given appropriate coverage.

Social indicators have been selected here to describe the degree of equality in Canada among class, status, ethnic, and sex groups with respect to educational opportunity, occupational mobility, and access to political power.[1] The choice of these three areas of social activity for analysis derives from three of the four tests for equality described in the introductory chapter: the degree to which educational advantages are based on ability to profit from them; the opportunity to compete for economic, social, or political position on the basis of completing any necessary educational preparation; and the opportunity to participate through all media of communication in the shaping of economic, social, and political opinion and policy.

Educational Inequalities

Opportunity to secure educational advantages based only on a person's ability to profit from them must be regarded as one of the most important parts of the opportunity structure of an advanced industrialized society. The modern industrial economy requires increasing numbers of workers with specialized technical education and skills necessary to employ the latest advances in modern technology, increasing numbers of managers with specialized professional education and skills necessary to organize production, and increasing numbers of researchers with specialized scientific education and skills necessary to create new technology.

A continuing, close relationship exists between occupational groupings and levels of schooling. Elementary schooling is usual for workers in the "blue-collar" occupational groups; most workers in the "white-collar" groups have secondary schooling, except for professional workers where the majority have post-secondary schooling. For each occupational group, however, the demand for more years of schooling has been increasing over time; and there has been a marked increase in the percentage of each occupational group with secondary or post-secondary schooling. With increasingly little place for the untrained at all levels, any social group which has relative difficulty in attaining the necessary educational qualifications will find itself relatively deprived with respect to the material and probably the psychic well-being of its members.

If class is defined by the occupations of family heads, the existence of inequalities between people in different classes with respect to access to education can be identified by examining the educational attainments of the children of parents belonging to different occupational groups. If opportunity for education were relatively equal, we would expect to find little variation in the proportions of children of different class backgrounds who are in school. In fact, we find that inequalities in access to education in Canada are clearly associated with differences in class background.

In Figure 5–1 the pattern and persistence of these inequalities for each of the census years from 1941 to 1961 is indicated by the percentage of young people living at home who were at school according to the occupational class of their fathers.[2] Because Figure 5–1 has been drawn on a semi-logarithmic scale, the rates of change in percentages of young people living at home who were attending school can be compared directly between occupational classes. The

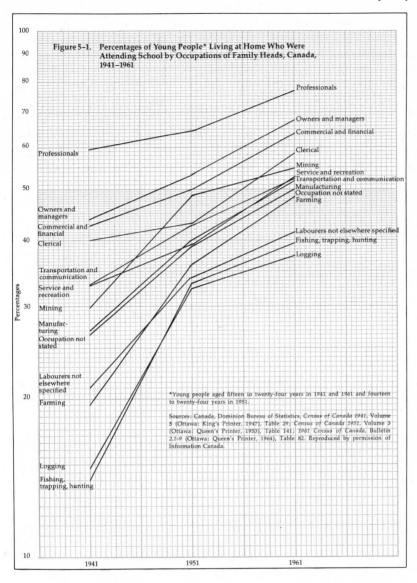

Figure 5-1. Percentages of Young People* Living at Home Who Were Attending School by Occupations of Family Heads, Canada, 1941-1961

*Young people aged fifteen to twenty-four years in 1941 and 1961 and fourteen to twenty-four years in 1951.

Sources: Canada, Dominion Bureau of Statistics, Census of Canada 1941, Volume 5 (Ottawa: King's Printer, 1947), Table 29; Census of Canada 1951, Volume 3 (Ottawa: Queen's Printer, 1953), Table 141; 1961 Census of Canada, Bulletin 2.1-9 (Ottawa: Queen's Printer, 1964), Table 82. Reproduced by permission of Information Canada.

slope of each occupational class line reflects the rate of change in the percentage of young people living at home who were at school, and the vertical distance between occupational class lines provides a measure of the relative disparity in access to schooling.

Between 1941 and 1961 the percentage of all young people living at home who were at school increased from 27.5 per cent in 1941 to 41.4 per cent in 1951 and 54.9 per cent in 1961, a trend which was consistent with the increase in the years of schooling of the labour force during this period; and this general increase for all occupational groups was reflected in increasing percentages in each class of young people living at home who were at school.

In general, according to this indicator, there was an improvement in equality of access to schooling between 1941 and 1951, but there was no further increase between 1951 and 1961. For the occupational classes which had the lowest percentages of young people in school in 1941 (fishing, trapping, and hunting; logging; farming; labourers; manufacturing; and mining), the rates of increase in the percentages of young people living at home who were at school were generally higher between 1941 and 1951 than they were for the occupational classes which had the highest percentages in school in 1941. As a result, Figure 5–1 shows a clear reduction in the disparities among occupational classes in access to schooling between 1941 and 1951. Between 1951 and 1961, however, the rates of increase in the percentage of young people living at home who were at school were more or less the same for each occupational class; and the disparities among occupational classes in access to education remained unchanged.

The changing pattern in access to schooling, still using as our indicator the census data on the proportions of young people living at home who were at school, is illustrated in another way in Figure 5–2, which shows the differences of the percentages for each occupational class from the national average. A trend for the differences from the national average to converge toward zero would be expected if inequalities between occupational classes were being reduced between 1941 and 1961, but no such trend is observable in Figure 5–2. There was some narrowing of class inequalities between 1941 and 1951 as the above-average classes, except for mining, moved closer to the average, and the below-average farming, logging, and fishing groups also moved closer to the average; but between 1951 and 1961 there was little further change in the position of the above-average classes, while those below average tended to lose their earlier gains. Taken together, Figures 5–1 and 5–2 indicate that access to education was much easier in 1961 than in 1941 for children of all class backgrounds, as is indicated by the increases in percentages shown in Figure 5–1; but the pattern of class inequalities in access to education in 1961 was not essentially different from that in 1941.

Another indicator of the existence of significant inequalities in opportunities for education among children of different class backgrounds is presented in Table 5–1, which shows the percentage distribution among occupational classes of the fathers of post-secondary students in 1968-69 compared with the percentage dis-

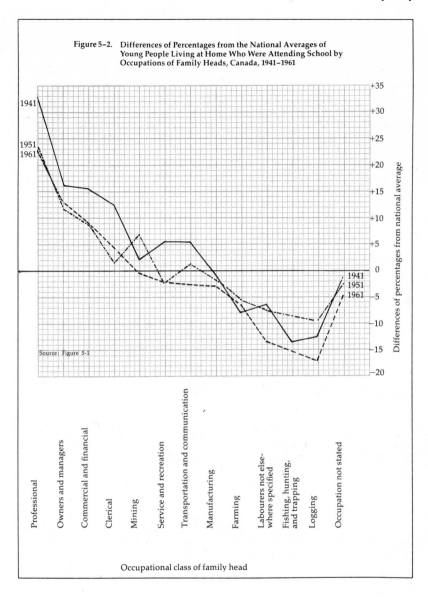

Figure 5-2. Differences of Percentages from the National Averages of Young People Living at Home Who Were Attending School by Occupations of Family Heads, Canada, 1941–1961

tribution of the 1961 labour force. If there were no association between class background and access to education, we would expect the occupational distribution of fathers of post-secondary students to approximate that of the entire male labour force, that is, being the child of a professional or a farmer would make no difference in proceeding to post-secondary education. Table 5-1 shows, however, that children whose fathers were owners, managers, and professionals were greatly over-represented in the post-secondary school

Table 5–1. *Occupational Class of Fathers of 1968–1969*
Post-secondary School Population Compared with
1961 Male Labour Force

(percentages)

Occupational class	Fathers of post-secondary school population, 1968–69*	Male labour force, 1961
Middle class (Professional, business, executive, managerial)	41.8	17.5
Lower middle class (Administrative, supervisory, clerical, service)	22.9	21.0
Working class (Processing, machining, assembling, labouring)	15.1	45.9
Farming	8.8	8.2
Other/no response	11.7	7.4
Total**	100.3	100.0

* Based on a sample of 32,786 students, 8.4 per cent of the total post-secondary population in 1968–69.

** Totals may not add to 100 per cent because of rounding errors.

Sources: Canada, Dominion Bureau of Statistics, *Post-Secondary School Population Survey 1968–69* (Ottawa: Queen's Printer, 1970), Table 23, p. 123; *1961 Census of Canada*, Bulletin 3.1–1 (Ottawa: Queen's Printer, 1964). Reproduced by permission of Information Canada.

population in 1968–69. In 1961, 17.5 per cent of the labour force could be classified as owners and managers or professionals; but the fathers of 41.8 per cent of students in post-secondary schools belonged to these occupational groups. In contrast, 45.9 per cent of the labour force could be classified as working class (manufacturing and mechanical, transportation and communication, construction, and labourers); but only 15.1 per cent of the fathers of post-secondary students belonged to the working class. The conclusion suggested by a study of Table 5–1 is one of marked inequality in access to higher education between children of the middle class on the one hand and those of the working class on the other, with the children of the lower middle class and farmers represented more or less as labour force statistics would lead one to expect if opportunities for access were equal.

If a person's status group is defined by his level of educational attainment, inequalities between people in different status groups with respect to access to education can be examined in terms of intergeneration changes in levels of educational attainment. One such indicator of inequalities in educational attainment is available from the results of the 1968–69 post-secondary school population survey. The percentage distributions of the educational attainments of the fathers and mothers of students in post-secondary school are shown in Table 5–2 according to the study programs in which the students were registered.

Two points are evident. First, the educational attainments of the fathers of post-secondary students were generally higher than those of the mothers because more fathers had attained one or more university degrees (15.6 per cent of the fathers compared with 5.9 per cent of the mothers) and mothers had tended to end their education with some university, trade, or vocational schooling after high school, or high school graduation (40.0 per cent of the mothers compared with 29.6 per cent of the fathers). Second, the percentage distributions for both fathers and mothers were rather different between students registered in university graduate and undergraduate programs on the one hand, and those registered in nursing, teacher training, and other post-secondary programs on the other hand. The percentages of students in university graduate and undergraduate programs whose fathers or mothers had one or more university degrees were higher than they were for students in other post-secondary programs; and the percentages of students in university programs, as well as in nursing, whose fathers or mothers had some post-secondary schooling or high school graduation were also higher than they were for students in teacher training and other post-secondary study programs.

If there were no association between the status (educational attainments) of parents and the access to education enjoyed by their children, we would expect the percentage distributions of educational attainments for the fathers and mothers of post-secondary students to approximate those for the male and female populations in general. A comparison between Tables 5–2 and 5–3, which show the distribution of schooling for males and females at the 1961 census, reveals that, in fact, the educational attainments of the parents of post-secondary students in 1968–69 were much higher than average.

One or more university degrees had been attained by 15.6 per cent of the fathers and 5.9 per cent of the mothers of post-secondary students, but only 4.2 per cent of the 1961 male population and 1.7 per cent of the female population (ten years of age and over not attending school) had a university degree. In contrast, 50.1 per cent of the male population and 43.9 per cent of the female population had elementary or no schooling in 1961; but only 22.2 per cent

Table 5–2. *Highest Schooling of Parents in Relation to Choice of Study Program of Post-secondary School Population, Canada, 1968–1969*

(percentages)

Study programs of post-secondary school population

Highest schooling of parents	University graduate	University under- graduate	Nursing	Teacher training	Other	Total
Fathers:						
One or more university degrees	22.2	18.1	8.0	6.8	9.1	15.6
Some university, trade or vocational schooling after high school, or high school graduation	33.0	31.5	27.4	21.0	24.5	29.6
Some high school or trade training after elementary school	24.2	29.1	38.3	31.4	29.6	29.4
Some elementary or no schooling	17.5	18.6	23.0	36.9	31.8	22.2
Other schooling or no response	3.1	2.7	3.3	3.8	5.0	3.2
TOTAL, fathers*	100.0	100.0	100.0	99.9	100.0	100.0
Mothers:						
One or more university degrees	9.4	7.2	2.9	1.4	2.3	5.9
Some university, trade or vocational schooling after high school, or high school graduation	41.5	43.1	41.1	29.4	31.1	40.0
Some high school or trade training after elementary school	25.2	29.1	31.9	33.4	33.3	30.0
Some elementary or no schooling	21.0	18.3	22.3	32.8	28.3	21.4
Other schooling or no response	2.8	2.2	1.9	3.1	5.1	2.8
TOTAL, mothers*	99.9	99.9	100.1	100.1	100.1	100.1

* Totals may not add to 100 per cent because of rounding errors.

Source: Canada, Dominion Bureau of Statistics, *Post-Secondary Student Population Survey 1968–69* (Ottawa: Queen's Printer, 1970), Table 24, p. 124. Reproduced by permission of Information Canada.

of the fathers and 21.4 per cent of the mothers of post-secondary students had elementary or no schooling. The differences between the percentage distributions for the parents of post-secondary students and those for the general population are most pronounced

Table 5–3. *Highest Schooling of Population Ten Years of Age and Over Not Attending School, Canada, 1961*

(percentages)

Level of schooling	Males	Females	Total population
University degree	4.2	1.7	2.9
Some university	3.3	2.9	3.1
Secondary, four to five years	13.7	18.8	16.2
Secondary, one to three years	28.7	32.7	30.7
Elementary or no schooling	50.1	43.9	47.0
TOTAL*	100.0	100.0	99.9

* Totals may not add to 100 per cent because of rounding errors.

Source: Canada, Dominion Bureau of Statistics, *1961 Census of Canada*, Bulletin 1.3–6 (Ottawa: Queen's Printer, 1963), Table 102. Reproduced by permission of Information Canada.

for the parents of students in the university programs and rather narrow for the parents of students in teacher training; but even for those in teacher training the percentage of parents with only elementary or no schooling was lower than the averages for the male and female populations.

Another indicator of educational mobility in Canada was obtained from the monthly labour force survey of January 1966 when people enumerated were asked to state the level of education attained by their parents and themselves. The data in Table 5–4 show the levels of education of sons and daughters aged twenty to sixty-four years and those of their fathers and mothers. The percentages along the diagonals sloping downward from left to right indicate the extent of educational inheritance between generations.

For sons the percentages along the diagonals are the highest whether the level of parental education considered is that of the fathers or the mothers. For daughters the percentages along the left–right diagonals are also high, but the overall pattern of educational inheritance is somewhat different. The majority of women whose fathers attended university have themselves only obtained a secondary school education, while almost 50 per cent of women whose parents had only an elementary education have obtained a secondary school education. Even with these differences for women, however, there is clearly a strong tendency for Canadians of both sexes to inherit their status groupings, which are based on level of educational attainment.

Table 5–5 presents the influence of parental background on educational attainment in relative rather than absolute terms. An

Table 5–4. *Educational Attainment of Sons and Daughters Aged
Twenty to Sixty-four Years by Levels of Education
of Fathers and Mothers, Canada, 1966*

| Parent and parent's level of education | Level of education of sons and daughters | | | | | | | |
| | Sons | | | | Daughters | | | |
	University	Secondary	Elementary	Total	University	Secondary	Elementary	Total
Fathers:								
University	55.8	37.5	6.7	100.0	37.1	56.0	6.9	100.0
Secondary	28.7	61.0	10.3	100.0	16.3	73.4	10.3	100.0
Elementary	7.4	41.8	50.8	100.0	5.2	49.1	45.7	100.0
Mothers:								
University	54.1	38.1	7.8	100.0	49.7	44.8	*	100.0
Secondary	29.4	58.9	11.7	100.0	17.1	73.1	9.8	100.0
Elementary	7.3	41.3	51.4	100.0	4.8	48.5	46.7	100.0
TOTALS	13.8	45.2	41.0	100.0	9.3	54.5	36.2	100.0

*Based on estimate of less than 10,000.

Source: Michel D. Lagacé, *Educational Attainment in Canada: Some Regional and
Social Aspects,* Dominion Bureau of Statistics, Special Labour Force Studies,
Number 7 (Ottawa: Queen's Printer, 1968), p. 18. Reproduced by permission of
Information Canada.

index of association has been calculated for each educational category
by expressing the proportion of sons or daughters of a given origin
as a ratio of the proportion of all sons or daughters in that category.
A situation of "perfect mobility" would exist only if there were no
link between the level of education of parents and that of sons and
daughters and the indices would all be one; an index greater than
one indicates a greater number of persons of given origin in a given
educational category than would obtain if there were no intergeneration relationship between educational attainments; and a value less
than one shows fewer persons in a category than expected.

Since the left–right diagonals in Table 5–5 all have values greater
than one, we may conclude that educational mobility is not perfect
and that some educational inheritance exists in Canada. Two features
of the pattern of indices suggest something of the nature of inter-
generation inequalities among educational status groups. First, by far
the highest degree of inheritance occurs between university-educated
parents and sons or daughters. The indices of association for university-educated fathers and sons, mothers and sons, and fathers
and daughters have values of four; and that for mothers and
daughters is the highest of all at 5.4. Second, the relatively low values

Table 5–5. *Indices of Association Between Educational Attainment of Sons and Daughters Aged Twenty to Sixty-four Years and Levels of Education of Fathers and Mothers, Canada, 1966*

Parent and parent's level of education	Level of education of sons and daughters					
	Sons			Daughters		
	University	Secondary	Elementary	University	Secondary	Elementary
Fathers:						
University	4.0	0.8	0.2	4.0	1.0	0.2
Secondary	2.1	1.3	0.3	1.8	1.3	0.3
Elementary	0.5	0.9	1.2	0.6	0.9	1.3
Mothers:						
University	3.9	0.8	0.2	5.4	0.8	*
Secondary	2.1	1.3	0.3	1.8	1.3	0.3
Elementary	0.5	0.9	1.3	0.5	0.9	1.3

* Based on estimate of less than 10,000.

Source: Michel D. Lagacé, *Educational Attainment in Canada: Some Regional and Social Aspects*, Dominion Bureau of Statistics, Special Labour Force Studies, Number 7 (Ottawa: Queen's Printer, 1968), p. 19. Reproduced by permission of Information Canada.

of the indices in the upper-right and lower-left cells of each quadrant of Table 5–5 suggest that short-distance moves are more common than long-distance ones. In general, the closer two categories are to one another the greater is the flow of persons between them.

To ascertain whether the pattern of inequalities in educational attainment between status groups has been changing over time, sons and daughters responding to the survey were divided into three age groups making it possible to examine the effects of educational stratification at three different periods in time. Table 5–6 shows only the outflow percentages and indices of association for fathers and sons by level of education and age group of the sons; but the general pattern found in Table 5–6 is also valid for mothers and sons, fathers and daughters, and mothers and daughters.

The total percentages for each age group in Table 5–6 show a marked increase in the proportion obtaining university and secondary school education and a decrease in the proportion with elementary education. The diagonals of the percentages suggest a slowly changing pattern of educational inheritance, and the indices of association show the direction in which change has been occurring. Among university-educated sons of university-educated fathers the index

Table 5–6. Educational Attainment of Sons Aged Twenty to Sixty-
four Years by Age and Father's Levels of Education,
Outflow Percentages and Indices of Association,
Canada, 1966

Age of son and father's level of education	Educational attainment of sons						
	Outflow percentages				Indices of association		
	University	Secondary	Elementary	Total	University	Secondary	Elementary
20–24 years:	22.0	56.8	21.2	100.0	—	—	—
University	63.2	34.8	*	100.0	2.9	0.6	*
Secondary	31.5	62.6	5.9	100.0	1.4	1.1	0.3
Elementary	11.8	56.2	32.0	100.0	0.5	1.0	1.5
25–44 years:	14.3	48.2	37.5	100.0	—	—	—
University	56.5	38.9	*	100.0	4.0	0.8	*
Secondary	27.9	62.5	9.6	100.0	2.0	1.3	0.3
Elementary	8.0	45.2	46.8	100.0	0.6	0.9	1.2
45–64 years:	9.7	36.2	54.1	100.0	—	—	—
University	48.4	37.1	*	100.0	5.0	1.0	*
Secondary	27.1	56.3	16.6	100.0	2.8	1.6	0.3
Elementary	5.2	32.9	61.9	100.0	6.5	0.9	1.1

* Based on estimate of less than 10,000.

Source: Michel D. Lagacé, *Educational Attainment in Canada: Some Regional and
Social Aspects*, Dominion Bureau of Statistics, Special Labour Force Studies,
Number 7 (Ottawa: Queen's Printer, 1968), pp. 20, 22. Reproduced by permission
of Information Canada.

fell from 5.0 in the oldest age group to 2.9 in the youngest. That of
university-educated sons and fathers who attended secondary school
declined from 2.8 in the oldest group to 1.4 in the youngest. A
slight decrease is also evident in the index of association of secondary-
educated fathers and sons from 1.6 in the oldest group to 1.1 in the
youngest.

On the whole, it is reasonable to conclude that there has been a
decrease over time in inequalities arising from the effects of educational inheritance; but this conclusion must be tempered by two
features of the data. First, while there was an increase over time
from 5.2 to 11.8 in the percentage of university-educated sons whose
fathers had obtained only an elementary education, that increase
did no more than match the general increase in university-educated
sons, so that the index of association remained relatively low at 0.5.
Second, while the percentage of elementary-educated sons of elementary-educated fathers declined from 61.9 per cent to 32.0 per cent,
this decline did not match the general decline in sons having ele-

mentary education (from 54.1 per cent to 21.2 per cent). As a result, there was a slight increase in the index of association for elementary-educated sons and fathers over time from 1.1 for the oldest group to 1.5 for the youngest, "suggesting a possible strengthening of educational inheritance among the most poorly educated, or, looking at it another way, indicating that the general increase in educational attainment noted above has been taking place less rapidly among sons whose fathers have no more than elementary schooling."[3] Thus, while equality of access to education seems in general to be increasing over time, the children of elementary-educated parents continue to experience special difficulties both in breaking out of the educational status group of their parents and in leaping over the middle (secondary school) status group to attain a university education.

The existence of a strong association between ethnic group membership and level of educational attainment in Canada is shown in Table 5–7. The ethnic groups have been ranked in reverse order of the percentages of each group attaining the elementary level of schooling. The rank order which results is the same as that obtained by ranking the ethnic groups by the percentages attaining the university level (or, except for the Jewish and British ethnic groups, by those having three to five years of secondary schooling).

In Table 5–8, the same six ethnic groups are ranked horizontally according to the average level of educational attainment of those of their members who were part of the male non-agricultural labour force in 1961. The rank order in terms of last grade attended was the same for Canada as a whole as the rank order in Table 5–7, and more or less the same pattern was repeated in different areas across the nation. The rank order of the groups varied somewhat

Table 5–7. *Percentage Distribution of the Labour Force by Ethnic Origin and Level of Schooling, Canada, 1961*

Ethnic origin	No schooling	Elementary	Secondary, 1–2 years	Secondary, 3–4 years	University	Totals
Jewish	1.1	25.8	15.2	34.7	23.2	100.0
British	0.2	27.0	25.5	35.8	11.5	100.0
German	0.3	37.6	22.6	31.4	8.2	100.0
Ukrainian	1.6	43.2	22.1	26.1	7.0	100.0
French	0.6	49.8	22.5	21.2	5.8	100.0
Italian	1.9	69.7	13.0	12.6	2.8	100.0
Other	1.4	39.9	19.7	29.0	10.1	100.0
All origins	0.6	37.5	23.1	29.6	9.3	100.0

Source: Canada, Royal Commission on Bilingualism and Biculturalism, *Report*, Volume IV (Ottawa: Queen's Printer, 1970), p. 103. Reproduced by permission of Information Canada.

Table 5–8. *Average Educational Levels Attained (Last Grade Attended) by the Male Non-agricultural Labour Force in Selected Provinces and Metropolitan Census Areas by Ethnic Origin, Canada, 1961*

Area of Canada	All origins	Jewish	British	German	Ukrain-ian	French	Italian	Other
Canada	8.45	10.08	9.43	8.69	8.07	7.08	6.15	8.46
Provinces:								
New Brunswick	7.50	*	8.19	8.00	*	5.88	*	8.81
Quebec	7.04	9.54	9.60	10.17	8.61	7.00	5.52	8.60
Ontario	8.81	10.09	9.42	8.71	7.85	7.44	6.17	8.44
British Columbia, Yukon, and Northwest Territories	9.35	*	10.13	9.04	7.82	8.79	7.32	8.61
Metropolitan Areas:								
Montreal	8.12	9.53	9.98	10.09	7.53	7.54	5.95	8.95
Ottawa	9.71	11.75	10.94	10.10	10.07	8.28	6.70	10.32
Toronto	9.23	9.92	9.83	9.61	8.08	8.38	5.74	9.06

* Sample too small to make a reliable estimate.

Source: Canada, Royal Commission on Bilingualism and Biculturalism, *Report*, Volume IIIA (Ottawa: Queen's Printer, 1969), p. 28. Reproduced by permission of Information Canada.

for the four provinces of New Brunswick, Quebec, Ontario, and British Columbia and for the three metropolitan areas of Toronto, Montreal, and Ottawa; but the Jewish, British, and German ethnic groups were consistently high in all areas while the Ukrainian, French, and Italian ethnic groups were consistently low.[4]

There are differences in the average educational attainments of men and women in Canada. We have seen that among the parents of the post-secondary students surveyed in 1968–69 the percentage of the fathers with one or more university degrees was much higher than it was for the mothers (Table 5–2). In the 1966 national labour force survey (Table 5–4), the percentage of sons with university degrees was higher than that of daughters, the percentage of daughters with secondary schooling was higher than that of sons, and the percentage of sons with elementary schooling was higher than that of daughters. A similar pattern of differences in educational attainment between males and females can be seen in Table 5–9. According to the findings of a 1967 labour force survey, women were better educated on the whole at the secondary level than men in most occupational groups; but the percentages of female workers

Table 5–9.   Estimated Percentage Distribution of the Male and
Female Labour Forces by Level of Schooling and by
Occupational Classification, Canada, 1967

Occupational class	Males			Females		
	Elementary*	Secondary	University	Elementary*	Secondary	University
Managerial	20.3	59.8	19.9	23.9	68.0	**
Professional and technical	3.1	35.5	61.4	**	52.0	45.8
Clerical	17.1	73.4	9.5	6.9	87.1	6.0
Sales	16.9	71.9	11.2	25.3	71.2	**
Service	42.2	54.2	3.6	45.0	52.6	2.4
Transportation and communication	49.6	48.6	**	**	87.5	**
Craftsmen, production process and related workers and labourers	48.1	49.3	2.6	55.2	44.3	**
Primary industries	62.7	34.7	2.5	54.4	44.1	**
All occupations	37.7	50.8	11.5	23.9	64.8	11.3

* Includes no schooling.
** Estimates based on fewer than 10,000 persons not included.

Source: Canada, Royal Commission on the Status of Women in Canada, *Report* (Ottawa: Queen's Printer, 1970), p. 60. Reproduced by permission of Information Canada.

who had attended university were lower than they were for male workers in the three occupational groups with enough respondents to make a comparison.

Differences in the educational attainments of men and women now result primarily from differential decisions about university education. Fewer women than men go on to university from high school, and fewer women than men continue beyond the undergraduate program to do graduate studies. The effect of these sex differences in choosing university studies is evident in the lower percentage of university enrolment which is female and the lower percentage of degrees awarded to women by Canadian universities. The proportion of female undergraduates increased from 16.3 per cent in 1920–21 to 23.5 per cent in 1930–31. It remained more or less at this figure for the next three decades, and then began increasing again from 24.9 per cent in 1960–61 to 34.9 per cent in 1968–69. The trend in the percentage of bachelor's and first professional degrees granted to women also shows this pattern of stag-

Table 5–10. *Women as Percentage of Undergraduate and Graduate Enrolment in Canadian Universities and Colleges, 1920–21 to 1968–69*

Academic year	Women as percentage of full-time under-graduate enrolment	Women as percentage of full-time and part-time graduate enrolment
1920–1	16.3	25.5
1925–6	21.2	26.0
1930–1	23.5	26.0
1935–6	22.4	24.5
1940–1	23.3	20.8
1945–6	20.8	22.0
1950–1	21.7	15.4
1955–6	21.3	15.9
1960–1	24.9	18.8
1965–6	32.8	21.7
1968–9	34.9	19.5

Sources: M. C. Urquhart and K. A. H. Buckley (eds.), *Historical Statistics of Canada* (Toronto: Macmillan Company of Canada Ltd., 1965), pp. 601–2; Dominion Bureau of Statistics, *Survey of Higher Education 1961–2* (Ottawa: Queen's Printer, 1964), Tables 14, 16; Dominion Bureau of Statistics, *Survey of Higher Education Part II, 1968–9* (Ottawa: Queen's Printer, 1970), Table 1, p. 15. Statistics from *Survey of Higher Education* reproduced by permission of Information Canada.

nation, even decline, between 1930–31 and 1960–61 and a marked increase during the 1960s.

At the graduate studies level, there was an increase in the percentage of female enrolment during the early 1960s; but this increase did not result in corresponding increases in the percentage of master's and doctoral degrees granted to women. As shown in Table 5–11, women have earned 20 per cent of the master's and about 8 per cent of the doctoral degrees in recent years. Moreover, the proportion of women in graduate school in 1968–69 had not yet regained the level achieved in the 1920s.

The first test of equality is the opportunity to secure educational advantages based only on a person's ability to profit from them. The above description of inequalities in Canada, which has reviewed the comparative educational attainment of women, ethnic groups, and children of parents belonging to different class and status groups, has implied that ability is randomly distributed in the population at birth and that differences among social groups therefore result from social inequalities. Indeed, in the presentation of such data as the over-representation of the children of professional workers in school and the under-representation of women in uni-

Table 5–11. *Percentage of University Degrees Granted to Women,*
Canada, 1920–21 to 1968–69

Academic year	Bachelor's and first professional degrees*	Master's degrees and licences**	Doctorates
1920–1	20.3	22.0	4.2
1925–6	22.6	20.7	14.3
1930–1	25.3	21.4	15.2
1935–6	25.3	17.1	7.3
1940–1	24.1	10.5	6.7
1945–6	26.9	11.3	11.5
1950–1	20.3	13.9	5.4
1955–6	22.9	20.8	6.4
1960–1	25.7	19.0	8.5
1965–6	32.9	19.0	10.9
1968–9	37.2	19.5	7.9

* Includes equivalent diplomas, in theology for example, and honours degrees.

** The licence in French-language universities was the next degree after the bachelor's prior to 1961 and corresponded more or less with the master's degree in English-language universities. Since 1961, the licence has been considered the equivalent of a bachelor's degree.

Sources: M. C. Urquhart and K. A. H. Buckley (eds.), *Historical Statistics of Canada* (Toronto: Macmillan Company of Canada Ltd., 1965), p. 603; Dominion Bureau of Statistics, *Survey of Higher Education, Part II, 1968–9* (Ottawa: Queen's Printer, 1970), Table 3, p. 16. Statistics from *Survey of Higher Education* reproduced by permission of Information Canada.

versity, the degree of over- and under-representation has been offered as a direct measure of the degree of inequality of opportunity.

The assumption of a random distribution of ability among social groups is justified with regard to ethnic and sex groups, but there is some evidence that ability is not randomly distributed among class and status groups.

Assuming that I.Q. tests do provide valid measures of ability, a matter for considerable dispute in itself, the positive correlation between social status and ability may be explained in large part by a positive correlation between occupation and ability.[5] Each occupation has people ranging greatly in ability as measured by I.Q., but some occupations require a minimum level of ability well above the minimum level required for other occupations. In a sample of American enlisted men drawn from seventy-four different civilian occupations during World War II, the top public relations man and the top truck driver, for example, both scored 149 on the Army General Classification Test; the lowest public relations man had a score of 100

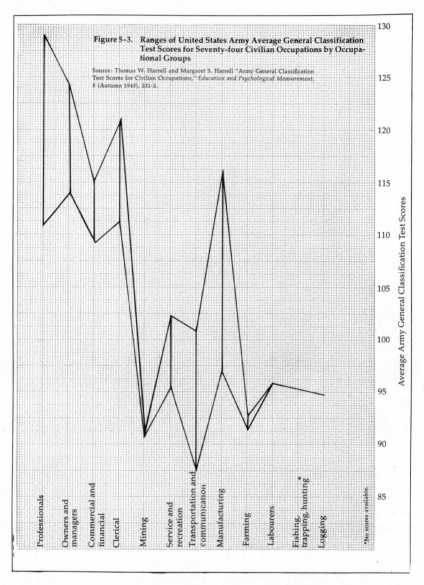

Figure 5–3. Ranges of United States Army Average General Classification Test Scores for Seventy-four Civilian Occupations by Occupational Groups

Source: Thomas W. Harrell and Margaret S. Harrell "Army General Classification Test Scores for Civilian Occupations," *Education and Psychological Measurement*, 5 (Autumn 1945), 231-2.

compared with 16 for the lowest truck driver; and the average for public relations men was 126.0 compared with 96.2 for truck drivers. As shown in Figure 5–3, where the average scores for the seventy-four civilian occupations have been grouped according to broad occupational groups, the upper-class managerial and professional occupations had higher ranges of average scores than the lower-class occupational groups.

The strong correlation between occupation and I.Q. means that we can regard measures of educational (and occupational) mobility as directly measuring social inequalities only if the resemblance of children and parents is no more than that of children and total strangers, but this we obviously cannot do.[6] General intelligence is a heritable trait. The usually accepted figures assign 75 to 80 per cent of the observed variation in the results of general intelligence tests to genetic factors and the rest to environmental, physical, and mental conditions and opportunities in the home.[7] Hence, genetic factors (and assortative mating) cannot be dismissed as irrelevant to the analysis of educational mobility. Through genetic processes and assortative mating, the higher average I.Q.s of managerial and professional people result in their children having higher I.Q.s, on the average, than the children of other occupational groups. Since a relatively high I.Q. is a necessary, if not a sufficient, condition for educational attainment, a higher proportion of the children of managerial and professional workers than of the children of lower-class workers would be expected to remain in school through university and then enter managerial and professional occupations themselves. The populations on which Figures 5–2 and 5–3 are based are not the same, so that no formal comparison is justified; but the general resemblance of the two figures is striking.

An assessment of the extent to which the measures of educational mobility used here have to be modified to take account of genetic processes and assortative mating must await research on the relationship between social class structure and the heritability of intelligence in Canada. Until the results of such research are available, indices of association and other similar measures of social mobility have to be interpreted with considerable caution.

Bearing in mind the need for caution, two comments may be made about the measures of educational inequality presented here. First, genetic variability guarantees a relatively large group of very bright children from lower-class backgrounds; and this group is larger than it would be on the basis of heritability alone as long as some social groups are relatively deprived of educational opportunity. Given some equality of opportunity, we may expect the children of parents in the upper occupational classes to have the largest relative representation at higher levels of education, but the greater absolute number of children would still probably come from the lower classes, simply because the lower classes have much larger populations than the professional and managerial classes.[8]

Second, the caution needed because of the heritability of intelligence in interpreting indicators of educational mobility for class and status groups is not required in interpreting the mobility indicators for sex and ethnic groups. There is no evidence that the relatively lower educational attainment of the French, the Italians, and women in Canada is the result of relatively lower average ability of the people in these groups. Combined with the modified indicators of inequalities among class and status groups, the indicators of educational mobility for ethnic and sex groups lead to the conclusion that opportunity to secure educational advantages based only on a person's ability to profit from them is still a long way from being realized in Canada.

Occupational Inequalities

With class groups defined by occupational categories, the first type of occupational inequality we shall examine is that arising from intergeneration occupational mobility. Admittedly, the existence of a distinctive pattern of occupational inheritance does not necessarily signify class inequalities in access to certain occupations, just as the absence of differences is not conclusive evidence of equality. A distinctive pattern of movement among occupations between generations might reflect personal preferences or economic imperatives rather than the relative inaccessibility of some occupations. However, evidence regarding occupational mobility between generations indicating that movement from lower class groups to higher class groups is relatively low may reasonably lead us to suspect that class origins rather than personal preferences or economic imperatives have created differential opportunities for access and account for the distinctive pattern of mobility. This is especially likely to be the case in advanced industrialized societies where accepted social custom has little place in dictating occupational choice.

The pattern of intergeneration occupational mobility can be described by comparing the occupational classes of children with those of their parents. Most studies of occupational mobility compare the occupational classes of fathers and sons, and this is the case with the analysis of intergeneration occupational mobility in the province of Quebec by Yves de Jocas and Guy Rocher which we shall review here.[9] Table 5–12 shows the percentage distribution of sons among eight occupational classes for each occupational class of the fathers. The percentages along the diagonal sloping downward from left to right show the extent of occupational inheritance between generations. For example, 47.5 per cent of the sons of fathers who were professionals, proprietors, and managers were themselves professionals, proprietors, or managers; and 26.6 per cent of the sons of farmers were farmers. Percentages above the diagonal show the movement from the lower to the higher classes in Table 5–12 and the percentages below the diagonal show the movement from higher to lower classes. In general, the percentages of upward movement

Table 5–12. *Percentage Distribution of French-Canadian Sons According to the Occupational Classes of Their Fathers*

Occupational class of sons	Occupational class of fathers								Totals, sons	
	Professionals, proprietors, and managers	Semi-professionals and lower administrators	Clerical and sales	Skilled and semi-skilled workers	Unskilled workers	Public service	Personal service	Farmers	Number	Percentage
Professionals, proprietors and managers	47.5	6.4	16.9	4.7	2.9	13.3	4.0	2.1	72	5.8
Semi-professionals and lower administrators	5.0	19.1	11.7	5.5	4.4	3.3	4.0	4.0	70	5.7
Clerical and sales	7.5	14.3	33.8	15.0	10.4	13.3	40.0	2.6	139	11.3
Skilled and semi-skilled workers	22.5	30.2	19.5	40.5	29.3	33.3	16.0	17.9	337	27.3
Unskilled workers	15.0	20.6	11.7	25.2	43.5	23.3	24.0	40.3	413	33.5
Public service	2.5	6.4	3.9	4.7	2.9	6.7	4.0	2.6	44	3.6
Personal service	0	1.6	2.6	3.3	5.5	6.7	4.0	4.0	49	4.0
Farmers	0	1.6	0	1.1	1.2	0	4.0	26.6	110	8.9
TOTALS, fathers										
Number	40	63	77	274	345	30	25	380	1,234	
Percentage	3.2	5.1	6.2	22.2	28.0	2.4	2.0	30.8		100.0

Source: Yves de Jocas and Guy Rocher, "Inter-Generation Occupational Mobility in the Province of Quebec", *Canadian Journal of Economics and Political Science, 27* (February 1957), 61.

(average 12.8 per cent) were higher than those of downward movement (average 7.8 per cent); but it is noteworthy that the percentages of sons who were in the highest classes and whose fathers were in the lower classes were relatively small. For example, only 2.1 per cent of the sons of farmers and 2.9 per cent of the sons of unskilled workers became professionals, proprietors, or managers.

Comparisons between generations using the percentage distribution of sons for each occupational class of the fathers can be misleading when the occupational structure for the generation of the sons is different from that of the fathers. For example, Table 5–12 shows that the working force for the generation of the sons had a larger group of professionals, proprietors, and managers (5.8 per cent of all workers) than that of the fathers (3.2 per cent), a larger group of clerical and sales workers (11.3 per cent compared with 6.2 per cent), and a much smaller group of farmers (8.9 per cent compared with 30.8 per cent). These differences between the generations in occupational structure can be controlled by expressing the proportion of sons in each cell of each occupational class as a ratio of the proportion of all sons in that class. As with the indices of association for intergeneration educational mobility, if chance alone were operating, each of the indices of association for intergeneration occupational mobility would be one; and we could describe the pattern as one of "perfect mobility". If the indices of association are greater than one, then the representation of sons in a given occupation from a given class background is greater than would be expected by chance alone; and, similarly, indices less than one indicate less representation of sons than would be expected by chance alone.

The indices of association for French-Canadian fathers and sons in the cells of Table 5–13 along the diagonal sloping downward from left to right show the degree of occupational inheritance for each class. What can be seen now but was not apparent in Table 5–12 is that the rate of occupational inheritance was much greater for the higher-class groups than it was for the lower ones. The index of association of 8.13 for professionals, proprietors, and managers is the highest by far in the table and indicates a high degree of occupational inheritance for this class. The indices of association above the diagonal in Table 5–13 show the degree of mobility from the lower to the higher occupational classes, and the indices below the diagonal show the degree of downward mobility. In general, upward mobility (the average of the indices equals 1.09) was greater than the downward mobility (the average of the indices equals 0.69); but the relatively low indices of association for professionals, proprietors, and managers whose fathers were unskilled workers (0.50), personal service workers (0.68), and farmers (0.36)

Table 5–13. Indices of Association for the Occupational Classes of French-Canadian Fathers and Sons

Occupational class of sons	Occupational class of fathers							
	Professionals, proprietors, and managers	Semi-professionals and lower administrators	Clerical and sales	Skilled and semi-skilled workers	Unskilled workers	Public service	Personal service	Farmers
Professionals, proprietors and managers	8.13	1.09	2.89	0.81	0.50	2.28	0.68	0.36
Semi-professionals and lower administrators	0.88	3.35	2.06	0.96	0.77	0.59	0.70	0.70
Clerical and sales	0.67	1.27	3.00	1.33	0.93	1.18	3.55	0.23
Skilled and semi-skilled workers	0.82	1.10	0.71	1.48	1.07	1.22	0.59	0.66
Unskilled workers	0.45	0.62	0.35	0.75	1.30	0.70	0.72	1.20
Public service	0.70	1.78	1.09	1.33	0.81	1.87	1.12	0.74
Personal service	0	0.40	0.65	0.83	1.39	1.68	1.01	0.99
Farmers	0	0.18	0	0.12	0.13	0	0.45	2.98

Source: Yves de Jocas and Guy Rocher, "Inter-Generation Occupational Mobility in the Province of Quebec," Canadian Journal of Economics and Political Science, 27 (February 1957), 61.

show the difficulties, noted above, of movement from the lower classes to the highest one.

De Jocas and Rocher also compared the patterns of occupational mobility of French-speaking and English-speaking sons in urban districts of the province of Quebec. The resulting indices of association are shown in Table 5–14, where classes one and two as well as five and seven have been combined because of the small size of the English-speaking sample. The patterns of mobility do not differ very much between the two language groups, although there are some peculiarities, such as the high index of association for English-speaking members of the upper class whose fathers were farmers (2.41), the high occupational inheritance for English-speaking public servants (index of association 4.39), the low occupational inheritance of English-speaking unskilled and personal service workers (0.52), and the high occupational inheritance of French-speaking farmers (6.17). The averages of the indices of association along the diagonals is 2.45 for the English and 2.42 for the French. The average of the indices above the diagonals is 1.17 for the English and 0.97 for the French. Below the diagonals the average is 0.80 for the English and 0.52 for the French.

Indices of association summarizing occupational inheritance for three occupational classes in Quebec are compared with indices for a number of countries in Table 5–15. As in Quebec, the indices of association for the highest occupational stratum are relatively high in other nations, a fact which indicates that occupational inheritance for the elite occupational classes is a cross-national phenomenon. Nonetheless, there is a considerable range among the countries from Puerto Rico to West Germany; and it is noteworthy that the index for Quebec tends towards the upper end of the range.

For all nations except Puerto Rico there is a significant drop in the indices of association between the elites on the one hand and the middle classes and manual workers on the other; and for the nations with the highest elite indices—Canada, West Germany, Sweden, and Denmark—the drop is substantial. Both the middle classes (non-manual workers excluding the elites) and the manual workers have relatively low levels of occupational inheritance; and, compared with the elite classes, the range of variation among nations is narrow.

Two conclusions seem to follow from the evidence in Table 5–15. First, occupational inheritance is greater for elite classes than for any others, a fact that indicates relative inaccessibility of the highest occupational classes and suggests significant inequalities in occupational opportunities. Second, although data for French-speaking Quebec should not perhaps be taken as broadly representative of the nation, the evidence does suggest that occupational inheritance

Table 5-14. *Indices of Association for French-speaking and English-speaking Fathers and Sons in Urban Districts of the Province of Quebec*

Occupational class of sons	French-speaking						English-speaking					
	Professionals, proprietors, managers, semi-professionals, and lower administrators	Clerical and sales	Skilled and semi-skilled workers	Unskilled workers and personal service	Public service	Farmers	Professionals, proprietors, managers, semi-professionals, and lower administrators	Clerical and sales	Skilled and semi-skilled workers	Unskilled workers and personal service	Public service	Farmers
Professionals, proprietors, managers, semi-professionals, and lower administrators	2.81	2.07	0.54	0.33	1.53	0.49	3.26	2.75	1.66	0.69	0.57	2.41
Clerical and sales	0.97	2.03	1.09	0.82	1.32	0.24	1.26	2.39	0.82	1.79	1.49	1.19
Skilled and semi-skilled workers	0.75	0.68	1.39	1.06	0.68	0.93	0.16	0.31	1.38	0.77	0.77	0.46
Unskilled workers and personal service	0.35	0.42	0.86	1.13	0.97	1.44	0.18	0	0.48	0.52	0.58	0.70
Public service	1.43	0.35	0.69	0.56	0.98	1.07	3.70	1.76	0.61	3.52	4.39	0.88
Farmers	0	0	0	0	0	6.17	0	0	0	0	0	2.78

Occupational class of fathers

Source: Yves de Jocas and Guy Rocher, "Inter-Generation Occupational Mobility in the Province of Quebec," *Canadian Journal of Economics and Political Science*, 27 (February 1957), 67.

Equality

Table 5–15. *Indices of Association for Fathers and Sons of the Same Occupational Classes, Selected Nations, 1946–1957**

Country	Elites I and II	Middle classes	Manual workers
Brazil (São Paulo)	4.179	1.613	1.487
Canada (French-Speaking Quebec)**	6.275	1.598	1.108
Denmark	9.559	1.485	1.304
France	5.714	1.821	2.335
Great Britain	5.981	1.442	1.195
Japan	3.277	2.179	1.195
Netherlands	4.805	1.985	1.160
Puerto Rico	2.561	3.100	1.567
Sweden	8.122	1.846	1.197
United States	3.295	1.645	1.462
West Germany	11.087	1.963	1.389

* Years of studies vary. See sources for details.
** Elites I and II includes professionals, proprietors, and managers; middle classes includes semi-professionals, lower administrators, clerical, sales, and public service; and manual workers includes skilled, semi-skilled, and unskilled workers and personal service.
Sources: S. M. Miller, "Comparative Social Mobility", *Current Sociology*, IX (Number 1, 1960), 54, reproduced by permission of Basil Blackwell and Mott Ltd., London; Yves de Jocas and Guy Rocher, "Inter-Generation Occupational Mobility in the Province of Quebec", *Canadian Journal of Economics and Political Science*, 27 (February 1957), 61.

for elite classes is slightly higher in Canada than in some other advanced industrial societies, while that for the middle classes and for manual workers is about the same.[10]

As with class groups, the existence of distinctive occupational patterns for ethnic groups does not necessarily signify unequal access to occupations, since differences in the distribution of members of each ethnic group might simply reflect the preferences and cultural characteristics of people in each ethnic group.[11] Again, however, the concentration of members of one ethnic group in the highest occupational classes and those from another group in the lower classes may be taken as a good indicator of ethnic inequalities. Such inequalities between ethnic groups in their occupational distribution have been found by a number of studies in Canada. Here we shall report the findings of three of them: those of de Jocas and Rocher, the Royal Commission on Bilingualism and Biculturalism, and John Porter.

Table 5–16, from the study by de Jocas and Rocher of French-speaking and English-speaking fathers and sons in urban districts of Quebec, shows a tendency for the English-speaking fathers and

Table 5–16. *Occupational Distribution of French-speaking and English-speaking Fathers and Sons in Urban Districts of the Province of Quebec*

(percentages)

Occupational class	French-speaking fathers	English-speaking fathers	French-speaking sons	English-speaking sons
Professionals, proprietors, and managers	3.2	11.8	6.8	17.3
Semi-professionals and lower administrators	5.6	5.5	5.2	10.0
Clerical and sales	9.0	9.1	15.6	22.7
Skilled and semi-skilled workers	27.4	26.4	34.2	23.6
Unskilled workers	30.5	17.3	26.0	7.3
Public service	3.2	10.9	4.3	12.7
Personal service	3.4	0.9	5.9	5.5
Farmers	17.7	18.2	2.0	0.9
TOTAL	100.0	100.0	100.0	100.0

Source: Yves de Jocas and Guy Rocher, "Inter-Generation Occupational Mobility in the Province of Quebec", *Canadian Journal of Economics and Political Science*, 27 (February 1957), 65.

sons to gravitate to the highest occupational categories, and this tendency seems to be stronger for the sons than for the fathers. In both ethnic groups, the non-manual occupational classes were generally more important for the sons than for their fathers; but the English-speaking sons were much more strongly represented in these classes than the French-speaking sons.

Table 5–17, taken from the Report of the Royal Commission on Bilingualism and Biculturalism, shows the percentage distribution of the male labour force in 1961 among various occupational categories for six ethnic groups. Because they are the occupational groups most associated with the nation's transition to an advanced industrial society, the groups of managers, professionals and technicians, craftsmen and production workers, and labourers are of particular interest.[12] In 1961, the average incomes of managers and professionals were $6,833 and $6,578 respectively while craftsmen were earning $3,723 and unskilled labourers $2,257. The percentage of the Jewish ethnic group working in the two highly paid, white-collar occupational groups in 1961 (53.1 per cent) was higher than that of any other ethnic group, followed by the British (21.4 per cent), the Germans (14.4 per cent), the French (13.5 per cent), the Ukrainians (12.9 per cent), and the Italians (9.4 per cent). In the two lower-paid, blue-collar groups the rank order of the ethnic groups was almost reversed, with 62.9 per cent of the Italian ethnic group working as

Table 5–17. *Percentage Distribution of the Male Labour Force by Ethnic Origin and Occupation, Canada, 1961*

Occupational class	All origins	British	French	German	Italian	Jewish	Ukrainian	Other
Professional and technical	7.6	9.3	5.9	6.1	2.8	13.7	5.8	6.9
Managerial	10.2	12.1	7.6	8.3	6.6	39.4	7.1	9.5
Clerical	6.9	8.2	6.7	5.0	3.7	6.8	5.7	5.1
Sales	5.6	6.6	5.2	4.4	3.2	14.1	3.5	4.2
Service	8.5	9.2	7.7	6.4	8.5	2.6	7.3	9.6
Transportation and communications	7.5	8.0	8.9	6.2	4.7	2.8	6.4	5.5
Craftsmen and production workers	28.8	25.5	31.4	32.5	43.7	15.6	29.6	29.8
Labourers	6.2	4.6	7.5	5.6	19.2	1.1	6.9	6.8
Farmers	12.2	10.8	10.8	21.0	2.7	0.5	23.0	15.8
Other primary	3.9	3.1	5.3	2.3	2.3	0.0	2.5	4.6
Not stated	2.6	2.6	3.0	3.0	2.6	3.4	2.2	2.2
TOTAL, all occupations								
Number	4,705,518	2,071,417	1,303,280	297,003	137,071	49,820	135,987	710,940
Percentage	100.0	100.0	100.0	100.0	100.0	100.0	100.0	100.0

Source: Canada, Royal Commission on Bilingualism and Biculturalism, *Report*, Volume IIIA (Ottawa: Queen's Printer, 1969), p. 38. Reproduced by permission of Information Canada.

skilled or unskilled labourers, followed by those of French (38.9 per cent), German (38.1 per cent), Ukrainian (36.5 per cent), British (30.1 per cent), and Jewish (16.7 per cent) origins.

After examining the occupational distribution of each ethnic group as reported at the censuses for 1931, 1951, and 1961, John Porter concluded that inequalities among ethnic groups in their access to upper-class occupations resulted in a "vertical mosaic" and that the rank order in the hierarchy of ethnic groups persisted over time.[13] Table 5–18 shows Porter's calculation of the percentage points by which members of each ethnic group were over-represented (+) or under-represented (−) relative to the proportion of the total male labour force in six occupational groups for the census years 1931, 1951, and 1961. The algebraic sums of the differences between the percentage distributions of each ethnic group and the percentage distribution of the total male labour force at each census have been added to Table 5–18 to provide a summary measure of the trend of ethnic group inequalities.

The differences in ethnic group representation in the professional and financial occupations which existed in 1931 were still very much in evidence in 1961. Members of the British and Jewish ethnic groups were over-represented in the professional and financial occupations in 1931, 1951, and 1961. Asians, under-represented in these two occupational groups in 1931 and again in 1951, were over-represented in 1961. Slight decreases in the under-representation of Germans, Dutch, Scandinavians, East Europeans, and other Europeans were also registered between 1931 and 1961. In contrast, those of French, Italian, Indian and Eskimo ethnic origins were even more under-represented in the professional and financial occupations in 1961 than they were in 1931. Overall, there was virtually no change in the inequalities with respect to the ethnic group representation in the professional and financial occupations between 1931 and 1961.

In the other occupational groups, inequalities in ethnic group representation were reduced between 1931 and 1961. The overall reductions in ethnic group inequalities were only slight ones in the personal service group between 1931 and 1951 and in the clerical group between 1951 and 1961; but they were very sizable during both periods in the primary and unskilled, agricultural, and other occupations. Except for the position of Asians, however, the reductions in inequalities did not much affect the structure of the vertical mosaic. The over-representation of the British and Jewish ethnic groups in upper-class occupations and their under-representation in lower-class occupations is evident in 1931 and 1961, as is the converse situation of Indians, Eskimos, Italians, and French.

Given the persistence of the vertical mosaic, an obvious trend

Table 5-18. Over-representation and Under-representation of Ethnic Groups in Selected Occupational Groups for the Male Labour Force, Canada, 1931-1961

(percentages)

Occupational group	British	French	German	Italian	Jewish	Dutch	Scandinavian	East European	Other European	Asian	Indian and Eskimo	Occupational group as percentage of total male labour force
1931:												
Professional and financial	+ 1.6	− 0.8	− 2.2	− 3.3	+ 2.2	− 1.1	− 2.9	− 3.9	− 4.4	− 4.3	− 4.5	4.8
Clerical	+ 1.5	− 0.8	− 2.2	− 2.5	+ 0.1	− 1.9	− 2.7	− 3.4	− 3.5	− 3.2	− 3.7	3.8
Personal service	− 0.3	− 0.3	− 1.2	+ 2.1	− 1.2	− 1.5	− 1.5	− 1.1	− 1.7	+27.8	− 3.1	3.5
Primary and unskilled	− 4.6	+ 3.3	− 5.3	+26.1	−14.5	− 4.8	+ 1.4	+12.4	+35.8	+10.2	+45.3	17.7
Agriculture	− 3.0	+ 0.1	+21.1	−27.6	−32.4	+18.5	+19.8	+14.5	+ 5.8	−20.9	− 4.9	34.0
All others	+ 4.8	− 1.5	−10.2	+ 5.2	+45.8	− 9.2	−14.1	−18.5	−20.4	− 9.6	−29.1	36.2
Algebraic sum of differences*	15.8	6.8	42.2	66.8	96.2	37.0	42.4	53.8	71.6	76.0	90.6	0.0
1951:												
Professional and financial	+ 1.6	− 1.5	− 2.2	− 3.1	+ 4.2	− 1.7	− 2.1	− 2.9	− 2.4	− 2.8	− 5.2	5.9
Clerical	+ 1.6	− 0.8	− 2.5	− 1.7	0.0	− 2.4	− 2.8	− 2.8	− 2.5	− 2.9	− 5.2	5.9
Personal service	− 0.3	− 0.2	− 1.2	+ 2.0	− 1.4	− 1.2	− 1.0	+ 0.6	+ 2.0	+23.9	− 0.6	3.4
Primary and unskilled	− 2.2	+ 3.0	− 3.7	+ 9.6	−11.5	− 1.7	+ 0.5	+ 2.3	+ 5.7	− 1.9	+47.0	13.3
Agriculture	− 3.2	− 0.3	+19.1	−14.7	−18.7	+17.3	+14.7	+11.2	+ 3.4	− 8.7	− 7.8	19.4
All others	+ 2.5	− 0.2	− 9.5	+ 7.9	+27.4	−10.3	− 9.3	− 8.4	− 6.2	− 7.6	−28.2	52.1

	11.4	6.0	38.2	39.0	63.2	34.6	30.4	28.2	22.2	47.8	94.0	0.0
Algebraic sum of differences*												
1961:												
Professional and financial	+ 2.0	− 1.9	− 1.8	− 5.2	+ 7.4	− 0.9	− 1.9	− 1.2	− 1.1	+ 1.7	− 7.5	8.6
Clerical	+ 1.3	− 0.2	− 1.8	− 3.2	− 0.1	− 1.7	− 2.4	− 1.7	− 2.0	− 1.5	− 5.9	6.9
Personal service	− 0.9	− 0.2	− 0.7	+ 2.9	− 2.4	− 0.5	− 1.1	+ 0.9	+ 5.1	+19.1	+ 1.3	4.3
Primary and unskilled	− 2.3	+ 2.8	− 2.1	+11.5	− 8.9	− 2.0	− 0.2	0.0	+ 1.8	− 3.6	+34.7	10.0
Agriculture	− 1.5	− 1.4	+ 8.8	− 9.5	−11.7	+10.3	+10.6	+ 6.9	+ 0.6	− 6.5	+ 6.9	12.2
All others	+ 1.4	+ 0.9	− 2.4	+ 3.5	+15.7	− 5.2	− 5.0	− 4.9	− 4.4	− 9.1	−29.5	58.0
Algebraic sum of differences*	9.4	7.4	17.6	35.8	46.2	20.6	21.2	15.6	15.0	41.5	85.8	0.0

* The algebraic sum of the differences between the percentage distribution of each ethnic group and the percentage distribution of the total male labour force.

Source: John Porter, *The Vertical Mosaic* (Toronto: University of Toronto Press, 1965), p. 87.

towards a reduction of occupational inequalities among ethnic groups is revealed in the algebraic sums of the differences between the percentage distributions of each ethnic group and the percentage distribution of the total male labour force at each census. If ethnicity were declining as a factor in occupational choices, we would expect the sums of differences to decrease towards zero as the percentage distribution of each ethnic group became more and more like the percentage distribution in the total male labour force. Table 5–18 shows that decreases were registered for nine of the eleven ethnic groups between 1931 and 1961, ranging from a modest reduction for the British groups (from 15.8 to 9.4) to an outstanding drop for the other European groups (from 71.6 to 15.0). The French and the Indian and Eskimo ethnic groups were the two exceptions to the general trend towards reductions in inequalities, but in the case of the French ethnic group (for which the sum of differences actually increased between 1951 and 1961), the percentage distribution was the one closest to the national average in each census year. The overall trend is important because some increases in opportunities for occupational choice evidently are occurring, but the speed of these changes should not be overstated. At the rate of reduction which prevailed between 1931 and 1961 for the nine ethnic groups showing decreases, it would be sometime around the end of the next century before the ethnic factor disappeared from occupational choices.

The vertical mosaic appears to have more or less the same structure in each province as it has in the nation at large. In 1961, for example, in each province and in Canada generally the French ethnic group had smaller than average proportions in the managerial, professional, clerical, and sales occupations; and it had greater than average proportions in the craftsmen, labourer, and primary (non-farming) occupations in all but one of the provinces.[14] Conversely, the British ethnic groups were over-represented in all provinces among professionals, clerks, and salesmen, and in all but one for the managerial class; while in the three blue-collar occupational groups they were under-represented in all but one of the provinces. Apparently, then, variations in industrial structure among the provinces have little effect on the relative positions of the ethnic groups with respect to their distributions among occupational classes.

Evidence of general differences in the occupational choices of men and women is shown in Figures 5–4 to 5–7. As Figure 5–4 shows, the participation of women in the labour force increased steadily after 1911 from 13.2 per cent of the labour force fifteen years of age and over to 27.3 per cent in 1961; but this increase in the percentage of the labour force which was female resulted mainly from an increase in the percentage of the white-collar occupational

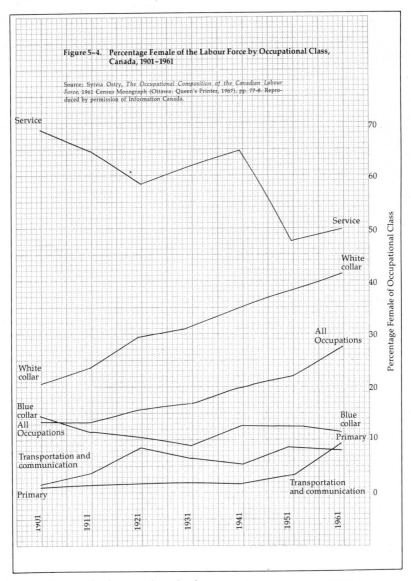

Figure 5-4. Percentage Female of the Labour Force by Occupational Class, Canada, 1901-1961

Source: Sylvia Ostry, *The Occupational Composition of the Canadian Labour Force*, 1961 Census Monograph (Ottawa: Queen's Printer, 1967), pp. 77-8. Reproduced by permission of Information Canada.

labour force which was female from 20.6 per cent in 1901 to 41.3 per cent in 1961.

Within the white-collar class, no change occurred in the percentage of the professional occupations which was female and only modest increases took place in the proprietory, managerial, and financial occupations. The change in the sex composition of the white-collar occupations was mainly the result of, first, a change in the clerical occupations from a predominantly male occupational group (only 22.1 per cent female in 1901) to a predominantly female

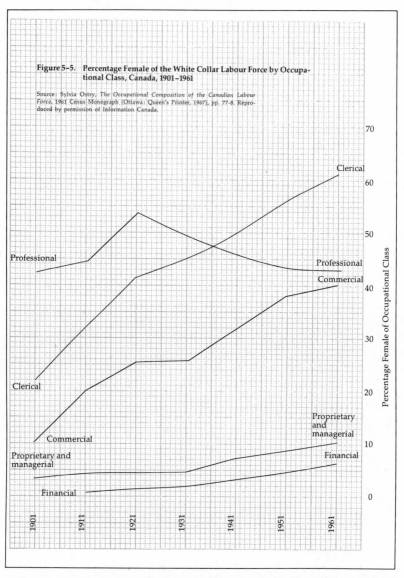

Figure 5-5. Percentage Female of the White Collar Labour Force by Occupational Class, Canada, 1901–1961

Source: Sylvia Ostry, The Occupational Composition of the Canadian Labour Force, 1961 Census Monograph (Ottawa: Queen's Printer, 1967), pp. 77-8. Reproduced by permission of Information Canada.

occupational group (61.5 per cent female in 1961) and, second, an almost equally marked change in the sex composition of the commercial occupations (from 10.4 per cent female in 1901 to 40.3 per cent in 1961).

The substantial increase in the importance of white-collar occupations in the provision of employment for women is indicated in Figure 5–6. While the service and blue-collar occupations declined in importance and there was little change in the importance of primary and transportation and communications occupations, the

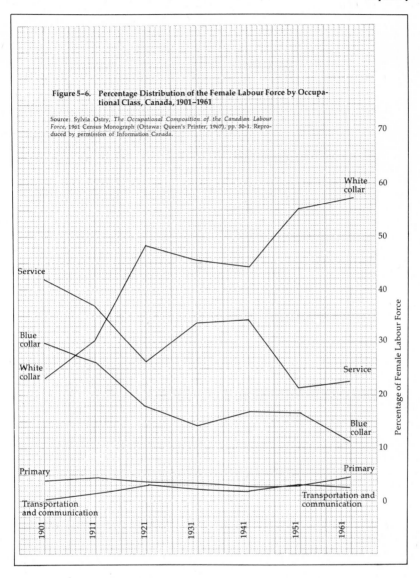

Figure 5–6. Percentage Distribution of the Female Labour Force by Occupational Class, Canada, 1901–1961

Source: Sylvia Ostry, *The Occupational Composition of the Canadian Labour Force*, 1961 Census Monograph (Ottawa: Queen's Printer, 1967), pp. 50-1. Reproduced by permission of Information Canada.

white-collar occupations which employed 23.6 per cent of the female labour force in 1901 became the most important occupational class for women, employing 57.3 per cent of the female labour force in 1961.

A comparison of Figures 5–6 and 5–7 indicates that the occupational distribution of the male labour force also changed considerably between 1901 and 1961, but in a direction opposite to that of the female labour force. The male labour force in 1901 was concentrated in the primary occupations (50.5 per cent), mainly agriculture, and

221

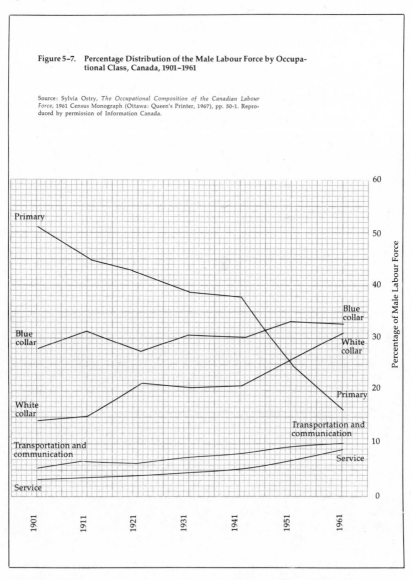

Figure 5–7. Percentage Distribution of the Male Labour Force by Occupational Class, Canada, 1901–1961

Source: Sylvia Ostry, *The Occupational Composition of the Canadian Labour Force*, 1961 Census Monograph (Ottawa: Queen's Printer, 1967), pp. 50-1. Reproduced by permission of Information Canada.

in blue-collar occupations (27.5 per cent). The secular decline in the importance of primary occupations to 16.1 per cent of the male labour force in 1961, the continuing importance of blue-collar occupations, and the increase in the importance of white-collar occupations had the effect of making the distribution of the male labour force in 1961 more balanced than it had been in 1901. In contrast, as Figure 5–6 shows, the distribution of the female labour force had become much more concentrated in one occupational division, the white-collar occupations, than it had been in 1901.

The general changes in the occupational choices of women result from two factors which work to ensure a general pattern of occupational segregation between men and women. First, many occupations, such as those of housekeeper, domestic, waitress, hairdresser, school teacher, nurse, dietitian, and home economist are considered female occupations because they are related to the customary functions of women in the home. Second, a few occupations, such as those of secretary, stenographer, typist, telephone operator, and sales clerk, have come to be considered female as a result of changes in the sex composition of the labour force. Sylvia Ostry has remarked,

> Although there are few jobs today earmarked "for men only", some occupations can still be characterized as primarily "women's work". Traditionally, women have been concerned with the care and training of children, cooking, cleaning, making and repairing clothes, ministering to the sick. Over time, as the performance of many of these functions has shifted from the home, they have continued to be regarded as predominantly "women's work". Women's activities in the world of work are, in other words, heavily concentrated in a few occupations and—with some notable exceptions—most of these are an extension of her traditional functions in the home. The major exceptions are, of course, the white-collar jobs: many clerical and some sales occupations are largely female preserves.[15]

The list of twenty-five leading occupations of the female labour force in 1961 illustrates the extent to which home-based functions have combined with modern clerical and commercial functions to provide the bulk of employment opportunities for women. The majority of the female labour force is located in predominantly female occupations which derive either from customary domestic segregation (maids, teachers, waitresses, and nurses) or from modern bureaucratic segregation (stenographers, sales clerks, and typists). It is also interesting to note that the only professional occupations listed in Table 5–19 are teaching and nursing, two customarily female occupations, and that in 1961 these two professions constituted three-quarters of the female work force in the professional field.

Sex differences in economic opportunity are evident not only in occupational choice but also in economic achievement as measured by income. Both women and men have always produced some goods and services without pay; but, for women, the unpaid production of goods and services has been and continues to be a major economic

Table 5–19. *Twenty-five Leading* Occupations of the Female Labour Force Fifteen Years of Age and Over, Canada, 1961***

Occupational class	Number of women	Per cent of total females in labour force	Per cent female of total in occupational class
Stenographers	160,666	9.11	97.2
Sales clerks	133,234	7.55	58.0
Maids and related services	120,161	6.81	88.1
School teachers	118,594	6.72	70.7
Farm labourers	66,081	3.75	29.7
Waitresses	61,802	3.50	78.6
Graduate nurses	59,201	3.36	96.2
Other production process and related workers	51,535	2.92	29.0
Nursing assistants and aides	49,267	2.79	78.9
Typists and clerk-typists	48,744	2.76	95.5
Telephone operators	33,682	1.91	95.2
Janitors and building cleaners	31,826	1.80	31.5
Cooks	24,528	1.39	49.5
Barbers, hairdressers, and manicurists	23,289	1.32	55.2
Owners and managers—retail trade	23,264	1.32	15.0
Nurses in training	22,667	1.29	98.6
Launderers and dry cleaners	22,547	1.28	71.4
Office appliance operators	22,367	1.27	78.8
Labourers (mainly in trade and manufacturing)	20,925	1.19	6.7
Owners and managers— community, business, and personal service	18,622	1.06	22.2
Millers, bakers, brewers, and related food workers	16,322	0.93	21.4
Dressmakers, seamstresses (not in factory)	15,504	0.88	95.8
Spinners, weavers, knitters, and related workers	14,571	0.83	43.1
Baby sitters	12,194	0.69	97.4
Housekeepers (except household), matrons, and stewards	12,171	0.69	75.1
TOTAL	1,183,764	67.12	

* Ten thousand or more women.

** Excluding Yukon and Northwest Territories.

Source: Sylvia Ostry, *The Occupaˑional Composition of the Canadian Labour Force*, Dominion Bureau of Statistics, 1961 Census Monograph (Ottawa: Queen's Printer, 1967), p. 76. Reproduced by permission of Information Canada.

activity.[16] More goods and services are produced without pay in the home than anywhere else, and most of them are produced by women. Women in the labour force spend a significant proportion of their time on household duties, and over half the adult female population are employed full-time in the care of their families and homes. A study for the Royal Commission on the Status of Women in Canada estimated that the unpaid work of housewives amounted to 11 per cent of the gross national product. In addition to unpaid services in the home, women also contribute substantially to the goods and services produced without pay in many family enterprises and volunteer associations.

In paid employment, the incomes of women are usually less than those of men. Table 5–20 gives the percentage distribution of male and female workers by income groups and occupational groups for 1969. In every occupational group, regardless of the measure of central tendency which is used, the average income of male workers was considerably higher than that of female workers.

The second test for measuring the advance towards a full realization of equality is the opportunity to compete for occupational positions on the basis of completing the necessary educational preparations. The question which obviously arises is to what extent the indicators of occupational inequalities set forth in this section show real discrimination in occupational mobility and to what extent they simply reflect the inequalities of educational attainment described in the previous section.

A detailed accounting for inequalities in intergeneration occupational mobility remains to be carried out, but the evidence of inequalities in intergeneration occupational mobility is consistent with our finding in the preceding section of inequalities in the educational attainment of the children of parents belonging to different class and status groups. It suggests that most of the differences in occupational mobility not explained by the heritability of intelligence may be explained by class and status differences in educational attainment. Two studies of ethnicity and economic achievement in Canada have also presented persuasive arguments that differences in the average educational attainment of ethnic groups explain much of the occupational and income differences between them.

In their comparison of the French and British ethnic groups arising out of a study for the Royal Commission on Bilingualism and Biculturalism, Raynauld, Marion, and Béland noted that among the university-educated of both ethnic groups the same proportion (70 per cent) was in the managerial and professional occupations.[17] They then advanced the hypothesis that the occupational distribution of both groups would be very similar if Canadians of French and

Table 5–20. Average Incomes and Percentage Distributions of Male and Female Workers by Income Groups and Occupation, Canada, 1969*

Income group (dollars)	Managerial		Professional and technical		Clerical		Sales		Services and recreation		Miners, craftsmen and production workers	
	Male	Female	Male	Female	Male	Female	Male	Female	Male	Female	Male	Female
Under 1,000	0.8	8.5	1.4	9.8	8.4	11.3	15.0	35.3	7.1	32.2	2.5	14.1
1,000—1,999	1.4	16.3	2.9	9.9	4.5	12.6	5.2	19.8	6.0	20.9	3.7	16.3
2,000—2,999	2.6	8.9	3.0	6.2	4.7	13.0	5.2	15.3	7.8	18.1	5.2	22.0
3,000—3,999	4.4	11.6	4.7	8.4	7.7	22.5	4.9	16.4	10.6	15.7	7.3	20.1
4,000—4,999	5.6	15.7	5.7	12.5	11.3	21.0	7.6	5.5	15.1	8.4	9.1	15.0
5,000—5,999	7.8	16.0	6.0	14.3	12.7	11.3	10.9	3.2	15.9	2.6	13.7	9.2
6,000—6,999	9.0	6.4	8.4	13.9	15.9	4.5	11.0	3.0	10.4	0.9	15.3	1.7
7,000—7,999	11.1	6.8	9.1	9.3	13.7	2.5	10.4	0.3	8.6	0.7	13.8	1.3
8,000—9,999	15.4	5.3	16.9	8.4	12.6	0.9	13.0	0.0	12.2	0.3	18.8	0.2
10,000—14,999	25.1	3.4	28.4	6.4	7.7	0.2	12.1	0.9	5.2	0.3	9.6	0.0
15,000 and over	16.8	1.0	13.4	1.2	0.7	0.1	4.8	0.3	0.9	0.0	0.8	0.0
TOTALS	100.0	100.0	100.0	100.0	100.0	100.0	100.0	100.0	100.0	100.0	100.0	100.0
Mean income	10,767	4,506	10,080	5,188	5,851	3,477	6,497	2,153	5,489	2,083	6,524	2,920
Median income	8,857	4,194	8,950	5,226	6,043	3,659	6,121	1,711	5,203	1,821	6,542	2,909
Mean earnings**	9,873	4,262	9,622	5,012	5,495	3,352	6,071	1,841	5,104	1,890	6,181	2,841
Mean earnings of full-year workers***	10,125	4,909	10,495	5,809	6,391	4,120	7,059	2,648	5,840	2,588	6,024	3,633

* Transporation and communication, farmers, loggers, fishermen, and labourers have been omitted because the female samples were too small for reliable estimates.

** Earnings include wages and salaries and net income from self-employment.

*** These are workers who reported having worked fifty to fifty-two weeks.

Source: Statistics Canada, *Income Distributions by Size in Canada 1969* (Ottawa: Information Canada, 1972), Table 37, p. 54. Reproduced by permission of Information Canada.

British origin had received equivalent schooling. The hypothesis was tested by giving those of French origin a hypothetical level of schooling equivalent to that of the British and recalculating French participation in the labour force on this revised educational basis. Table 5–21 shows that the overall difference between the hypothetical distribution for the French and the actual distribution for the British is much less than that between the actual distributions for the two ethnic groups. If the labour force of French origin had a level of schooling equivalent to the British, the observed differences in the occupational distribution of the two groups would be reduced by about 60 per cent.

In another study carried out for the Royal Commission on Bi-

Table 5–21. *Influence of Schooling Level on Access to Occupations for British and French Ethnic Groups, Canada, 1961*

| Occupational class | Percentage distribution of non-agricultural labour force of French and British origins | | |
	Actual labour force of French origin given present schooling	Hypothetical labour force of French origin given schooling equivalent to British ethnic group	Actual labour force of British origin
Professional and technical	6.1	10.5	10.4
Managerial	8.9	10.9	13.9
Clerical	7.7	10.3	9.5
Sales	6.1	7.2	7.7
Service	7.7	7.5	8.8
Transport and communication	10.3	9.1	9.2
Craftsmen and production workers	36.7	31.4	28.4
Labourers	8.2	6.4	4.8
Farmers	0.4	0.3	0.9
Other primary	6.2	4.4	4.6
Not stated	1.8	1.9	1.8
All occupations	100.0	100.0	100.0
Algebraic sum of the differences between the British and the French groups	28.7	11.3	

Source: Andre Raynauld, Gérald Marion, and Richard Béland "La Repartition des Revenus Selon Les Groups Ethniques au Canada", cited in the Royal Commission on Bilingualism and Biculturalism, *Report*, Volume IIIA (Ottawa: Queen's Printer, 1969), p. 47. Reproduced by permission of Information Canada.

lingualism and Biculturalism, Donald Armstrong attempted to hold the effects of education constant by comparing university graduates in architecture, science, and engineering, since in these fields the educational backgrounds of those from French-language and other universities would be very similar. The average income of French Canadians was found to be slightly lower than that of English-speaking Canadians; but Armstrong's analysis indicated that the closer he was able to come to comparing like with like in terms of education, the better French Canadians did compared with other ethnic groups.

The largest and most homogeneous group of French-speaking and other Canadians which Armstrong studied was engineering, particularly civil engineering. From his analysis of their economic experience, which is summarized in part in Tables 5–22 and 5–23, Armstrong advanced five conclusions:

1. *Taken together, the French-Canadian managers and professional engineers under the age of fifty have an income advantage over all other groups.*
2. *When the managers in this group are considered separately, the French Canadians are at an advantage in obtaining management positions, but they are at a disadvantage with regard to income ranging from zero for people who graduated in the last ten years to 3.5 per cent for people who graduated ten to twenty-five years ago.*
3. *French-speaking civil engineers over the age of fifty, that is, those graduating before 1940, are at a 6 per cent income disadvantage taking managers and professional people together, whereas the managers in this group are at an income disadvantage of about 10 per cent. However, if we look at those who have gone on to do graduate work (most of which would be done in English), the income disadvantage of this older group disappears both in management and in the management plus professional groups taken together.*
4. *Considering all age groups together, 100 French-Canadian civil engineers chosen at random would earn the same number of management dollars as 100 non-French-Canadian civil engineers.*
5. *In accounting for achievement, ethnicity is not nearly so important as education. The average university graduate of any ethnic group in Canada will probably earn about the same pay as the average graduate of any other ethnic group with the same training.*[18]

Table 5–22. *Average Salaries of Engineering Graduates of French-language and Other Universities Working in Management and Non-management Positions, Quebec, 1961–1963*

Year of graduation	Non-management				Management			
	All branches		Civil engineers		All branches		Civil engineers	
	French	Others	French	Others	French	Others	French	Others
Pre 1940	12,212	11,865	12,014	12,574	14,173	18,558	14,700	17,795
1940–1944	12,815	11,387	14,190	11,902	14,470	15,809	14,670	15,216
1945–1949	11,366	11,074	13,054	11,845	12,645	13,028	12,318	13,438
1950–1954	9,942	9,646	10,738	9,922	10,650	11,463	10,301	11,056
1955–1959	7,700	7,665	8,142	7,965	8,274	9,592	8,650	8,833
1960	6,347	6,289	6,650	6,500	6,323	6,571	6,388	5,750
1961	6,232	6,287	6,561	6,571	6,227	7,357	6,500	7,166
1962	6,166	6,862	6,730	11,750	6,166	6,000	7,500	5,500

Source: Donald E. Armstrong, *Education and Economic Achievement*, Documents of the Royal Commission on Bilingualism and Biculturalism, Number 7 (Ottawa: Information Canada, 1970), pp. 39, 41, 79, 80. Reproduced by permission of Information Canada.

Table 5–23. *Percentages of Engineering Graduates of French-language and Other Universities Working in Management Positions, Quebec, 1962–1964*

Year of graduation	All branches		Civil engineering	
	French	Others	French	Others
Pre 1940	58	53	61	52
1940–1944	47	42	49	47
1945–1949	42	37	41	34
1950–1954	28	24	33	31
1955–1959	19	10	22	17
1960	10	7	13	10
1961	8	5	9	10
1962	7	9	7	14

Source: Donald E. Armstrong, *Education and Economic Achievement*, Documents of the Royal Commission on Bilingualism and Biculturalism, Number 7 (Ottawa: Information Canada, 1970), pp. 79, 80. Reproduced by permission of Information Canada.

Armstrong concluded that the main explanation of the economic achievement of an ethnic group in Canada must be the amount and kind of education its members have obtained. According to him, "the policy implication is equally clear. If any ethnic group wishes to improve its total economic achievement it must provide its members with the amount and kind of education appropriate to the needs of a modern, progressing economy."[19]

Equality

Table 5–24. *Sex Ratios in Annual Earnings, Adjusted and Unadjusted Data for 256 Major Occupations, Canada, 1961*

| Occupation | Ratio of average annual earnings of female wage earners to earnings of male wage earners | | | |
	All wage earners	Full-year wage earners	Full-year wage earners adjusted* Female weights	Male weights
Managerial	48.1	51.6	67.3	63.1
Professional and technical	43.3	61.2	66.9	74.1
Clerical	60.8	74.1	90.0	87.2
Sales	35.2	44.8	70.8	67.4
Service and recreation	47.9	47.2	76.9	61.9
Transportation and communication	62.2	67.4	**	**
Farmers and farm workers	43.3	59.6	51.2	52.0
Craftsmen, production, and related workers	50.1	55.7	115.1	105.3
Labourers	67.2	66.9	98.1	86.2
All occupations	54.2	59.3	85.0	77.5

* Adjusted for male–female differences in occupational distribution, age, and education.

** Excluded because of the very different distribution of male and female workers. Almost 94 per cent of women but less than 1 per cent of men in this class were in one occupation: telephone operators.

Source: Sylvia Ostry, *The Female Worker in Canada*, Dominion Bureau of Statistics, 1961 Census Monograph (Ottawa: Queen's Printer, 1968), pp. 41, 44. Reproduced by permission of Information Canada.

The combined evidence of occupational and economic inequalities between men and women indicate that inequalities in economic achievement continue to exist even where educational attainment is relatively equal. Table 5–20 showed wide differences in income between men and women in 1969 in every occupational class. This same pattern of differences in economic achievement can be seen in the first column of Table 5–24. The average annual earnings of female wage earners in 1961 for all occupations were 54.2 per cent of those for male wage earners, varying from 35.2 per cent in the sales occupations to 67.2 per cent for labourers.

The percentages shown in Table 5–24 overstate sex differences in earnings because they do not take account of differences between men and women with respect to such factors as hours worked, occupational deployment, educational qualifications, and work experience. In an attempt to specify more exactly what were the pay differences between men and women for comparable work performed in 1961, Sylvia Ostry adjusted the 1961 average for these four factors.

First, women on average worked fewer hours per year in paid work than men, and this reduced their annual earnings relative to men. When full-year wage earners only were compared, the sex ratio increased from 54.2 per cent to 59.3 per cent, varying from 44.8 per cent in the sales occupations to 74.1 per cent in the clerical occupations.

Second, the occupational distribution of women in the labour force reduced their average earnings relative to those of men, because they tended to work in low-paid occupations. Sex differences in occupational distribution can be adjusted by weighting the earnings of both sexes according to the distribution of females among the occupations or according to the distribution of males among the

Table 5–25. *Summary of Sex Ratios in Annual Earnings by Adjustment Factors, Canada, 1961*

	Sex ratio	
Adjustment factor	Female weights[1]	Male weights[2]
Unadjusted	54.2	
Annual hours worked[3]	59.3	
Occupational distribution	67.2	65.6
Age[4]	72.5	68.5
Education[5]	79.2	74.1
Age and education	85.0	77.5

1. $\Sigma p_f q_f / \Sigma p_m q_f$ where p_m and p_f are the mean earnings of full-time, full-year males and females respectively in each of the 256 occupational classes and q_f is the proportion of females in each of the selected classes.

2. $\Sigma p_f q_m / \Sigma p_m q_m$ where q_m is the proportion of men in each of the selected occupational classes.

3. Ratio based on annual wages and salaries of wage earners who had worked forty-nine to fifty-two weeks, usually thirty-five hours or more per week.

4. Earnings of females in each occupational class were multiplied by the ratio of median male age to median female age, and new weighted averages calculated.

5. Earnings of females were adjusted by the ratio of male educational level to female educational level. The indicator of educational level used was the per cent of the work force having completed high school education or better.

Source: Sylvia Ostry, *The Female Worker in Canada*, Dominion Bureau of Statistics, 1961 Census Monograph (Ottawa: Queen's Printer, 1968), p. 43. Reproduced by permission of Information Canada.

occupations. The results differ slightly, depending on whether the female or the male occupational distribution is used to weight earnings; but, if the occupational distributions of the female and male work force had been identical in 1961, the sex ratio in earnings for full-time wage earners would have been 65.6 to 67.2 per cent.

Third, the longer work experience of men presumably accounts for some differences in annual earnings between men and women in 1961. In the absence of data on the length of work experience, age was substituted as an adjustive weight. In 1961, men were older on the average and, therefore, presumably more experienced in their jobs than women. Adjusting for these age differences between men and women raised the sex ratio by another 2.9 to 5.3 percentage points.

Fourth, the greater educational attainment of men also accounts for differences in annual earnings between men and women in 1961. By weighting female earnings to correspond to the superior male educational levels, in addition to taking account of differences in occupational distribution, the sex ratios were increased from 65.6 and 67.2 to 74.1 and 79.2 per cent.

Finally, the effects of age and sex differences were found to be additive. When adjustments for these two factors were combined with adjustments for annual hours worked and occupational distribution, the overall result was to increase the ratio of average annual earnings of female wage earners from 54.2 per cent of the average annual earnings of male wage earners to 77.5 to 85.0 per cent of the average annual earnings of male wage earners.

The combined effects of the adjustments were quite different in different occupational classes. For the two manual occupational classes of craftsmen and labourers, differences between men and women disappeared completely; and the sex ratios after adjustment were also very high for the clerical occupations. In the managerial, professional, sales, service and recreation, and farming occupational classes, however, the sex differentials in earnings remained substantial even after accounting for differences in the work year, occupational deployment, age, and education. Ostry concludes,

> the adjustments which were made were very rough—
> distributional differences other than occupational were not
> taken into account nor were a number of important
> "quality" factors such as those stemming from male–female
> differences in turnover, work experience, absenteeism, etc.
> More detailed adjustments would no doubt have reduced
> the "unexplained" gap even further. However it seems
> clear that some portion of the residual differential stemmed

from "discrimination", i.e. from the fact that women were paid less than men for comparable work.[20]

Political Inequalities

The distribution of political power results inevitably in social stratification; and, as Gaetano Mosca remarked, every political community has its ruling class and its ruled.

Among the constant facts and tendencies that are to be found in all political organisms, one is so obvious that it is apparent to the most casual eye. In all societies—from societies that are very meagerly developed and have barely attained the dawnings of civilization, down to the most advanced and powerful societies—two classes of people appear—a class that rules and a class that is ruled. The first class, always the less numerous, performs all the political functions, monopolizes power and enjoys the advantages that power brings, whereas the second, the more numerous class, is directed and controlled by the first, in a manner that is now more or less legal, now more or less arbitrary and violent, and supplies the first, in appearance at least, with material means of subsistence and with the instrumentalities that are essential to the vitality of the political organism.[21]

The seeming inevitability of inequalities in the distribution of political power raises several questions concerning access to political power which have preoccupied students of politics over many centuries. Who are the rulers in the community? Are there important differences between rulers and ruled? Is the ruling class homogeneous or are there differences among the rulers? What is the relationship between rulers and ruled?

Such questions must be asked to understand the provision of the political good equality because positions of great political power are relatively few and highly valued and because we expect people in positions of power to use them to accomplish the goals they prefer. The perception of the problems of the community, the definition of the issues arising from them, the consideration of acceptable solutions, and the manner of implementing solutions to the problems all are affected by which individuals in the community are doing the perceiving, considering, deciding, and implementing. The life experiences and social values of people in Canada are likely to differ between citizen and outsider, native and foreign-born, rich and poor, French-speaking and English-speaking, easterner and westerner;

and we can expect that the issues advocated by leaders of interest groups and the decisions taken by politicians and administrators will reflect these varying life experiences and social values.

Questions as to how representative the ruling class of a political community is with respect to important social groups are particularly relevant in a political democracy, the code of morality of which includes the ideal of universal participation. As with occupation and education, any social group the members of which have persistent difficulties in gaining access to political power will probably find itself relatively deprived with respect to the material goods and services allocated to citizens through the political system and certainly deprived with respect to the esteem and the self-esteem enjoyed by the members of the group. In a political democracy, political equality is an especially salient aspect of general equality.

Studies of political participation in several countries have shown that membership in different class and status groups is associated with different levels of political activity. No matter how class is measured, these studies consistently show that higher-class persons are more likely to participate in politics than lower-class persons.[22] To illustrate this point, the relationship between self-class identification and campaign activity for a 1956 American sample is shown in Table 5–56. With a rise in class, the percentage of non-voters declines and the percentage of those most active rises correspondingly.

A similar tendency for campaign activity to increase with rising

Table 5–26. Campaign Activity by Self-class Identification, United States, 1956

(percentages)

Degree of campaign activity	Average working class	Upper working class	Average middle class	Upper middle class	Total
Non-voting	34	16	15	12	25
Voting, discussing politics, displaying button or sticker	58	68	65	57	61
Voting and donating money, attending meetings, working for party, or joining a club	8	16	20	31	14
TOTAL	100	100	100	100	100

Source: Lester W. Milbrath, Political Participation © 1965 by Rand McNally and Company, Chicago, pp. 117, 155–6.

Table 5–27. *Campaign Activity by Self-class Identification,
Canada, 1965*

(percentages)

Campaign activity	Lower class	Working class	Middle class	Upper middle class
Low	84	77	71	58
Medium	12	19	23	35
High	4	4	5	6
TOTAL*	100	100	99	99

* Totals may not add to 100 per cent because of rounding errors.

Source: Rick Van Loon, "Political Participation in Canada: the 1965 Elections", *Canadian Journal of Political Science*, III (September 1970), 384.

social class can be seen in Table 5–27 for a 1965 sample of the Canadian electorate. The percentage with low campaign activity (voting and discussing politics) declined from 84 per cent in the lower class to 58 per cent in the upper middle class, while the percentage with medium activity (not only voting and discussing politics but also trying to convince someone how to vote or perhaps belonging to a political party or working during an election) increased from 12 per cent to 35 per cent.

A tendency for those with higher education to be more likely to participate in politics has also been found in many western countries.[23] After a comparative study of political orientations in the United States, Britain, West Germany, Italy, and Mexico, Almond and Verba concluded that education had a stronger effect on patterns of political participation than income or occupation. Their evidence indicated substantial cross-national uniformity in the political orientations of the more educated person:

(1) *the more educated person is more aware of the impact of government on the individual than is the person of less education . . . ;*
(2) *the more educated individual is more likely to report that he follows politics and pays attention to election campaigns than is the individual of less education . . . ;*
(3) *the more educated individual has more political information . . . ;*
(4) *the more educated individual has opinions on a wider range of political subjects; the focus of his attention to politics is wider . . . ;*
(5) *the more educated individual is more likely to engage in political discussion . . . ;*

(6) *the more educated individual feels free to discuss politics with a wider range of people . . . . Those with less education are more likely to report that there are many people with whom they avoid such discussions;*

(7) *the more educated individual is more likely to consider himself capable of influencing the government; this is reflected both in responses to questions on what one could do about an unjust law . . . and in respondents' scores on the subjective competence scale . . . ;*

(8) *the more educated individual is more likely to be a member—and an active member—of some organization . . . and*

(9) *the more educated individual is more likely to express confidence in his social environment: to believe that other people are trustworthy and helpful . . . .*[24]

Table 5–28 shows the connection between education and voting in federal elections found in the 1965 Canadian survey. In view of the more general findings of Almond and Verba, the results of the Canadian study should not be surprising: the greater the number of years of education the respondent had, the more likely he was to have voted in federal elections. The positive connection between education and turnout can perhaps be seen most easily by noting that the pattern of turnout for those with nine to eleven years of education is almost the same as the national average. For those with more than eleven years of education, the percentage voting

Table 5–28. Voting Frequency in Federal Elections by Educational Attainment, Canada, 1965

(percentages)

Frequency of voting in federal elections	Years of education						
	0–5	6–8	9–11	12–13	14-16	Over 17	National average
All	51	50	55	63	64	69	56
Most	36	26	29	25	26	16	27
Some	11	20	13	8	8	12	13
None	1	4	3	4	3	4	3
TOTAL*	99	100	100	100	101	101	99

* Totals may not add to 100 per cent because of rounding errors.

Source: Rick Van Loon, "Political Participation in Canada: the 1965 Election", *Canadian Journal of Political Science,* III (September 1970), 385.

in all federal elections (63 to 69 per cent) is markedly above the national average while the percentage of those voting in most or some elections (28 to 34 per cent) is below it. Conversely, for those with less than nine years of education, the percentage voting in all federal elections (50 or 51 per cent) is below the national average, and the percentage of those voting in most or some elections (46 or 47 per cent) is above it.

The evidence from sample surveys on the association between the class and status position of citizens and the extent of their political participation leads clearly to the conclusion that, in general, there are important socio-economic differences between people at different levels of participation. Those describing themselves as lower class or working class and having relatively few years of education are more likely to limit their political participation to the "passive" or "spectator" activities of voting and discussing politics, if indeed they do that much. Those describing themselves as middle class or upper middle class and having more years of education are more likely to be found trying to persuade another person how to vote, belonging to a political party, or working in an election campaign.

The association between socio-economic position and participation in politics is crucial because the power or influence of participants to affect policy outcomes is, of course, greater at the higher levels of participation; but it is in the competition for the highest political offices of the nation that political inequalities are most in evidence. Although the opportunity to compete for high political office is legally open to almost every adult, inequalities between classes limit the distribution of political opportunities in the same way that they limit the distribution of economic and educational opportunities.

Certainly, the available evidence indicates a persistent bias in the occupational classes of the people who gain political power in Canada. Table 5–29, for example, shows the composition of the House of Commons from 1867 to 1945 classified according to the main economic and occupational interests of the members. A comparison of the percentage distribution of economic and occupational interests for the years 1867 to 1878, covering the first to the fourth Parliaments, with that for the years 1930 to 1945, covering the seventeenth to the twentieth Parliaments, reveals very little change in the occupational composition of the Commons, as the same groups tended to dominate throughout.

In general, the main economic interests of Members in the first twenty Parliaments were in the professional occupations, business, and farming. Law accounted for the largest percentage of the occupational interests of Members of the first four Parliaments, and it retained its predominance at about one-quarter of the known inter-

Table 5–29. *Percentage Distributions of the Economic and Occupational Interests of Members of Parliament, Canada, 1867–1945*

	Parliaments and time periods				
Occupation	First to fourth, 1867–1878	Fifth to eighth, 1882–1896	Ninth to twelfth, 1900–1911	Thirteenth to sixteenth, 1917–1926	Seventeenth to twentieth, 1930–1945
Accountants	0	0.4	0.2	0.6	0.6
Agriculture	5.9	11.8	11.7	18.9	16.5
Clergy	0	0.1	0.1	0.9	1.6
Druggists	0	0.1	0.6	0.9	0.6
Engineering	1.5	0.4	0.2	0.2	1.4
Finance and insurance	12.8	9.5	7.4	8.8	7.0
Labour	0	0.1	0.6	0.4	2.1
Law	24.6	23.6	27.6	23.6	27.7
Manufacturing	7.1	8.6	14.0	10.9	9.5
Medicine and dentistry	5.8	7.0	6.6	8.2	6.9
Merchants	16.2	14.9	15.1	10.7	9.2
Mining	1.0	1.8	1.1	1.7	1.7
Public service	3.2	1.3	1.4	1.6	1.8
Publishing and journalism	6.1	5.5	5.0	4.2	3.4
Real estate	0	0.1	0.5	0.9	0.8
Service industries	2.7	3.3	2.0	2.8	2.3
Teaching	1.6	2.2	2.2	2.6	4.4
Transportation	11.3	8.6	2.8	1.1	0.5
Other	0.2	0.7	1.0	1.0	2.0
Total known interests*	100.0	100.0	100.1	100.0	100.0

* Totals may not add to 100 per cent because of rounding errors.

Source: Norman Ward, *The Canadian House of Commons: Representation* (Toronto: University of Toronto Press, 1950), p. 132.

ests in each period. The most notable increase in representation was that of agricultural interests from 5.9 per cent in the first four Parliaments to an average of 18.9 per cent between 1917 and 1926. In fact, the peak for the agricultural interest occurred in the fourteenth Parliament, elected in 1921, when the success of the Progressive Party temporarily made agriculture the predominant economic interest in the Commons, accounting for 25.3 per cent of the interests represented compared with 24.4 per cent for law. Most business interests remained more or less consistently represented throughout, but one notable decline was that of transportation interests from 11.3 per cent between 1867 and 1878 to 0.5 per cent in the period 1930 to 1945. The decrease in the representation of transportation interests around the turn of the century reflects the declining opportunities for railway promotion through the Commons because of the slow-down in railway construction, the integration of smaller companies into larger ones which could gain direct access to governments without recourse to the Commons, and the increasing direct involvement of the State in railway operations.

The data in Table 5-29 do not permit us to identify all the lower-class occupational interests which may have been represented in the Commons between 1867 and 1945, but it is obvious that labour as a broad economic interest was consistently under-represented in the occupational interests during this period. Even after 1930, when the experience of the Great Depression might have been expected to mobilize a greater representation for labour in the Commons, its representation remained a token one.

Studies of the twenty-fifth Parliament, elected in 1962, and the twenty-sixth Parliament, elected in 1963, have shown that the composition of occupational interests of Members has changed very little since 1945. In a sample of the Members elected in 1962, 51 per cent were engaged in one of the professions before entering politics, 25 per cent were businessmen, 12 per cent were farmers, and 12 per cent were lower middle class or manual workers.[25] A study of the Members elected in 1963 classified 33 per cent of the Members as upper professionals, 41 per cent as professionals and upper white-collar workers, 7 per cent as white-collar and upper blue-collar workers, and 17 per cent as lower white-collar and blue-collar workers.[26] Since the occupational class scale used for the 1963 study included farmers among lower white-collar and blue-collar workers, the results of the two studies are consistent with Table 5-29 in their findings of primarily professional work and secondarily business and farming as the occupational backgrounds of Canadian Members of Parliament.

Consistent with the general trend for opportunities for entry to narrow as the power of political offices increases, the Canadian federal Cabinet has always been recruited from an even more narrow range of economic interests and occupational classes than the House of Commons. Leon Epstein analyzed the occupations of 275 federal Cabinet Ministers for the period 1867 to 1957 and found 140 (50.9 per cent) of them were lawyers, 51 (18.5 per cent) were in other professions including medicine and journalism, and 65 (23.6 per cent) were businessmen.[27] Only 11 of the Cabinet Ministers from 1867 to 1957 were farmers and 4 had manual or clerical occupational backgrounds. Thus, only 7 per cent of the Ministers at most could be said to have had anything but middle-class occupations; and the proportion of Ministers with lower-class occupations remained low throughout the ninety-year period.

John Porter's study of the social background of Canadian federal Cabinet Ministers supports Epstein's findings.[28] Porter found that 50 of the 88 Ministers between 1940 and 1960 were lawyers; 11 were in other professions including the military, teaching, medicine, and the public service; and 16 were businessmen; 5 Ministers were farmers; and only 1 was a skilled worker.

A classification by Richard Van Loon of the non-political occupations of Canadian Cabinet Ministers appointed between 1867 and 1965 confirms these findings of Epstein and Porter. Van Loon's classification (Table 5-30) shows that professional workers and businessmen completely dominated the Cabinet appointments made by the Prime Ministers of both parties. Over the entire period, 65.2 per cent of Conservative appointments and 72.3 per cent of Liberal appointments went to professional men or public servants, and 26.1 per cent of Conservative appointments and 17.9 per cent of Liberal appointments went to businessmen. It is also evident from Table 5-30 that the pattern of appointing primarily professional men and secondarily businessmen to the Canadian federal Cabinet has existed in both parties since the time of Confederation.

Nor is any change in this pattern found in the appointments to the Liberal Cabinets of Prime Ministers Pearson and Trudeau. In studying the occupational backgrounds of the members of the 1966 Pearson Cabinet, Van Loon and Whittington found that nine Ministers had been lawyers before entering politics, seven had been in other professions, five in the civil service, five in business, and one had been a labour organizer. In the 1970 Trudeau Cabinet, there were still nine lawyers, five businessmen, and one labour organizer; and there were ten other professional workers, two civil servants, and one farmer.[29]

Studies of the economic and occupational interests in a number of provincial legislatures indicate that the biases are slightly different but the range of interests represented is just as limited as that found in the national legislature. Table 5-31 summarizes data on the occupational groups represented in the legislatures of Manitoba and Nova Scotia between 1870 and 1960. In both provinces the representation of business interests has declined historically from about two-fifths of each legislature to one-fifth. As the business interest declined in Manitoba, the election of several teachers to the legislature after 1920 caused a slight increase in the representation of the professions; but the more important increase was that of agricultural interests. The decline of business interests directly represented in the Nova Scotia legislature seems to have led only

Table 5–30. Non-political Occupations of Canadian Cabinet Ministers by Party and by Period in Which They Were First Appointed to Cabinet, 1867–1965

(percentages)

Party and period	Profes-sional	Merchan-dising	Manufac-turing*	Service industry*	Finance and in-surance	Public service	Agricul-ture	Labour	Other	Totals** Percentage	Number
1867–1896:											
Conservative	66.1	22.6	1.6	1.6	1.6	1.6	4.8	0	0	99.9	62
Liberal	60.9	21.7	0	8.7	4.3	0	4.3	0	0	99.9	23
1896–1921:											
Conservative	63.3	3.3	10.0	0	6.7	6.7	3.3	3.3	3.3	99.9	30
Liberal	76.7	13.3	0	0	0	0	6.7	0	3.3	100.0	30
1921–1948:											
Conservative	61.7	10.6	4.3	0	8.5	2.1	12.8	0	0	100.0	47
Liberal	67.6	5.9	4.4	1.5	1.5	4.4	10.3	4.4	0	100.0	68
1948–1965:											
Conservative	60.5	15.8	7.9	0	7.9	2.6	5.3	0	0	100.0	38
Liberal	65.0	12.5	5.0	2.5	0	12.5	2.5	0	0	100.0	40
TOTAL:											
Conservative	62.3	14.7	5.1	0.6	5.7	2.9	6.8	0.6	0.6	99.3	177
Liberal	67.4	11.1	3.1	2.5	1.2	4.9	6.2	1.9	1.2	99.5	161

* Managers or proprietors.

** Totals may not add to 100 per cent because of rounding errors.

Source: From an unpublished study, The Structure and Membership of the Canadian Cabinet, by Richard Van Loon, prepared for the Royal Commission on Bilingualism and Biculturalism, with permission of the author.

Table 5–31. *Occupational Groups in the Legislatures of Manitoba and Nova Scotia, 1870–1960*

(percentages)

Occupational groups	Manitoba			Nova Scotia			
	1870–90	1890–1920	1920–60	1878–90	1901–28	1933–41	1949–53
Professions	26	23	32	27	46	40	44
Business	43	36	20	39	38	33	22
Agriculture	18	33	42	10	7	5	10
Labour	–	–	–	–	–	2	8
Miscellaneous and unclassified	12	8	6	25	9	20	15
TOTALS*	99	100	100	101	100	100	99

* Totals may not add to 100 per cent because of rounding errors.

Sources: J. Murray Beck, *The Government of Nova Scotia* (Toronto: University of Toronto Press, 1957), p. 356; M.S. Donnelly, *The Government of Manitoba* (Toronto: University of Toronto Press, 1963), p. 82.

Table 5–32. *Non-political Occupations of Quebec Parliamentarians, 1904–1962*

(percentages)

Occupational group	1904	1944	1956	1962
Professional	58.1	39.3	44.0	55.7
Managerial	19.0	19.1	27.9	24.9
Clerical and sales	1.3	5.6	4.3	9.4
Workers	17.5	11.2	8.6	7.3
Agricultural	0	5.6	2.1	2.1
Not Known	4.0	19.1	12.9	1.0
TOTAL*	99.9	99.9	99.8	100.4

* Totals may not add to 100 per cent because of rounding errors.

Source: André Gélinas, *Les Parlementaires et l'Administration au Québec* (Québec: Les Presses de l'Université Laval, 1969), p. 45

to an increase in the representation of the professions, especially of law, as lawyers formed 21 per cent of the Assembly during 1949–1953. As in the federal legislature, labour interests have not been much represented in either of these provincial legislatures.

In Quebec during the twentieth century the Assembly has represented primarily middle-class occupational groups as Table 5–32 shows. The professions were much the largest occupational classification for Quebec Parliamentarians between 1904 and 1962, farmers were represented less and businessmen more in 1962 than in 1904, and workers had a very low percentage of representation throughout.

Table 5–33. *Non-political Occupations of Members of the 1962 Quebec and 1963 Ontario Legislatures Compared with 1961 Provincial Labour Forces*

(percentages)

Occupational group	Ontario Legislature	Ontario Labour force	Quebec Legislature	Quebec Labour force
Professional	38.0	9.9	55.7	10.1
Managerial	27.9	8.8	24.9	7.8
Clerical and sales	12.9	21.6	9.4	18.4
Agricultural	12.9	7.2	7.3	7.5
Workers	8.3	50.3	2.1	53.1
Not Known	–	2.3	1.0	3.0
TOTALS*	100.0	100.1	100.4	99.9

* Totals may not add to 100 per cent because of rounding errors.

Sources: Canada, Dominion Bureau of Statistics, *1961 Census of Canada*, Bulletin 3.1–1 (Ottawa: Queen's Printer, 1964), Table 3; F.F. Schindeler, *Responsible Government in Ontario* (Toronto: University of Toronto Press, 1969), p. 39; André Gélinas, *Les Parlementaires et l'Administration au Québec* (Quebec; Les Presses de l'Université Laval, 1969), p. 45.

As in many other legislatures, lawyers have been the single most important occupational group in the Quebec Assembly, as they formed 41 per cent of the 1904 Assembly, 28 per cent in 1944, 23 per cent in 1956, and 27 per cent in 1962.[30]

The comparison in Table 5–33 between the occupational distributions of the Quebec and Ontario legislatures in the early 1960s and the occupational distributions of the respective provincial labour forces also shows a familiar pattern of over-representation of upper middle-class occupational groups and under-representation of lower middle-class and working-class groups. The most over-represented groups in both provincial legislatures were professional workers, who comprised 38.0 per cent of the Ontario and 55.7 per cent of the Quebec legislature but only 10 per cent of the provincial labour forces. The most under-represented in both provinces were workers, who comprised half of the labour force in each province but only 8.3 per cent of the Ontario and 2.1 per cent of the Quebec legislature.

Like the federal Cabinet, the provincial Cabinets tend to be recruited from a more narrow range of occupational interests than their legislatures. At least in Ontario in 1963, the professions (47 per cent), sales (16 per cent), and farmers (16 per cent) were all better represented in the Cabinet than in the legislature; and within the predominant professional group, which was represented by 47.0 per cent of the Cabinet, eight members or 42 per cent were lawyers compared with 22 per cent of the legislature.[31] The Quebec Cabinet in 1962 represented an even more narrow occupational range, as 79 per cent of the Ministers had been in one of the professions before entering politics and the rest were businessmen.[32]

The chances for Canadians of differing class backgrounds to gain high political office are obviously not equal, but studies of the social background of legislators and Cabinet Ministers in other political democracies indicate that the pattern of recruitment found in Canada is a common one. The principal non-political occupations of the 180 United States Senators who held office from 1947 to 1957 were: 97 law, 17 other professions, 53 business, 13 farmers, and no manual or clerical workers.[33] Among the Deputies to the French National Assembly from 1898 to 1940, the percentage of lawyers was a relatively low 25 per cent; but 60 per cent of the Deputies were professional men, 21 per cent were businessmen or large landowners, 10 per cent were middle-size farmers; and only 9 per cent were workers, clerical employees, or lower-level functionaries.[34] In the Assemblies of the Fourth Republic, 1945 to 1958, law was the original occupation of 142 Deputies, 12.8 per cent of the total. The total representation of professionals was 47.8 per cent; that of businessmen was 15.7 per cent; 136 Deputies were farmers, 12.2 per cent of the total; and 21.1 per cent of the Deputies had a lower-class occupational background.

French Cabinets from 1898 to 1940 were composed of men whose original occupations were in the professions (83 per cent) and business (12 per cent). Only 2 per cent were middle-size farmers and 3 per cent were lower-class workers. Of the 88 British Cabinet Ministers who held office between 1918 and 1959, 52.0 per cent were professional men in their non-political occupations; 9.3 per cent were in business; 20.0 per cent were manual or clerical workers; and 18.7 per cent were in other white-collar jobs, had private means, or were professional politicians.[35] Among 259 federal and state Cabinet Ministers in Australia between 1901 and 1961, 37 per cent were professional or semi-professional men; 16 per cent were administrators, including senior government officials, and businessmen; 21 per cent were rural proprietors; 8 per cent had been commercial and clerical (lower middle-class) workers; and 18 per cent had been manual workers.[36] The occupational backgrounds of German Cabinet members during the periods of the Weimar and the Federal Republics show a similar emphasis on business and professional men. The civil service (48.4 per cent) and law (31.1 per cent) were the most important non-political occupations of German Cabinet members during the Weimar Republic; but journalism (19.7 per cent), business (16.4 per cent), teaching (12.3 per cent), and labour (10.7 per cent) were also well-represented in the backgrounds of members.[37] The civil service (27.2 per cent), law (21.9 per cent), and business (21.9 per cent) were also the most important non-political occupations of Cabinet members in Germany during the first decade of the Federal Republic, 1949 to 1960; and engineering (11.4 per cent), teaching (9.1 per cent), and banking or insurance (6.8 per cent) accounted for most of the rest.[38]

Enough examples have been given to make the point that the Canadian pattern of political recruitment from elite occupational classes is not unique. Lawyers seem to be slightly more favoured in North American politics than they are in Europe, but in all countries legislatures and Cabinets are drawn primarily from the business and professional classes. Even so, the lower classes have had markedly better representation in the political elites of Britain, France, Australia, and even Germany than they have had in Canada or the United States.

The greater representation of lower-class occupations in the Australian, British, and German Cabinets is probably explained by the existence of a socialist working-class party which provided the channel for a few to move directly from lower-class occupations to positions of political power.[39] The Australian Labour Party accounts for almost all the lower-class workers who became federal Cabinet Ministers in Australia between 1901 and 1961. Only 3 per cent of the Liberal–Country Party Ministers had lower-class occupations before entering politics, but 16 per cent of the Labour Party's Ministers had commercial or clerical occupations and 42 per cent were manual workers. Similarly, the Labour Party in Britain with 44.3 per cent of its Ministers between 1918 and 1959 having original occupations as manual or clerical workers accounted for all the Ministers from these occupational groups. Fewer ex-workers have been included in German Cabinets than in those of Australia or Britain, but this reflects the lesser success of the German Social Democratic Party. Before 1960, the Social Democrats formed the Government only during the Weimar Republic and then in coalition; and this seems to account for the relatively large 10.7 per cent of ex-workers in German Cabinets during Weimar compared with 2.6 per cent during the monarchy (1890–1918), 3.0 per cent under Hitler (1933–1945), and 2.3 per cent in the post-war Federal Republic (1945–1960).

In the case of the Cabinets formed from the governing parties of Canada, differences in occupational background of the sort which are found between party leaders on the left and on the right in Australia, Germany, and Britain are simply not present. Epstein has reported that between 1867 and 1957 eighty Liberal and seventy-six

Equality

Conservative Cabinet Ministers were professionals while twenty-nine Liberal and thirty-six Conservative Ministers were businessmen.[40] Van Loon's classification for the period 1867 to 1965 (Table 5–30) shows that a higher proportion of Liberal Cabinet Ministers had professional occupations and the Conservative Cabinets had relatively more businessmen, but the differences between the two parties were slight.

Given the weakness or absence of a socialist working-class party, high political offices with only few exceptions go to those who have an upper-class occupational position. Such an upper-class position may be inherited or acquired, but the odds appear to be against the latter course. Matthews found that only 7 per cent of the fathers of American Senators had lower-class occupations, 24 per cent were themselves professional men, 35 per cent were in business, and 32 per cent were farmers.[41] Schmidt reports that 18.2 per cent of the fathers of post-war German Cabinet Ministers were workers; but, on the whole, professional and business occupations were more common—civil service, 20.4 per cent; business 22.3 per cent; and law and teaching, 6.8 per cent each.[42]

In Canada, the chances of rising from lower-class origins first to a middle-class occupation and then into political office seem somewhat better for Members of Parliament than is the case for American Senators. Kornberg and Thomas found that 34 per cent of the Members of the twenty-fifth Parliament had fathers whose occupations were lower class, 32 per cent of their fathers were farmers, 17 per cent were businessmen, and 18 per cent were professional men.[43] Gélinas also reports evidence of intergeneration occupational mobility for Quebec Parliamentarians. As Table 5–34 shows, many fathers who were farmers, workers, and office employees have had sons become members of the professions and then enter politics.

Table 5–34. Non-political Occupations of Quebec Parliamentarians Compared with the Occupations of their Fathers, 1965*

(percentages)

	Professional	Managerial	Clerical and sales	Agriculture	Workers	Not known	Total**
Fathers	8	28	20	24	20	0	100
Parliamentarians	56	24	9	7	2	1	99

* Based on information obtained from interviews with fifty backbench Members in 1964–65.

** Totals may not add to 100 per cent because of rounding errors.

Source: André Gélinas, *Les Parlementaires et l'Administration au Québec* (Quebec: Les Presses de l'Université Laval, 1969), p. 46.

Kornberg and Thomas have suggested that the differences between American Senators and Canadian M.P.s in intergeneration occupational mobility may be due, in part, to Canada's relatively less developed economy.[44] During the period when the legislators were growing up, relatively more Canadians were engaged in primary and secondary occupations, for example, in farming and manufacturing, and fewer in tertiary occupations. Therefore, more contemporary Canadian legislators would be likely to have lower-class backgrounds than would their American counterparts; but this difference would tend to disappear as the Canadian economy developed and Canadian society lost some of its mobility.

Another possible explanation for the differences between American Senators and Canadian Members of Parliament is that the political positions of Senators and M.P.s in the power structures of their respective countries are not directly comparable. If Senators occupy a higher level in the American pyramid of power than M.P.s do in the Canadian one, then the lesser representation of Senators of humble origins should not be surprising. This possible explanation gains some support from Epstein's evidence that only 8 to 12 per cent of the 275 Cabinet Ministers in Canada from 1867 to 1957 could be said to be of modest or humble origins, if not exactly from working-class backgrounds, and that almost all the rest appear to have come from the middle or upper class.[45]

In view of the strong association between occupation and education and the high proportion of professionals in the Canadian House of Commons, it is not surprising to find that 49 per cent of the Members elected to the Commons in 1963 had professional or graduate degrees or some professional qualification; another 16 per cent had university training, including bachelor's degrees; 23 per cent had secondary education; and only 4 per cent had no more than an elementary education.[46] Kornberg and Thomas report that 72 per cent of 165 Members questioned in a 1962 survey had college degrees with 60 per cent of them having law degrees.[47]

Among federal Cabinet Ministers the proportion having university education is even higher than it is in the Commons. Porter reports that 86 per cent of the Ministers who held office between 1940 and 1960 and 52 per cent of the Ministers from 1867 to 1940 had university education, and Epstein found that 72.4 per cent of the ministers who held office between 1867 and 1957 had university education and only 2.2 per cent had elementary education.[48]

As with occupational backgrounds, the recruitment of Canadian legislators and Cabinet Ministers from upper-status educational groups is a pattern commonly found in other political democracies. Of the 180 American Senators who held office from 1947 to 1957, 84 per cent had attended college, including 23 per cent who had attended college only, 8 per cent law school only, 45 per cent college and law school, and 8 per cent post-graduate.[49] In the British House of Commons elected in 1964, 32.7 per cent had an education combining public school with university, another 20.2 per cent had a combination of secondary school and university education, 12.9 per cent had a public school education, 18.1 per cent had a secondary school education, and 16.2 per cent had an elementary education.[50] In the German Federal Republic the proportion who had a higher education rose steadily since the time of the Weimar Republic, from 37 per cent in the Reichstag of 1928 to 41 per cent in the 1949 Bundestag, 47 per cent in 1953, and 52 per cent in 1957.[51] In the Japanese House of Representatives elected in 1958, 48 per cent of the Liberal-Democrats were graduates of national or public universities or colleges and 33 per cent were graduates of private universities or colleges, while 30 per cent of the Socialists were graduates of public and 32 per cent of private universities or colleges.[52]

Data on the levels of educational attainment for Cabinet Ministers in Australia, the Weimar and Federal Republics of Germany, and the United Kingdom provide a useful comparative perspective on the educational status of Canadian Ministers. The percentage of Ministers having a university education is relatively high in all countries, but not uniformly so. In particular, the levels of educational attainment for Australian federal Cabinet Ministers are lower than those in the other countries, especially considering that almost one-third of the total shown for "university" actually had some "other tertiary" education. This may be a reflection of an anti-intellectualism common historically in many important Australian social movements and organizations.

The distributions of educational attainment by party for Australia, Canada, and the United Kingdom once again indicate the effects of having a governing socialist party. The Labour Party has been the means of attaining high political office for the 18.7 per cent of Cabinet Ministers in the United Kingdom who had an elementary education, while in Australia a remarkable 51 per cent of the Labour Ministers had only a primary education. In Canada, as with occupation so with education, no significant differences appear between the two governing parties. Seen in comparative perspective, the relatively small proportion of Canadian Ministers with secondary or primary education is especially remarkable, since the Canadian data extend further into the past than those for Australia, Germany, or the United Kingdom; and the chances of getting more than an elementary education were much lower in the nineteenth century.

Canadians of the British ethnic groups have been consistently

Table 5–35. *Educational Attainment of Cabinet Ministers in Australia, Canada, Germany, and the United Kingdom*

(percentages)

Nation	University	Secondary	Primary	Not known	Total*
Australia, Federal Cabinet, 1901–1961:**					
Liberal-Country Party	49	34	7	10	100
Labour	19	25	51	5	100
Total	37	31	24	8	100
Canada, Federal Cabinet, 1867–1957:					
Liberals	76	9	3	12	100
Conservatives	68	13	2	17	100
Total	72	11	2	14	99
Germany, Weimar (1918–1933) and Federal (1949–1960) Republics:					
Weimar	70	12	12	5	99
Federal	80	11	9	0	100
United Kingdom, 1918–1959:***					
Conservative	84	16	0	0	100
Labour	52	6	42	0	100
Total	69	12	19	0	100

Column group header: Educational attainment of Cabinet Ministers

* Totals may not add to 100 per cent because of rounding errors.

** University includes university and "other tertiary".

*** Secondary includes secondary and public school education.

Source: S. Encel, "The Political Elite in Australia" in Colin A. Hughes (ed.), *Readings in Australian Government* (St. Lucia, Queensland: University of Queensland Press, 1968), p. 104; Leon D. Epstein, *Political Parties in Western Democracies* (New York: Praeger Publishers 1967), p. 198; Maxwell E. Knight, *The German Executive 1890–1933* (Stanford, California; Stanford University Press, 1952), p. 36; Hannelore Schmidt, "Die Deutsche Exekutive 1949–1960", *European Journal of Sociology*, IV (1963, No. 1), 173; Philip W. Buck, *Amateurs and Professionals in British Politics* (Chicago and London: University of Chicago Press, © 1963 by the University of Chicago), p. 121.

over-represented, those of the French ethnic group on the whole have been slightly under-represented, and those belonging to other ethnic groups have been very much under-represented in the highest political offices of the nation. In the first period after Confederation, the new Members of the Canadian House of Commons were 24.9

per cent French, 31.5 per cent English, 26.2 per cent Scottish, 14.5 per cent Irish, and 2.8 per cent other ethnic groups. Over the following ninety years this original pattern of ethnic group representation persisted with surprisingly little change. Overall, the representation of the French ethnic group between 1867 and 1964 was 27.0 per cent of new Members; 69.1 per cent of the new Members belonged to the British ethnic groups (27.6 per cent English, 24.9 per cent Scottish, and 16.6 per cent Irish); and only 3.8 per cent had other ethnic origins.

According to the first national census in 1871, the ethnic group composition of the national population was 31 per cent French, 60 per cent British (20 per cent English, 16 per cent Scottish, and 24 per cent Irish), and 8 per cent other ethnic groups. Even at the outset, then, the British ethnic groups were over-represented and the French and other ethnic groups were under-represented. Over the entire period from 1867 to 1964, the French ethnic group, with 28 to 31 per cent of the national population, continued to be slightly under-represented in the House of Commons. As the proportion of the

Table 5–36. Ethnic Origins of New Members of the Canadian House of Commons by Period During Which They Were First Elected, 1867–1964

(percentages)

Period	French	English	Scottish	Irish	Other	Total* Per-centage	Total* Num-ber
1867–1873	24.9	31.5	26.2	14.5	2.8	99.9	317
1874–1877	25.3	16.5	35.2	22.0	1.1	100.1	91
1878–1895	27.2	25.3	23.5	20.9	3.1	100.0	383
1896–1899	24.8	23.9	26.5	20.4	4.4	100.0	113
1900–1910	20.5	26.9	26.9	22.4	3.2	99.9	308
1911–1929	21.7	26.2	29.7	19.5	2.9	100.0	512
1930–1939	30.8	24.2	27.9	14.6	2.5	100.0	240
1940–1953	28.7	32.3	22.5	11.6	4.9	100.0	387
1954–1958	31.3	30.8	15.9	12.6	9.3	99.9	214
1959–1964	48.1	29.1	13.3	5.1	4.4	100.0	158
Percentage of total Members of Parliament	27.0	27.6	24.9	16.6	3.8	99.9	
Total Number	736	751	679	453	104		2,723

* Totals may not add to 100 per cent because of rounding errors.

Source: From an unpublished study, The Structure and Membership of the Canadian Cabinet, by Richard Van Loon, prepared for the Royal Commission on Bilingualism and Biculturalism, with the permission of the author.

Table 5–37. Ethnic Group Composition of the Canadian Population, 1871–1961

(percentages)

Ethnic groups	1871	1901	1931	1961
British	60.5	57.0	51.9	43.8
French	31.1	30.7	28.2	30.4
Other	8.4	12.3	19.9	25.8
TOTAL	100.0	100.0	100.0	100.0

Source: Canada, Dominion Bureau of Statistics, *Census of Canada 1951*, Volume I (Ottawa: Queen's Printer, 1953), Table 31; *1961 Census of Canada*, Bulletin 1.2–5 (Ottawa: Queen's Printer, 1962), Introduction. Reproduced by permission of Information Canada.

British ethnic groups in the national population declined and that of the non-British, non-French ethnic groups rose, the British ethnic groups became increasingly over-represented in the House of Commons by maintaining virtually their original proportions; and the non-British, non-French ethnic groups became increasingly under-represented by failing to increase their political representation in anything like the same degree as they increased in the national population.

The representation of the non-British, non-French ethnic groups in the Canadian House of Commons does appear to have been increasing in recent years. Table 5–36 shows that almost 5.8 per cent of the new Members elected from 1940 to 1964 belonged to the other ethnic groups compared with 3.0 per cent in the period 1867 to 1940. A study for the Royal Commission on Bilingualism and Biculturalism reported that between November 1965 and June 1968 there were at least twenty-four Members in the House of Commons with ethnic origins other than British or French.[53] This was "considerably more than in previous Canadian Parliaments," but it was still only 9 per cent of the Commons' total membership compared with the 26 per cent of the national population which was neither British nor French. Two surveys of Members of Parliament made in the early 1960s also support this finding by the Royal Commission study of a modest increase in the representation of non-British, non-French ethnic groups. In Kornberg's sample of 165 backbench Members of the House of Commons elected in 1962, 51 per cent of them belonged to the British ethnic group compared with 44 per cent of the national population, 34 per cent belonged to the French ethnic group compared with 30 per cent of the population, and 16 per cent belonged to other ethnic groups.[54] In Andrew's sample of the backbenchers elected to the Commons in 1963, 52 per cent were of British ethnic origin, 31 per cent were French, and 11 per cent were from other ethnic groups.[55]

Among the members of Parliament of non-British, non-French origin, some ethnic groups have been more represented than others. Table 5–38 shows that between 1867 and 1964 the German, Ukrainian, and Jewish ethnic groups were those most represented. Between 1945 and 1964 there were at least seven Members of Parliament of German origin, five of Scandinavian origin, nine of Ukrainian origin, and four of Jewish origin.[56]

In appointments to the federal Cabinet, the British ethnic groups usually have been more over-represented than has been the case in the House of Commons; and the non-British, non-French ethnic groups have been even more under-represented. Overall, 71.7 per cent of the Cabinet Ministers appointed between 1867 and 1965 belonged to one of the British ethnic groups; 26.9 per cent were French; and only 1.5 per cent had other ethnic origins.

The greatest imbalance of ethnic representation in the federal Cabinet resulted from the appointments made by Prime Minister

Table 5–38. Number of Members of the Canadian House of Commons of Non-British, Non-French Ethnic Origins, 1867–1964

Ethnic origin	Atlantic Provinces	Que-bec	Ontario	Mani-toba	Saskat-chewan	Alberta	British Columbia	Total
German	7	2	21	4	3	1	2	40
Ukrainian		2		3		6		11
Jewish		5	2	2				9
Scandinavian				2	1	1	2	6
Swiss		1	5					6
Dutch	1	1	1		1		1	5
Polish		3	1		1			5
Icelandic				3			1	4
Italian			3					3
Austrian					1			1
Belgian		1						1
Chinese							1	1
Czech				1				1
Lebanese					1			1
Portuguese		1						1
Rumanian		1						1
Yugoslav					1			1
TOTAL	8	15	35	15	9	8	7	97

Source: Royal Commission on Bilingualism and Biculturalism, Report, Volume 4 (Ottawa: Queen's Printer, 1970), p. 272. Reproduced by permission of Information Canada.

Macdonald, 80.3 per cent of which went to the British ethnic groups. Conversely, with 50 per cent British and 45 per cent French, there was virtually a balance between the two "founding" ethnic groups in the new appointments made up to 1965 by Prime Minister Pearson; and both were over-represented at the expense of the other ethnic groups.

No trend is yet evident to indicate that the under-representation of the non-British, non-French ethnic groups in the federal Cabinet will soon be terminated; but at least the token representation of these ethnic groups now seems to have been firmly established. Although only five Cabinet Ministers who had non-British, non-French ethnic origins were appointed from 1867 to 1965, Prime Ministers Diefenbaker and Pearson each appointed one Cabinet Minister who had ethnic origins other than British or French. Moreover, among the twenty-five Cabinet Ministers first appointed to office by Prime Minister Trudeau from 1968 to 1973, there were four (16 per cent) from the non-British, non-French ethnic groups, and there were six French (24 per cent), and fifteen British (60 per cent). Including the eleven British and seven French Cabinet Ministers who were reappointed from previous Ministries, the overall ethnic composition of the forty-three Ministers who served in the Trudeau Cabinets from 1968 to 1973 was 60.5 per cent British, 30.2 per cent French, and 9.3 per cent other ethnic groups.

Nowhere are political inequalities more apparent in the social backgrounds of political decision-makers than in the differences in the representation of men and women in high public office. Women first received the right to vote in Manitoba in provincial elections in January 1916. This right was extended in the next few years to voting in federal elections and in other provincial elections, except in Quebec where women were not permitted to vote until 1940. The right to run for public office accompanied the right to vote; but, while the turnout of women to vote in federal and provincial elections is not very different from that of men, few women have been elected to public office.

The discrimination against women in politics clearly begins in the political parties. Of the total of 12,262 candidates in the fifteen federal general elections from 1921 (when women first could run) to 1968, only 300 or 2.4 per cent were women.[57] In the 1968 federal election only 34 of the 967 candidates (3.5 per cent) were women, but there was a noticeable increase in the 1972 federal election when 68 of the 1,116 candidates (6.1 per cent) were women.

The proportion of women elected to Parliament since 1921 has been even smaller than the proportion of women candidates. Between 1921 and 1968, 18 women were elected to the House of

Table 5–39. Ethnic Origins of Canadian Cabinet Ministers by Prime Ministers Who First Appointed Them to Cabinet, 1867–1965

(percentages)

Prime Minister	English	Irish	Scottish	United Empire Loyalist	Anglo-Saxon not specified	French	Other European	Totals* Percentage	Number
Macdonald	14.9	19.1	25.5	12.8	8.5	19.1	0	99.9	47
Mackenzie	8.7	0	17.4	21.7	17.4	34.8	0	100.0	23
Abbott, Bowell, Thompson, Tupper	13.3	13.3	20.0	6.7	13.3	26.7	6.7	100.0	15
Laurier	13.3	20.0	20.0	6.7	13.3	26.7	0	100.0	30
Borden	13.3	20.0	13.3	6.7	23.3	23.3	0	99.9	30
Meighen	26.9	3.8	26.9	15.4	3.8	23.1	0	99.9	26
King	7.5	7.5	23.9	1.5	31.3	25.4	3.0	100.1	67
Bennett	23.8	4.8	28.6	0	14.3	28.6	0	100.1	21
St. Laurent	23.5	0	17.6	0	29.4	29.4	0	99.9	17
Diefenbaker	8.1	5.4	8.1		48.6	27.0	2.7	99.9	37
Pearson	4.5	0	13.6	0	31.8	45.0	4.5	99.4	22
Percentage of total Cabinet Ministers	13.1	9.6	20.0	6.3	22.7	26.9	1.5	100.1	
Total number	44	32	67	21	76	90	5		335

* Totals may not add to 100 per cent because of rounding errors.

Source: From an unpublished study, *The Structure and Membership of the Canadian Cabinet*, by Richard Van Loon, prepared for the Royal Commission on Bilingualism and Biculturalism, with permission of the author.

Commons, 0.8 per cent of the Members elected. In addition, 49 women were elected to provincial legislatures between 1917 and 1970, 1.9 per cent of the provincial legislative membership. Altogether between 1917 and 1970 there were 134 federal and provincial elections and 6,845 people elected to legislative offices. Only 67 of those elected, just under 1 per cent of the total, were women.

A slight increase above historical norms was noticeable in the legislative representation of women in the early 1970s. Only one woman held a seat in the House of Commons elected in 1968, but four others were elected in the federal election of 1972, giving women their largest representation ever at 2 per cent of the Commons membership. Twelve of the forty-nine women elected to provincial legislatures between 1917 and 1970 were in fact holding seats in June 1970; and there were fourteen women (six of them in British Columbia) represented in seven provincial legislatures as of January 1973, 2.2 per cent of the total provincial legislative membership. In addition, token representation of women in federal and provincial Cabinets appears to be now generally accepted. At the federal level, only three women have been named Cabinet Ministers, and they were appointed by the last three Prime Ministers: Ellen Fairclough to the Diefenbaker Ministries of 1957, 1958, and 1962; Judy LaMarsh to the Pearson Ministries of 1963 and 1965; and Jeanne Sauve to the Trudeau Ministry of 1972. As of January 1973, a woman had been appointed to the Cabinet in six of the seven provinces where women held legislative office; and together they represented 3.5 per cent of all provincial ministers.

The slight increase in recent years in the candidacies and election of women to the federal and provincial legislatures may signal a beginning towards rectifying the under-representation of women in Canadian political life; but, given the evidence to date, the conclusion of the Royal Commission on the Status of Women in Canada still seems fair enough.

> *The last fifty years, since woman suffrage was introduced, have seen no appreciable change in the political activities of women beyond the exercise of the right to vote. In the decision-making positions, and most conspicuously in the government and Parliament of Canada, the presence of a mere handful of women is no more than a token acknowledgement of their right to be there. The voice of government is still a man's voice. The formulation of policies affecting the lives of all Canadians is still the prerogative of men. The absurdity of this situation was illustrated when debate in the House of Commons on a change in abortion*

*law was conducted by 263 men and one woman. Nowhere
else in Canadian life is the persistent distinction between
male and female roles of more consequence. No country
can make a claim to having equal status for its women so
long as its government lies entirely in the hands of men.*[58]

The very low proportion of women holding high public office
is similar to the situation found in other western democracies.[59]
Normally 5 to 6 per cent of the candidates for election to the British
House of Commons since 1945 have been women, the peak being
6.7 per cent (126 women candidates) in the election of 1950; and
4 to 5 per cent of the candidates elected have been women, the
largest number being 28 in 1964 and 1970. In the Bundestag of
the German Federal Republic, 7.6 per cent of the members were
women in 1949, 9.2 per cent in 1957, and 6.9 per cent in 1965.
Women formed 6.1 per cent of the 1945 Constituent Assembly in
France and 3.5 per cent of the National Assembly in 1956, 1.3
per cent in 1958, and 1.6 per cent in 1968. Women held 2.3 per
cent of the combined seats of the United States Senate and the
House of Representatives in 1953, and 2.1 per cent of the seats
after the 1968 elections. Only 2 women have ever been appointed
to the Cabinet by Presidents of the United States. In Britain, 4
women were appointed Cabinet Ministers between 1918 and 1967;
and 7 women were appointed Ministers without Cabinet rank. In
Australia, 3 out of the 259 federal and state Cabinet Ministers
holding office between 1901 and 1961 were women; and all of them
were appointed after World War II. Only Sweden appears to be
somewhat exceptional in its representation of women in high public
office, but even there only 25 per cent of the Lower House and
10 per cent of the Senate were women in 1968.

The third test of the advance of equality is the opportunity to
participate through all media of communication in the shaping of
economic, social, and political opinion and policy. There is no doubt
that opportunities to participate in the shaping of opinion and
policy in all areas of social activity are markedly enhanced for those
who occupy the most important political offices of the nation. Thus,
to the extent that the members of any social group find themselves
relatively deprived of access to high public office, they will also find
themselves relatively deprived of the access necessary to influence
public opinion and policy.[60]

Indicators of the social background of politicians in Canada provide unmistakable evidence that lower-class, lower-status groups;
non-French, non-British ethnic groups; and women are relatively
deprived of access to high political office in Canada. Historically,
the bias in national politics against lower-class, lower-status groups

has been greater in Canada than in some other industrialized democracies because the Government has never been formed by a socialist working-class party; but, given the tendency toward a decline in the class character of contemporary socialist parties, these differences between Canada and other nations are tending at least to diminish if not disappear entirely. Political inequalities affecting women in Canada appear little different from those existing, in other industrialized democracies. Nor is there as yet any obvious mechanism for their reduction which would be comparable in effect to that, say, of the working-class party with respect to class and status differences.[61] In the case of ethnicity there is some evidence of a trend to rectify inequalities of access. Gradually, it seems, the under-representation of the members of non-French, non-British ethnic groups is being corrected but at a rate which makes it unlikely that this type of political inequality will soon disappear.

Tests of Equality

Applying each of the tests of equality in turn, we find that different class, status, ethnic, and sex groups are not equally represented among those who have achieved higher levels of schooling; they are not equally represented among those who have attained positions in the higher-paid, upper-class, professional and managerial occupations; and they are not equally represented among those who have gained the highest levels of elected public office.

Inequalities result from one group consciously exercising its social, economic, and political power in its own interests at the expense of other groups, a situation which is perhaps most commonly found in the construction of the norms and regulations governing the pursuit of formal education. Inequalities also result from the unconscious, mutual acceptance of stereotyped roles among the members of different social groups, a situation which is perhaps most commonly found in the segregation of social, economic, and political activities between the sexes. However the inequalities arise, discrimination among class, status, ethnic, and sex groups is evidently a common feature of the Canadian political community.

Two factors in the Canadian situation may be suggested to modify this charge of discrimination. First, there is some evidence that occupational inequalities derive from educational inequalities and that educational inequalities, in turn, reflect variations in the distribution of general intelligence among social groups. Second, when the Canadian situation is viewed in a comparative perspective, the existing educational, occupational, and political inequalities appear to be little different from inequalities which are commonly found in other advanced industrialized societies.

These two factors may modify the general charge of discrimination against the Canadian political community, but neither serves to answer it. The occupational inequalities among ethnic and sex groups are only partly explained by group differences in levels of educational attainment; and the best interpretation of the unexplained differences is simply discrimination, conscious or unconscious. Variations in the intergeneration educational and occupational achievements of class and status groups appear too great to be explained simply (and conveniently) by class or status group differences in average general intelligence; and such an explanation is irrelevant for explaining ethnic and sex group differences in the levels of occupational and educational attainment because there are no ethnic or sex group differences in average general intelligence. Again, therefore, conscious or unconscious discrimination must be included as an essential part of any explanation of inequalities in Canada. Finally, the comparative perspective is sobering but not conclusive. While the differences are not perhaps great, some nations have done noticeably better than Canada in reducing barriers to education, occupation, and political office. Moreover, it is just at this point that one must be reminded that our ultimate test is not some international league standing but the creation of real possibilities for human development. Wherever such possibilities can be realized, social change continues to be justified.

The existence of discrimination in Canada provides justification for governmental intervention to reduce inequalities and correct long-standing patterns of need deprivation. A variety of public policies have been undertaken by governments in Canada to reduce inequalities among class, status, ethnic, and sex groups. Probably the most important set of policies has been that taken by provincial governments since the 1930s respecting the provision of facilities for formal education. The reports of the Royal Commission on Bilingualism and Biculturalism and the Royal Commission on the Status of Women in Canada and the response of governmental authorities to their recommendations provide other examples of public concern for reducing inequalities among social groups in Canada.

Any generalizations about the effectiveness of these public policies designed to promote equality obviously must be tentative and inconclusive. Nonetheless, a number of the main social indicators used here are consistent in suggesting that general reductions in inequalities affecting ethnic and sex groups are occurring but only at rates of change which would ensure their presence as important factors in Canadian society for a long time to come. In addition, although the evidence is slight, there seems to have been a decrease in class and status inequalities during the war and the immediate post-war period, but very little if any reduction thereafter. This pattern was first in evidence in the second chapter with respect to the distribution of family incomes in Canada, and it has reappeared in this chapter in the indicator of differential class access to educational opportunities (the percentage of young people living at home who were at school by occupational groups, 1941 to 1961).

If this interpretation of social trends in Canada should prove to be a valid one, then the immediate response should be an attempt to devise a set of public policies aimed at creating an environment of social flexibility, generosity among social groups, and rejection of stereotyped roles within which social change could flourish. When the need for equality is put in terms of such a political demand, however, it becomes evident how far existing, "disjointed incremental" policies fall short of creating such an environment and how great the challenge to political leadership is to move us toward the creation of more possibilities for human development through a more equal society.

NOTES

1. Class groups are determined by relations of property ownership and economic production. According to Max Weber, all persons in the same class situation have a typical probability of procuring goods, gaining a position in life and finding inner satisfaction "which derives from the relative control over goods and skills and from their income-producing uses within a given economic order." [Max Weber, *Economy and Society*, Guenther Roth and Claus Wittich (eds.) (New York: Bedminister Press, 1968), vol. I, p. 302. Positively privileged classes are typically rentiers who derive their income from property whether it be slaves, land, mines, or securities; entrepreneurs, such as merchants, shipowners, bankers, and financiers; or professionals with valued expertise. Negatively privileged classes are typically the propertyless who are slaves, serfs, and paupers or the labourers who are variously skilled, semi-skilled, or unskilled.

    Status groups are determined by objective claims of pluralities of persons within a large social group to social esteem in terms of positive or negative privileges. Again according to Weber, status is typically founded on style of life, formal education, and hereditary or occupational prestige. Status may rest on class position, but it is not solely determined by it.

    "Money and an entrepreneurial position are not in themselves status qualifications, although they may lead to them; and the lack of property is not in itself a status qualification, although this may be a reason for it. Conversely, status may influence, if not completely determine, a class position without being identical with it. The classification of an officer, a civil servant or a student may vary greatly according to their wealth and yet not lead to a different status since upbringing and education create a common style of life." (Max Weber, *ibid.*, p. 306.)

    Thus stratification into classes results from modes of acquiring income whether through property ownership or position in the processes of production; but stratification into status groups results from attributions of social esteem deriving from distinctive patterns of consumption. As Runciman sums it up, "the members of your class are those who share your location in the process of production, distribution and exchange; the members of your status group are those who share your style of life and your relative position in terms of social estimation and prestige." [W. G. Runciman, *Social Science and Political Theory*, 2d ed., (Cambridge: Cambridge University Press, 1969), p. 138.]

Ethnic group is a term most frequently applied to any social group which differs in one or more aspects of its patterned, socially-transmitted way of life so as to exhibit a complex of "ethnic traits" distinguishing it from other groups in the community. [Melvin M. Tumin, "Ethnic Group," in Julius Gould and William L. Kolb (eds.), *A Dictionary of the Social Sciences*, (New York: The Free Press, 1964), pp. 243–4. Copyright © 1964 by the United Nations Educational, Scientific, and Cultural Association.] Ethnic traits are diverse but may include religious or linguistic characteristics, distinctive skin pigmentation, or the national or geographic origins of members or their forebears. Thus, for example, French-speaking Canadians, Jews, and Indians have ethnic traits which make it possible to distinguish them from other groups in the Canadian community.

2. In analyzing the data of Fig. 5–1 as meaningful and comparable we should remember the shortcomings arising from changes in the definitions of occupational classifications, the changes in the age groupings of the young people included, and the inclusion of children living at home rather than of all children. In spite of these limitations, the series of percentages in Figure 5–1 represent a useful quantitative indicator of the pattern, if not the precise degree, of inequalities in access to education among young people of different class backgrounds in each census year, and of the persistence of inequalities over time even as levels of educational attainment were rising for all classes.

3. Michel D. Lagacé, *Educational Attainment in Canada: Some Regional and Social Aspects*, Dominion Bureau of Statistics, Special Labour Force Studies, Number 7 (Ottawa: Queen's Printer, 1968), p. 20. Reproduced by permission of Information Canada.

4. Canada, Royal Commission on Bilingualism and Biculturalism, *Report*, vol. IV (Ottawa: Queen's Printer, 1970), p. 102; vol. III (Ottawa: Queen's Printer, 1969), pp. 27, 29.

5. Richard Herrnstein, "I.Q.," *The Atlantic*, 228 (September 1971), 50–1.

6. Bruce K. Ecklund, "Genetics and Sociology: A Reconsideration," *American Sociological Review*, 32 (April 1967), 189.

7. *Encyclopaedia Britannica* (Chicago: Encyclopaedia Britannica, Inc., 1965), vol. 12, p. 345.

8. B. K. Ecklund, *loc. cit.*

9. For the report of their study see Yves de Jocas and Guy Rocher, "Inter-Generation Occupational Mobility in the Province of Quebec," *Canadian Journal of Economics and Political Science*, 27 (February 1957), 57–68.

10. Indirect evidence suggests that the data for French-speaking Quebec are representative for English-speaking Quebec at least. The indices of association for classes one and two in Table 5–14 were 2.81 for French-speaking and 3.26 for English-speaking urban Quebec. If we combine the two upper classes for all French-speaking fathers and sons from Table 5–12, the combined index of association is 3.11. Thus, if we were able to calculate a separate index of association for the upper class in English-speaking Quebec, the index would likely be comparable to that obtained for the French-speak-

ing sample. It may also be noted that the percentage of the Quebec labour force in the highest occupational classes is similar to that in the other provinces, and this indicates that the structure of occupational opportunities at least is more or less the same in all the provinces. A comparison of the labour forces of Quebec and Ontario is given in Tables 5–33 for 1961. For percentage distributions for all provinces, 1911 to 1961, see Canada, Dominion Bureau of Statistics, *1961 Census of Canada*, Bulletin 3.1–1 (Ottawa: Queen's Printer, 1964), Table 3.

11. This point is made by the Royal Commission on Bilingualism and Biculturalism, *Report*, vol. III, p. 35.

12. *Ibid.*, p. 37.

13. John Porter, *The Vertical Mosaic* (Toronto: University of Toronto Press, 1965), pp. 73–91.

14. Royal Commission on Bilingualism and Biculturalism, *Report*, vol. III, pp. 40–1.

15. Sylvia Ostry, *The Occupational Composition of the Canadian Labour Force*, Dominion Bureau of Statistics, 1961 Census Monograph (Ottawa: Queen's Printer, 1967), p. 27. Reproduced by permission of Information Canada.

16. Canada, Royal Commission on the Status of Women in Canada, *Report* (Ottawa: Information Canada, 1970), p. 30.

17. Andre Raynauld, Gérald Marion and Richard Béland, "La répartition des revenus selon les groupes ethniques au Canada," cited in the Royal Commission on Bilingualism and Biculturalism, *Report*, vol. III, pp. 46-7.

18. Donald E. Armstrong, *Education and Economic Achievement*, Documents of the Royal Commission on Bilingualism and Biculturalism, Number 7 (Ottawa: Information Canada, 1970), pp. 92-3. Reproduced by permission of Information Canada.

19. *Ibid.*, p. 97. Reproduced by permission of Information Canada.

20. Sylvia Ostry, *The Female Worker in Canada*, Dominion Bureau of Statistics, 1961 Census Monograph (Ottawa: Queen's Printer, 1968), p. 42. Reproduced by permission of Information Canada.

21. Gaetano Mosca, *The Ruling Class* (New York: McGraw-Hill Book Company, 1939), p. 50 .

22. Lester W. Milbrath, *Political Participation* (Chicago: Rand McNally and Company, 1965), p. 116.

23. *Ibid.*, p. 122.

24. Gabriel A. Almond and Sidney Verba, *The Civic Culture: Political Attitudes and Democracy in Five Nations* (copyright © 1963 by Princeton University Press) for the Center of International Studies, Princeton University, pp. 380–381.

25. Allan Kornberg, *Canadian Legislative Behaviour* (New York: Holt, Rinehart and Winston, 1967), p. 45.

26. Caroline Andrew, "The Political Background of Members of the Twenty-Sixth House of Commons," cited in David Hoffman and Norman Ward, *Bilingualism and Biculturalism in the Canadian House of Commons*, Documents of the Royal Commission on Bilingualism and Biculturalism, Number 3 (Ottawa: Queen's Printer, 1970), p. 27.

27. Leon D. Epstein, *Political Parties in Western Democracies* (New York: Frederick A. Praeger, 1967), p. 197.

28. J. Porter, *The Vertical Mosaic*, p. 391.

29. Richard J. Van Loon and Michael S. Whittington, *The Canadian Political System: Environment, Structure and Process* (Toronto: McGraw-Hill Company of Canada Ltd., 1971), p. 351.

30. André Gélinas, *Les Parlementaires et l'Administration au Québec* (Québec: Les Presses de l'Université Laval, 1969), p. 45.
31. Fred F. Schindeler, *Responsible Government in Ontario* (Toronto: University of Toronto Press, 1969), pp. 41-2. It should be noted that 21 per cent of the Cabinet had managerial occupations, somewhat less than the group represented in the legislature.
32. A. Gélinas, *op. cit.*, p. 46.
33. Donald R. Matthews, *U. S. Senators and Their World* (New York: Vintage Books, 1960), p. 282.
34. Mattei Dogan, "Political Ascent in a Class Society: French Deputies 1870–1958," in Duane Marvick (ed.), *Political Decisionmakers* (Glencoe: Free Press, 1961), p. 73.
35. Philip W. Buck, *Amateurs and Professionals in British Politics, 1918–59* (Chicago and London: University of Chicago Press, 1963), p. 121.
36. S. Encel, "The Political Elite in Australia," in Colin A. Hughes (ed.), *Readings in Australian Government* (St. Lucia, Queensland: University of Queensland Press, 1968), p. 102.
37. Maxwell E. Knight, *The German Executive 1890–1933* (Stanford, California: Stanford University Press, 1952), p. 41. Note that the percentages do not add to 100 per cent because one person might have engaged in several occupations in the course of his career.
38. Hannelore Schmidt, "Die Deutsche Exekutive 1949–1960," *Archives Européennes de Sociologie*, IV (November 1963), 175.
39. L. D. Epstein, *Political Parties in Western Democracies*, pp. 167–200.
40. *Ibid.*, p. 197.
41. D. R. Matthews, *op. cit.*, p. 20.
42. H. Schmidt, *op. cit.*, p. 176.
43. Allan Kornberg and Norman Thomas, "Representative Democracy and Political Elites in Canada and the United States," *Parliamentary Affairs*, 19 (Winter 1965–6), 95.
44. *Ibid.*, p. 96.
45. L. D. Epstein, *op. cit.*, p. 197.
46. D. Hoffman and N. Ward, *Bilingualism and Biculturalism in the Canadian House of Commons*, p. 24.
47. A. Kornberg and N. Thomas, *op. cit.*, p. 94.
48. J. Porter, *The Vertical Mosaic*, p. 388; L. D. Epstein, *op. cit.*, p. 198.
49. D. R. Matthews, *op. cit.*, p. 26.
50. David E. Butler and Anthony King, *The British General Election of 1964* (London: Macmillan and Company Ltd., 1965) p. 237.
51. Gerhard Loewenberg, *Parliament in the German Political System* (Ithaca, New York: Cornell University Press, 1967), p. 103.
52. Robert A. Scalapino and Junnosuke Masumi, *Parties and Politics in Contemporary Japan* (Berkeley and Los Angeles: University of California Press, 1964), p. 167.
53. Royal Commission on Bilingualism and Biculturalism, *Report*, vol. IV, p. 79.
54. A. Kornberg, *Canadian Legislative Behaviour*, p. 46.
55. D. Hoffman and N. Ward, *op. cit.*, p. 22.
56. Royal Commission on Bilingualism and Biculturalism, *Report*, vol. IV, p. 78.
57. Royal Commission on the Status of Women in Canada, *Report*, pp. 339–340.
58. *Ibid.*, p. 355. Reproduced by permission of Information Canada.
59. The evidence reported in this paragraph is taken from the following sources: Royal Commission on the Status of Women in Canada, *Report*, p. 344; P. W. Buck, *Amateurs and Professionals in British Politics*, pp. 32–35, 101, 107; G.

4

Loewenberg, *Parliament in the German Political System*, pp. 95–6; Pamela Brookes, *Women at Westminster* (London: Peter Davies, 1967), pp. 271–8; S. Encel, "The Political Elite in Australia," p. 105.

60. The indicators of political inequalities might also be applied to the second test as evidence of a lack of equality in access to political positions given appropriate educational preparation. Since what is appropriate educational preparation for membership in the political occupations is not at all clear, however, I have preferred to relate the evidence only to the third test.

61. It should be noted that socialist parties have represented women somewhat better in legislatures than parties of the right, but the differences are not very great.

Chapter Six

LIBERTY

At least two different aspects of freedom can be evaluated in any political community.[1] One is the probability of a person's being interfered with by other people. The more actions a person can take in a given sphere of action without interference by others, the greater is his degree of freedom. A citizen who enjoys, for example, the constitutional rights of free speech and free assembly has more freedom of independence to express his personal interests and more freedom of participation to influence the political life of his community than a citizen without those rights. Before the reform of the federal franchise law in 1960, the citizen of Canada who could vote had more freedom of participation than a Canadian Indian living on a reservation who could not vote; and a Canadian who could order alcoholic beverages in taverns, purchase them in the government's stores, and consume them in the privacy of his home had more freedom of independence than an Indian who could order drinks in a tavern but could not purchase alcohol in the government's stores or drink in his home on the reservation.

Another aspect of freedom concerns the scope or extent of the sphere of action. The greater the scope or extent of a person's sphere of action in terms of range of activities, size of territory, or number of people, the greater is the person's degree of freedom. The citizen of Canada who is able to travel with minor difficulties in obtaining a passport and visas to other nations has more freedom of independence than a citizen whose government issues no travel permits. Other things being equal, a citizen of a political community which has a multi-level system of government has more freedom of participation than a citizen of a unitary state. A businessman in Canada had somewhat more freedom of independence before the enactment of combines legislation and consumer protection legislation than he has had afterwards. Since the establishment of administrative tribunals such as the Income Tax Appeal Board, the ordinary citizen has had more freedom of participation than he had formerly to assert his personal interests against bureaucratic decisions.

A comparative evaluation of the two aspects of freedom is difficult because quantitative social indicators are not readily available. At best it is possible to form judgements of "more" or "less" about an aspect of freedom by using the extent of conforming behaviour as a rough index.[2] Beyond that a complete assessment of freedom of independence and participation in a political community is rarely possible because the aspects of freedom are closely interrelated and their relative importance is difficult to establish for any given comparison.

Governments are not the only source of coercion in a community. Extra-governmental efforts to ensure conformity in economic and social relationships are common in all societies; and, while interference by governments with freedom should properly be the focus of consideration in a study of political goods, any attempt at a complete assessment of freedom in a community obviously requires consideration of both governmental and extra-governmental interference with personal liberties. Regrettably, I have not found it possible to undertake such a burdensome and challenging task in this brief survey of political goods and have confined my consideration to governmental actions which restrict personal liberties.

Permissiveness and Coerciveness

Whether freedom of independence or freedom of participation is being considered, the lower the probability of interference by others, the greater is a person's degree of freedom. The Feierabend study group at San Diego State College has tried to make systematically comparative judgements for this aspect of freedom by compiling and scaling data on the permissiveness and coerciveness of governmental regimes and related political structures in seventy-five countries for the period from 1945 to 1966.[3]

The Feierabend study group classified the coercion observable in national political and social events as they were reported in the yearbooks of *Collier's Encyclopedia* and *Encyclopaedia Britannica* and supplemented by the reports of four other sources dealing specifically with press freedom. For making its classifications, the group used preconceived code sheets which required its coders to rate the degree of coercion observable in a number of different spheres of action for each country and year studied. These "more" or "less" ratings of governmental permissiveness or coerciveness were based on the coders' interpretations of the events reviewed and their understanding of the entire national situation for the indicator and year under review. The ratings for each indicator were made according to a scale having six positions:

(1) most permissive: little or no coercion of the private, social, and political sectors of the society;
(2) moderately permissive: few restrictions by the government on basic freedoms such as freedom of assembly, speech, and action;
(3) slightly permissive: controls in existence over the socio-political freedoms of the society but considered to be necessary to the well-being of the society by the majority of the population;
(4) slightly coercive: controls over the socio-political freedoms of the society considered to be beyond the bounds of acceptable governmental control by the majority of the population combined with considerable resistance to this control and reaction by the government in terms of physical coercive action;
(5) moderately coercive: governmental control over a majority of the socio-political freedoms of the society backed up with considerable use of force, actual or potential, against the population;
(6) most coercive: governmental controls over all or almost all of the socio-political freedoms of the society, allowing no opposition in any sector, and controls expedited by the application of extreme force if necessary.

Among the many indicators for which the Feierabend study group collected data, five may be taken as especially representative of governmental permissiveness and coerciveness: restraints on civil rights, degree of executive coercion, oppression of party opposition, restraints on suffrage, and internal press censorship.[4] The indicator of restraints on civil rights involves a general rating of the personal freedom of the individual citizen in relation to speech, religion, press, assembly, and occupational choice. Degree of executive coercion refers to the general regulatory control exercised by the government and includes consideration of the manner of recruiting the chief political executive (whether by election, assassination of his predecessor, coup d'état, or otherwise) and evaluation of his performance and general policy orientation. Oppression of party opposition refers to the attitude and actions of the government towards political parties not belonging to or controlled by the political party in power. The indicator of restrictions on suffrage provides a measure of the degree of governmental control over voting, including an approximation of the number of people disfranchised and an assessment of the regularity and authenticity of elections. Internal press censorship refers to the amount of governmental control directed at regulating the publication of printed news but does not cover restrictions imposed on foreign correspondents or by occupation governments.

Summary average scores for the five indicators of permissiveness–

coerciveness—restraints on civil rights, degree of executive coercion, oppression of party opposition, restraints on suffrage, and internal press censorship—have been calculated by Robert Kauffman; and the results are shown in Table 6-1 for seventy-five nations for the period 1945-1966. In order to obtain these summary scores, each coder's rating of permissiveness–coerciveness was assigned an appropriate score on the six-point scale. Then the average score for each indicator was calculated for each nation for the entire 1945–1966 period, and these average scores for each of the five indicators were in turn averaged for each nation to produce an overall score of permissiveness–coerciveness. The summary scores which resulted from taking these successive averages thus provide a rough index for ranking the seventy-five nations by their degree of permissiveness–coerciveness; and, although it would be unwise to attach too much importance to the exact ranks attained by this method, the general pattern of scores does reveal significant variations in the extent to which different regimes resorted to coercion between 1945 and 1966.

According to the indicators of permissiveness and coerciveness which are summarized in Table 6–1, the nations which are industrialized political democracies are distinguished by their relatively low levels of coercion. Twenty of the first twenty-four nations listed in Table 6–1 are industrialized political democracies. Their summary average scores of permissiveness–coerciveness are all well below the median score (Ecuador = 3.121); and, indeed, all but three of them have scores which fall in the first quartile.

The relatively low score ascribed to Canada by the index of permissiveness–coerciveness may reasonably be thought to place Canada among that most permissive group of nations in which the citizens experienced little or no coercion between 1945 and 1966. Canada's score of 1.075 placed it tenth on the index, with 87 per cent of the seventy-five nations having higher scores and only 12 per cent having lower scores. Even within the relatively permissive sub-group of twenty industrialized political democracies, which had a median score of 1.078, the Canadian score was a moderately favourable one. This particular cross-national investigation, then, leads clearly to the conclusion that compared with other nations the probability of governmental interference in Canada is relatively low.

Our study of the probability of governmental interference in Canada can be extended by using the comparative categories developed by the Feierabend study group to classify the historical stages in the growth of freedom in Canada. The low probability of governmental interference which the Feierabend study group found in post-war Canada is the culmination of over three centuries of political history during which the character of governmental regimes

Table 6–1. *Summary Average Scores for Five Indicators of Permissiveness–Coerciveness in Seventy-five Nations, 1945–1966*

Nation	Score	Nation	Score
Iceland	1.000	Lebanon	3.275
Luxembourg	1.000	Ethiopia	3.326
New Zealand	1.000	Morocco	3.327
Norway	1.000	Honduras	3.427
Sweden	1.000	Colombia	3.437
Finland	1.018	Venezuela	3.456
Ireland	1.022	Peru	3.467
United States	1.025	Argentina	3.729
Netherlands	1.036	Pakistan	3.810
Canada	1.075	Cambodia	3.816
Belgium	1.081	Jordan	3.834
United Kingdom	1.135	Poland	3.895
Australia	1.173	Thailand	3.970
Italy	1.209	Sudan	4.083
Costa Rica	1.227	Union of South Africa	4.092
Uruguay	1.273	Tunisia	4.184
Israel	1.357	Ghana	4.222
France	1.408	Egypt	4.238
Japan	1.414	USSR	4.370
Austria	1.476	Indonesia	4.446
Philippines	1.476	Syria	4.478
Switzerland	1.543	Nicaragua	4.537
Mexico	1.588	Dominican Republic	4.575
West Germany	1.654	Cuba	4.595
Chile	2.077	Paraguay	4.599
Malaya	2.105	Iraq	4.741
Ceylon	2.266	Afghanistan	4.765
India	2.340	Portugal	4.972
Panama	2.523	Saudi Arabia	4.974
Brazil	2.738	Spain	4.997
El Salvador	2.854	Haiti	4.998
Cyprus	2.910	Czechoslovakia	5.052
Liberia	2.931	Hungary	5.277
Bolivia	2.948	Rumania	5.288
Libya	3.011	Bulgaria	5.356
Laos	3.103	East Germany	5.779
Turkey	3.113	Albania	5.991
Ecuador	3.121		

Source: Robert E. Kauffman, *Level and Fluctuation of Government Coercion and Systemic Political Instability: A Cross-National Study* (San Diego: San Diego State College, 1970).

slowly changed from most coercive to most permissive. Generally speaking, the colonial regime of France may be characterized as moderately to most coercive; the colonial regime of Britain was slightly coercive; and, except for the slightly permissive periods of world war, the modern Canadian democratic regime has been moderately to most permissive. Without attempting a detailed history of governmental interference in Canada, it may be possible to indicate this growth of freedom by using the six positions on the scale developed by the Feierabend study group to make comparative ratings for four indicators for which historical studies are readily available: freedom of religion, internal press censorship, oppression of party opposition, and restraints on suffrage.

Freedom of religion.[5] Religious freedom in Canada has developed in three stages. With respect to religious freedom, Canada was most coercive under the French colonial regime, slightly coercive between 1760 and 1854, and it has been moderately permissive since 1854.

Under the French colonial regime, the government carefully controlled religious practices and permitted no opposition. A brief period of tension between Catholics and Protestants in the colony ended in 1627 when the royal charter of the Company of One Hundred Associates provided for the exclusion of all Protestants and the establishment of the Roman Catholic Church under royal auspices. The Society of Jesus was given a monopoly of all religious functions in the colony and instituted a religious regime "as puritanical as that of Calvin and his followers in Geneva."[6] The government of New France became a virtual theocracy as the Jesuits nominated acceptable governors, controlled finance, and employed company officers to impose civil punishments for religious crimes.

After the dissolution of the Company in 1663, ecclesiastical supremacy was gradually undermined; and after 1727 the supremacy of the state over the church was so completely established that the local parish became a mere extension of the central political authority at Quebec. However, this progressive shift from ultramontane theocracy to Gallican authoritarianism did not alter the high degree of coerciveness in the colony. Both Bishops Laval and Saint-Vallier (1659–1725) were vigilant in detecting vice and combatting heresy; and the pious Governor Denonville was able to report to French authorities that "Praise be God, there is not a heretic here."[7]

The British conquest changed the relationship of church and state in Canada. In Britain Roman Catholicism was still illegal, but the French colonists were permitted to practise their religion without having equal political rights. After the arrival of the Loyalists, an annual statutory grant was made for the support of the Church of England, but the imperial policy of an established church could not be put into practice. On the one hand, in Lower Canada the loyalty of the Roman Catholic Church during the War of 1812 brought it the rewards of legal recognition and financial support from the state. On the other hand, the religiously pluralistic society of Upper Canada produced a persistent opposition to the privileged position of the Church of England over such matters as the clergy reserves, which contributed to causing the 1837 Rebellion and which only ended with the secularization of the clergy reserves in 1854.

The conflict between voluntarism and establishmentarianism was less acrimonious in the Maritimes than it was in Upper Canada, but there was also greater intolerance shown towards Catholics. After the expulsion of the Catholic Acadians in 1755, the Church of England was officially established in Nova Scotia (1758), New Brunswick (1786) and Prince Edward Island (1802). Protestant dissenters were granted liberty of conscience, but Roman Catholics were prohibited from owning property and operating schools and Catholic priests were banned from the colonies. Between 1783 and 1830 the civil disabilities against Catholics were gradually removed in Nova Scotia, and the provisions of the British Catholic Relief Act were extended to New Brunswick and Prince Edward Island by Acts of the colonial assemblies in 1830.

Since 1854, few restrictions have been placed on religious freedom by Canadian governments. The British North America Act contains no guarantee of religious freedom, but Section 1(a) of the Canadian Bill of Rights does recognize and protect freedom of religion. By a legal oddity, no statutes have ever disestablished the Church of England in the three Maritime Provinces; but the situation has no practical significance, as all religious bodies are treated with complete equality and the Church of England claims no preferential treatment.[8] Outside the Maritime Provinces, there is no established church, although in the province of Quebec the political authority of the Catholic hierarchy, the entrenched position of Catholic schools in the public educational system, and the subsidies received by Church welfare enterprises from public funds have provided certain similarities to a state church.[9] Various religious groups have been targets of discrimination by majority groups, for example, Jews and Jehovah's Witnesses in Quebec, Doukhobors in British Columbia, and Hutterites in Alberta; but such intolerance is now rare. Undoubtedly the most important of the residual issues is that of denominational education, which has constantly raised serious problems of religious liberty in all provinces. Limitations on state aid to separate schools now present the last substantial barrier to the achievement of the highest degree of permissiveness in religious freedom.

Internal press censorship.[10] Internal press censorship was moderately coercive in Canada in the eighteenth century, developed from slightly coercive to moderately permissive during the nineteenth century, and became most permissive in the twentieth century. The subservient role of the newspapers as agents of the government was taken for granted in British North America during the second half of the eighteenth century. Governors and other public officials subjected newspapers to a humiliating domination which was reinforced by the almost complete dependence of the early press on the financial support and patronage of the colonial ruling elite.

In the early nineteenth century, a new kind of editor who printed advertisements and sold subscriptions instead of depending on public patronage appeared. Editorial comment on contentious social and political issues, especially on the struggle for responsible government, openly challenged governmental controls over news publication and resulted in many conflicts between editors and public officials. Coercion of newspaper publishers, editors, and journalists was common and at first effective; but it also tended to evoke sympathy and opposition, as was illustrated by the acquittal of Joseph Howe on criminal charges of libel in 1835, a critical precedent for the freedom of the press.

In the latter part of the nineteenth century, attempts at governmental denomination of the press ended; and freedom of the press increased markedly with the passage of progressive legislation explicitly defining a broad licence within which Canadian journalism could function. As one contemporary observer suggested, the new legislation was "presumably a recognition by the Local and Federal legislatures of the exceptional position occupied by the newspaper press, the public, and, at times, perilous nature of its duties, and its public usefulness."[11]

Governmental censorship of the press during the two world wars of the twentieth century was accepted in Canada as a patriotic necessity. Censorship was particularly strict during World War I, as one paper and a press were seized for infractions; 151 newspapers were denied use of the mails and possession of copies of them was made illegal; and in 1918 it was made a crime to import, publish, post, or possess a publication in an enemy language. About fifteen Communist weeklies were suppressed in the early months of World War II before the Soviet Union became an ally, but otherwise there were only a few convictions for minor security violations which resulted in small fines but did not interrupt publishing schedules.

Except for the periods of the world wars, restrictions on the freedom of the press in the twentieth century in Canada have been relatively few. The laws on defamatory libel and contempt of court have provided useful legal standards without undue restrictions for the press, although journalists do remain vulnerable by having no statutory right to protect the sources of their information. Occasional attempts to interfere with the freedom of the press, such as the Alberta Press Bill, have been strongly and successfully resisted. The trend clearly has been towards a libertarian, most permissive treatment of the press.

Oppression of party opposition.[12] Oppression of party opposition in Canada was moderately coercive under the French and early British colonial regimes, slightly coercive from 1790 to 1840, and moderately permissive from 1840 to 1920. Since 1920 it has been most permissive.

During the French colonial regime, the authoritarian controls of state and church made the development of opposition movements impossible. Before 1690 the authorities did experience difficulties enforcing some of their controls, particularly those directed at the trading activities of the *coureurs de bois* in the interior. "Organized within fur trading parties, with a strong sense of comradeship and loyalty to their leaders, and with their own distinctive rules of conduct and code of honour, these rangers of the wood were able to exert a powerful collective force in resisting the regulations of the state and church."[13] After 1690 even this resistance disappeared as the French military presence on the frontier was strengthened, the fur trade was brought under close control, and the *coureurs de bois* became *voyageurs*.

The defeat of the French regime by the British did not immediately affect the authoritarian character of colonial government. An assembly was granted to Nova Scotia in 1758, but for three decades it represented no opposition. In Canada there was an even more determined effort than in Nova Scotia to maintain authoritarian government, and by 1774 governmental and ecclesiastical control was wider and stronger than anything which had existed under French rule.[14]

Between 1790 and 1840 open opposition movements developed inside the colonial assemblies, but they were subjected to continual harassment by governmental authorities. Movements of political opposition, such as those of James Glenie in New Brunswick (1789–1805), Cottnam Tonge in Nova Scotia (1792–1807), Robert Gourlay in Upper Canada (1817–1819), Louis Joseph Papineau in Lower Canada (1807–1837), and William Lyon Mackenzie in Upper Canada (1828–1837), were variously met by governmental authorities with suspension of the reformers from official positions, their expulsion from the assemblies, rejection of policies proposed by reformist assemblies, charges of seditious libel, and banishment from the colonies. In Nova Scotia, for example, Cottnam Tonge carried his opposition against the prevailing system of political preferment and arbitrary rule into the country, succeeded in building up the rudimentary organization of a reform party and was elected speaker of the assembly in 1805; but following the election of 1806, the Governor refused to accept Tonge as speaker, dismissed him as Naval Officer, enforced an old law against town meetings to prevent demonstrations of public opposition, and suspended a number of justices of the peace who supported Tonge. In 1827 the Governor of Lower Canada also refused to accept Papineau as speaker, prorogued the legislature, and brought charges of seditious libel against the editor and printer of a newspaper carrying accounts of protest meetings. The following year the first reform assembly in Upper Canada passed fifty-seven bills which were vetoed by the Legislative Council, and the reform leader Mackenzie was expelled five times from the anti-reform assembly of 1830.

Probably the most oppressive policy of the Canadian authorities was their tolerance of anti-reform mob violence. As a result of the activities of the reactionary Orange Order "something closely approaching gangsterism was introduced into the politics of Upper Canada, and mob violence came increasingly to be relied upon in the two years before the rebellion as a means of suppressing efforts to secure by free and open discussion a solution of public questions."[15] It was the violence involving reformers and reactionaries after a mass meeting which caused Papineau to leave Montreal in November 1837; but the Government, believing the reformers to be on the verge of rebellion, issued warrants for the arrest of Papineau and other reform leaders. A series of bitter clashes followed and the insurrection was ruthlessly suppressed. A clumsy insurrection by the reformers of Upper Canada was also easily and decisively suppressed. The leaders of the insurrections escaped to the United States, and the ensuing border agitation was without effect. At the end of the 1830s the oppression of party opposition had reverted temporarily to being rather more than "slightly" coercive.

During the 1840s party competition was accepted with responsible government, and governmental coercion of opposition parties was replaced by a more subtle manipulation of electoral rules and public resources. The four main techniques used to advance the position of the governing party and inconvenience the opposition were deferred elections, gerrymandering, the alteration of franchise qualifications, and the distribution of patronage.

Voting was not simultaneous in all constituencies in the first three national elections of 1867, 1872, and 1874. The government was able to call the election first in favourable constituencies and afterwards take the campaign to marginal and then to dangerous constituencies.

In 1878 simultaneous voting was established throughout the east for all but a few constituencies, Manitoba voted with the east in 1882, and by 1908 deferred elections had been discontinued in the majority of western constituencies.[16]

In 1872, 1882, and 1892, the Government clearly abused its power to redistribute seats in the House of Commons by altering constituency boundaries so that they greatly favoured the governing party; and this was especially flagrant in 1882 when forty-six constituencies in Ontario were gerrymandered.[17] The potential for abuse was greatly reduced in 1903, however, when the Laurier Government assigned the task of redistribution to a Select Committee of the House of Commons including representatives of both parties; and gerrymandering on a grand scale disappeared.

The most blatant example of manipulating the rules of voting eligibility was the Wartime Elections Act which was passed just before the 1917 election. Under the 1917 amendments, the franchise was granted to all women who had husbands, sons, brothers, or fathers in the Canadian or British armed forces and to any men disqualified by provincial property or income qualifications who had sons or grandsons in the services. The franchise was also extended to virtually all members of the armed forces whether or not they were ordinarily residents of Canada, minors, or Indians. The disfranchised groups included conscientious objectors, Mennonites, Doukhobors, all naturalized British subjects born in an enemy country and naturalized after March 1902, and anyone who habitually spoke an enemy language and had been naturalized after 1902. Newly franchised soldiers and the wives, mothers, sisters, and daughters of soldiers were expected to vote for the Government, whereas the disfranchised naturalized aliens according to their record between 1900 and 1911 would have been likely to vote for the Liberal opposition. As Ward has remarked, these changes produced "the most remarkable franchise act ever passed in Canada and very possibly in the democratic world" and could hardly fail to return a majority for the Union Government enacting it.[18]

Political patronage included the use of civil servants as party workers, the appointment of party supporters to the civil service, the use of public works appropriations for "pork barrel" purposes, and the granting of contracts in return for financial or electoral support.[19] The first important step to reduce patronage was taken in 1918 when most of the civil service was placed under the Civil Service Commission and the recruitment of officials was based on its open competitive tests. Since then patronage has declined steadily but has not disappeared entirely.

Only a few instances of direct oppression of party opposition can be documented in the late nineteenth and early twentieth centuries. The most important instance of oppression occurred during the "red scare" period at the end of World War I. Fifteen radical associations were banned by Order-in-Council in 1918–19 under the authority of the War Measures Act.[20] Among the seven leaders of the Winnipeg Strike who were convicted of seditious conspiracy in 1920, four were also leaders in the radical Socialist Party of Canada and one was a Social Democrat. In 1919, following the strike, a section aimed at unlawful association was added to the Criminal Code enacting that any organization

whose professed purpose or one of whose purposes is to bring about any governmental industrial or economic change within Canada by use of force, violence or physical injury to person or property, or by threats of such injury, or which teaches, advocates, advises or defends the use of force, violence, terrorism, or physical injury to person or property, or threats of such injury, in order to accomplish such change, or for any other purpose, or which shall by any means prosecute or pursue such purpose or professed purpose, or shall so teach, advocate, advise or defend, shall be an unlawful association.

The electoral and civil service reforms achieved by the end of World War I were probably sufficient to merit the conclusion that the shift from a moderately to a most permissive position with respect to restrictions on party opposition occurred in national politics at about this time. The much slower achievement of these reforms by provincial governments delayed a comparable reduction of indirect restrictions on provincial party oppositions until after World War II, and patronage has continued to be much more important in most provincial than in federal politics.

One measure of the freedom of party opposition in Canada can be found in the multi-party system which has characterized national politics since 1921, with the Liberals and Conservatives joined permanently in the House of Commons by members of the Social Credit Party and the Co-operative Commonwealth Federation (later New Democratic Party) since 1935, and variously at other times by members of the Progressive Party, United Farmers of Alberta, Canadian Communist Party, Bloc Populaire, Reconstruction Party, United Farmers of Ontario-Labour, Unity Party, Labour Party, and Liberal-Progressive Party. During the same period, provincial governments have been controlled by Liberals, Conservatives, C.C.F., N.D.P., Social Credit, United Farmers of Alberta, Farmer-Labour Party of Ontario, and Union Nationale.

The direct oppression of opposition parties in modern Canadian politics has continued to be sporadic and transitory. It is perhaps significant that in the Manitoba elections of 1920 four of the socialist leaders of the Winnipeg Strike won seats in the legislature while still serving jail terms, and in the 1921 federal election J. S. Woodsworth became the first socialist member of the House of Commons. There were three reported instances of prosecutions under the 1919 "unlawful association" section of the Criminal Code, all against Communists with two convictions resulting, before the section was repealed in 1936.[21] The following year the Quebec Government passed the Communistic Propaganda Act ("Padlock Law") empowering the Government to close any house being used to propagate Communism and to confiscate propaganda materials, and it was not until 1957 that this Act was declared *ultra vires* of the Quebec legislature by the Supreme Court of Canada. By far the most serious governmental coercion of political opposition occurred in October 1970 when two political kidnappings led the Government to invoke the War Measures Act, briefly imprison four hundred and fifty supporters of the political left, and ban the Front de Libération du Québec. The political environment which resulted from resorting to these controls produced a slightly permissive situation for party opposition for several months in 1970–71.

Restraints on suffrage.[22] Restrictions on the right to vote and seek elected public office have been progressively reduced in four stages, from moderately coercive between 1758 and 1830 to most permissive at present when virtually all responsible citizens can vote in both federal and provincial elections. At various times in Canadian history, Roman Catholics, Quakers, Jews, Mennonites, Doukhobors, Eskimos, Indians, Chinese, Japanese, women, and people without property have been by law ineligible to vote. The progressive inclusion of each of these disqualified groups over the past two centuries has constituted an important element in the general decline of governmental coercion. It has also made a significant contribution towards the expansion of freedom of participation.

The franchise acts which followed the granting of representative assemblies from 1758 to 1830 may be described as moderately coercive because of their highly discriminatory property, sexual, and religious qualifications. The freehold franchise prevalent in rural England was extended to the colonies of Nova Scotia, New Brunswick, and the Canadas while freeholders, leaseholders, and householders were allowed to vote in Prince Edward Island; but this property qualification was perhaps more significant in principle than it was in practice until the 1830s when free land ceased to be available. Although there was no statutory prohibition against female suffrage at this time, women were effectively excluded from voting as a result of acceptance in the colonies of the British policy of disfranchising women by convention and the rule of the Common Law. The first franchises in the colonies also included religious disqualifications similar to those existing in Britain which especially affected Quakers, Roman Catholics, and Jews. Because of their numbers, the ineligibility of Roman Catholics was by far the most important result of the religious disqualifications in the colonial franchises.

Following the introduction of more liberal policies in Britain after 1749, legislation which permitted an affirmation to be substituted for an oath was passed by the assembly of Nova Scotia in 1759, New Brunswick in 1786, Prince Edward Island in 1785, Lower Canada in 1793, and finally Upper Canada in 1833; and the colonial franchises and legislatures were thereby opened to Quakers, Moravians, Mennonites, and other religious sects refusing to swear an oath. Roman Catholics were first enfranchised in Nova Scotia in 1789. The Constitutional Act of 1791 granted all citizens in Lower and Upper Canada the rights of franchise and election to the colonial assembly regardless of religious persuasion, and New Brunswick passed legislation allowing Roman Catholics to vote in 1810. Finally, following the example of the Catholic Emancipation Act in Britain, Prince Edward Island opened its franchise and all elective offices to Catholics in 1829; and Nova Scotia and New Brunswick granted them the right of election the following year. The disfranchisement of Jews in British North America had been an incidental effect of the policies intended to disfranchise Catholics; and as Catholics obtained the right to vote so did Jews, although there continued to be indirect restrictions on their right of election in New Brunswick and Nova Scotia until 1846.

With the virtual end of religious disqualifications in the 1830s, a second, slightly coercive stage of restraints on suffrage began. The disfranchisement of women by convention and the rule of the Common Law was converted into their disfranchisement by law in Prince Edward Island in 1836, New Brunswick in 1843, the Province of Canada in 1849, and Nova Scotia in 1851. An end to grants of free land also made the property qualification more restrictive after the 1830s.

Franchise provisions were gradually liberalized in all the colonies in the middle of the nineteenth century but a property qualification was retained. Prince Edward Island had the most liberal provisions when its occupancy franchise was extended after 1853 to include all citizens liable for statute labour on the roads, in effect, virtually the entire male population. The most restrictive qualifications existed

Liberty

in New Brunswick where the assessment franchise adopted in 1855 did not enfranchise the labouring class representing one-fifth of the male population, and in British Columbia, where a very complex franchise came close to producing manhood suffrage for whites only in a province having a very large proportion of non-whites. Property qualifications remained an important restriction until 1898 when the federal government returned to using provincial franchises for federal elections; and, since manhood suffrage had been adopted in all the provinces except Quebec and Nova Scotia, the notion that the franchise was a trust accompanying property rather than a right of citizenship soon disappeared from Canadian politics except at the municipal level.

Campaigns for female suffrage were well underway in Canada by 1880; but it was not until 1916 that the first legislation granting female suffrage was passed in Manitoba. Similar legislation soon followed in other jurisdictions, and by 1922 women had the right to vote and seek election at the federal level and in all the provinces except Quebec.

A third, moderately permissive stage of restraints on suffrage in Canada may be dated from the 1920s to the 1960s. Unlike the effects of the improvements which terminated the second stage of suffrage restrictions, no significant increase in the percentage of the voting-age population eligible to vote marked the end of this period, as Tables 6–3 and 6–4 taken together show; but a number of specific restrictions on the franchise after 1920, while not affecting very large groups of citizens, infringed principles which are sufficiently important to prevent rating Canadian suffrage as most permissive.

Table 6–2. Percentage of the Population Enfranchised in Selected Constituencies at the Federal Elections of 1867, 1882, 1891, and 1900

| Province | Eligible voters as a percentage of total population in selected constituencies | | | |
	1867	1882	1891	1900
Nova Scotia	14.0	15.1	22.1	24.8
New Brunswick	15.2	16.9	21.1	27.3
Quebec	16.1	16.6	20.1	21.1
Ontario	16.5	20.2	26.4	27.1
Manitoba	—	34.8	30.3	27.9
British Columbia	—	11.0	13.3	21.9
Number of constituencies in sample	30	35	37	36

Source: Norman Ward, The Canadian House of Commons: Representation (Toronto: University of Toronto Press, 1950), pp. 212, 214, 221, 225.

Table 6–3. *Percentage of Total Population Enfranchised at the Federal Elections of 1911, 1921, and 1930*

Province	Eligible voters as a percentage of total population		
	1911	1921	1930
Prince Edward Island	—	52.9	53.4
Nova Scotia	27.8	56.2	53.8
New Brunswick	28.7	52.7	50.7
Quebec	22.7	44.8	47.0
Ontario	27.4	58.6	55.2
Manitoba	21.4	41.8	46.9
Saskatchewan	28.9	44.0	44.5
Alberta	28.6	46.5	41.6
British Columbia	21.2	44.0	48.0
Canada	25.2	50.6	49.7

Source: Norman Ward, *The Canadian House of Commons: Representation* (Toronto: University of Toronto Press, 1950), p. 230.

Table 6–4. *Percentage of the Voting-age Population Registered on the Voters' Lists at the Federal Elections of 1940, 1957, and 1972*

Province	Registered voters as percentage of voting-age population		
	1940	1957	1972
Newfoundland	—	96.8	99.9
Prince Edward Island	99.7	98.5	100.2
Nova Scotia	98.5	98.0	98.7
New Brunswick	99.2	98.9	99.8
Quebec	97.1	97.8	95.8
Ontario	95.3	92.0	91.0
Manitoba	94.3	92.3	95.1
Saskatchewan	93.9	94.4	95.6
Alberta	89.4	90.4	94.4
British Columbia	84.2	90.2	90.6
Canada	94.6	94.0	93.7

Sources: Canada, Dominion Bureau of Statistics, *Canada Year Book 1948–49* (Ottawa: King's Printer, 1949), p. 94; *Canada Year Book 1957* (Ottawa: Queen's Printer 1957), p. 71; Canada, Chief Electoral Officer, *Twenty-Ninth General Election 1972: Report of the Chief Electoral Officer* (Ottawa: Information Canada, 1973), p. ix; *Eighth Census of Canada 1941* (Ottawa: King's Printer, 1946), Volume III, Table 3; *Census of Canada 1956* (Ottawa: Queen's Printer, 1957), Bulletin 1-10, Table 21; Statistics Canada, *1971 Census of Canada*, Volume I–Part 2 (Bulletin 1.2-4) (Ottawa: Information Canada, 1973), Table 14. Reproduced by permission of Information Canada.

One shortcoming of suffrage legislation after 1920 resulted from the slowness of Quebec to accept reforms previously adopted in other jurisdictions. The property qualification, which had been removed from the provincial franchise in Nova Scotia in 1920, lasted in Quebec until 1936; and women in Quebec were not accorded voting rights on equal terms with men until 1940.

A more serious shortcoming of suffrage legislation after 1920 was the persistence of a number of discriminatory qualifications based on ethnicity which were only gradually amended after World War II. Until 1948, Canadians of the Chinese, Japanese, and East Indian ethnic groups had no vote unless they had served in the armed forces; and it was not until 1953 that all references to race were finally removed from franchise legislation in British Columbia. Doukhobors were also enfranchised in British Columbia in 1953, and in 1955 the federal provision was repealed which had disqualified from voting any persons entitled to claim exemption from military service because of their religious affiliations. The provision of the federal franchise act which had prevented Eskimos from voting after 1934 was repealed in 1950, but the disfranchisement of Indians living on reservations continued for federal elections until 1960 and was maintained for provincial elections in Quebec until 1969.

In terms of the number of people who were previously disqualified, the most important changes in suffrage qualifications since 1920 have been those which have greatly increased the population eligible to vote and seek elective office by lowering the age limit from the customary twenty-one years to eighteen years or nineteen years. Alberta (nineteen in 1944), Saskatchewan (eighteen in 1945), British Columbia (nineteen in 1953), and Quebec (eighteen in 1963) were the first provinces to lower the age limits; and at the end of the 1960s there were similar amendments in other jurisdictions. By 1972 the age to qualify for suffrage had been lowered to eighteen years for federal elections and for provincial elections in Prince Edward Island, New Brunswick, Ontario, Manitoba, and Alberta, and to nineteen years in Newfoundland and Nova Scotia.

Although certain election officers and people who are non-residents, insane, or confined in penal institutions are unable to vote, most of the people who are disfranchised in Canada at present are accounted for by those who are not citizens and those who are under-age. Given its recent amendment, the age limit is not likely to be soon further reduced. Nor is there any sign of an impending relaxation of existing requirements for citizenship. Indeed, an amendment to the Canada Elections Act in 1970 which removed the long-standing provision exempting non-citizen British subjects from the requirement of Canadian citizenship ended a point of discrimination among non-citizens with respect to voting qualifications; but it also added to the group of people who are disqualified. Even with these remaining restrictions, however, suffrage qualifications in contemporary Canada fully merit an unqualified rating of most permissive.

Libertarian Attitudes

No doubt the probability of governmental interference is measured most reliably by estimates derived from historical analysis of the experience of the people who have lived in a given political community, but another useful approach to estimating the probability of governmental interference is to study the attitudes toward individual liberties and civil rights which are prevalent in the community. As Ted G. Harvey has remarked,

> *students of politics have long realized that individual orienta-tions towards rules of the political process produce important effects on the quality of political relations. Such orientations may be of considerable importance in determining whether political relations are peaceful, expansive, and productive, or turbulent, restrictive, and destructive. Beliefs regarding civil liberties fall into this category, particularly in a society which loosely defines itself as "democratic."*[23]

The classic study of popular attitudes towards civil liberties in a political democracy was that directed by Samuel Stouffer in the United States in 1954. Based on a national sample of the American population and a separate sample of community leaders, Stouffer found, first, that a majority of the national sample approved of giving certain individual freedoms to socialists but were much less tolerant of atheists and communists and, second, that all categories of community leaders tended on average to be more respectful of the civil rights of non-conformists than the average person in the general population.[24] To analyze the patterns of response, Stouffer constructed a scale of willingness to tolerate non-conformists based on fifteen items from the questionnaire (which included seven of the nine items shown in Table 6–5). When the samples were divided into three groups of more tolerant, middle, and less tolerant, 66 per cent of the community leaders and 31 per cent of the national sample fell into the more tolerant group, while 5 per cent of the community leaders and 19 per cent of the national sample had scale scores low enough to be in the less tolerant group.

The marked differences in attitudes towards civil liberties which Stouffer found between community leaders and ordinary citizens in the United States were also found by Herbert McCloskey in his study of the values and beliefs of political influentials (based on a sample of over 3,000 drawn from the delegates and alternates who had attended the Democratic and Republican conventions of 1956) compared with those held by the general electorate. As Table 6–6 shows, McCloskey found remarkably high support expressed by both groups on abstract statements about freedom. However, when both groups

Table 6–5. Opinions of Americans on Civil Rights for Three Types of Non-conformists, United States, 1954

Item	Type of non-conformist	Percentage of respondents expressing agreement	
		Community leaders	National sample
If non-conformist wanted to make a speech in our community, he should be allowed to speak	Socialist	84	58
	Atheist	64	37
	Communist	51	27
If people suggested removing a book written by the non-conformist from the local public library, would not approve	Socialist	79	52
	Atheist	64	35
	Communist	42	27
Non-conformist should be allowed to teach in a college or university*	Socialist	48	33
	Atheist	25	12
	Communist	11	6

* The question concerning admitted Communist was "Suppose he is teaching in a college. Should he be fired or not?" The percentages shown are those responding that he should not be fired.

Source: Samuel A. Stouffer, *Communism, Conformism and Civil Liberties* (New York: John Wiley and Sons, Inc., 1966), pp. 29–30, 32–3, 40, 43.

Table 6–6. Political Influentials Versus the Electorate: Responses to Items Expressing Support for General Statements of Free Speech and Opinion, United States, 1956–1957

Item	Percentage expressing agreement	
	Political influentials	General electorate
People who hate our way of life should still have a chance to talk and be heard.	86.9	81.8
No matter what a person's political beliefs are, he is entitled to the same legal rights and protections as anyone else.	96.4	94.3
I believe in free speech for all no matter what their views might be.	89.4	88.9
Nobody has a right to tell another person what he should and should not read.	81.4	80.7
You can't really be sure whether an opinion is true or not unless people are free to argue against it.	94.9	90.8
Unless there is freedom for many points of view to be presented, there is little chance that the truth can ever be known.	90.6	85.2
I would not trust any person or group to decide what opinions can be freely expressed and what must be silenced.	79.1	64.6
Freedom of conscience should mean freedom to be an atheist as well as freedom to worship in the church of one's choice.	87.8	77.0

Source: Herbert McCloskey, "Consensus and Ideology in American Politics," *American Political Science Review*, 58 (June 1964), 366.

were presented with the items shown in Table 6–7, involving more specific applications of free speech and procedural rights, the political influentials were much more consistent in applying the general principles to the specific instances and exhibited stronger support for specific democratic values than did the electorate in general.

A community survey which was carried out by Ted G. Harvey in a large city in Western Canada in early 1970 had the objective of providing at least partial information about popular attitudes towards freedom of speech in Canada along the lines of the survey developed by Stouffer and others with respect to the United States. Harvey asked the respondents to his survey to indicate the extent to which they endorsed free speech for eight more or less deviant political types. The distribution of responses from the endorsement of a minimum to a maximum of free speech for each of the eight political types is shown in Table 6–8.

Table 6–7. *Political Influentials Versus the Electorate: Responses to Items Expressing Support for Specific Applications of Free Speech and Procedural Rights, United States 1956–1957*

| | Percentage expressing agreement | |
| | Political influentials | General electorate |
Item		
Freedom does not give anyone the right to teach foreign ideas in our schools.	45.5	56.7
A man oughtn't to be allowed to speak if he doesn't know what he is talking about.	17.3	36.7
A book that contains wrong political views cannot be a good book and does not deserve to be published.	17.9	50.3
When the country is in great danger we may have to force people to testify against themselves even if it violates their rights.	28.5	36.3
No matter what crime a person is accused of, he should never be convicted unless he has been given the right to face and question his accusers.	90.1	88.1
If a person is convicted of a crime by illegal evidence, he should be set free and the evidence thrown out of court.	79.6	66.1
If someone is suspected of treason or other serious crimes, he shouldn't be entitled to be let out on bail.	33.3	68.9
Any person who hides behind the laws when he is questioned about his activities doesn't deserve much consideration.	55.9	75.7
In dealing with dangerous enemies like the communists, we can't afford to depend on the courts, the laws and their slow and unreliable methods.	7.4	25.5

Source: Herbert McCloskey, "Consensus and Ideology in American Politics," *American Political Science Review*, 58 (June 1964), 367.

Liberty

Table 6–8.   Attitudes in a Canadian Community Towards Freedom
of Speech for Eight Deviant Political Types, 1970

(percentages)

Deviant political type	Extent to which free speech is endorsed for deviant political types*			
	Minimum	Medium low	Medium high	Maximum
A Quebec separatist	22	22	18	32
An American draft dodger	28	16	16	34
A Nazi	50	18	13	14
A retired military officer	5	4	9	77
A Communist	44	19	14	18
A person campaigning for harsher penalties for drug use	10	8	14	64
An atheist	26	12	14	43
A person campaigning to restrict coloured immigration to Canada	36	18	16	24

* Row percentages add up to less than 100 per cent because of 5 per cent
incomplete responses.

Source: Ted G. Harvey, "Attitudes Towards Freedom of Speech in a Canadian
Community: A Study of Social, Political, and Psychological Correlates," *Papers
Presented at the Forty-Third Annual Meeting of the Canadian Political Science
Association*, Volume 3 (Ottawa: mimeographed), Table I.

Two points emerge from the distribution of attitudes toward freedom of speech summarized in Table 6–8.[25] First, the restrictions on
free speech endorsed by the respondents seemed to be related more
to the degree of political deviancy than they were to the left-wing or
right-wing ideological stance of the type. The strongest support for
freedom of speech was forthcoming for the least deviant types, a
retired military officer and a person campaigning for harsher penalties
for drug use. An atheist, a Quebec separatist, and an American draft
dodger received more hypothetical support for their freedom to speak
than did a person campaigning to restrict coloured immigration into
Canada. A Communist and a Nazi, at opposite ends of the ideological
spectrum, were the two most deviant political types and had the
weakest support for their freedom of speech. Second, both an overall
predisposition to restrain freedom of speech and a considerable potential for conflict appeared to exist in the community arising from the
division of opinion over the desirability of free speech for the various
deviant political types. Harvey observes that

> in dealing with the question: "How do Canadians feel about
> freedom of speech?" it became clear that sharp polarization
> was evident in the community studied. Many persons were

classified as strong supporters of free speech, but many others appeared to be strong opponents of free speech. Most importantly large segments of the population endorsed broad restrictions on free expression. Several deviant types were severely restricted in free speech: "a Nazi", "a Communist", and "a person campaigning to restrict coloured immigration to Canada". Two others were restricted by near majorities: "a Quebec Separatist", and "an American draft dodger". Only 7.2 per cent of the population examined favoured free expression in every instance. In general the community studied reflected a broad base of potential popular support for anti-civil libertarian actions.[26]

With the exception of Harvey's study, no systematic comparison of the attitudes toward civil liberties of community leaders and the general electorate has been carried out yet in Canada; but a number of different surveys have provided hints of an overall pattern similar to that found in the United States.

Perhaps the most interesting survey results are those which were reported by the Canadian Television Network on its public affairs program "W5" on November 15, 1970 after the Trudeau Government had invoked the War Measures Act on October 16th to deal with acts of terrorism in Quebec by the F.L.Q. A formidable 87 per cent of the 1,650 people interviewed in ten major cities across the nation said they had approved the Government's decision to invoke the War Measures Act, and 80 per cent still approved it. Only 10 per cent felt the imposition of the Act had reduced their personal civil liberties and half of that 10 per cent said they were not concerned about these restrictions.

The overwhelming approval of this strong exercise of governmental authority during a period perceived as a severe crisis in domestic security is perhaps to be expected, but other attitudes towards civil liberties expressed by the respondents to this survey revealed surprisingly widespread support for repressive measures against nonconformists in general. Fifty-three per cent of the respondents said they favoured the prevention or suppression of Communist demonstrations, 51 per cent favoured similar measures being taken against student militants, 43 per cent supported suppression of public demonstrations by hippies, 39 per cent of the respondents agreed with the government's taking steps to prevent or suppress public demonstrations by labour militants, 39 per cent of the respondents also felt the government should suppress public demonstrations by anti-Vietnam-war groups, and 31 per cent expressed support for governmental suppression of demonstrations by women's liberation groups.

The C.T.V. survey also indicated a general predisposition towards greater censorship of the mass media. Sixty-eight per cent of those interviewed expressed the belief that newspapers, magazines, radio, and television in Canada provided excessive coverage to such groups as demonstrators against the war in Vietnam, student militants, women's liberation groups, the Communist Party of Canada, labour militants, and hippies. Under the War Measures Act, the federal government had the power to censor and suppress the news media; and 49 per cent of the sample were in favour of the government's exercising such censorship at that time. The survey also found 59 per cent of the respondents were in favour of the reimposition of the death penalty.

The results of the C.T.V. survey indicate that attitudes of the Canadian electorate towards civil liberties and individual freedoms are not as tolerant as the actual experience of liberty might lead one to expect. However, the timing of the C.T.V. survey, with interviews shortly after the invoking of the War Measures Act, raises the question as to how much the expressions of unwillingness to tolerate non-conformists were affected by the prevailing atmosphere of a national security emergency.

In assessing the possible transience of the opinions expressed by the respondents to the C.T.V. survey, one point to keep in mind is that the sample was based on respondents living in ten Canadian cities. Stouffer and others have found that urban respondents on average are more tolerant in their attitudes toward civil liberties than are rural respondents.[27] Thus, we could expect a completely representative national sample which included respondents from small towns and rural areas to have showed itself even more willing to support repressive measures against non-conformist demonstrations than the C.T.V. sample was.

Another point which implies that the opinions expressed in the C.T.V. survey may well be representative of long-term views is that other surveys have produced responses on a number of items which are very similar to those found in the C.T.V. survey. Table 6–9, for example, shows that a majority of Canadians have opposed abolition of the death penalty for many years, and that the 59 per cent favouring restoration of the death penalty in November 1970 was actually less than the percentage favouring its restoration in 1972. Among the respondents to a national sample interviewed in 1969 for the Special Senate Committee on Mass Media, 76 per cent favoured censorship of television; and 49 per cent expressed support for censorship of radio and newspapers.[28] Early in 1971, 56 per cent of a national sample (76 per cent in Quebec) expressed their support for a program in their province similar to a plan then being discussed in Quebec to

Table 6–9. Opinions of Canadians on the Abolition of the Death Penalty, 1943–1972

Opinion	1943	1953	1958	1960	1965	1966	1972*
Should abolish death penalty	18	22	33	41	35	37	30
Should retain death penalty	73	71	52	51	56	53	63
No opinion	9	7	15	8	9	10	7

* The question in 1972 concerned the restoration of the death penalty.

Source: Canadian Institute of Public Opinion, *The Gallup Report* (Toronto: mimeographed), February 24, 1965; February 23, 1966; February 2, 1972.

register all citizens and issue identity cards showing fingerprints and photographs.[29]

The responses to a question put by the Canadian Institute of Public Opinion to a national sample early in 1971 on the desirability of the Government's renewing the Emergency Public Order Act (which had replaced the War Measures Act as the legislative authority for the extraordinary governmental powers deemed necessary to resolve the "October crisis") revealed that most citizens were more worried about law and order than they were about civil liberties. Support for the continuance of the Emergency Public Order Act was expressed by 58 per cent of the respondents compared with 28 per cent who favoured its withdrawal.[30] The phrasing of the question posed directly the problem of restricting civil liberties to facilitate law and order, and the percentage distribution of reasons given by the majority of respondents for supporting continuance of the Act showed unmistakably their willingness to continue with limitations on civil rights.[31]

—we still need its protection: the trouble is not over yet, we need the power to control violence in a sudden emergency   65%

—the police need the powers granted by the Act to keep down sudden revolt or disorder: they can do a better job if they're not handicapped—they do not without it have enough authority in a crisis   30%

—other reasons (including the innocent have nothing to fear—we can trust the government to do what is necessary, etc.)   2%

—can't say why   8%

In contrast, the percentage distribution of the reasons why the minority supported withdrawal of the Public Order Act also showed that their concern was for the effects of the Act on civil rights.

—it's an infringement of civil rights and liberties—it is

not democratic—we do not want a police state in Canada—not needed in peace time   32%

—the present laws are sufficient without the special powers of the Act—it creates injustice—the crisis is over—the Act has served its purpose   29%

—the police can abuse the provisions in the Act—gives them too much power   13%

—the Act should never have been invoked—wasn't necessary—causing too much trouble—should be withdrawn and re-evaluated   13%

—other reasons   2%

—can't say why   7%

The 1968 federal election survey asked respondents to give their reactions to four statements which may be considered relevant in evaluating the prevalence of a tolerant public opinion in Canada: first, "Communists should be outlawed"; second, "Homosexuals should be imprisoned"; third "Canada would be a better place if all people had the same religion"; and, fourth, "Canada would be a better place if all people had the same national origin". The distribution of opinions ranging from strong agreement to strong disagreement with each of these four statements is shown in Table 6–10. Over one-half of the respondents agreed that Communists should be outlawed, 42 per cent of them expressing strong agreement; and one-third said that they thought homosexuals should be imprisoned. On the issues involving ethnic and religious tolerance, 46 to 47 per cent of the respondents expressed a tolerant attitude by disagreeing strongly with the statements that Canada would be a better place if all people had the same religion and national origin; but one-tenth strongly agreed and another tenth mildly agreed with the two statements.

When the opinions of each respondent on the four issues are combined according to their disagreement, either mild or strong, with each statement, a rough index of tolerance is produced which has a range from the very tolerant position of disagreement with all four statements to the very intolerant position of disagreement with none of the statements. The frequency distribution of the respondents to the 1968 federal election survey along this index of tolerance places 22 per cent at the very tolerant position and 12 per cent at the very intolerant position. The 27 per cent of the respondents who disagreed with three of the four statements may be thought to be moderately tolerant; in the middle, 24 per cent disagreed with two of the four statements; and the 15 per cent who disagreed with only one of the four statements are perhaps justly described as moderately intolerant. Taking the distributions of opinion on the four issues of tolerance

Table 6–10. Attitudes of Canadians on Four Issues of Social and Political Tolerance, 1968

(percentages)

Issue-statement	Agree strongly	Agree mildly	Disagree mildly	Disagree strongly	No opinion	No answer	Total*
Communists should be outlawed.	42	12	21	15	9	**	99
Homosexuals should be imprisoned.	20	11	26	29	14	**	100
Canada would be a better place if all people had the same religion.	11	11	23	46	9	**	100
Canada would be a better place if all people had the same national origin.	9	9	24	47	10	1	100

* Totals may not add to 100 per cent because of rounding errors. Number of respondents = 2,767.

** Less than 0.5 per cent.

Source: John Meisel, Queen's University, 1968 Federal Election Survey.

both as separate items and as a combined index, they tend to support the existence of a sizable body of public opinion which is more or less intolerant and to imply at least some potential for conflict over the use of public power to interfere with the social freedom of "outsiders" in the community.

A common finding of surveys of attitudes toward civil liberties is that the better educated and the younger respondents tend on average to be more tolerant than less educated and older respondents. Stouffer, for example, found that 47 per cent of his respondents aged twenty-one to twenty-nine years scored as more tolerant compared with only 18 per cent among those aged sixty and over, and that 66 per cent of college graduates were more tolerant compared with 16 per cent of those with elementary education.[32]

In his study of attitudes towards freedom of speech in a city in Western Canada, Harvey combined the attitudes expressed by his respondents towards freedom of speech for the eight deviant political types into an overall index of support for freedom of speech with four positions from low to high. In Tables 6–11 and 6–12 the percentage distributions of the respondents along this index of support for freedom of speech are shown for different age and schooling groups, and the strong correlation of both age and schooling with the degree of support for freedom of speech is evident. In Table 6–11, for example, 38 per cent of the group aged twenty-one to thirty showed high support for freedom of speech while 43 per cent of the respondents over sixty-five were low in their support; and in Table 6–12 the 40 per cent of the respondents with elementary schooling who

Table 6–11. Support in a Canadian Community for Freedom of Speech by Age Group, 1970

(percentages)

		Support for freedom of speech			
Age group	Low	Medium low	Medium high	High	Total*
21–30	12	19	32	38	101
31–40	17	22	35	26	100
41–50	23	26	28	22	99
51–65	30	32	22	16	100
Over 65	43	37	16	4	100

* Totals may not add to 100 per cent because of rounding errors.

Source: Ted G. Harvey, "Attitudes Towards Freedom of Speech in a Canadian Community: A Study of Social, Political, and Psychological Correlates," *Papers Presented at the Forty-Third Annual Meeting of the Canadian Political Science Association*, Volume 3 (Ottawa: mimeographed), Table VI.

Table 6–12. *Support in a Canadian Community for Freedom of Speech by Level of Schooling, 1970*

(percentages)

| Level of schooling | Support for freedom of speech | | | | |
	Low	Medium low	Medium high	High	Total*
Grade school	40	35	14	12	101
Junior high school	37	33	20	10	100
High school	19	26	33	22	100
Some university	7	14	35	44	100
Completed university or attended graduate school	6	5	19	69	99

* Totals may not add to 100 per cent because of rounding errors.

Source: Ted G. Harvey, "Attitudes Towards Freedom of Speech in a Canadian Community: A Study of Social, Political, and Psychological Correlates," *Papers Presented at the Forty-Third Annual Meeting of the Canadian Political Science Association*, Volume 3 (Ottawa: mimeographed), Table V.

expressed low support for freedom of speech may be contrasted with the 44 per cent who expressed high support among those with some university and the 69 per cent who expressed high support among those who had completed university or attended graduate school.

Selected items from national surveys in Canada indicate that Harvey's finding of more tolerant attitudes among the young and the better educated in his Western Canadian community study probably can be generalized to the entire nation. Tables 6–13 and 6–14 show six items which raise issues of social or political tolerance from national polls taken by the Canadian Institute of Public Opinion in recent years. Young people were more likely than older people to say that they would vote to abolish capital punishment, that they agreed with marriage between whites and non-whites, that they would not move their home because of an influx of non-white neighbours, and that the Emergency Public Order Act should be withdrawn. The same percentage of respondents (46 to 47 per cent) at each level of schooling in 1966 expressed the belief that personal rights were fully protected in Canada, but those with more schooling were more likely to think that personal rights were in danger. On the issue of reinstating the death penalty for political kidnapping put to a sample in 1971, there was no significant difference in the pattern of responses between those with public-school and those with high-school education—over 70 per cent of both groups favoured reinstatement. The majority of the university-educated group also favoured reinstating

Table 6–13. Opinions of Canadians on Interethnic Relations,
Abolition of Death Penalty, and Withdrawal of
Public Order Act by Age Group of Respondents,
1966–1971

| Release date | Item | Percentage of respondents expressing agreement by age group | | | | |
		21–29	30–39	40–49	Over 50	Total
23/2/66	Would vote in a national referendum to abolish the death penalty	43	37	35	36	37
11/9/68	Agree with marriage between whites and non-whites	50	40	30	29	36
16/7/69	Would not move home if coloured people came in great numbers to live in area	74	62	52	57	61
28/4/71	Believe Emergency Public Order Act should be withdrawn	46	27	24	20	28

Source: Canadian Institute of Public Opinion, The Gallup Report (Toronto: mimeographed).

Table 6–14. Opinions of Canadians on Rights in Danger and
Reinstatement of the Death Penalty by Level of
Education, 1966 and 1971

| Release date | Item | Percentage distribution of responses by level of education of respondents | | | |
		Public school	High school	University	Total
3/8/66	Do you think personal rights are being fully protected in Canada or do you think they are in danger?				
	Rights fully protected	46	47	46	47
	Rights in danger	28	37	45	34
	No opinion	26	16	9	19
	Total	100	100	100	100
9/1/71	Do you or do you not think that the death penalty should be reinstated for the kidnapping of people in public or political life?				
	Approve reinstatement	71	73	55	70
	Disapprove reinstatement	15	19	37	20
	Undecided	14	8	8	10
	Total	100	100	100	100

Source: Canadian Institute of Public Opinion, The Gallup Report (Toronto: mimeographed).

the death penalty for this crime, but the disapproving minority (37 per cent) was significantly larger than it was in the other two groups.

Table 6–15 shows the relationships of age and schooling with the rough index of tolerance which was constructed from the four items in the 1968 federal election survey involving tolerance for Communists, homosexuals, and ethnic and religious diversity. The very tolerant group which disagreed with all four items in Table 6–10 was younger and much better educated on average than the sample taken as a whole, and the intolerant groups which disagreed with none or only one of the statements were older and much less well-educated than the average for the total sample.[33]

The positive associations of age and education with attitudes toward civil liberties imply that university students, young and well educated, should be highly libertarian in their attitudes; and two studies in Canada and the United States support this hypothesis. The first survey, carried out in 1957, consisted of a sample of 894 students at the University of California at Berkeley. The students were asked to agree or disagree with fifteen statements, each of which involved an implicit conflict of values concerning provisions in the American Bill of Rights. The percentage distribution of responses for each item is shown in Table 6–16, with the proportion giving what was

Table 6–15. Cross-tabulations of Age and Years of Schooling with an Index of Tolerance, Canada, 1968

(percentages)

	Low				High	Total
	0	1	2	3	4	
Age:						
21–30	18	21	23	25	26	23
31–40	18	18	19	22	27	21
41—50	20	21	21	21	24	22
51–60	14	19	18	16	14	16
Over 60	31	22	18	16	9	18
TOTAL*	101	101	99	100	100	100
Schooling:						
0–5 years	23	14	11	4	1	9
6–10 years	62	63	58	45	27	49
11–15 years	14	23	30	44	55	36
Over 15 years	1	**	2	6	17	6
TOTAL*	100	100	101	99	100	100
Number of respondents	328	411	660	732	615	2,746

Rank on the index of tolerance

* Totals may not add to 100 per cent because of rounding errors.

** Less than 0.5 per cent.

Source: John Meisel, Queen's University, 1968 Federal Election Survey.

Table 6–16. *Attitudes Towards Principles of the Bill of Rights Expressed by Students at the University of California, Berkeley, 1957*

(percentages)

Item	Agree	Disagree	Don't know
1. The Government should have the right to prohibit any group of persons who disagree with our form of government from holding public meetings.	10	85	4
2. State governments should have the power to pass laws making it illegal to speak against racial or religious groups.	10	85	5
3. It unduly hampers the police in their efforts to apprehend criminals when they have to have a warrant to search a house.	11	84	4
4. The police are justified in holding a man with a long criminal record until they have enough evidence to indict him.	12	80	7
5. Large-scale police round-ups of "undesirables" are proper as long as they are restricted to people with known criminal records.	19	63	18
6. Legislative committees should not investigate the political beliefs of university faculty members.	61	29	9
7. It is wrong for government investigators to take pictures of people listening to a street-corner speech.	56	30	13
8. "Crime" comic books should be screened by some government agency before publication.	45	47	7
9. The circulation of Russian or Chinese newspapers in this country should be restricted to scholars.	6	87	6
10. It is reasonable to suspect the loyalty of a lawyer who represents accused Communists before a Congressional Committee.	13	79	8
11. A high school teacher who "pleads the Fifth Amendment" while being questioned by a Congressional Committee should be fired at once.	13	75	11
12. The government is acting properly in refusing a passport to a Socialist.	10	67	21
13. A former member of the Communist Party who refuses to reveal the names of Party members he has known should not be allowed to teach in a private university.	27	60	13
14. If a person accused of a major crime is acquitted, and if new evidence is then found that the prosecution claims indicates that he was guilty, he should be retried.	53	39	13
15. The government should have the right to withhold relevant FBI files from defendants in criminal			

cases, when opening files to them might reveal the names of confidential informants.   56   24   20

Source: Hanan C. Selvin and Warren O. Hagstrom, "Determinants of Support for Civil Liberties," *British Journal of Sociology*, 11 (March 1960), 52–3.

Table 6–17. Opinions of English-speaking Canadian University Students on Civil Libertarian Items, 1969

(percentages)

Item	Agree	Disagree	Don't know
1. The government should have the right to prohibit any group of persons who disagree with our form of government from holding public meetings.	3	94	3
2. The government should have the power to pass laws making it illegal to speak against racial and religious groups.	20	72	8
3. It unduly hampers the police in their efforts to apprehend criminals when they have to have a warrant to search a house.	17	73	8
4. The police are justified in holding a man with a long criminal record until they have enough evidence to indict him.	12	76	11
5. Large-scale police round-ups of "undesirables" are proper as long as they are restricted to people with known criminal records.	13	73	13
6. Legislative committees should not investigate the political beliefs of university faculty members.	69	20	10
7. It is wrong for government investigators to take pictures of people listening to a street-corner speech.	40	39	20
8. "Crime" comic books should be screened by some government agency before they are put on the news stands.	25	56	18
9. A book which an admitted communist wrote should be removed from the public library.	1	97	2
10. A person who is against all churches and religion should not be allowed to speak on this campus.	1	96	3
11. The government should hire defence counsel for people who cannot afford to hire their own counsel in criminal cases.	94	2	4
12. The government should hire defence counsel for admitted rapists and murderers who cannot afford their own counsel.	82	11	7
13. The government should be able to censor movies before they are released to the public.	32	59	8
14. Only taxpayers should be allowed to vote in a city referendum deciding on a tax-supported undertaking.	65	25	8

Source: W.B. Devall, "Support for Civil Liberties Among English-Speaking Canadian University Students," *Canadian Journal of Political Science*, III (September 1970), 437.

considered the libertarian response italicized. Overall, the responses were decidedly libertarian, with a majority of the respondents taking a libertarian stand on all but three of the fifteen statements.

The second survey, carried out in 1969, consisted of a sample of 832 English-speaking university students from all regions of Canada. In this survey, the Canadian students were asked to agree or disagree with fourteen statements involving a conflict of values relating to civil liberties; and, as shown in Table 6–17, a majority of the respondents expressed a libertarian attitude on twelve of the fourteen items. As with the Berkeley sample, then, the percentage distribution of the responses of Canadian students to each item, reveals a generally high level of positive support for civil liberties.

The responses of the two groups of university students can be directly compared for each of the first eight items in Tables 6–16 and 6–17. There are no significant differences between the two samples. The percentage of Berkeley students giving libertarian responses was greater for items two, three, four, and seven; that of Canadian students was greater for items one, five, six, and eight.

The authors of each study prepared indices of libertarianism for their samples; and, as the division of responses on the first eight items would suggest, the percentage distributions of scores on each index were closely similar. The mean score for each sample was 9.9 libertarian responses, 66 per cent of fifteen items and 71 per cent of fourteen items. On his index of libertarianism, Devall rated 24 per cent of the Canadian students as slightly libertarian (zero to eight libertarian responses), 30 per cent mediumly libertarian (nine or ten libertarian responses), 31 per cent moderately libertarian (eleven or twelve libertarian responses), and 15 per cent highly libertarian (thirteen or fourteen libertarian responses).[34] On the index proposed by Selvin and Hagstrom, 20 per cent of the Berkeley students were rated slightly libertarian (zero to seven libertarian responses), 46 per cent moderately libertarian (eight to eleven libertarian responses), and 34 per cent highly libertarian (twelve to fifteen libertarian responses).[35]

The authors of each study used their scales of libertarianism to assess the relationship between libertarian attitudes and other attributes of the students. For example, Devall found that Jewish students tended to give more civil libertarian responses than Catholic or Protestant students, those who felt religion was very important in their lives and attended church frequently gave fewer libertarian responses on average than students saying religion was of little importance in their lives, and students who preferred the New Democratic Party were much more likely to appear high on the civil libertarian index than those who preferred the Progressive Conservative

Party.[36] The most pertinent of the several relationships found between libertarian attitudes and social background was the identification of differences in attitudes between leaders and followers in both of the surveys of university students. The findings in these surveys are consistent with those of Stouffer and McCloskey in their national (United States) samples.

Selvin and Hagstrom found that student leaders on average were more libertarian than non-leaders. Among students who held three or more elected positions in groups or organizations on or off campus, 67 per cent were highly libertarian compared with 42 per cent highly libertarian among those holding two elected positions, 38 per cent among those holding one elected position, and 31 per cent among those holding no elected positions.[37]

For his analysis, Devall employed a scale of political activity which included a wide range of possible activities such as informal discussion of politics, participation in demonstrations or campaigns, and holding leadership positions in political groups. As shown in Table 6–18, he found a very strong relationship between the number of civil libertarian responses given by students and the degree of their political activity.

Not only are university students on average more libertarian than the electorate in general, but also within the university community students who are politically active are more likely to be highly libertarian than students who engage in few or no political activities. Future elites will be recruited predominantly from among the university-trained group, and most student political activists will be more politically active through their adult lives than other students.

Table 6–18. Support for Civil Liberties and Political Activity of English-speaking Canadian University Students, 1969

Number of civil libertarian responses	Percentage distribution of respondents at each level of political activity			
	None	Low	Moderate	High
Low (0–8)	44	23	16	15
Medium (9–10)	24	34	23	13
Moderate (11–12)	25	31	38	32
High (13–14)	7	12	23	40
TOTAL	100	100	100	100

Source: W.B. Devall, "Support for Civil Liberties Among English-Speaking Canadian University Students," *Canadian Journal of Political Science*, III (September 1970), 441.

Consequently, a set of attitudes highly favourable towards civil liberties would appear to be a probable attribute of any future Canadian political elite, if not so assuredly of the general electorate.

The Scope of Action

Whether freedom of independence or freedom of participation is considered, the greater the scope of a person's sphere of action the greater is his degree of freedom. Within the Canadian political community, the historical experience has been a marked decline in the probability of governmental interference as the political orientation of regimes evolved from most coercive to most permissive; but there has also been a correspondingly marked increase in the range of activities over which governmental rather than personal preferences are decisive. A description of the development of modern, positive government properly belongs to a consideration of public policies rather than political goods; but brief reference to some indicators of the growth of government in Canada over the past century will serve to suggest the seriousness of the problem created for freedom by the enlargement in the scope of public decision-making and the corresponding reduction in the scope of personal action.

Governmental expenditures to purchase goods and services for both current consumption and capital formation provide a useful indicator of the increasing scope of governmental activities. Expenditures by all levels of government on goods and services were $21 million in 1870, $77 million in 1900, and $496 million in 1926.[38] There were decreases in expenditures during the depression in the early 1930s and the post-war reconstruction of the late 1940s and an acceleration because of defense spending during World War II; but, with these exceptions, governmental expenditures have risen gradually but steadily since 1926, reaching $22,012 million by 1971. Compared with the total volume of expenditures for all goods and services produced in the economy, governmental expenditures increased from 4.6 per cent of gross national expenditures in 1867 to 9.6 per cent in 1926 and 23.6 per cent in 1971.

As Figure 6-1 shows, the relative importance of the federal government as a purchaser of goods and services has been decreasing since 1952 but the increase in expenditures by the regional governments has more than made up for this. Overall, governments have continued to take a moderately rising share of the total production of goods and services, a fact that implies a steady increase in the scope of their activities.

The increasing scope of governmental activity is also indicated by the growth of governmental employment. At Confederation, less than one out of every hundred of the labour force was employed at any

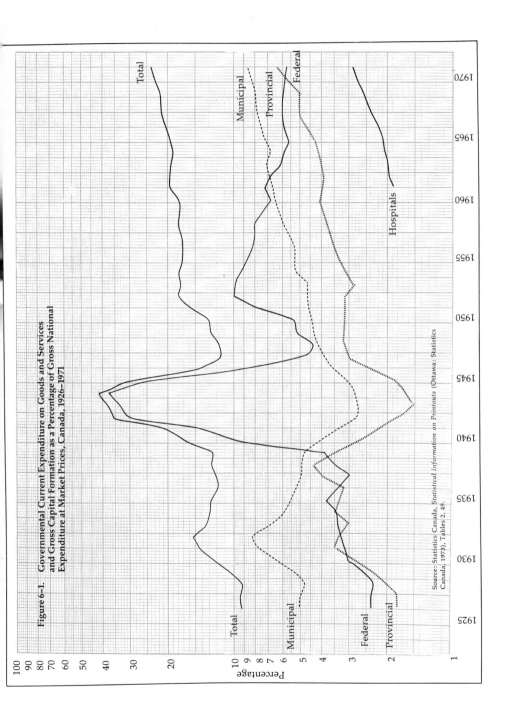

Figure 6-1. Governmental Current Expenditure on Goods and Services and Gross Capital Formation as a Percentage of Gross National Expenditure at Market Prices, Canada, 1926–1971

Source: Statistics Canada, *Statistical Information on Printouts* (Ottawa: Statistics Canada, 1973), Tables 2, 49.

level of government; a century later, more than one in every eight members of the labour force was on a government payroll.[39] Considering only the years from 1946 to 1970, the total number of governmental employees in Canada (excluding persons employed in the armed forces, public enterprises, and educational institutions) tripled from 223,458 to 884,358. Taking account of the growth of the population and labour force, Table 6–19 shows that the number of governmental employees per thousand population rose from 18.2 to 41.5 and the number of governmental employees per thousand members of the labour force rose from 46.0 to 105.6 between 1946 and 1970.

As with the increases in governmental expenditures, the most significant feature of the growth in governmental employment was that combined provincial and municipal governmental employment increased at a much more rapid rate than employment by the federal government.[40] Between 1946 and 1970 federal employment only increased from 9.5 to 12.2 employees per thousand population and from 24.0 to 31.0 employees per thousand members of the labour force, while combined provincial and municipal employment increased from 8.7 to 29.7 employees per thousand population and from 22.0 to 74.6 employees per thousand members of the labour force.

Indicators of increases in both expenditures and employment are consistent in pointing to a remarkable expansion in the scope of gov-

Table 6-19. *Number of Governmental Employees per Thousand Population and per Thousand Labour Force, Canada, 1946–1970*

Fiscal year	Number of employees at all levels of government*	Number of employees per thousand population		Number of employees per thousand labour force	
		All governments	Federal government	All governments	Federal government
1946	223,458	18.2	9.5	46.0	24.0
1950	212,390	15.5	6.9	40.9	18.3
1955	352,929	22.5	9.5	63.2	26.7
1960	484,523	27.1	10.5	75.8	29.2
1965	649,293	33.2	11.0	90.9	30.1
1970	884,358	41.5	12.2	105.6	31.0

*Employees filing taxable returns according to Department of National Revenue taxation statistics.

Sources: J. E. Hodgetts and O. P. Dwivedi, "The Growth of Government Employment in Canada," *Canadian Public Administration*, XI (Summer 1969), 231; Canada, Department of National Revenue, *Taxation Statistics 1972 Edition* (Ottawa: Information Canada, 1972), Table 13; Statistics Canada, *Statistical Information on Printouts*, Tables A, B.

ernmental activities in the twentieth century. As Dawson and Ward
have said,

> the negative laissez-faire state has been more and more
> transformed into the positive state which is continually
> recognizing a greater and greater responsibility for the wel-
> fare of its citizens. The government is becoming yearly more
> assertive and its activities more widespread; it has long since
> ceased to regard as its sole or even its chief function the
> enunciation of general rules of conduct and the assigning of
> punishments for their breach, and it is quite prepared to
> direct and drive people into righteousness; it has taken the
> position that it will not only punish deviations from its rules,
> but it will endeavour in many areas of social life to prevent
> such deviations taking place on any significant scale. The ex-
> treme application of this principle occurred during the
> Second World War and the succeeding period of emergency,
> when virtually every activity of the citizen came to a greater
> or less degree under the direction of the state; and there is
> little or no reason to believe that government participation
> in the life of the citizen will ever return to the level it was in
> 1939. The chief uncertainty for the future is the point at
> which this participation will stop.[41]

The progressive enlargement of the scope of modern government
has been accompanied by a corresponding increase in its administrative powers. Acts of the federal and provincial legislatures commonly
empower the executive to enact subsidiary legislation within the limits
of enabling statutes by Order-in-Council or by departmental regulation and to make judicial or quasi-judicial decisions in disputes about
administrative matters with little or no opportunity for appeal to the
courts. At least one-half of the 225 public acts of the Dominion in
force in 1933 empowered the federal executive to legislate by Order-
in-Council or departmental regulation.[42] In 1969 the House of Commons Special Committee on Statutory Instruments reported that it
had examined 601 Acts of Parliament, virtually all of the statutes then
in force, and found that 420 of them provided for delegated legislation.[43]

In answer to the Special Committee's questionnaire on how much
use was made of these delegated powers, a substantial majority of the
governmental commissions and departments replied that statutory
powers to make regulations had been used very extensively. Perhaps
the extent of their use is indicated by the fact that 6,892 regulations
covering 19,972 pages were published in the Canada Gazette between

January 1, 1956, and December 31, 1968, an average of 530 regulations a year; and this does not include those regulations expressly exempted from publication nor those having a legislative aspect but not considered by the regulation-making authority to require publication.

Probably Parliament and the provincial legislatures have been too ready to delegate their law-making powers to administrative bodies, although the reasons given to justify delegation are generally valid ones: lack of legislative time, lack of legislative knowledge on technical matters, the need for rapid decisions in cases of emergency, the need to experiment with legislation especially if it is in a new field of governmental activity, the need for flexibility in the application of laws, and unforeseen situations which may arise during the introduction of new and complex pieces of legislation.[44] What needs to be made clear, however are the implications which these increases in governmental activities and public administrative powers have for the total of freedom in the community. Inevitably, the progressive transfer of many spheres of choice-making from the private and personal to the public and political realm has reduced freedom of independence; and, as a result, the total of freedom could be maintained only if there were some corresponding increase elsewhere to offset the reduction.

One possibility is that a decline in the probability of governmental interference during recent years has compensated for the loss of freedom resulting from the greater scope of governmental activity. However, considering the historical experience with respect to the declining probability of governmental interference, it seems most unlikely that this aspect did in fact compensate for the increasing scope of governmental activity. The marked increases in governmental activity have been a phenomenon of the twentieth century, especially the years after World War II, whereas most of the important advances from coerciveness to permissiveness in the relationship of governments and citizens had been achieved in Canada by 1920.

The total of freedom could also have been maintained if the loss in freedom of independence caused by the greater scope of governmental activity had been matched by a corresponding increase in freedom of participation in the public sphere. There have been some important extensions and additions to the system of political representation achieved in the middle of the nineteenth century which undoubtedly have had some effect on freedom of participation: the termination of restrictions on suffrage, greater democracy in the organization of political parties, the acceptance of pressure groups as media of interest articulation, the establishment of governmental advisory committees representing relevant public interests and clienteles, the evolution of the federal constitution which has divided the increasing activities among multiple levels of government, and the appearance of the ombudsman to receive citizens' complaints and rectify their grievances. Important as these developments in our system of representation have been, if actual participation in politics is any indication of participatory opportunities, existing political arrangements still appear to be quite inadequate to provide a structure of participatory opportunities sufficient to compensate for the losses in freedom of independence caused by the greater scope of governmental activity.

Participation in politics may vary from none for extremely apathetic or parochial citizens to incessant for those who hold high political office. If we examine democratic political participation in a comparative perspective, a pyramid of involvement is immediately evident with most citizens limiting their political activities to voting and political discussion, a minority becoming involved in election campaigning and party work, and only a very small group becoming engaged in politics on a full-time basis.

A study of political participation by Milbrath concluded that in the United States 40 to 70 per cent of American adults perceive political messages and vote in any given election, 25 or 30 per cent may try to convince others to vote in a certain way, 15 per cent may display a campaign button or sticker during an election, 13 per cent may contact a public official, 10 per cent make monetary contributions to political parties, only 4 or 5 per cent are active in party work and election campaigns or attend political meetings, and 1 per cent become candidates and hold public or party office.[45]

Richard Rose has reported that 78 per cent of the British electorate identified with a party and voted in 1959, 22 per cent were members of a political party including those who belonged to the Labour Party through a trade union, 9 per cent were individual members of a party, and 0.5 per cent were active workers in local organizations.[46]

A study of political participation in West Germany estimated that 70 per cent of the population were eligible voters, 60 per cent of the population voted in federal elections, 9 per cent attended meetings on public affairs, 3 per cent were active in politics, 3 per cent were members of political groups, 2 per cent were members of parties, 0.4 per cent were members of local and district councils, 0.003 per cent were members of state and federal legislatures, and 0.001 per cent belonged to national elites.[47]

As is to be expected, the pattern of large numbers of citizens with very limited participation and relatively few with an intensive commitment which is found in the politics of the United States, Britain, and West Germany can also be found in Canadian political life.[48] In the national samples interviewed following the 1965 and 1968 federal elections, 83 to 84 per cent of the respondents reported that they voted in all or most federal elections, and 75 to 77 per cent said that they voted in all or most provincial elections. Only 3 to 4 per cent said they never voted in federal elections, and 8 to 10 per cent reported not voting in any provincial elections. Also, 79 per cent of the respondents expressed an identification with one of the four main parties competing for votes, and 7 per cent said that they had read some political party literature during the 1965 election campaign. Half of the electorate reported in 1965 that politics was rarely or never a subject of conversation for them.[49] During the 1965 election campaign, 22 per cent of the respondents had tried to convince others how to vote; 14 per cent had attended one or more political meetings; 5 per cent had helped in the election campaign; 4 per cent said that they belonged to a political organization; 3 per cent reported donating money to the campaign of a political party; and 1 per cent had canvassed for campaign contributions.

The very limited participation by ordinary citizens in the political life of their community is accompanied by widespread feelings of inability to influence the actions of their governments. Table 6–20 lists four statements which tried to probe the sense of subjective political efficacy included in the questionnaires of the federal election surveys of 1965 and 1968. Disagreement with these efficacy-probing statements may be taken to indicate directly the existence of some sense of freedom for ordinary citizens to participate in politics and government. In both 1965 and 1968, sizable majorities of respondents agreed that voting was the only means they had of influencing the government and that politics and government were sometimes too complicated to understand; and they were about equally divided as to whether the government cares much what they think and whether they have any influence on what the government does.

As with the index of tolerance, the separate responses to each of the four efficacy-probing statements in Table 6–20 may be combined to form an index of the sense of political efficacy and provide a summary indicator of ordinary citizens' perceptions of their freedom of participation. A respondent who disagreed with each of the items listed in Table 6–20 may be thought to have expressed a positive, optimistic opinion about the ability of the ordinary citizen to influence politics and government. A respondent who disagreed with none of the four items may be thought to have expressed a very negative, pessimistic opinion about the political efficacy of ordinary citizens. Table 6–21 shows that one-quarter of the respondents in the federal election surveys of 1965 and 1968 ranked at the low position on this index of political efficacy, and another one-quarter were moderately low. Only 5 to 6 per cent of the respondents ranked high in their sense of efficacy to influence political and governmental affairs. These

Table 6–20. Responses to Four Statements Probing a Sense of Political Efficacy, Canada, 1965 and 1968

(percentages)

Statement	Percentage distribution of responses, 1965						Percentage distribution of responses, 1968					
	Agree	Disagree	Don't know	No answer	Total* Percentage	Number	Agree	Disagree	Don't know	No answer	Total* Percentage	Number
Voting is the only way that people like me can have any say about how the government runs things.	76	22	2	**	100	2,721	76	20	3	**	99	2,767
I don't think that the government cares much what people like me think.	46	49	5	**	100	2,721	42	51	7	**	100	2,767
Sometimes politics and government seem so complicated that a person like me can't really understand what is going on.	69	28	3		101	2,721	69	26	3	1	99	2,767
People like me don't have any say about what the government does.	49	47	3	**	99	2,721	47	49	4	1	101	2,767

* Totals may not add to 100 per cent because of rounding errors.

** Less than 0.5 per cent.

Sources: Philip E. Converse, John Meisel, Maurice Pinard, Peter Regenstreif, and Mildred Schwartz, 1965 Federal Election Survey; John Meisel, Queen's University, 1968 Federal Election Survey.

Table 6–21. Percentage Distribution of Canadians According to the
Number of Efficacy-probing Statements with Which
They Disagreed, 1965 and 1968

	1965	1968
Disagreed with all four statements	5	6
Disagreed with three of the statements	17	15
Disagreed with two of the statements	24	25
Disagreed with one of the statements	25	26
Disagreed with none of the statements	27	27
Incomplete response	1	2
TOTAL		
Percentage*	99	101
Number	2,721	2,767

* Totals do not add to 100 per cent because of rounding errors.

Sources: Philip E. Converse, John Meisel, Maurice Pinard, Peter Regenstreif, and Mildred Schwartz, 1965 Federal Election survey; John Meisel,
Queen's University, 1968 Federal Election Survey.

results seem to imply that the feeling of power to participate in political affairs and to influence governmental policies is not widespread
among Canadian citizens but is instead limited to a relatively small
proportion of the electorate.[50]

Citizens with positive feelings of political efficacy are more likely
to hold favourable attitudes towards their government. According to
the evidence of the 1968 federal election survey, most Canadians
hold rather mixed views of their national government; but the perceptions of government held by the respondents who had a high
sense of political efficacy were generally more favourable than those
of respondents ranking low in political efficacy. Those with a high
sense of political efficacy were more likely to think that the activities
of the federal government made a good deal of difference to people
and more inclined to believe that most of the time the government
could be trusted to do what is right. They were less likely to express
the opinions that quite a few people running the government are a
little crooked and that university graduates take up too large a position
in government. People with a high sense of political efficacy seem to
be somewhat more likely to think that governmental officials know
what they are doing and less likely to think that their taxes are being
wasted. People with a strong sense of political efficacy also were
slightly less likely than others to hold the view that high governmental officials pay more attention to big interests than to ordinary
citizens; but, even so, approximately nine-tenths of the respondents
at each position on the index of political efficacy agreed that the big
interests received preferential treatment.

Table 6–22. *Attitudes of Canadians Towards Their Government According to Their Rank on an Index of Political Efficacy, 1968*

Attitude	Percentage expressing agreement by rank on the scale of political efficacy					
	Low				High	Total
	0	1	2	3	4	
What the government in Ottawa does makes a good deal of difference to people.	36	53	64	73	81	56
Most of the time you can trust the government to do what is right.	35	48	63	66	68	52
Quite a few people running the government are a little crooked.	41	29	19	17	13	26
People with university degrees take up too large a position in our governments.	57	41	27	14	13	35
Almost all of the people running the government are smart people who usually know what they are doing.	43	43	59	62	59	51
People in the government waste a lot of the money we pay in taxes.	56	49	40	35	37	46
Some people who are high in government pay more attention to what the big interests want rather than give everyone a fair break.	91	92	88	86	87	89

Source: John Meisel, Queen's University, 1968 Federal Election Survey.

An important indicator of the way in which citizens' feelings of political efficacy are an expression of their perceptions of their freedom of participation in political and governmental affairs is illustrated by their views of the measures which could be taken against an unfair Parliamentary Bill. Table 6–23 shows the very limited range of the means for political influence which are perceived to be available by most citizens, but it also shows that people with a high sense of political efficacy are much more likely to be aware of some means for political action than are people with a low sense of political efficacy.

According to the norms of liberal democracy, the primary source of assistance for citizens who aim to influence an unfair legislative proposal should be their elected representatives; and 27 per cent of the respondents to the 1968 federal election survey did say that they could contact a Member of Parliament. One-tenth suggested taking action through contacting other citizens (5 per cent), an unspecified representative (3 per cent), the mass media (1 per cent), or the Prime Minister or the Minister responsible for the Bill (1 per cent); 8 per cent suggested making some sort of petition, direct action, or referendum to represent their interests; and 11 per cent offered a hotchpot

Liberty

Table 6–23. *Opinions of Canadians on the Initial and Additional Measures Which Citizens Could Take Against an Unfair Parliamentary Bill According to Their Rank on an Index of Political Efficacy, 1968*

(percentages)

Measures which could be taken	Rank on scale of political efficacy					Total
	Low 0	1	2	3	High 4	
Initial measure:						
Contact M.P.	10	23	34	38	58	27
Contact representative (unspecified), other citizens, Prime Minister, Minister, mass media	6	7	10	19	22	10
Petition, direct action, or referendum	5	8	10	13	8	8
Other	11	13	11	11	5	11
Nothing could be done	55	40	27	15	5	35
Don't know/no answer	14	8	8	4	2	9
TOTAL*	101	99	100	100	100	100
Additional measure:						
Contact M.P.	1	4	5	7	8	4
Contact other citizens	1	4	4	11	18	5
Contact representative (unspecified), Prime Minister, Minister, mass media	1	2	4	8	16	4
Petition, direct action, or referendum	2	6	9	11	15	7
Other	1	2	5	5	6	3
Don't know/no answer	94	82	74	59	36	77
TOTAL*	100	100	101	101	99	100
Number of respondents	744	707	695	411	166	2,723

* Totals may not add to 100 per cent because of rounding errors.

Source: John Meisel, Queen's University, 1968 Federal Election Survey.

of other measures which might be taken. The remaining two-fifths of the respondents gave no answer, did not know what could be done, or said that nothing could be done to prevent the passage of an unfair Bill.

When a supplementary question about the possible measures against an unfair Bill was put to the respondents in 1968, 77 per cent gave no answer or said that they did not know of any measures which might be taken in addition to the first one mentioned. Among the 23 per cent of the respondents who did offer an additional measure for citizens to take against an unfair Bill, 5 per cent suggested contacting other citizens; 4 per cent proposed to contact their Member of Parliament; 4 per cent suggested some other elitist contact; and 7 per cent mentioned a petition, direct action, or a referendum.

The results clearly indicate that most citizens have a very restricted view of the means available to them to influence unfair legislative proposals, but the cross-tabulation of the various types of political action mentioned by the 1968 respondents with their rank on the index of political efficacy shows that the respondents with a high sense of political efficacy were much more likely to perceive measures which could be taken against an unfair Bill than were the respondents low in political efficacy. In response to the original question, fully 69 per cent of the respondents ranking low in political efficacy but only 7 per cent of the respondents ranking high in political efficacy gave no answer, did not know, or said nothing could be done. On the question about additional measures which could be taken, 94 per cent of those low in political efficacy but only 36 per cent of those high in political efficacy made no answer or said that they did not know of any. The pattern of responses indicates that in the first instance politically efficacious citizens more often perceive their Members of Parliament as the primary medium for action against an unfair Bill, but that in addition to this, they are also much more aware of other measures which could be taken to represent their interests.

The restricted sense of political efficacy held by most citizens is important, not only because it would appear to be a direct indicator of the sense of freedom of participation felt by ordinary citizens, but also because of the correlation which has been found to exist between positive feelings of political efficacy and engagement in political activities. People who feel politically efficacious are much more likely to become actively involved in politics, as a number of studies in different nations have found.[51] Table 6–24 shows, for example, that in the United States in 1956 the incidence of political activity increased significantly among those respondents ranking higher on the index of political efficacy.

The drop in rates of participation in Canada as political activities become more demanding in terms of the opportunities, resources, and motivation required of participants is evident in Table 6–25; but the influence of a positive sense of political efficacy on participation is also clear. For nine of the twelve activities listed in Table 6–25 the rate of participation was higher among those who had a higher sense of political efficacy.

According to the information obtained from the 1965 and 1968 federal election surveys, citizens with a high sense of political efficacy are more likely to vote in a given election as well as to vote in all federal and provincial elections. They are more likely to read political

*Table 6–24. Percentages of Americans at Different Levels of
Political Participation by Rank on an Index of Political
Efficacy, United States, 1956*

(percentages)

| Campaign activity | Rank on the index of political efficacy* | | | | | Total |
	Low 0	1	2	3	High 4	
Non-voting	46	38	23	15	6	25
Voting, discussing, displaying button or sticker	51	54	65	64	66	61
Voting and donating money, attending meetings, working for party, or joining political club	3	8	12	21	28	14
TOTAL	100	100	100	100	100	100

* The index of political efficacy was constructed from the responses made to
the same items shown in Table 6–20.

Source: Lester W. Milbrath, *Political Participation,* © 1965 by Rand McNally and
Company, Chicago, p. 56.

party literature during an election campaign, attend a political meeting, or contribute money to a political party. They are more likely
to be members of organizations which could serve as political pressure
groups, and they are more likely to try to influence the passage of
legislation through Parliament. Only in connection with helping a
party during an election campaign, belonging to a political organization, and canvassing others for campaign contributions did the evidence from the 1965 federal election survey fail to show a significant
association (on the chi square test with $p = 0.01$) between political
activity and sense of political efficacy.

The importance that sense of political efficacy has as an indicator
of freedom of participation through its strong association with a
variegated set of governmental orientations and political activities
makes the pattern of its distribution a matter of considerable importance for the shape of political life in the community. Obviously, how
many of the citizens feel politically efficacious will affect the rate of
participation in a political community; but exactly who among the
citizens feels politically efficacious will also affect what issues reach
the political agenda of the community, what viewpoints are expressed,
and what collective decisions are made. Tables 6–26 to 6–28 show
that people who have a high sense of political efficacy tend to have
superior social backgrounds, exhibit greater social and political tolerance, and show more interest in political and governmental affairs
than people with a low sense of political efficacy.

Table 6–25. Percentages of Canadians Who Participated in Selected Political Activities According to Their Rank on an Index of Political Efficacy, 1965 and 1968

| Political activities | Percentage participating by rank on the scale of political efficacy | | | | | |
	Low 0	1	2	3	High 4	Total
In 1968 had voted in the last federal election	82	84	86	91	90	85
Read political party material during the 1965 election campaign	60	74	79	84	91	74
In 1968 had voted in all federal elections since becoming eligible to vote	52	54	58	67	74	58
In 1968 had voted in all provincial elections since becoming eligible to vote	50	50	49	56	69	52
Tried to influence others how to vote during the 1965 election campaign	15	19	26	33	41	23
Belonged in 1968 to an organization such as trade union, professional association, or church group through which an unwanted law could be opposed	8	13	18	26	40	17
Attended one or more political meetings during the 1965 election campaign	9	15	12	14	31	14
As of 1968 had done something to try to influence an Act of Parliament, such as contact M.P. or other citizens	5	6	8	15	26	9
Helped in the 1965 election campaign	4	6	5	6	4	5
Belonged to a political organization in 1965	4	4	4	4	7	4
Contributed money to a political party during the 1965 election campaign	1	2	4	5	3	3
Canvassed others for campaign contributions in 1965	*	1	1	2	1	1

* Less than 0.5 per cent.

Sources: Philip E. Converse, John Meisel, Maurice Pinard, Peter Regenstreif, and Mildred Schwartz, 1965 Federal Election Survey; John Meisel, Queen's University, 1968 Federal Election Survey.

In the first place, strong feelings of political efficacy are not randomly distributed among all class and status groups in the community. Table 6–26 shows that upper-class professionals, owners, and managers are over-represented and skilled and unskilled labourers are under-represented among those ranking high in political efficacy; that those describing themselves as belonging to the upper and middle classes are over-represented and those placing themselves in the working and lower classes are under-represented in the higher positions on the index of political efficacy; and that those with post-secondary

Table 6–26. *Cross-tabulations of Occupation, Schooling, and Subjective Social Class with an Index of Political Efficacy, Canada, 1965*

(percentages)

	Rank on the index of political effciency					
	Low				High	Total
	0	1	2	3	4	
Occupation:						
Professionals	3	5	11	14	26	9
Owners and managers	8	10	11	16	16	11
Clerical and sales	9	15	16	24	23	16
Skilled and unskilled labour	50	41	36	28	19	39
Farmers	8	8	8	5	1	7
Others	23	20	19	11	15	19
Total*	101	99	101	98	100	101
Schooling:						
0–8 years	52	40	25	19	8	34
9–11 years	34	33	38	30	18	33
12–13 years	11	18	21	27	24	19
Over 13 years	3	9	16	24	50	14
Total	100	100	100	100	100	100
Subjective social class:						
Upper or upper middle	4	6	11	16	24	9
Middle	27	36	40	53	51	38
Working	57	51	44	27	20	45
Lower	8	2	2	1	1	4
Other	5	5	4	3	4	4
Total*	101	100	101	100	100	100
Number of respondents	744	681	664	457	140	2,687

*Totals may not add to 100 per cent because of rounding errors.

Source: Philip E. Converse, John Meisel, Maurice Pinard, Peter Regenstreif, and Mildred Schwartz, 1965 Federal Election Survey.

schooling are very much over-represented and those with no schooling, primary schooling, and even some secondary schooling are under-represented among citizens having the highest sense of political efficacy.

People who have a stronger sense of political efficacy appear to be more likely to exhibit a greater degree of social and political tolerance in their attitudes towards other members of the community. Table 6–27 shows the cross-tabulation for the respondents to the 1968 federal election survey between their rank on the index of political efficacy and their rank on the index of tolerance. Among the respondents who ranked low on the index of political efficacy, 45 per cent were also low or moderately low on the index of tolerance, and only 29 per cent were high or moderately high. In contrast, among the

Table 6–27. *Cross-tabulation of the Positions on an Index of Political Efficacy and an Index of Tolerance for Respondents to the 1968 Canadian Federal Election Survey*

(percentages)

Rank on the index of political efficacy	Rank on the index of tolerance						
	Low 0	1	2	3	High 4	Total Percent-age*	Number
Low 0	23	22	27	19	10	101	738
1	13	18	29	24	16	100	704
2	8	11	22	34	26	101	688
3	2	7	18	32	40	99	408
High 4	1	7	10	30	53	101	165
TOTAL	12	15	24	27	22	100	2,703

* Totals may not add to 100 per cent because of rounding errors.

Source: John Meisel, Queen's University, 1968 Federal Election Survey.

respondents who ranked high on the index of political efficacy, 83 per cent were also high or moderately high on the index of tolerance; and only 8 per cent were low or moderately low.

People who have a higher sense of political efficacy are also more likely to express a greater degree of interest in the political affairs of their community. In Table 6–28, the degree of interest expressed by the respondents with respect to the 1965 and 1968 election campaign is employed as an indicator of their general interest in the political affairs of the community. The level of campaign interest was generally higher in 1968 than it was in 1965, but the positive association between efficacy and interest is evident in both samples. In 1965, only 14 per cent of the respondents who were low in political efficacy expressed a good deal of interest in the election campaign, whereas 56 per cent of those high in political efficacy expressed a strong interest in the campaign. In 1968, the percentage of respondents low in political efficacy who said that they had been very much interested in the campaign increased to 28 per cent; but the percentage of highly efficacious respondents who were very much interested also increased to 78 per cent. In both 1965 and 1968, then, at each successive position on the index of political efficacy, there was an increasing percentage of respondents who expressed high interest in the election campaign.

The widespread feelings of their inability to influence government and politics form an important part of the explanation for the very limited political participation by most citizens, but the positive

Table 6–28. *Cross-tabulation of the Positions on an Index of Political Efficacy with Interest in the Election Campaign for Respondents to the 1965 and 1968 Canadian Federal Election Surveys*

(percentages)

Rank on the index of political efficacy	Interest expressed in the 1965 election campaign					Interest expressed in the 1968 election campaign				
	Much	Some	Not much	Total Percentage*	Number	Much	Some	Not much	Total Percentage*	Number
Low 0	14	38	47	99	741	28	36	37	101	740
1	19	45	36	100	679	40	38	22	100	706
2	27	52	20	99	660	47	40	14	101	693
3	45	40	15	100	457	63	29	8	99	410
High 4	56	39	4	99	140	78	18	4	100	166
TOTAL	26	44	30	100	2,677	44	35	21	100	2,715

* Totals may not add to 100 per cent because of rounding errors.

Sources: Philip E. Converse, John Meisel, Maurice Pinard, Peter Regenstreif, and Mildred Schwartz, 1965 Federal Election Survey; John Meisel, Queen's University, 1968 Federal Election Survey.

association between sense of political efficacy and degree of interest in political affairs suggests that the efficacy–participation relationship need not be inevitable. Richard Van Loon has pointed out that interest in politics can be stimulated in a variety of social settings.

Interest in politics is stimulated early in life by the family, peer groups, and the schools. This stimulation is much more likely to occur with middle class than with lower class children and the working class lies somewhere between. An important point, however, is that the stimulation of interest in politics can occur in virtually any environment and, we might hypothesize, at any time during a person's life. Most important, once that interest has been stimulated, involvement in the electoral and probably in the non-electoral part of the political process as well, is much more likely to occur. Participation in Canadian politics can be induced even among people who would not normally be considered to have the resources or the necessary propensity to show interest.[52]

The potential for widening political participation by arousing greater interest in the political affairs of the community is indicated by the positive association between the degree of interest in the 1965 and 1968 election campaigns expressed by respondents to the two federal election surveys and the extent of their involvement in a variety of political activities. Respondents who were more interested in the election campaigns were more likely to have engaged in every type of political activity listed in Table 6–29 than the respondents who were less interested. Moreover, the degree of association is generally stronger for each cross-tabulation between degree of interest and political activity than it is for the corresponding cross-tabulations between sense of political efficacy and political activity.[53]

The positive correlation between political interest and political activity may offer a potentially important means of breaking up the widespread pattern of low efficacy, low interest, and unfavourable perceptions of government and of turning political passivity into participation; but for the present, the pattern of distribution for political interest among social groups is very similar to that for political efficacy. Table 6–30 shows that, like political efficacy, political interest tends to be higher in the upper-class occupational groups, the upper-status educational groups, and the upper and middle social classes than it is in the lower-class, lower-status groups. The degree of association between the variables of political interest and social background is not quite as strong as it is in the case of the association between political efficacy and social background,[54] but the social and

Table 6–29. Percentages of Canadians Who Participated in Selected Political Activities According to Their Amount of Interest in the Election Campaign, 1965 and 1968

(percentages)

Political activities	Interest expressed in the election campaign			
	Not much	Some	Much	Total
In 1968 had voted in the last federal election	66	87	94	86
Read political party material during the 1965 election campaign	50	79	92	74
In 1968 had voted in all federal elections since becoming eligible to vote	39	54	69	58
In 1968 had voted in all provincial elections since becoming eligible to vote	41	48	60	52
Tried to influence others how to vote during the 1965 election campaign	10	19	44	23
Belonged in 1968 to an organization such as trade union, professional association, or church group through which an unwanted law could be opposed	6	14	24	17
Attended one or more political meetings during the 1965 election campaign	7	12	25	14
As of 1968 had done something to try to influence an Act of Parliament, such as contact M.P. or other citizens	2	4	15	9
Helped in the 1965 election campaign	3	3	10	5
Belonged to a political organization in 1965	1	3	10	4
Contributed money to a political party during the 1965 election campaign	1	2	5	3
Canvassed others for campaign contributions in 1965	*	1	3	1

* Less than 0.5 per cent.

Source: Philip E. Converse, John Meisel, Maurice Pinard, Peter Regenstreif, and Mildred Schwartz, 1965 Federal Election Survey; John Meisel, Queen's University, 1968 Federal Election Survey.

political consequences which seem to derive at present from the effects of political interest on participation are probably not very different from those which result from the effects of political efficacy.

The Political Problem of Liberty

The historical experience of liberty in the Canadian political community over three hundred years has included the moderately and, at times, most coercive policies of the French and British colonial regimes, the transition from coerciveness to moderate permissiveness which accompanied the emergence of a nascent liberal democratic

Table 6–30. *Cross-tabulations of Occupation, Schooling, and Subjective Social Class with Amount of Interest Expressed in the Election Campaign, Canada, 1965*

(percentages)

| | Interest expressed in the election campaign | | | |
	Not much	Some	Much	Total
Occupation:				
Professionals	5	8	13	9
Owners and managers	9	11	15	11
Clerical and sales	11	18	17	15
Skilled and unskilled labour	45	40	29	39
Farmers	8	7	7	7
Others	22	17	19	19
Total*	100	101	100	100
Schooling:				
0–8 years	48	31	24	34
9–11 years	33	34	32	33
12–13 years	12	21	21	18
Over 13 years	6	13	22	14
Total*	100	99	99	99
Subjective social class				
Upper or upper middle	5	8	16	9
Middle	29	40	46	38
Working	54	46	32	45
Lower	6	3	2	4
Other	6	3	5	4
Total*	100	100	101	100
Number of respondents	820	1,180	711	2,711

* Totals may not add to 100 per cent because of rounding errors.

Source: Philip E. Converse, John Meisel, Maurice Pinard, Peter Regenstreif, and Mildred Schwartz, 1965 Federal Election Survey.

regime in the nineteenth century, and a steady reduction in remaining obstacles to political freedom throughout the twentieth century.

The outstanding advance in this growth of liberty surely occurred in the three decades between 1837 and 1867 which witnessed the critical transformation of a society on the verge of rebellion into one engaged in the peaceful negotiation of a new national political constitution. In the 1830s, irritating restrictions on religious freedom were a leading political issue, governmental attempts at internal press censorship were commonplace, and the political executive regularly resorted to oppressing opposition parties. By the 1860s, restrictions on religious freedom were no longer a ranking political issue, outright attempts at press censorship were clearly beyond accepted political norms, and oppression of opposition parties had been converted into relatively open competition.

From the base of the fundamental constitutional achievements of the mid-nineteenth century, there has been during the twentieth century a progressive, though not uninterrupted and still unfinished, realization of the basic rights of every citizen to the due process of law; equality before the law; and freedom of personal expression in religion, speech, assembly, and press. Although there are a number of specific issues outstanding, the most important of which is public support for denominational education, governmental interference in the personal sphere of religious beliefs and practices has virtually disappeared from the community. Even with the controls applied and accepted during the exceptional conditions of world war, governmental censorship of the press has ceased to be a barrier to freedom of expression. The use of governmental authority to bias the open competition of political parties has decreased steadily from the establishment of the Civil Service Commission in 1908 to the creation of the Electoral Boundaries Commissions in 1965. Removing material disqualifications by property ownership, sex, ethnicity, and even age has produced effectively universal suffrage. The inclusion of additional indicators would simply confirm the generalization. The likelihood of governmental action to prejudice the rights of certain social groups or specific individuals continues to decrease, and by any standard Canada has become one of the most permissive political communities in human history. Yet a number of disturbing factors threaten to inhibit the further growth of liberty and to prevent the realization of social conditions generally more favourable to satisfying the need for self-actualization.

One disturbing factor is the existence of a public opinion which seems to imply a considerable potential for collective interference with the fundamental rights of certain social groups or specific individuals. Although the rights to life and liberty, due process, and free expression have been gradually realized in Canada, a disturbingly large percentage of citizens continue to express their approval of censoring the mass media, interfering with the free expression of political deviants, and exercising the power of the state through capital punishment. Moreover, in spite of the secular growth of freedom of independence, governments in the twentieth century have acted retrogradely, for example, to repress the Winnipeg General Strike in 1919; to deprive Japanese Canadians during World War II of their rights to liberty, enjoyment of property, and equality before the law; and to deny liberty and free expression to the left-wing (but not extremist) political opponents of the regime during the "October crisis" of 1970. The overwhelming public support for the acts of governmental coercion committed on each of these occasions serves to emphasize that freedom in a political democracy is not yet achieved when human rights acquire a legislative existence or when political elites accept the limitation of the state's coercive power; freedom is only completely realized when the public opinion very largely if not unanimously accepts the norms of liberty and understands the meaning of their specific applications to the political life of the community.

The existence of a strong streak of intolerance in Canadian public opinion brings to mind both Erich Fromm's argument that concentration on eliminating external restraints on freedom has blinded us to the existence of inner restraints, compulsions, and fears and Christian Bay's argument that defensiveness restricting psychological freedom represents an obstacle to freedom as deserving of our attention as the more widely recognized external obstacles. Social science research in Canada so far has provided little evidence to document the patterns of apathy, alienation, and authoritarianism which derive from the limited political consciousness of a personality incapable of coping with the responsibilities and anxieties of citizenship in a modern political democracy.[55] Yet the evidence of a significant component of irrationality in mass political attitudes persists throughout the survey data reported in this chapter.

The social distribution of respondents along the indices of tolerance and political efficacy which were constructed from the responses to the 1965 and 1968 federal election surveys may be taken to illustrate the large irrational component of mass political thinking. The index of tolerance is an indicator of the potential limits to freedom of independence which are implicit in public attitudes towards coercing "outsiders", those who do not belong to one's ethnic or religious group, or who do not adhere to one's political and social conventions. The index of political efficacy is an indicator of the potential limits to freedom of participation which are implicit in public attitudes towards the likelihood of governmental responsiveness to the representations of ordinary citizens.

Respondents from different social groups were not randomly distributed along either the index of tolerance or the index of political efficacy. Upper-class, upper-status respondents were much more likely to be highly tolerant and feel politically efficacious than lower-class, lower-status respondents. When such class and status differences occur with respect to the allocation of national income or the allocation of social roles, they may be expected. In such a context they seem to derive from rational self-interest; and, consequently, no attribution of irrationality to the attitudes of one interest group or another would seem to be merited. When these class and status differences occur in the context of attitudes of tolerance and political efficacy, however, their rational component is much less easy to locate.

The strongly positive relationships between years of schooling and the indices of tolerance and political efficacy are especially instructive. Since schooling has the professed objective of developing individual rational capacity and this objective becomes more precise with advancing years, it is not surprising to find that people with more years of schooling tend to be more tolerant and feel more efficacious with respect to the political and governmental affairs of the community. Yet the effects of schooling on attitudes of tolerance and efficacy also serve to emphasize that the members of different social groups have very different access to the advantages of this social environment which facilitates the reduction of irrationality and prejudice in social and political orientations. The double result of our failure to develop in the community a more generalized environment conducive to the reduction of the irrational component in mass political and social attitudes is to deprive the members of disadvantaged social groups of their psychological freedom and to threaten the permanence of the social freedom already achieved through elite leadership.

Just as the failure to take account of the psychological aspect of freedom may lead one to over-estimate the total of freedom achieved through the reduction of external obstacles to social freedom, so the failure to take account of the provision of freedom of participation as an essential counterpart of freedom of independence may also lead one to over-estimate the total of freedom in the community. The probability of governmental interference with such accepted fundamental rights as due process and free expression has declined; but the scope of governmental action has increased as a result of the acceptance of additional social and economic rights which impose mounting obligations upon governments to expand services, reallocate incomes, and extend controls. As the scope of social action which is subject to individual decision is progressively restricted and the scope of social action which is subject to collective action is widened, the total of freedom can only be maintained if the decrease in freedom of independence is offset by an increase in freedom of participation.

Reducing restrictions on suffrage, improving party competition, and promoting free expression signal both a decrease in the probability of governmental interference and an increase in the freedom of participation. Freedom of participation has also been increased by the more democratic organization of political parties and pressure groups, the growing freedom and popular responsiveness of the mass media, and the establishment of administrative structures specifically to promote interaction with departmental clienteles. Yet these new structures for wider participation by ordinary citizens in collective decision-making do not appear to have increased freedom of participation in anything like the degree to which the growth of modern, positive government has decreased it by reducing the scope of individual action. Even when the significant reductions in the probability of governmental interference with basic human rights are taken into account, overall freedom appears to have declined in recent years.

A good test of the existence of widespread freedom of participation is the extent to which ordinary citizens feel capable of influencing political affairs and governmental activities in their community. The evidence from the 1965 and 1968 federal election surveys in Canada indicates that very few Canadians have a high sense of political efficacy. Most are skeptical about the responsiveness of governmental authorities to the opinions of ordinary citizens and have a very limited view of the means available to ordinary citizens to represent their interests in the political process. Of course, the small proportion of Canadians who feel politically efficacious does not mean that the modern structures for wider participation should be written off as failures; but it does show plainly how very far short of the objective of a genuinely participatory democracy we are at present.

The overall failure to increase freedom of participation for ordinary citizens and the resulting persistence of a widespread sense of political inefficacy are compounded by the social bias which accompanies the distribution of the freedom of participation. The evidence is very clear that a sense of freedom of participation is much stronger among people in upper-class, upper-status groups than it is among those belonging to lower-class, lower-status groups. Political action is the outcome for each participant of a variable interaction of opportunities, resources and motivation;[56] and we are merely beginning to sort out contributing factors and causal relationships. Yet even a cursory analysis of the evidence from the 1965 and 1968 federal election surveys has revealed among lower-class, lower-status groups a syndrome of lower interest in political affairs, weaker sense of political efficacy, and lower rates of political participation. A virtual political culture of poverty appears to undermine the freedom of participation of the very group of citizens which stands most in need of forceful and effective representation of their interests in the processes of community decision-making. Richard Van Loon has correctly identified the vicious circle which entraps people who have fewer resources, weaker motivation, and lower rates of participation.

> *In addition to not expressing their discontent through the electoral system, then, a high proportion of the Canadians who have the most to be discontented about do not feel that they are capable of having any influence over political allocations. To some extent, they may be right. Their lack of efficacy combined with a lack of resources leads them to abstain from participating in politics and their abstention makes their low level of efficacy a self-fulfilling prophecy.*

321

> *The political system pays relatively little attention to them because they do not matter as much as middle class citizens. They do not matter as much to many decision-makers because they do not participate, and they do not participate because they lack the personal and economic resources.*[57]

The present political constitution of liberal democratic regimes, not surprisingly given its evolution out of class societies, is elitist in its orientation and inhibiting to mass political participation; and reforms of existing political institutions and procedures must surely accompany any serious efforts to achieve a participatory liberal democracy. Yet what seems even more important than reformation of the democratic constitution is reflection on its unrealized assumption of rational, freely acting citizens. What follows from that reflection is the recognition of a cruel pattern of unsatisfied needs which robs many citizens of the capacity to act in accordance with the basic assumptions of liberal democratic theory.

A prime requisite for creating a more liberal, more participatory democracy is the development in the community of a more intensive, generalized political education aimed at the widest dissemination of attitudes of tolerance and political efficacy. One of the strongest impressions which arises from studying the correlations between social background and the indices of tolerance and political efficacy is that the concern expressed for education and the development of common schools by the founding philosophers and statesmen of liberal democracy was not misplaced. Schooling is associated with the emergence of the attitudes of rationality, tolerance, and sense of efficacy which are crucial attributes of enlightened, responsible citizenship in a modern political democracy; but the institutions of formal schooling are also now clearly inadequate to the enormous tasks of political education which, however, are still left virtually to them alone.

The strong association of political interest with rates of participation and feelings of efficacy implies that a promising course for reform may lie in systematically promoting political interest. The significant effects on participation which result from popular interest in such personalities as John Diefenbaker and Pierre Trudeau show what even political leadership in search of partisan advantage can accomplish. Unfortunately, the interest created for partisan advantage, however useful, has neither the scope nor the durability to provide a sure foundation for imparting the kind of political education now required for people to cope with the responsibilities and anxieties of citizenship in a fully realized participatory democracy. Yet, outside of the hortatory manifestoes of provincial educational systems, one looks in vain in Canada for any public declaration of the goals of a political education for freely acting, responsible citizenship or for any integrated and sustained set of public policies designed to promote rationality and liberality in mass political thought and interest and efficacy in mass political action.

Obviously, the leadership of elite groups is a prerequisite for developing the relevant sub-goals and effective policies for mass political education. For the elites the costs of sharing power will not be inconsequential; but the penalty for their failure to do so is a political community in which general feelings of powerlessness will rise as the scope of government inevitably continues to increase, in which public policy and human development continue to be severely biased by the exceptional deprivation of freedom experienced by disadvantaged social groups, and in which the achievement of the social and psychological freedom conducive to human growth is constantly threatened by a potential backlash of ignorance and intolerance.

NOTES

1. Carl J. Friedrich, *Man and His Government* (New York: McGraw-Hill Book Company, 1963), p. 353. Friedrich also describes a third aspect of freedom which concerns the conflict of values in a given political situation. The greater the value a person places on carrying out acts of non-compliance in a given situation compared with the value he attributes to obtaining the reward for compliance or avoiding the punishment for non-compliance, the greater will be his degree of freedom. For example, when Doukhobors were threatened with jail for failure to comply with a hated law, they may yet have remained relatively free by going to jail if they valued non-compliance more than they feared imprisonment. In providing social indicators of freedom as a political good in Canada, I have not found it possible to include this third aspect of freedom and have limited my survey to the probability of interference and the scope of action.
2. *Ibid.*, p. 353.
3. Robert E. Kauffman, *Level and Fluctuation of Governmental Coercion and Systemic Political Instability: A Cross-National Study* (San Diego: San Diego State College, 1970).
4. *Ibid.*, pp. 34–6.
5. My description of religious freedom is based primarily on John S. Moir (ed.), *Church and State in Canada, 1627–1867* (Toronto: McClelland and Stewart Limited, 1967); H. H. Walsh, *The Christian Church in Canada* (Toronto: Ryerson Press, 1968); and D. A. Schmeiser, *Civil Liberties in Canada* (London: Oxford University Press, 1964).
6. J. S. Moir, *op. cit.*, p. xiv.
7. Quoted by H. H. Walsh, *op. cit.*, p. 57.
8. D. A. Schmeiser, *op. cit.*, p. 70.
9. M. Searle Bates, *Religious Liberty: An Inquiry* (New York: International Missionary Council, 1945), pp. 88–9.
10. My description of internal press censorship is based primarily on W. H. Kesterton, *A History of Journalism in Canada* (Toronto: McClelland and Stewart Limited, 1967).

Liberty

11. John King, quoted by W. H. Kesterton in *A History of Journalism in Canada,* p. 61.
12. My description of the moderately coercive and slightly coercive periods in the oppression of party opposition is based primarily on S. D. Clark, *Movements of Political Protest in Canada 1640–1840* (Toronto: University of Toronto Press, 1959) and that of the moderately permissive and most permissive periods on Hugh G. Thorburn (ed.), *Party Politics in Canada* (Toronto: Prentice-Hall of Canada Ltd., 1963); R. MacGregor Dawson and Norman Ward, *The Government of Canada,* 5th ed., (Toronto: University of Toronto Press, 1970); and D. A. Schmeiser, *Civil Liberties in Canada.*
13. S. D. Clark, *op. cit.,* p. 17.
14. *Ibid.,* pp. 42, 44.
15. *Ibid.,* p. 488.
16. Escott Reid, "The Rise of National Parties in Canada," in H. G. Thorburn (ed.), *op. cit.,* p. 14.
17. R. M. Dawson and N. Ward, *op. cit.,* p. 312.
18. Norman Ward, *The Canadian House of Commons: Representation* (Toronto: University of Toronto Press, 1950), pp. 226–7.
19. Escott Reid, "The Saskatchewan Liberal Machine Before 1929," in H. G. Thorburn (ed.), *op. cit.,* p. 57.
20. For a complete list see William Rodney, *Soldiers of the International* (Toronto: University of Toronto Press, 1968), p. 18, note.
21. D. A. Schmeiser, *op. cit.,* p. 218.
22. My description of restraints on suffrage is based on John Garner, *The Franchise and Politics in British North America 1755–1867* (Toronto: University of Toronto Press, 1969); Norman Ward, *The Canadian House of Commons: Representation* (Toronto: University of Toronto Press, 1950), pp. 211–39; Terence H. Qualter, *The Election Process in Canada* (Toronto: McGraw-Hill Company of Canada Limited, 1970); and Canada, Royal Commission on the Status of Women in Canada, *Report* (Ottawa: Information Canada, 1970).
23. Ted G. Harvey, "Attitudes Towards Freedom of Speech in a Canadian Community: A Study of Social, Political, and Psychological Correlates," *Papers Presented at the Forty-Third Annual Meeting of the Canadian Political Science Association,* vol. 3 (Ottawa: mimeographed), pp. 2–3.
24. The sample of community leaders included mayors; presidents of school boards, library boards, chambers of commerce, labour unions, bar associations, women's clubs, and parent-teacher associations; chairmen of Democratic and Republican county central committees; chairmen of community chests; commanders of the American Legion; Regents of the Daughters of the American Revolution; and newspaper publishers.
25. T. G. Harvey, *op. cit.,* p. 14.
26. *Ibid.,* pp. 61–2.
27. Samuel Stouffer, *Communism, Conformism and Civil Liberties* (New York: John Wiley and Sons, Inc., 1966), pp. 111–13, 130.
28. Canada, Special Senate Committee on Mass Media, *Report,* vol. III (Ottawa: Queen's Printer, 1970), p. 125.
29. Canadian Institute of Public Opinion, *The Gallup Report* (Toronto: mimeographed, February 20, 1971).
30. Canadian Institute of Public Opinion, *The Gallup Report,* April 28, 1971. The question was: "Canada's Emergency Public Order Act, passed to deal with the F.L.Q. crisis in Quebec, ends in April. At the expense of certain civil rights, this act makes it easier for police authorities to arrest suspects, and

keep them in jail. Do you think this act should be withdrawn, or do you think it should be continued in some form?"

31. Canadian Institute of Public Opinion, *The Gallup Report*, May 1, 1971.
32. S. Stouffer, *op. cit.*, pp. 89–90.
33. Because of their immediate relevance in providing a context for the discussion below of tolerance among Canadian university students, age and schooling are the only social background characteristics considered in relation to the index of tolerance here. An analysis of the relationship between the index and other variables also turned up a number of other positive associations between social background and the index of tolerance. Perhaps the most interesting of these relationships was that revealed between the index of tolerance and language most often spoken at home.

Language most often spoken at home	Rank on the index of tolerance					Total
	Low				High	
	0	1	2	3	4	
English	46	56	66	74	87	69
French	45	39	27	21	11	26
Other	8	5	7	4	2	5
Total	99	100	100	99	100	100

Given the items which comprise the index, the over-representation of the English and the under-representation of the French among the very tolerant (and the opposite among the intolerant groups) may be interpreted as yet another expression of the Canadian dualism discussed in chapter four. Whereas the English tended to express a preference for the tolerant, multicultural society which is the prevailing ideal of English Canada, the French seemed to be expressing their preference for a more homogeneous, French, Catholic community.

34. W. B. Devall, "Support for Civil Liberties Among English-Speaking Canadian University Students," *Canadian Journal of Political Science*, III (September 1970), 438.
35. Hanan C. Selvin and Warren O. Hagstrom, "Determinants of Support for Civil Liberties," *British Journal of Sociology*, 11 (March 1960), 55. If "highly libertarian" in this study were limited to those giving thirteen to fifteen libertarian responses, thus corresponding more closely to the four-part scale used by Devall, the percentage highly libertarian in the Berkeley sample would be 20 per cent.
36. W. B. Devall, *op. cit.*, pp. 448–9.
37. H. C. Selvin and W. O. Hagstrom, *op. cit.*, p. 70.
38. O. J. Firestone, *Canada's Economic Development 1867–1953*, Income and Wealth Series VII (London: Bowes and Bowes, 1958), p. 127; Canada, Statistics Canada, *Statistical Information on Printouts* (Ottawa: Statistics Canada, 1973), Table 49.
39. J. J. Deutsch, "The Public Service in a Changing Society," *Canadian Public Administration*, IX (Spring 1968), 1.
40. J. E. Hodgetts and O. P. Dwivedi, "The Growth of Government Employment in Canada," *Canadian Public Administration*, XI (Summer 1969), 229–230.
41. R. M. Dawson and N. Ward, *op. cit.*, pp. 264–5.
42. J. A. Corry, "Administrative Law in Canada," *Proceedings: Canadian Politi-*

cal Science Association, 1933, p. 196, cited by R. M. Dawson and N. Ward, *op. cit.,* p. 267.

43. Canada, Parliament, House of Commons, Special Committee on Statutory Instruments, *Third Report* (Ottawa: Queen's Printer, 1969), p. 4.

44. *Ibid.*

45. Lester W. Milbrath, *Political Participation* (Chicago: Rand McNally and Company, 1965), p. 19.

46. Richard Rose, *Politics in England* (Boston: Little, Brown and Company, 1964), p. 89.

47. Lewis J. Edinger, *Politics in Germany* (Boston: Little, Brown and Company, 1968), p. 168.

48. With the exception of the reference in note 49, the evidence on participation in Canada reported here is based on Philip E. Converse, John Meisel, Maurice Pinard, Peter Regenstreif, and Mildred Schwartz, 1965 Federal Election Survey; and on John Meisel, Queen's University, 1968 Federal Election Survey.

49. Social Research Group, *A Study of Interethnic Relations in Canada,* Research Report for the Royal Commission on Bilingualism and Biculturalism, Division IX, Contract 2 (Montreal: mimeographed, 1965), Table 11–17.

50. Two other questions asked in the 1968 federal election survey are indicators of a sense of political efficacy but were omitted from the index constructed here. Respondents were invited to express their opinions on the amount of correspondence between elections and the attention paid by government to the ideas of ordinary people and on the statement that in general those elected to Parliament soon lose touch with the people. Given the implications of these two statements for a sense of efficacy, it is not surprising to find that the responses to them were strongly correlated with the respondents' positions on the index of political efficacy. The percentages of respondents at each position on the efficacy index who agreed with the statements were as follows:

Rank on the scale of political efficacy

	Low				High	Total
	0	1	2	3	4	
Generally, those elected to Parliament soon lose touch with the people.	84	71	49	36	30	61
A good deal of correspondence exists between elections and the amount of attention paid by government to the ideas of ordinary people.	29	45	57	67	72	49

51. L. W. Milbrath, *op. cit.,* pp. 56–7.

52. R. Van Loon, "Political Participation in Canada: the 1965 Election," *Canadian Journal of Political Science,* III (Sept. 1970), 396.

53. If we use gamma as a measure of the strength of association between variables, we find gammas for the twelve variables of political activity cross-tabulated with the variables of political interest and political efficacy respectively as follows: voting in the last federal election, interest=0.58 and efficacy=0.17; reading political party material, interest=0.63 and efficacy=0.35; voting in federal elections, interest=0.37 and efficacy=0.17; voting in

provincial elections, interest=0.24 and efficacy=0.07; trying to influence others how to vote, interest =0.55 and efficacy=0.30; belonging to an organization which could be a pressure group, interest=0.36 and efficacy=0.30; attending political meetings, interest=0.45 and efficacy=0.18; doing something to influence an Act of Parliament, interest=0.63 and efficacy=0.40; helping in the election campaign, interest=0.40 and efficacy=0.05; belonging to a political organization, interest=0.57 and efficacy=0.08; contributing money to the election campaign, interest=0.54 and efficacy=0.32; and canvassing others for contributions, interest=0.74 and efficacy=0.36. These results are consistent with Van Loon's conclusion from his study of participation in the 1965 election that a high level of interest in politics completely obliterated the effect of a variable as important as efficacy in its effects on campaign activity. Van Loon argues that, if level of interest were not an important factor, people having low levels of political efficacy would be unlikely to participate no matter what their level of interest. In fact, 15 per cent of those respondents in the 1965 federal election survey who had a low level of efficacy and a high level of interest rated high on a campaign activity index compared with 11 per cent rated high among those who had a high level of efficacy and a high level of interest. Similar results were found when levels of campaign activity were examined for different combinations of political interest, social class, and educational attainment. (See R. Van Loon, *op. cit.*, pp. 395-6.)

54. The gammas for the cross-tabulations between the variables of social background and the variables of political interest and political efficacy respectively are as follows: occupation, interest=0.16 and efficacy=0.26; schooling, interest=0.30 and efficacy=0.42; and subjective social class, interest=0.30 and efficacy=0.36.

55. Nor has social science research in Canada yet provided evidence about the extent of manipulation of consumers and voters which could be applied to an evaluation of the existence of the third type of freedom mentioned by Bay, potential freedom or freedom from manipulation.

56. This approach to thinking about political participation has been suggested by James D. Barber, *Citizen Politics: An Introduction to Political Behavior* (Chicago: Markham Publishing Company, 1969), pp. 1–25. See also Barber's other works, *The Lawmakers: Recruitment and Adaptation to Legislative Life* (New Haven: Yale University Press, 1965) and *The Presidential Character: Predicting Performance in the White House* (Englewood Cliffs, N.J.: Prentice-Hall, 1972).

57. R. Van Loon, *op. cit.*, p. 394.

ENVOI

Viewed from the comparative perspective of Canadian history and the experience of other political communities, the people who live in contemporary Canada enjoy a remarkably high provision of basic political goods. The social indicators of the Canadian socio-political environment show that sizable advances have been made in the provision of welfare, equality, and liberty, and that these improvements have been accompanied by approximately constant, if not increasing, levels of security and fraternity.

Advances in welfare have resulted from sizable increases in the average income of Canadians. Canadian standards of housing and nutrition are second only to those of the United States. Compared with some other advanced industrial nations, mortality and morbidity statistics indicate a more modest achievement in improving the health status of Canadians; but the comparative position of Canada among all the nations is highly favourable and shows a great advance over conditions which prevailed earlier in this century.

Equality has increased in Canada because occupational access in a technological society tends to rest on educational attainment, and educational advantages are now more open to those who can profit from them. The political elite continues to consist mainly of men recruited from the upper middle classes, but this class pattern of recruitment appears to derive much more from educational mobility and much less from social bias than was the case in the past. At least the social background of the Canadian political elite is not very different from that found in other western democracies, and the differences occasioned by the presence in other countries of governing socialist parties have been fading as the recruitment patterns of contemporary socialist parties increasingly resemble those of their bourgeois competitors.

Liberty has increased as the authority relationships between Canadian citizens and their governments have developed over two centuries from moderate coerciveness to high permissiveness. The goal of minimizing the probability of governmental interference has not yet been realized; but the improvement in the basic rights of every citizen to the due process of law; equality before the law; and freedom of expression in religion, speech, assembly, and press has placed Canadians among the most favoured peoples in the enjoyment of this political good.

The increasing enjoyment of welfare, equality, and liberty has occurred in a context of relatively high security. Contemporary violence may have several political meanings, but among the least likely is the general breakdown of law and order in Canada and the loss of our customary political stability. Admittedly, rates of crime have been increasing in contemporary Canada; but the crimes causing the rate increases have been mainly traffic violations and crimes against property without violence, that is, crimes which reflect our increasing urbanization, the changing age composition of the population, the greater opportunities for such crimes, and better law enforcement but which probably do not affect the personal security of citizens very much. Political violence has been low in Canada compared with other countries, and the recent incidents of violence in Quebec should not affect this ranking. In political communities where stability is the norm, the occurrence of violence causes temporary dislocation of a sort which we in Canada have experienced before and soon forgotten; and the violence in Quebec appears to be no exception. Combined with the relatively low and diminishing profile of Canada in external affairs, the modest increases in rates of violent crime and the maintenance of a comparatively high level of political stability appear to ensure Canadians a place among the favoured peoples who enjoy the security of citizenship in the small, industrialized, liberal democracies.

Only in the supply of fraternity does the Canadian political community fail to meet a standard comparable to that enjoyed in the few most favoured political communities. Comparative evidence on the intensities of national identity are not readily available, but it would be difficult to deny that national identity is more intense and more widely shared in most other advanced industrial nations and even in many developing nations than it is in Canada.

Yet weakness of national identity is not unique to contemporary Canada, and its enervating effects should not be exaggerated. We have always been two nations, perhaps more; but this has not prevented us from defining boundaries, establishing public authority, and effecting national policies. Consequently, the rise in public discussion and political disagreement about our national identity should not be mistaken for waning fraternity. More likely, it reflects some displacement of a closed, elitist politics of accommodation by more open political procedures.[1] Our recent circumstances have only made more explicit the depth and persistence of our communal and regional divisions while renewing the challenge of their accommodation; and the social indicators do reveal a slowly growing popular awareness of these national differences, acceptance of them, and willingness to accommodate them.

Satisfaction at the high enjoyment of political goods in Canada is obviously justified. Only a few other political communities could claim to provide on balance a comparable set of goods. Yet the satisfaction must inevitably be diminished by the substantial shortcomings in the present distribution of political goods among Canadians and by some disquieting indicators of even greater inadequacies for the future. Even the most cautious speculations about trends in the provision of political goods suggest quite forcibly that, even if they were adequate for the present, contemporary patterns of provision for welfare, security, fraternity, equality, and liberty cannot be taken for granted for the future. At every turn we confront more difficult problems of political choice.

In spite of the high average enjoyment of welfare in Canada, at least 15 per cent and probably more of the population have less than the minimum standard acceptable in a modern industrial state. This incidence of poverty is not unique for Canada among the advanced industrial societies, but it does represent a group of several million people living in one of the most affluent nations in history who do not have their most basic physiological needs adequately satisfied.

In the past, we have relied primarily on economic expansion rather than redistribution of income to alleviate the problem of poverty in our community, and contemporary public and private policies continue to promote economic growth in order to provide more welfare. But the option of this choice for welfare through economic growth must sooner or later be closed. Even with advances in technology and resource conservation, the potential for industrial expansion appears to be strictly limited in the long-term by the interacting factors of resource depletion, population growth, availability of arable land, and environmental pollution.[2] If collapse is to be avoided, policies placing limits on growth have to be adopted; but, once economic growth is limited, issues about the redistribution of income become more insistent, both within the community between rich and poor social groups and without the community between rich and poor nations.

The intensification of distributional questions in political life appears likely to occur in a social context in which the realization of equality of opportunity, especially in education, will have reduced social mobility and heightened status consciousness. Inequalities among ethnic groups in access to occupation, education, and political office are declining and will eventually disappear. Sexual inequalities are perhaps the most evident in contemporary Canada but, given the resolution, also will disappear. However, inequalities among class and status groups have not been much reduced, especially in the provision of education and in access to political power; and they may be expected to persist or even to increase in the future.[3]

The question for politics is whether the persistence of class and status inequalities will or should be accepted as just, even though they are based on real differences in individual ability and effort. My belief is that they will and should be challenged. The inequalities of a meritocracy rest on the assumption that in a situation of equal opportunity income and status are the rewards for successful achievement. That assumption is directly contradicted by the socialist belief that each should contribute to society according to his ability and be rewarded according to his need. Although many people dismiss the socialist ethic as unrealistic, many others do not; and one can confidently anticipate a revivified articulation of the socialist commonwealth as an alternative to meritocratic inequality. Thus, a pronounced ideological division and derivative disagreements over public policies between advocates of socialist equality and supporters of meritocratic inequality may become a common feature of politics in industrialized societies, including Canada, as equality of opportunity fails to satisfy the general need for esteem.

The advances which have been achieved in the provision of liberty in modern Canada have been devalued by the progressive transfer of power from private to public agencies. However great the benefits have been in terms of welfare, security, fraternity, and equality, the public collectivization of decision-making which has characterized modern Canadian government has reduced freedom of independence without as yet providing an offsetting enhancement of freedom of participation.

The problems of maintaining welfare as the limits to growth are approached ensure further politicization of social decision-making, and the resulting growth of government combined with a reduction in social mobility promises to intensify the already serious problem of the freedom of participation. As an upper-status group possessing a monopoly of ability and expertise becomes ever more firmly in control of political power, growth of alienation and apathy among ordinary citizens may be expected to follow. Unless new forms and degrees of citizen participation in political life are created and promoted, elite predominance in politics will steadily erode the democratic principle beyond the possibility of resurrection. Since such a prospect will surely not go unchallenged, again one may confidently predict an ideological division and related policy disagreements between the supporters of elitism and the advocates of mass participation in politics.

The intrusion of the political community into the lives of its citizens also implies greater concern for each person's sense of identification with the community. Charles Tilley has noted that separatist movements have sprung up with great energy in recent years, making demands for autonomy, cohesion, and insulation from the control of the nation-state. He speculates on the possibility that these movements "record a transfer of power away from the national State, perhaps in part because its own weight keeps it from dealing with the most burning aspirations of its own citizens, and in part because power is devolving to international blocs of states."[4]

If this speculation is well-founded, there is reason to believe that separatist movements, both violent and non-violent, will become a more prominent feature of future politics. According to this argument, the growth of the separatist movement in Quebec—where there exists a communal situation particularly conducive to demands for autonomy, cohesion, and insulation from federal control—should be seen as the precedent for similar movements in other regions as political cleavages are deepened over the distribution of welfare, the strengthening of elites, and the influence of citizens in policy formation.

Obviously, the Canadian nation-state is especially vulnerable to the pressures of such separatist movements; and dismemberment might be the result. What seems more likely, however, is a gradual renegotiation of the federal bargain resulting in much greater power for all regional governments, not only that of Quebec. At the same time, the imperatives of human survival may be eroding the national power from the other direction through the transfer of more governmental functions to the jurisdiction of international and supranational organizations. The potential of these trends for disagreement over constitutional policy is obvious.

The issues in the provision of welfare, fraternity, equality, and liberty imply problems for the provision of security. Domestic political stability will be challenged by the intensification of the issues of welfare distribution, the growth of separatist movements, the conflict of social classes, and demands for greater mass participation in politics. External political involvements will be complicated by rising tensions between poor and wealthy nations and by bloc strains among the wealthy nations over the control of the human environment, the growth of separatist movements, and the decline of national state power.

Living in contemporary Canada, we have been fortunate in the skills and values of our people, the richness of our physical resources, and the general benignity of our external relationships which have permitted the growth of our prosperity; but we have also been generally fortunate in the political choices which have been made here. The federal constitution, for example, has provided a framework for national economic development and regional accommodation. The public agency has been willingly used to promote national development and integration from the building of canals and railroads to the encouragement of bilingualism and biculturalism. A system of public schooling has been fashioned which is beginning to make a reality of the value ascribed to equality of opportunity. These choices are representative of the array of public policies which have been instrumental to our achieving the present levels of political goods.

The resolution of the problems which can be foreseen in maintaining and enhancing our supply of political goods will require the continuance of a certain benignity in our political environment, especially in view of the growing interdependence of nation-states. Their resolution will also demand imaginative domestic public policies and difficult political choices by the Canadian people. Political creativity has played a modest part in the modern political development of Canada. The future demand for this quality of political leadership promises a continuing challenge both for those who seek to wield public authority and for those who concede it.

NOTES

1. S. J. R. Noel, "Consociational Democracy and Canadian Federalism," *Canadian Journal of Political Science*, IV (March 1971), 17–18.
2. Donella H. Meadows et al., *The Limits to Growth* (New York: Universe Books, 1972), pp. 23–4.
3. That class and status inequalities would persist or even increase in spite of the existence of opportunities for social, including educational, mobility would follow from differences in individual abilities and the heritability of intelligence in a society based on disproportionate rewards for successful people. The emergence of a "meritocracy" is the subject of an excellent satirical essay by Michael Young, *The Rise of the Meritocracy* (London: Thames and Hudson, 1958). For another recent approach see Richard Herrnstein, *I.Q. in the Meritocracy* (Boston: Little, Brown and Atlantic Monthly Press, 1973).
4. Charles Tilley, "Collective Violence in European Perspective," in Hugh Davis Graham and Ted Robert Gurr (eds.), *Violence in America: Historical and Comparative Perspectives* (New York: Bantam Books, 1970), p. 43.

BIBLIOGRAPHICAL NOTES

The conceptual framework relating human needs to political goods was developed from the motivational theories of Abraham Maslow as set forth in *Motivation and Personality* (New York: Harper and Brothers, 1954), especially chapter five, "A Theory of Human Motivation," and chapter twelve, "Self-Actualizing People: A Study of Psychological Health." Maslow's later work *Toward A Psychology of Being* (Princeton: D. van Nostrand Company, 1962) extends his argument for a psychology of growth and actualization as an alternative to the limited perspective of a behavioral or Freudian psychology.

The usefulness of Maslow's theory of human motivation for political studies is argued persuasively by James C. Davies, *Human Nature in Politics* (New York: John Wiley and Sons, 1963). In the first two chapters he discusses some of the political implications of the existence of basic human needs. In the remainder of the book he deals with the concepts of tension and perception and explores the psychological relevance of groups, religion, status, leadership, and instability for political behaviour.

Christian Bay has also suggested the usefulness of Maslow's theory of motivation for political studies in his criticism of behavioral political science, "Politics and Pseudopolitics: A Critical Evaluation of Some Behavioral Literature," *American Political Science Review*, 59 (March 1965), 39–51. Bay concedes that politics should refer to power, but he argues that it should also refer to some conception of human welfare or the public good and insists on the need for a political theory that deals with basic human needs as well as overt desires and other observable aspects of behaviour. He enlarges on this theme in his very challenging article "Needs, Wants and Political Legitimacy," *Canadian Journal of Political Science*, I (September 1968), 241–260 and advances a model of individual intellectual and political development which culminates in self-governing individuals and responsible citizenship.

The concept of political goods is discussed by Roland Pennock, "Political Development, Political Systems and Political Goods," *World Politics*, 18 (April 1966), 415–434; and Amitai Etzioni provides a useful discussion of the requirement for some conception of human needs in social research and makes some suggestions for satisfying this requirement in "Basic Human Needs, Alienation and Inauthenticity," *American Sociological Review*, 33 (December 1968), 870–885.

My definition of political goods and the exploration of the various dimensions of each political good owes a substantial debt to Carl J. Friedrich, *Man and His Government* (New York: McGraw-Hill Book Company, 1963). Friedrich blends philosophical and empirical studies of politics into an outstanding review of the fundamental ideas, institutions, and procedures which have emerged from the human experience of politics.

The movement in the middle of the 1960s to develop quantitative social indicators to describe political outcomes and assess public policies reflected a growing realization among policy-analysts and policy-makers that measures of social performance are increasingly important in a post-industrial society which seeks to satisfy broad human interests and values as well as narrow economic goals and that social accounting information was markedly inferior in quantity and quality to existing economic indicators.

The first comprehensive survey of the field was *Social Indicators* (Cambridge, Mass.: The M.I.T. Press, 1966) edited by Raymond Bauer. The essays in this volume by Albert D. Biderman, "Social Indicators and Goals" and Bertram M. Gross, "The State of the Nation: Social Systems Accounting" are especially useful. Two issues of *The Annals* of the American Academy of Political and Social Science edited by Bertram Gross, Numbers 371 (May 1967) and 373 (September 1967) were devoted to the question of social goals and indicators for American society; and the result is an impressive collection of papers covering general arguments for social indicators, problems arising from their use in the analysis and formation of public policy, suggestions for social indicators in a variety of specific policy areas, and illustrations of the use of social indicators to evaluate policy performance. These papers are also available in Bertram M. Gross (ed.), *Social Intelligence for America's Future: Explorations in Social Problems* (Boston Allyn and Bacon, 1969). Another important collection reflecting many of the same concerns is Eleanor B. Sheldon and Wilbert E. Moore (eds.), *Indicators of Social Change: Concepts and Measurements* (New York: Russell Sage Foundation, 1968).

The best short introduction to the use of social indicators for policy analysis is United States, Department of Health, Education, and Welfare, *Toward A Social Report* (Washington: United States Government Printing Office, 1969) which was published in the final hours of the Johnson administration. The Report was offered as a first step in the development of a national system of social accounting in the United States, and it has been followed by *Social Indicators 1973* (Washington: United States Government Printing Office, 1974), produced by the United States Office of Management and Budget.

Some indication of recent efforts to improve the data available for public decision-making and a reminder of the continuing, serious need for better performance measures to improve the delivery of social services are given by Alice M. Rivlin, *Systematic Thinking for Social Action* (Washington: The Brookings Institution, 1971). The author concludes that relatively little effort has gone into devising such measures so far despite their importance and the apparent intellectual challenge of the task. This argument is repeated in an abbreviated form in Alice Rivlin, *New Approaches to Public Decision-Making*, Economic Council of Canada, Special Study Number 18 (Ottawa: Information Canada, 1972).

The need for improvement in the quantity and quality of social data for public decision-making in Canada has been advanced by the Economic Council of Canada in its *Eighth Annual Review: Design for Decision-Making* (Ottawa: Information Canada, 1971). The Council reviews new approaches to decision-making and the evolution of systematic analysis by governments in the United States and Canada, suggests a model system of decision-making for the federal government, and strongly recommends the development of a comprehensive set of statistical measures ("goal indicators") to monitor the changing conditions of our society over a broad spectrum of goal areas.

Two other reports reflect a rising interest in Canada in establishing a comprehensive system of social accounting. The Canadian Council of Social Development sponsored a seminar on social indicators in Canada in January 1972; and the proceedings of that seminar edited by Novia A. M. Carter, *Social Indicators* (Ottawa: Canadian Council of Social Development, 1972), present an interesting review of the issues and problems of social accounting in a Canadian context (see especially Dorothy Walters, "Social Intelligence and Social Policy" and Gail Stewart, "On Looking Before Leaping") together with some discussion of the efforts to develop social indicators in Canada (K. Scott Wood, "Social Indicators and Social Reporting in the Canadian North" and Hans Adler, "The Development of Social Indicators at Statistics Canada"). Earle L. Snider, *Towards the Development of a Socio-Political Data Bank for Alberta* (Edmonton: mimeographed, 1972) is a report commissioned by the Human Resources Council of the Alberta Government which summarizes the problems of developing comprehensive systems of social information and provides an inventory of relevant data being collected by public and private agencies in that province.

The best source of comparative social indicators for students of politics is the *World Handbook of Political and Social Indicators* (New Haven and London: Yale University Press), both the first (1964) edition by Bruce M. Russett, Hayward M. Alker, Karl W. Deutsch, and Harold D. Lasswell, and the second (1972) edition by Charles L. Taylor and Michael C. Hudson. These two volumes provide quantitative data for comparing nations on a great variety of politically relevant indicators including human resources, wealth and natural resources, social patterns, and government and politics. The first edition includes a preliminary analysis of the data to explore trends and patterns of political development which is omitted from the second edition. The second edition presents many more politically relevant variables with respect to political structure and performance and political protest and executive change, and it includes excellent discussions defining each political variable and assessing the quality of the data. The *Statistical Yearbook* and the *Demographic Yearbook* published annually by the Statistical Office of the United Nations Department of Economic and Social Affairs are also valuable collections of comparative social indicators.

For developing social indicators with respect to the Canadian economy and society, an indispensable source is *Canadian Historical Statistics* (Toronto: Macmillan Company of Canada, 1965) edited by M. C. Urquhart and K. A. H. Buckley. Unfortunately, the data series stop at 1960; but a much needed revision of this work is now in progress. More recent information is generally available in the *Canada Year Book*, published annually by Statistics Canada, which conveniently summarizes many of the data series collected by the federal statistical agency and published separately in profuse detail throughout each year.

The importance of the decennial census as a source of information for describing and evaluating economic and social conditions in Canada scarcely needs to be mentioned. The census data have the immense attraction of permitting analysis of secular changes since censuses have been carried out for many years to collect information on the size and selected characteristics of the population.

As valuable as a complete census can be in providing basic information to develop social indicators, in most cases a smaller sample survey is more useful and less expensive. Fred Schindeler and C. Michael Lanphier, in "Social Science Research and Participatory Democracy in Canada," *Canadian Public Administration*, 12 (Winter 1969), 481–498, trace the state of social science research in Canada as it relates to the formation of public policy and consider the ways in which sample surveys are being fostered in Canada and how their use is affecting the decision-making process at the federal level of government.

The most important sources of data for social indicators of the Canadian polity undoubtedly are the Federal Election Surveys carried out in 1965 by Philip E. Converse, John Meisel, Maurice Pinard, Peter Regenstreif, and Mildred Schwartz and in 1968 by John Meisel. The computer tapes containing the results of the interviews are now generally available in the data banks of a number of Canadian universities. The locations of these tapes as well as other quantitative data relevant for political research are recorded in the *Newsletter* of the Canadian Political Science Association. Unfortunately, no national survey was conducted in connection with the 1972 federal election because of a failure to obtain necessary financial support. The importance of the data arising from these sample surveys in developing indicators of Canadian political development make it imperative that such gaps in our system of socio-political intelligence should not be repeated.

On specific social indicators the references in footnotes and tables in the text will suggest sources for further reading, but a number of studies may be especially useful. Among the several studies of poverty in Canada, Ian Adams, William Cameron, Brian Hull, and Peter Penz, *The Real Poverty Report* (Edmonton: M. G. Hurtig Limited, 1971) combines a good general description of the dimensions of poverty in Canada with a sharp criticism of existing policies and proposals for change. *Poverty in Canada* (Scarborough, Ontario: Prentice-Hall of Canada Limited, 1971), edited by John Harp and John R. Hofley, is an excellent collection of readings which adopts a sociological perspective on poverty, explores the sources and culture of poverty in Canada, and reviews programs and strategies for remedial public action.

On the subjects of war and domestic political violence, probably the best approach is to study Canada in a comparative perspective in J. David Singer and Melvin Small, *The Wages of War, 1816–1965: A Statistical Handbook* (New York: John Wiley and Sons, 1972) and in Hugh Davis Graham and Ted Robert Gurr (eds.), *Violence in America: Historical and Comparative Perspectives* (New York: Bantam Books, 1970), Part VII. P. J. Giffin, "Rates of Crime and Delinquency," in W. T. McGrath (ed.), *Crime and Its Treatment in Canada* (Toronto: Macmillan Company of Canada, 1965), Chapter 4, is still the best introduction describing the incidence of crime in Canada. The Report of the Canadian Committee on Corrections, *Toward Unity: Criminal Justice and Corrections* (Ottawa: Information Canada, 1969), Chapter 3, provides more recent information; but this Report is much more interesting for its discussion of social goals and proposals for reform in the area of criminal justice and corrections than it is for its use of goal indicators in policy analysis.

The problem of fraternity in Canada is stated plainly by the Royal Commission on Bilingualism and Biculturalism in its *Preliminary Report* (Ottawa: Queen's Printer, 1965). It is also analyzed in two perceptive essays by John Meisel, "Values, Language and Politics in Canada" and " 'Cancel Out and Pass On': A View of Canada's Present Options" which are included in his *Working Papers on Canadian Politics*, enlarged ed. (Montreal: McGill–Queen's University Press, 1973). Richard Joy, *Languages in Conflict* (Toronto and Montreal: McClelland and Stewart Limited, 1972) provides a concise statement of the Canadian problem of two unilingualisms divided by a bilingual belt which is based on a skilful analysis of Canadian census records from 1851 to 1961.

The classic study of inequality in Canada is John Porter, *The Vertical Mosaic* (Toronto: University of Toronto Press, 1965). Much of the work of the Royal Commission on Bilingualism and Biculturalism is also relevant to the problem of describing and assessing the effects of inequalities in Canada. An excellent analysis of one of the most important aspects of inequality in Canada is contributed by Robert M. Pike, *Who Doesn't Get To University–and Why: A Study*

Bibliographical Notes

on Accessibility to Higher Education in Canada (Ottawa: Association of Universities and Colleges of Canada, 1970). The first part of Pike's study describes the extent of social inequalities in access to higher education in Canada and tries to identify the factors which help to perpetuate class and group inequalities in educational opportunities and choices. The second part analyzes student financial aid in the context of existing inequalities.

As an alternative to general historical analysis or sample surveys directed at eliciting libertarian attitudes, a useful approach to measuring liberty in Canada is to study the changing socio-political position of marginal groups. Morris Davis and Joseph F. Krauter, *The Other Canadians* (Toronto: Meuthen, 1971) review the pattern of discrimination against Indians, Eskimos, Negroes, Chinese and Japanese, Doukhobors, and Hutterites and assess the changes in public policies which have occurred in recent years. Two other studies of minority groups in Canada, Forrest La Violette, *The Canadian Japanese and World War II* (Toronto: University of Toronto Press, 1948) and Harry B. Hawthorn (ed.), *A Survey of the Contemporary Indians of Canada* (Ottawa: Indian Affairs Branch, 1966, 1967), are especially valuable for the perspective they provide on the psychological dimension of freedom. Richard Van Loon, "Political Participation in Canada: the 1965 Election," *Canadian Journal of Political Science*, III (September 1970), 376–399, is a pioneering effort to explore some of the sources of political participation in Canada based on data from the 1965 Federal Election Survey. Maurice Pinard, *The Rise of a Third Party: A Study in Crisis Politics* (Englewood Cliffs: Prentice-Hall, 1971) provides a brilliant analysis from survey research of the social and psychological bases of the Social Credit protest movement in Quebec. Peter Russell, in "A Democratic Approach to Civil Liberties," *University of Toronto Law Journal*, XIX (1969), 109–131, presents a persuasive statement of our need to make governmental activity thoroughly responsive to public demand and our requirement for a new political technology for both organizing and gauging public demands and interest and for identifying and correcting abuses of public authority.

INDEX